Hydrogen Regulation in Europe

Hydrogen Regulation in Europe

Emerging Issues and Best Practices for the Clean Energy Transition

Edited by

RUVEN FLEMING

Associate Professor and Scientific Coordinator of the Groningen Center of Energy Law and Sustainability, University of Groningen

OXFORD
UNIVERSITY PRESS

OXFORD
UNIVERSITY PRESS

Great Clarendon Street, Oxford, OX2 6DP,
United Kingdom

Oxford University Press is a department of the University of Oxford.
It furthers the University's objective of excellence in research, scholarship,
and education by publishing worldwide. Oxford is a registered trade mark of
Oxford University Press in the UK and in certain other countries.

Published in the United States of America by Oxford University Press
198 Madison Avenue, New York, NY 10016, United States of America.

British Library Cataloguing in Publication Data
Data available

Library of Congress Control Number: 2025943639

ISBN 978–0–19–895696–9

DOI: 10.1093/law/9780198956969.001.0001

Printed and bound by
CPI Group (UK) Ltd., Croydon, CR0 4YY

The manufacturer's authorised representative in the EU for product safety is
Oxford University Press España S.A. of Parque Empresarial San Fernando de Henares,
Avenida de Castilla, 2 – 28830 Madrid (www.oup.es/en or product.safety@oup.com).
OUP España S.A. also acts as importer into Spain of products made by the manufacturer.

MIX
Paper | Supporting
responsible forestry
FSC
www.fsc.org
FSC® C013604

To

Leon König

Acknowledgements

Books are rarely written and produced quickly. The one that you are reading now is the result of a long process that has required support, dedication, and teamwork. It is important to me to make this visible as there have been many people that were instrumental to its creation along the way.

This book proves that lawyers can play a proactive role in facilitating the energy transition in hydrogen. The idea to write this book and its shape and form is the result of numerous discussions with people working in government, industry organizations, law firms, lobby groups, non-governmental organizations, universities, and academic publishing companies.

In particular, I would like to thank Ivan-Petar Yovchev, Josephine Glandien, Daniel Schulz, Jens Hüttenrauch, Lorenzo Squintani, Fay Gibbons, Lindsay Glick, and everybody participating in the hydrogen research line of the Groningen Center of Energy Law and Sustainability—the world's first energy law research line on hydrogen regulation.

Furthermore, this book would be less interesting and less useful had it been written by me alone. My sincere thanks goes to all of the great authors who produced beautiful chapters and who will therefore make a direct contribution to the hydrogen energy transition. Most of the chapter authors who contributed their work here are not academics but legal experts on particular aspects of hydrogen regulation in certain parts of the EU. They all took time out of their busy schedules to produce their contributions to this book and all have been very open and responsive to feedback; and none got despaired at the numerous revisions and drafts that have been asked of them. Thank you!

Particular thanks are extended to everyone at the Groningen Centre of Energy Law and Sustainability for having so much patience with me and my ideas. This book would not have come together at its final stages without the precise and relentless work of Leopold L. Doebler. Working with Leo was a great experience.

Finally, this book is dedicated to Leon König, a curious and aspiring law student at the University of Göttingen in Germany. You make Ida and me, Dana, Winnie, and Edwin, as well as your family and friends very proud of the marvellous person that you have become.

Contents

PART 2 HYDROGEN DOWNSTREAM: KEY REGULATORY ISSUES

Table of Cases

EUROPEAN COMMISSION

COURT OF JUSTICE OF THE EUROPEAN UNION

UNITED KINGDOM

Table of Legislation

EUROPEAN UNION

Directive

Regulations

GERMANY

GREECE

ITALY

NORWAY

POLAND

SPAIN

UNITED KINGDOM

Statutes

STATUTORY INSTRUMENTS

International Instruments

Abbreviations

General Abbreviations

BAT	Best Available Technique
BREF	Best Available Techniques Reference Document
CBAM	Carbon Border Adjustment Mechanism
CCU	Carbon capture and utilization
CCS	Carbon capture and storage
dB(A)	Decibel
DSO	Distribution System Operator
EIA	Environmental Impact Assessment
GATT	General Agreement on Tariffs and Trade
GHG	Greenhouse gas
Gw	Gigawatt
IED	Industrial Emissions Directive
MW	Megawatt
NOX	Nitrogen oxides
PAS	Simplified Authorisation Procedure
PAUR	Regional single authorisation procedure
PEM	Proton Exchange Membrane
P2G	Power-to-gas
G2P	Gas-to-power
QRA	Quantitative Risk Assessment
RES	Renewable Energy Systems
RFNBO	Renewable fuel of non-biological origin
SUER	Single Desk for Renewable Energies
TPA	Third party access
TSO	Transmission System Operator
TWh	Terawatt-hour
WTO	World Trade Organization

Country-Specific Abbreviations

Denmark

AWG	Authority Working Group
DEA	Danish Energy Authority
PtX	Power-to-X
SF	Stakeholder Forum

Germany

A List of Abbreviations, including English translations, can be found in Chapter IV's Appendix.

Greece

MPPR	Major-Accident Prevention Policy Report
SEA	Special Ecological Assessment

Italy

AU	Single Authorisation
AIA	Integrated Environmental Authorisation
AUA	Single Environmental Authorisation
D.P.C.M.	Council of Ministers Presidential Decree
NTC	Technical Standards for Construction
PAUR	Regional Single Authorisation Procedure
PNIEC	National Integrated Plan for Energy and Climate
PNRR	National Recovery and Resilience Plan
PAS	Simplified Authorisation Procedure
VIA	Environmental Impact Assessment
VAS	Strategic Environmental Assessment
SUAP	One-Stop Shop for Productive Activities

The Netherlands

Awb	Algemene wet bestuursrecht
Bal	Besluit activiteiten leefomgeving
Bkl	Besluit kwaliteit leefomgeving
MBA	Milieubelastende activiteit
Ow	Omgevingswet
Ob	Omgevingsbesluit
Or	Omgevingsregeling
PGS	Publicatiereeks Gevaarlijke Stoffen

English translations can be found in Chapter II's Appendix.

Norway

EEZ	Exclusive Economic Zone
ME	Ministry of Energy
NCS	Norwegian Continental Shelf
OEA	Offshore Energy Act
PA	Petroleum Act
PCA	Pollution Control Act
PCR	Pollution Control Regulations

UK

COMAH	Control of Major Accident Hazards Regulations 2015
CPO	Compulsory Purchase Order
DCO	Development Consent Order
GPDO	Town and Country Planning (General Permitted Development) Order 2015
NPPF	National Planning Policy Framework
NPS	National Policy Statement
NSIP	Nationally Significant Infrastructure Projects

Spain

A List of Abbreviations, including English translations, can be found in Chapter VI's Appendix.

Editor and Author Biographies

Editor

Ruven Fleming
Ruven Fleming is Associate Professor of Energy Law at the University of Groningen and Scientific Coordinator of the Groningen Centre of Energy Law and Sustainability. Dr. Fleming`s research interest is energy law, with a particular focus on hydrogen, 'unconventional' forms of energy production, renewable energy, and energy investment and trade law.

Dr Fleming is the author and editor of standard reference works like the *Cambridge Handbook of Hydrogen and the Law* (CUP 2024) and the *Encyclopedia of Energy Law, Climate Change and the Environment* (Edward Elgar Publishing 2021) as well as numerous other energy law books. He has published articles in the most renowned international and national energy and climate law journals and written numerous book chapters. Dr Fleming is a member of the editorial board of the *European Energy & Climate Journal.* He advises the European Commission, national governments and parliaments on energy law-related issues on a regular basis.

Dr Fleming has received grants from the European Commission and the NWO (Dutch Science Organization) as well as other European or national organizations for various research and educational projects that he either led or in which he has participated. He is Secretary of the North Sea Energy Law Partnership, a Member of the IUCN World Commission on Environmental Law, a Member of the Operating Committee of the International Association of Energy Law, and a frequent speaker at events of the Dutch Association for Energy Law and Reviewer for public funding bodies and international publications.

Dr Fleming undertook undergraduate law studies in Germany at the University of Marburg and went on to conduct Russian language studies at Moscow State University Lomonossow/Russia as well as gaining work experience at a Russian/German law firm in Moscow. Prior to the commencement of his research in Groningen, Dr Fleming received a Master's in Oil and Gas Law (LLM) as well as a PhD in law from the University of Aberdeen, United Kingdom.

Authors

Diomidis Afentoulis
Diomidis Afentoulis holds a Bachelor of Laws from the Aristotle University of Thessaloniki (2015–2021) and has earned a Master of Laws (LLM) in energy and climate law from the University of Groningen (2022–2023). He works as a Contract Lead at Equinor, an international broad energy company.

Laura Bucher
Laura Bucher is currently an advisor at the German International Cooperation Society (GIZ), specializing in access to climate financing, with a particular focus on the Green Climate Fund. She studied law in the Netherlands and Spain and holds an LLM in energy and climate law from the University of Groningen (2023), where her primary research focused on the hydrogen permitting regime in Spain and carbon capture and storage. Over the past two years, her work has primarily

focused on carbon markets in Laos, carbon funds at the World Bank, and hydrogen projects in Morocco carried out in collaboration with Germany.

Dimitra Douka

Dimitra Douka is an attorney-at-law specializing in energy and environmental law, with extensive experience providing legal advice to multinational companies. She holds an LLM in energy and climate law from the University of Groningen and an LLM in public law from the National University of Athens. Having worked with organizations such as Hydrogen Europe and Holcim Group, she combines legal expertise with a strategic focus on sustainability in the energy sector.

Emilie Victoria Nørgaard Elkjær

Emilie Victoria Nørgaard Elkjær holds a bachelor's degree in law from Copenhagen University and a master's degree in law from Groningen University. During her studies in the Netherlands, she engaged in an academic internship in which the permitting regime for electrolysers in Denmark was analysed. Additionally, she has gained valuable experience during her studies working at institutions such as the Danish Energy Agency and completing an internship at the European Parliament, where she focused on the Energy Committee (ITRE). Emilie is currently pursuing a Master's degree in Danish law

Silke Goldberg

Silke Goldberg is a partner at Herbert Smith Freehills LLP and a visiting professor at the University of Groningen and Queen Mary University of London. Her practice focuses on clean energy across the entire value chain and the energy transition. Dr Goldberg is admitted to practice in Germany, France, and England and advises in English, Dutch, German, and French. She is listed in the Legal 500 UK Hall of Fame for her work on both power and renewables.

Inigo del Guayo

Iñigo del Guayo is Professor in Administrative Law at the University of Almería (Spain). He obtained his two law degrees (LLM and PhD) from the University of Navarre (Spain). He has researched and published widely in the areas of energy law, public law instruments to deal with insolvency, public services, and town and urban planning law, within a wider interest in public economic law and regulation (he is author of more than 250 publications, among them monographs, chapters in edited books, and articles in journals). He is the editor and a co-author of the three editions of the book *Energy Law in Europe. National, European Union and International Law and Regulation* (OUP 2001, 2007, and 2016). He is Chair of the Academic Advisory Group (AAG) of the Section on Energy, Environment, Resources and Infrastructure Law (SEERIL) of the International Bar Association (IBA). He has produced many reports on a variety of legal issues for public and private institutions, and is Director of the Master on Energy Law, of the Spanish Energy Club. He is a founding member and currently vice-president of the Spanish Energy Law Association (AEDEN); a member of the scientific committee of the European Federation of Energy Law Associations (EFELA); and is a member of the Latin American Forum for Administrative Law. He was the recipient of a grant from the British Academy for a research period in the United Kingdom. He was Director of the Spanish National Institute for Public Administration.

Ignacio Herrera Anchustegui

Ignacio Herrera Anchustegui is Professor of Law and leader of the Research Group for Energy, Climate, and Environmental Law at the University of Bergen. He specializes in offshore energy, market regulation, and new energy technologies. His PhD thesis, 'Buyer Power in EU Competition Law', received the 2017 Concurrences Award for best thesis in Competition Law and Economics and was awarded the Meltzer Prize for Young Researchers in 2017 at the University of Bergen. He is the author of over 60 publications and edited the *Routledge Handbook of Energy Law* (Routledge 2020), *Offshore Wind Licensing* (Edward Elgar 2024), the *Research Handbook on EU Competition Law and the Energy Transition* (Edward Elgar 2025), and *Offshore Energy: Law Challenges and Opportunities for Renewables and Hydrocarbons* (Bloomsbury/Hart 2025).

Jeanette Maria Jansen

Jeanette Maria Jansen holds a background in international relations and energy and climate law. She has worked in the public sector at both regional and European Union levels, as well as in the private sector. Her experience at an energy-intensive industrial company—where she encountered the challenges of decarbonization and integrating hydrogen into high-temperature heating processes—sparked her interest in researching hydrogen for such applications. She now works in the energy field at a Brussels-based trade association.

Martyn Jarvis

Martyn Jarvis is a Partner at Town Legal LLP in London. Martyn graduated from the University of Leicester with an LLB in law in 2010 and qualified as a solicitor in 2014. Since then, Martyn has focused his legal practice on the consenting and delivery of Nationally Significant Infrastructure Projects and major mixed-use regeneration projects and has worked on some of the most significant development projects in England of the last 10 years. This has included advising on the promotion of nuclear power stations, electricity interconnectors, airport expansion projects, hyperscale data centres, the delivery of legacy development in the Olympic Park in Stratford, and on major brownfield regeneration projects at Canada Water in the London Borough of Southwark and more recently in north-east Cambridge. Martyn has consistently been ranked as a Leading Associate for Planning in London in the Legal 500.

Konstantinos Kounelis

Konstantinos Kounelis is a Greek lawyer who studied law with a particular focus on Energy and Climate Law at the University of Groningen. His professional and academic interests include the legal frameworks surrounding renewable energy, with an emphasis on the permitting regimes for hydrogen production plants in Greece.

Torhild Nordtveit

Torhild Nordtveit holds a Master of Laws from the University of Bergen (2007–2013), an LL.M. from the University of Heidelberg (2011–2013), and a PhD from the University of Bergen (2021). Her PhD thesis concerned the transferral of debts, which is the Norwegian approach to discharge of debts by novation. Since August 2024, she has been employed at the Faculty of Law at the University of Bergen as a postdoctoral researcher at the NFR-funded FME HyValue.

Yegór Osipov-Gipsh

Yegór Osipov-Gipsh is a PhD researcher in energy law at the University of Groningen, focusing on floating offshore wind and hydrogen. He is also a journalist, writing for *De Groene Amsterdammer*, a leading Dutch weekly magazine.

Maciej Owidzki

Maciej Owidzki works as a business developer within Equinor's Polish offshore wind division, where he navigates the intersection of legal frameworks and commercial ventures. He holds two master's degrees, having studied energy and commercial law in the Netherlands and Norway; Maciej specializes in distilling regulations into actionable commercial language, ensuring strategic alignment with the evolving dynamics of Poland's energy and hydrogen markets.

Monika Radomska

Originally from Poland, Monika undertook law studies in the Netherlands. She specialized in energy infrastructure and its decarbonization. In this context she worked on the permitting regime for CO_2 and hydrogen pipelines in various capacities. Her origins in Poland made it possible for her to specialize in Polish permitting processes for energy facilities specifically. Her research interest lies in the interlinkage and the nexus between environmental permitting procedures (egetc EIA) on the one hand and energy regulation on the other hand.

Giovanni Volpi

Giovanni Volpi is an Italian trainee lawyer based in Verona, specializing in environmental and energy law with a strong interest in the sustainable development of the Alpine region. In this context, he has been actively engaged in analysing the regulatory framework for hydrogen production in Italy, identifying various challenges and opportunities for improvement.

I

Introduction

Ruven Fleming

1. Introduction

The European Union (EU) has had ambitious plans for hydrogen for some time. In July 2020 the EU adopted a common Hydrogen Strategy.[1] The strategy is structured into twenty key actions across four major areas, ranging from an investment agenda for the EU to measures aimed at boosting demand for hydrogen and scaling up production. It also includes eight key actions devoted to the design of an enabling and supportive framework, and five additional key actions addressing the international dimension.

The Hydrogen Strategy is part of a larger policy initiative for a climate-neutral EU, namely the European Green Deal.[2] Under the Green Deal, the Commission introduced in 2021 its 'Fit for 55' initiative—a set of proposals to reduce net greenhouse gas (GHG) emissions by at least 55% by 2030. This initiative also promotes demand for, and production of, renewable and low-carbon gases, including hydrogen.

These policy aims were supported by various legal initiatives at the EU level, including the introduction of new laws and regulations. The most prominent is arguably the Hydrogen and Decarbonized Gas Markets package, which came into force in 2024 after nearly three years of deliberation.[3] This package, also known as the 'Fourth Gas

[1] Communication from the Commission to the European Parliament, the Council, the European Economic and Social Committee and the Committee of the Regions, *A Hydrogen Strategy for a Climate-Neutral Europe* COM(2020) 301 final.

[2] Commission, *The European Green Deal* COM(2019) 640 final.

[3] For details on the process and the package see Leigh Hancher and Simina Suciu 'Hydrogen Regulation in Europe—the EU's "Hydrogen and Decarbonized Gas" Package: Best Practice or Missed Opportunity?' in Ruven Fleming (ed), *Cambridge Handbook of Hydrogen and the Law* (CUP 2024) 13–29.

Package', introduced both a new Gas Directive and a new Gas Regulation. Together, they establish common internal market rules for renewable gases, natural gas, and hydrogen to foster decarbonization, create the conditions for a more cost-effective transition, and achieve the EU's 2050 goal of climate neutrality.[4] Essentially, it is a recast of the 'Third Gas Package', extended in scope to cover hydrogen networks.[5]

With ambitious targets for hydrogen production and imports, and a comprehensive regulatory framework for hydrogen and decarbonized gases, the EU aimed—together with the United States—to be among the world's leading jurisdictions in hydrogen policy development. This objective is further underpinned by at least two key refinements of policy aims and actions.

First, in March 2022 the EU launched its 'RepowerEU' plan, triggered by the global energy crisis. This initiative called for a rapid expansion of renewable energy generation capacity, as well as ensuring enhanced integration of renewable sources into final energy uses.[6] A major pillar of RepowerEU is the so-called Hydrogen Accelerator, which sets out an ambitious strategy to double the EU's domestic renewable hydrogen production target for 2030 from 5 million to 10 million tonnes per annum, and to supplement this with an additional 10 million tonnes per annum of imports.[7]

Second, on 26 February 2025 the European Commission announced its Clean Industrial Deal.[8] This includes investment measures implemented via the Hydrogen Bank and promises a long-awaited new delegated act setting regulatory conditions for low-carbon hydrogen, along with a review of the delegated act for renewable fuels of non-biological origin (RFNBOs).[9] Perhaps even more pertinent is the Commission's commitment, under the Clean Industrial Deal, to resolve the Industrial Decarbonisation Accelerator Act by the end of 2025,[10] which will propose concrete measures to address permitting bottlenecks related to industrial energy access and decarbonization.[11] This development is worth watching, and if implemented effectively, could prove highly valuable in resolving the key permitting issues identified in this book.

Achieving these targets and executing the planned actions requires the EU to ramp up manufacturing capacity significantly and accelerate the development and retrofitting of infrastructure to accommodate future hydrogen deployment.[12] However, there is growing scepticism about whether these targets are realistic and whether their ever-increasing trajectory genuinely advances the development of a hydrogen economy.[13]

[4] ibid 14.
[5] ibid.
[6] Commission, *REPowerEU: Joint European Action for More Affordable, Secure and Sustainable Energy* COM(2022) 108 final, 8 March 2022.
[7] DG ENER, 'In Focus: Renewable Hydrogen to Decarbonise the EU's Energy System' https://commission.europa.eu/news/focus-renewable-hydrogen-decarbonise-eus-energy-system-2022-11-15-0_en accessed 7 March 2025.
[8] Commission, *The Clean Industrial Deal: A Joint Roadmap for Competitiveness and Decarbonisation* COM(2025) 85 final.
[9] ibid 8, 9.
[10] ibid 6.
[11] ibid 5.
[12] Hancher and Suciu (n 3) 15.
[13] ibid.

2. Critical Key Observations

There are two reasons for this increasing scepticism. First, some Member States simply reacted by doubling their domestic targets, without sufficiently rigorous consideration of the implementation issues that might arise. Second, despite investments being the first key action area of the EU Hydrogen Strategy of 2020, five years on we observe a slower-than-expected level of hydrogen investment in the EU, due to demand being lower than initially anticipated, which endangers the 2030 targets.[14]

Both issues are visible in Europe's largest Member State, Germany. Hydrogen is viewed as a cornerstone of Germany's energy transition plans, regardless of changes in government in recent years. This prominence is reflected in the National Hydrogen Strategy of June 2020 and its update in 2023.[15] Demand for hydrogen in Germany is estimated to reach 95–130 TWh by 2030, with 10 (GW of hydrogen production to be domestic; imports (and their derivatives) are expected to cover the remaining demand that cannot be met domestically.[16] Ten GW does not sound like much, but this goal has effectively been doubled by the German government—only within three years. The original 2020 strategy anticipated five GW of domestic hydrogen production, whereas the updated 2023 strategy raised this to ten GW.[17]

This requires a rapid expansion of production capacity, as well as the build-up of transport and end-use infrastructure for hydrogen. While the national government can set ambitious targets, it has also recognized that implementation ultimately depends on market players launching projects and on local two authorities issuing permits for those projects.[18] This observation is not unique to Germany; it holds true across all EU Member States.

Assuming these goals are highly ambitious and given indications (eg the cited ACER study of late 2024) that a gap exists between where we should be and where we are, a central legal question emerges: what can be done to accelerate the hydrogen transition in Europe? One key answer is improved information for all stakeholders—including project developers and public authorities—on the permitting processes for hydrogen projects. What is the duration of these permitting processes? What permits are needed for hydrogen projects? How do the individual permitting frameworks compare? Answering these questions is at the heart of this book's motivation.

[14] See eg ACER, *European Hydrogen Markets 2024 Market Monitoring Report* (November–December 2024) 4–5 https://www.acer.europa.eu/monitoring/MMR/european_hydrogen_markets_2024 accessed 26 February 2025.

[15] German Government, *The National Hydrogen Strategy* https://www.bmwk.de/Navigation/EN/hydrogen/national-hydrogen-strategy.html accessed 17 February 2025.

[16] German Hydrogen Strategy 2023, 3, 5, and 6.

[17] ibid 3 and 4.

[18] ibid 26.

3. Literature Review on Hydrogen Regulation in Europe

Having outlined some key questions for European hydrogen regulation, we now turn to a literature review to see if and how these questions have been addressed in the past and how this book will build upon that work. Fortunately, over the last two years there has been a significant increase in legal literature addressing hydrogen. This recent surge in literature on hydrogen regulation in Europe is a positive trend, since the industry has lamented the lack of information on applicable regulatory frameworks at every hydrogen event in recent years. The growth in legal literature facilitates market players' understanding and comparison of different aspects of hydrogen frameworks.

With this increase in literature, it is now possible to conduct a more targeted review. This chapter and book will therefore provide only an overview of the available legal literature on hydrogen regulation in Europe. For readers interested in global perspectives or legal frameworks in other regions, there is good news: a comprehensive overview of global hydrogen regulation literature and non-European regional perspectives was already provided elsewhere by the end of 2024.[19] Here, the focus will hence be on literature specifically dedicated to Europe, and this overview aims to convey the current status while highlighting common themes and emerging trends.

The legal literature on hydrogen regulation in Europe can be broadly clustered into six categories:

- regulatory and methodological approaches to hydrogen regulation in Europe;
- environmental and efficiency aspects of hydrogen regulation;
- public participation aspects of European hydrogen regulation;
- offshore hydrogen regulation in Europe;
- the regulation of hydrogen trade in Europe;
- comparative research on the European approach to hydrogen regulation compared to other regions of the world.

The available literature in each of these six categories will now be discussed in turn.

3.1 Regulatory and Methodological Approaches to Hydrogen Regulation in Europe

As might be expected, a significant body of legal literature has followed both the legislative process and the eventual outcome, namely the EU's Hydrogen and Decarbonized Gas Markets package. This central legislative package introduced both a new Gas Directive and a new Gas Regulation.

[19] Ruven Fleming, 'Introduction' in Ruven Fleming (ed), *Cambridge Handbook of Hydrogen and the Law* (CUP 2024) 4–8 https://doi.org/10.1017/9781009459259 accessed 26 February 2025.

There are at least two authoritative general analyses of the package. The first, by Hancher and Suciu,[20] thoroughly describes how the EU established a comprehensive legal framework for hydrogen and clear rules for Member States. They express scepticism about two main issues: first, the legislative process, which they argue was derailed by the war in Ukraine; this crisis shifted co-legislators' attention to emergency legislation addressing security-of-supply issues and rising gas prices.[21] Second, they question whether the ambitious timelines and targets are realistic, given that even after formal adoption the Gas Package must still be transposed into national law by Member States—a process that will take another one to two years.[22]

The second piece is by Tanase and Herrera Anchustegui, who discuss regulatory principles applicable to hydrogen—for example, in the context of hydrogen transmission through pipelines.[23] They observe that these principles are largely adapted from existing frameworks in the natural gas and electricity sectors.[24]

Beyond these general treatments, the package has also been analysed from various specific perspectives. For example, Yafimava focuses on issues of flexibility and security of supply.[25] She points out shortcomings that restrict a flexible, stepwise development of hydrogen networks.[26] She warns that this could prevent a coordinated network decarbonization process—phasing out natural gas and phasing in hydrogen networks—without negatively affecting natural gas supply security.[27] In particular, regarding flexibility, she regards the transition period (or 'regulatory holidays', as Hancher and Suciu similarly term it) until 2033 as far too brief.[28]

The short transition period is also a focal point for Iakovenko, who examines a different aspect of the package.[29] He considers the implications of the package for private investment in hydrogen infrastructure, warning that politically driven projects often result in market distortions and asset redundancy.[30] He argues that the lack of genuine market involvement and the additional costs of constructing and maintaining such infrastructure can adversely affect price trends and gas-consuming sectors in the countries concerned. He cautions that similar issues could arise for hydrogen infrastructure under the package.[31]

[20] Hancher and Suciu (n 3).
[21] ibid 28.
[22] ibid.
[23] Lavinia Tanase and Ignacio Herrera Anchustegui, 'EU Hydrogen and Decarbonised Gas Market Package: Unbundling, Third-Party Access, Tariffs and Discounts Rules at the Core of Transport of Hydrogen' in Íñigo del Guayo Castiella and Lorenzo Mellado Ruiz (eds), *Retos Regulatorios de los Gases Renovables en la Economía Circular* (Marcial Pons 2023) 8.
[24] ibid.
[25] Katja Yafimava, 'The EU Decarbonised Gas and Hydrogen Package: Do the New Rules for European Gas Network Decarbonisation Ensure Flexibility and Security of Supply?' (2024) OGEL 3 https://www.ogel.org/journal-advance-publication-article.asp?key=793 accessed 5 March 2025.
[26] ibid 22.
[27] ibid.
[28] ibid.
[29] Mykola Iakovenko, 'The EU Hydrogen and Decarbonised Gases' Legislative Package and its Implications for Private Investment in Hydrogen Infrastructure Development' (2024) OGEL 3 https://www.ogel.org/journal-advance-publication-article.asp?key=813 accessed 5 March 2025.
[30] ibid 14.
[31] ibid.

Pinto's work is concerned with how regulatory failure in hydrogen can be avoided.[32] She proposes cross-sectoral dynamic regulation, including mechanisms like regulatory sandboxes (eg hydrogen valleys).[33] She observes that this approach could produce meaningful and effective legal frameworks for hydrogen, both in the EU and the United States,[34] by identifying regulatory hurdles and simultaneously preventing regulatory arbitrage.[35]

Pailman takes a conceptual approach by proposing a new methodology for designing regulatory and legal frameworks for hydrogen in Europe. Her 'hydrogen prism' consists of three components: cohesiveness, risk mitigation, and possibility for compliance.[36] These serve as benchmark parameters for hydrogen legal frameworks in the mobility sector.[37] Although this framework is applied to one sector (mobility), Pailman argues it has significant potential for legislators and stakeholders in other sectors.[38] The issues she describes (the pacing problem and the chicken-and-egg dilemma) exist wherever hydrogen regulation is introduced.

Finally, Jiménez Casanova connects these conceptual questions to practical concerns, focusing on the integration of gas, electricity, and hydrogen network planning.[39] She argues that the challenges of integration should be addressed through 'hydrogen system planning'.[40] This approach is essentially one of legal systems integration; she advocates a governance structure to manage the interrelations between gas and electricity networks in integrated planning, using existing European instruments.[41]

3.2 Environmental and Efficiency Aspects of Hydrogen Regulation in Europe

In the literature, these conceptual questions have been examined with respect to two concrete principles: the circular economy principle and the energy efficiency principle. Martín Morán analyses hydrogen regulation from a circular economy perspective. He concludes that current European hydrogen regulation does not adhere to the principle of technological neutrality, creating path dependency risks and potentially stifling

[32] Jacqueline Pinto, 'Dynamic Regulation: Instruments to Foster a Cross-Sectoral Hydrogen Economy?' (2024) 21(3-4) Journal for European Environmental & Planning Law 215–38 https://brill.com/view/journals/jeep/21/3-4/jeep.21.issue-3-4.xml accessed 5 March 2025.

[33] ibid 220.

[34] ibid 238.

[35] ibid 235, 236.

[36] Kelsey Pailman, 'The Hydrogen Prism: Angles of EU Hydrogen Regulation for Sustainable Mobility' (2024) 21(3-4) Journal for European Environmental & Planning Law 274–96 https://doi.org/10.1163/18760104-21030011 accessed 5 March 2025.

[37] ibid 278.

[38] ibid 295.

[39] Paola Jiménez Casanova, 'Towards a Sustainable, Integrated, and Decarbonized Energy System in the EU: Addressing Structural Challenges Through Hydrogen System Planning' (2024) 21(3-4) Journal for European Environmental & Planning Law 193–214 https://doi.org/10.1163/18760104-21030004 accessed 7 March 2025.

[40] ibid 212.

[41] ibid 211, 212.

future innovation.[42] He is particularly critical of the legislature's apparent preoccupation with electrolysers.[43] According to him, this bias causes the current regulatory framework to distort competition, disadvantaging hydrogen production from biomass and other non-organic methods.[44] From a circular economy perspective, such a distortion is undesirable in the EU.[45]

Jiménez Casanova and Pinto examine the 'energy efficiency first' principle and its effect on the hydrogen economy[46]—a pertinent issue given the heated stakeholder debates. They ask whether this principle helps or hinders hydrogen development. They note that although the energy efficiency first principle is explicitly supported in EU law, its implementation is inconsistent across Member States, due to challenges such as insufficient guidelines and enforcement procedures, as identified by the European Commission.[47] They further contend that applying this principle to hydrogen infrastructure can help prevent excessive investments and optimise hydrogen's integration into the broader energy system.[48]

3.3 Public Participation and European Hydrogen Regulation

One of the fundamental principles of European environmental and energy law is public participation. Two publications by Forns Gómez and Rehage (interestingly by the same authors in swapped order) address this topic specifically. The first publication examines two case studies to identify common issues and best practices concerning public participation in European hydrogen regulation.[49] This article confronts a core issue in the hydrogen transition: whether certain layers of public participation can be sacrificed for the greater goal of accelerating permitting procedures and, thus, the hydrogen transition itself. While law-makers in Europe's key hydrogen countries answered this question with a resounding 'yes', Rehage and Forns Gómez remain sceptical. In the case studies of Germany and Spain, they observe that accelerating approvals for renewable hydrogen projects is occurring at the expense of public participation.[50] They identify an 'acceleration dilemma': the understandable attempt to speed up

[42] Álvaro Martín Morán, 'Diversifying Clean Hydrogen: Regulatory Barriers for a Circular Hydrogen Economy' (2024) 21(3-4) Journal for European Environmental & Planning Law 167–92 https://doi.org/10.1163/18760104-21030003 accessed 7 March 2025.

[43] ibid 192.

[44] ibid.

[45] ibid.

[46] Paola Jiménez Casanova and Jacqueline Pinto, 'Interpreting the Energy Efficiency First Principle: Help or Hindrance for the Hydrogen Economy?' (2024) 33(6) European Energy and Environmental Law Review 274–88 https://kluwerlawonline-com.ezproxy.uef.fi:2443/journalarticle/European+Energy+and+Environmental+Law+Review/33.6/EELR2024022 accessed 7 March 2025.

[47] ibid 283.

[48] ibid 285.

[49] Ruben Rehage and Alba Forns Gómez, 'Accelerating Authorizations vs Public Participation in the Decision-Making Chain of Renewable Hydrogen in Germany and Spain: A Dilemma' (2024) 21(3-4) Journal for European Environmental & Planning Law 297–317 https://doi.org/10.1163/18760104-21030007 accessed 7 March 2025.

[50] ibid 317.

authorizations could lead to decreased acceptance, increased resistance, and ultimately slower processes.[51]

In their second joint publication (authors Forns Gómez and Rehage in opposite order), they focus on the inclusiveness of European hydrogen transitions, specifically on justice for vulnerable and marginalized individuals in Spain and Germany.[52] They conclude that a one-size-fits-all approach—treating everyone the same—fails to account for vulnerable groups and thereby perpetuates inequality of opportunity in the hydrogen economy.[53]

3.4 Offshore Hydrogen Regulation in Europe

Hydrogen is not only produced and transported onshore; offshore hydrogen is also of interest. Offshore hydrogen production and transport have become important subjects for European coastal countries. In recent years, Andreasson has addressed this topic in two publications (2022 and 2024).

In the first piece, Andreasson, together with Lisa van Nieuwkoop, investigates the integration of renewable energy systems in the Dutch North Sea.[54] They explain that technical integration of different energy systems must be supported and facilitated by legal system integration. Technically, they note that electricity from offshore wind farms can be used to produce hydrogen on existing offshore hydrocarbon platforms via electrolysis, thereby facilitating green hydrogen production.[55] Regarding offshore-produced hydrogen, they find that transporting it to shore via existing offshore natural gas pipelines may require adapting admixing restrictions in onshore gas networks.[56] Similarly, reusing disused offshore gas pipelines for hydrogen transport faces challenges: they observe that Dutch law currently lacks a standardized procedure for such reuse, offering only ad hoc solutions.[57]

In 2024, Andreasson revisited the Dutch regulatory framework for hydrogen and compared it to the Danish system; unfortunately, the situation remained unsatisfactory.[58] She found that offshore green hydrogen development in both Denmark and the

[51] ibid.

[52] Alba Forns Gómez and Ruven Rehage, 'Is Public Participation in Hydrogen Matters (Un)just? Evaluating the Ex-/Inclusion of the Vulnerable and Marginalised Individuals in the Hydrogen Decision-Chains of the EU, Spain and Germany' (2024) 21(3-4) Journal for European Environmental & Planning Law 318–42 https://doi.org/10.1163/18760104-21030006 accessed 7 March 2025.

[53] ibid 341, 342.

[54] Liv Malin Andreasson and Lisa van Nieuwkoop, 'Transitioning to an Integrated Renewable Energy System in the Dutch North Sea' in Ruven Fleming and others (eds), *A Force of Energy: Essays in Energy Law in Honour of Professor Martha Roggenkamp* (University of Groningen Press 2022) 182–90 https://books.ugp.rug.nl/ugp/catalog/book/87 accessed 7 March 2025.

[55] ibid 186.

[56] ibid 187.

[57] ibid.

[58] Liv Malin Andreasson, 'Offshore Production and Transport of Green Hydrogen: A Case Study on Denmark and the Netherlands' in Ruven Fleming (ed), *The Cambridge Handbook of Hydrogen and the Law* (CUP 2024) 173–88 https://pure.rug.nl/ws/portalfiles/portal/1157871830/offshore-production-and-transport-of-green-hydrogen.pdf accessed 7 March 2025.

Netherlands still faced legal uncertainties. She recommended, as the simplest regulatory option, installing electrolysers on existing offshore hydrocarbon platforms.[59] Regarding transport, she noted Denmark's progress in amending its Gas Supply Act to develop dedicated hydrogen infrastructure and allow hydrogen injection into the natural gas network.[60] However, she identified a need to clarify the permissible hydrogen content in the existing network. Conversely, the Netherlands has clarified the permissible hydrogen content in its gas network, but faces uncertainty because its Gas Act does not apply to dedicated hydrogen transport infrastructure.[61]

3.5 The Regulation of Hydrogen Trade in Europe

Large-scale hydrogen transport infrastructure (eg pipelines) is crucial for hydrogen trade, whether offshore or onshore. Given the EU's target of importing 10 million tonnes of renewable hydrogen by 2030,[62] the rules for international hydrogen trade take centre stage. In his work, Noël examined the compatibility of hydrogen trade with World Trade Organization (WTO) rules, particularly the question of 'like products' under the General Agreement on Tariffs and Trade (GATT), in the context of fossil-fuel-based, low-carbon, and renewable hydrogen.[63]

He concludes that a WTO panel would likely consider all types of hydrogen as 'like products'; however, EU regulations (RED III, ReFuelEU Aviation, FuelEU Maritime) do not immediately and unconditionally grant the same advantages to all hydrogen types.[64] Specifically, advantages granted to RFNBO and low-carbon hydrogen are not extended to 'green' hydrogen imports (because their electricity cannot be counted as 'fully renewable'), and economic benefits are similarly not extended to imported black, brown, or grey hydrogen.[65] These barriers could severely impact third countries with limited low-emission renewable technologies. The RFNBO and low-carbon hydrogen requirements could also discriminate de facto among WTO members, potentially violating GATT Article I.[66]

Another crucial aspect of trade in any product is standardization and labelling. Accordingly, in 2024 Pereira, Fossa, Muinzer, and Olujobi discussed hydrogen product labelling.[67] They argue that hydrogen labelling can be used as part of a country's energy transition strategy, and should be implemented on the basis of lifecycle assessment.[68]

59 ibid 187.
60 ibid.
61 ibid 188.
62 Commission (EU), *REPowerEU Plan* COM(2022) 230 final, 7.
63 Sebastian Noël, 'Achieving Greenhouse Gas Emission Reductions Through the Utilization of Hydrogen: Are Fossil, Low-Carbon and Renewable Hydrogen "Like Products" Under the GATT?' (2024) OGEL 3 www.ogel.org/article.asp?key=4144 accessed 5 March 2025.
64 ibid 21.
65 ibid.
66 ibid.
67 Eduardo G Pereira and others, 'A Road to Energy Transition with Hydrogen and Carbon Capture and Utilization (CCU) Products Labelling' (2024) OGEL 3 https://www.ogel.org/journal-advance-publication-article.asp?key=805 accessed 5 March 2025.
68 ibid 26/27.

They call for obligations to promote hydrogen and carbon capture and utilization (CCU) -based products with detailed criteria; support mechanisms (such as subsidies and tax measures); sustainability and transparency requirements; and both domestic and international regulatory collaboration.[69]

Gallegos takes a similar approach by examining how hydrogen is certified as sustainable in international trade with the EU.[70] She highlights the need for certification to differentiate hydrogen by environmental credentials.[71] She examines hydrogen certification schemes that track and trace sustainability attributes through the value chain, and identifies regulatory barriers.[72] As of June 2024, five voluntary schemes have applied for RFNBO certification recognition by the European Commission, pending technical assessment, which will establish detailed rules for treating and categorizing imported and domestically produced RFNBO.[73]

Gallegos notes that this divergence of schemes is even more pronounced globally and is likely to persist, since each scheme is tailored to different regions, stakeholders, and regulatory frameworks.[74] This results in substantial differences in how hydrogen's environmental characteristics are defined, raising concerns about cross-border comparability and potential barriers to trade.[75] She proposes introducing—and legally recognizing—a Digital Product Passport for traded hydrogen. This would streamline the certification process and reduce the number of schemes, leading to harmonization.[76]

3.6 Comparative Works on European Hydrogen Regulation

Comparing the EU's hydrogen framework with those under development elsewhere is a growing component of the hydrogen legal literature. Two regions have been particularly scrutinized: North America and Australia. An example is an article by Talus, Gallegos, and Pinto, which discusses legal barriers to importing US hydrogen into the EU.[77] The issue of certification schemes and differing methodologies for calculating GHG emissions also plays a key role, as do other potential barriers such as applying the Carbon Border Adjustment Mechanism (CBAM) to US hydrogen.[78] They conclude that in EU–US trade, the EU must ensure that the cost and technical requirements

[69] ibid 28.
[70] Francisca Gallegos, 'Bridging the Gap: Certification Schemes for Sustainable Hydrogen in Global Trade' (2024) 21(3-4) Journal for European Environmental & Planning Law 239–73 https://doi.org/10.1163/18760104-21030005 accessed 5 March 2025.
[71] ibid 246.
[72] ibid 239.
[73] ibid 268.
[74] ibid 272.
[75] ibid.
[76] ibid 273.
[77] Kim Talus, Francisca Gallegos, and Jacqueline Pinto, 'Importing US-produced Hydrogen and Its Derivatives into the EU—Examples of Unnecessary Complications, Barriers and Distinctions' (2024) Journal of Energy & Natural Resources Law https://doi.org/10.1080/02646811.2024.2341544 accessed 7 March 2025.
[78] ibid 19–22.

for producing RFNBOs are not so burdensome that producers are driven to sell their hydrogen and derivatives elsewhere.[79]

A similar conclusion can be drawn from comparisons with the emerging Australian framework. First, for renewable hydrogen export contracts in Australia; second, for regulatory choices generally in both markets. Kelly and Pettit discuss the first point:[80] they emphasize the need for contractual interoperability across jurisdictions and observe that green ammonia is likely to remain the most cost-effective method for hydrogen imports (EU) and exports (Australia), and is also the most legally secure option given existing, well-regulated frameworks.[81]

Hunter, Pettit, and Taylor,[82] and separately Penttinen, Pettit, and Talus,[83] all compare the EU and Australian hydrogen frameworks in their respective articles. Hunter, Pettit, and Taylor find that the EU framework could serve as a model for Australia in some respects; however, in other respects (such as the CBAM), it creates hurdles noted by the authors.[84] Penttinen, Pettit, and Talus acknowledge the complexities in developing hydrogen legal frameworks. They find that the hydrogen economy's development in both the EU and Australia is strongly influenced by pre-existing regulatory frameworks and the division of legislative competences.[85] In the EU, the hydrogen regulatory framework largely mirrors EU-level legislation, imposing strict rules and targets for hydrogen production and market creation, thus ensuring uniformity across Member States.[86] By contrast, Australia employs a cooperative federalism model, with both federal and state governments sharing crucial roles and responsibilities.[87] They find that, compared to the EU system, the Australian model gives states more discretion for tailored solutions, whereas the EU system can act as an effective 'block' on hydrogen.[88]

4. The Contribution of this Book

This book's discussion of hydrogen regulation in Europe not only provides an overview of the status quo but also examines in depth the regulatory issues for two key segments of the hydrogen economy: production and transport. This book's unique contribution

[79] ibid 23.

[80] Cameron Kelly and Jordie Pettit, 'A Model for Renewable Hydrogen Export Contracts: Towards International Best Practice' in Kim Talus (ed), *A Research Agenda for International Energy Law* (Edward Elgar Publishing 2024) 147–85 https://doi.org/10.4337/9781803924960.00012 accessed 7 March 2025.

[81] ibid 185.

[82] Tina Soliman Hunter, Jordie Pettit, and Madeline Taylor, 'Implications of "Net-Zero Emissions by 2050" for the Hydrocarbon Industry: A Case Study of Hydrogen in Mature Petroleum Jurisdictions' (2023) 16 Journal of World Energy Law and Business 280–301 https://doi.org/10.1093/jwelb/jwad007 accessed 7 March 2025.

[83] Sirja Lena Penttinen, Jordie Pettit, and Kim Talus, 'Creating the Hydrogen Market from Scratch in the EU and Australia: How Legislative Authority Shapes the Regulatory Choices' (2024) OGEL 3 <www.ogel.org/article.asp?key=4145> accessed 5 March 2025.

[84] Hunter, Pettit, and Taylor (n 82) 292, 293.

[85] Penttinen, Pettit, and Talus (n 83) 19.

[86] ibid.

[87] ibid.

[88] ibid.

lies in its detailed treatment of hydrogen value chain regulation in Europe, with a particular focus on permitting regimes for the relevant infrastructure components.

On the one hand, it is the first to provide a holistic legal overview of permitting regimes for hydrogen production, transport, and end use in Europe. On the other hand, it includes case studies from which best practice examples for certain elements of the hydrogen value chain can be drawn. The chapters (apart from the Introduction and the Conclusion) are organized into two parts. Given the diverse nature of end-use applications, the book focuses on production/upstream (Part 1) and infrastructure/downstream (Part 2) aspects of the hydrogen value chain.

The primary focus of Part 1 is the applicable permitting regimes for electrolysers in Europe. Focusing on electrolysers—rather than other production technologies—is informed by the European Hydrogen Strategy, which targets domestic hydrogen production from electrolysers. Since the Commission views electrolysers as a key tool for achieving Europe's renewable hydrogen ambitions by 2030, understanding the conditions and permitting regimes in each Member State is pivotal.

Focusing on production capacity's legal status is justified by the topic's importance. Without production, there can be no transport or end use. A recent study indicates that permitting regimes for green hydrogen production are indeed the bottleneck.[89] It is therefore crucial to identify barriers in electrolyser permitting regimes in order to streamline and accelerate procedures.

The book provides an overview of relevant production permitting regimes. Part 1's chapters compare the requirements of seven different EU Member States for the same project: installing and operating an electrolyser in country X. This enables project developers to understand and compare the permitting regimes of individual countries. Key insights and conclusions about these features will be presented in the book's final chapter.

Part 2 of the book shifts focus to key regulatory issues in transport and end use of hydrogen—in other words, downstream issues. This section includes diverse chapters discussing aspects such as hydrogen transport and infrastructure, offshore hydrogen production, industrial end use of hydrogen, and hydrogen contracting strategies. Each aspect is explored through case studies from different EU Member States. Among these is an example of one of the most promising end uses of green (renewable) hydrogen: high-temperature industrial applications. This case study reveals general insights about hydrogen end-use regulation that go beyond individual cases. In addition, there is a chapter on hydrogen contracting strategies, offering insights into both the physical and contractual/legal infrastructure required for the European hydrogen transition. This variety of topics indicates the breadth of key issues. The aim of Part 2 is to highlight key legal issues and to offer recommendations or existing best practices for addressing them.

[89] PWC Strategy& (2023) *H2 Readiness of German Industry* 13 https://www.strategyand.pwc.com/de/en/industries/energy-utilities/hydrogen-economy.html accessed 26 February 2025.

5. Conclusion

The EU has been developing hydrogen policies and legal frameworks relentlessly since 2020. This has arguably resulted in regulation preceding market development. Moreover, national legal frameworks now must incorporate rules for a new energy carrier and enable progress toward EU-wide hydrogen targets. All of this puts legal systems, authorities, and project developers to a stress test.

If this stress test is to be managed effectively, it is crucial to examine what is working and what is not—and to do so among countries with comparable legal systems. Given that Member States share the influence of EU law, they provide valuable case studies and comparisons.

However, this is not just an academic exercise. An in-depth examination of national hydrogen regimes can provide crucial guidance for project developers with hydrogen business interests, and can highlight to policymakers where other countries may be performing better or taking different approaches. If the hydrogen goals set by the EU and its Member States for 2030 are still to be reached, this exercise must be undertaken urgently. Moreover, it can be beneficial in the long run—for meeting hydrogen targets beyond 2030, since the energy transition will by no means be complete by then.

PART 1
HYDROGEN UPSTREAM
Permitting Regimes for Electrolysers

II
The Netherlands

Yegór Osipov-Gipsh and Jeanette Maria Jansen

1. Introduction

On 1 January 2024, the Netherlands enacted its new comprehensive environmental legislation, the *Omgevingswet* (the Environment and Planning Act; hereafter Ow).[1] Replacing twenty-six existing laws with one law, the Ow aims to simplify the regulation of all physical activities in the country, including constructing and operating electrolysers onshore. Aiming to streamline permitting procedures, the Ow allows applicants to submit one application with one authority for all necessary environmental permits. It also entrenches the key role of Dutch municipalities (*gemeenten*) in the permitting process by giving them broad powers to determine rules for their respective physical environments and, consequentially, to shape the assessment criteria for granting the required permit(s). The Ow is complemented by secondary environmental legislation that provides more detailed regulations; an overview of these laws is provided in Table II.1 in this chapter's Appendix.

Further change is on the way. In December 2024, the Dutch Senate approved the new Energy Act, which replaced the country's pre-existing electricity and gas legislation.[2] Transposing the 2024 EU Gas Directive,[3] this Act introduced unbundling and

[1] Environment and Planning Act (*Omgevingswet*) of 23 March 2016 (as adopted on 1 January 2024).
[2] Energy Act (*Energiewet*) of 11 December 2024.
[3] Directive (EU) 2024/1788 of the European Parliament and of the Council of 13 June 2024 on common rules for the internal markets for renewable gas, natural gas and hydrogen, amending Directive (EU) 2023/1791 and repealing Directive 2009/73/EC (recast) OJ L 2024/1789.

third-party access rules for hydrogen, which were previously lacking in European and Dutch law. Those who directly or indirectly exercise control over electrolysers are prevented from owning or controlling parts of hydrogen transmission and distribution systems.[4] The Energy Act also gives a Dutch Minister the power to streamline the permitting for electrolysers.[5] Both these aspects are discussed in section 3 of this chapter (subsections 3.1 and 3.3), which considers all areas of law that are relevant to planning, building, operating, and decommissioning an electrolyser in the Netherlands. Prior to that, section 2 provides brief general observations. Section 4 features a short list of recommendations to improve the existing system, and section 5 concludes the chapter.

For this chapter, three approved electrolyser permits were consulted alongside the Ow and the accompanying legislation.[6] However, all three were approved under the pre-2024 regime and may provide inductive guidance only. Brief information about the permits is provided in Table II.2 in the Appendix.

2. General Observations on the Permitting Regime

Before discussing the Dutch permitting regime, one of its key elements must be mentioned. As of 20 January 2025, Dutch law considers electrolysers to be IPPC installations.[7] This means that hydrogen production through the electrolysis of water is deemed to be a so-called environmentally harmful activity (*milieubelastende activiteit*; hereafter MBA).[8] Various regulations apply to electrolysers because of this designation across several areas of law. The nature of MBA and forthcoming related changes are discussed in subsection 3.4 of this chapter, but they are already relevant in other sections and hence must be mentioned now.

[4] Art 3.10 Energy Act.

[5] ibid art 6.1(1)(k).

[6] Provincie Friesland, 'Besluit Omgevingsvergunning' (Z2021-002320, 8 September 2021) <https://www.planviewer.nl/imro/files/NL.IMRO.9921.EcomunityWaterstof-VA01/d_NL.IMRO.9921.EcomunityWaterstof-VA01.pdf> accessed 20 January 2025 (hereafter Permit Oosterwolde); Provincie Groningen, 'Besluit Omgevingsvergunning' (Z2022-001022, 4 October 2023) <https://bestanden.provinciegroningen.nl/bestanden-openbaar/publicatievoorstel/KIWI_PublicatieVoorstel_IPPC_000000210003/D2023-104321%20GEANONIMISEERD%20-%20DEFINITIEF%20-%20Besluit%20%20Kloosterlaan%2012%20te%20Farmsum.pdf> accessed 20 January 2025 (hereafter Permit Farmsum);

Provincie Groningen, 'Besluit Omgevingsvergunning' (Z2023-010955, 2 April 2024) <https://bestanden.provinciegroningen.nl/bestanden-openbaar/publicatievoorstel/KIWI_PublicatieVoorstel_IPPC_000000450002/D2024-024381%20GEANONIMISEERD%20-%20DEFINITIEF%20-%20Ontwerpbesluit%20%20Synergieweg%2011%20%209979XD%20te%20Eemshaven.pdf> accessed 20 January 2025 (hereafter Permit Eemshaven).

[7] Annex to art 1.1 of Environment and Planning Act contains the definition of '*ippc-installatie*', which refers to the definition of 'installation' as given in art 3(3) of Directive 2010/75/EU of the European Parliament and of the Council of 24 November 2010 on industrial emissions (integrated pollution prevention and control) (recast) OJ L 334/17 (Industrial Emissions Directive; hereafter IED) as initially adopted. There, 'installation' is defined as 'stationary technical unit within which one or more activities listed in Annex I or in Part 1 of Annex VII are carried out'. Annex I of the IED features Category 4(2)(a), which covers production on an industrial scale of inorganic chemicals, including hydrogen. So far, any production of hydrogen in electrolysers was considered to be of industrial scale, and electrolysers were deemed to be IPPC installations. For forthcoming changes, see subsection 3.4.

[8] Annex to art 1.1 Environment and Planning Act; art 3.72(1)(b) Environmental Activities Decree (*Besluit activiteiten leefomgeving*) of 3 July 2018.

Dutch administrative law prescribes two types of permitting procedures: the standard procedure (eight weeks)[9] and the extended procedure (six months).[10] To install and operate an electrolyser, an applicant will have to submit several permit applications. To make this process smoother, the Ow allows the applicant to submit several applications jointly (thus making one application only).[11] If a joint application involves permits assessed under both procedures, the overall waiting time will be that of the extended one (six months).[12] *Under the Ow, as long as electrolyser is an IPPC-installation, joint permit applications for electrolysers will fall under the extended procedure of six months.*[13] Later in this chapter we indicate waiting times for each relevant permit in case of individual application.

Applications are submitted to and must be reviewed by competent authorities, most often municipalities.[14] In practice, municipalities often pass on the examination of applications to regional branches of *Omgevingsdienst* (Environmental Service), a bureaucratic extension of the competent authority.[15] Therefore, permit applicants must be ready to engage in dialogue with both the relevant municipality and the relevant branch of *Omgevingsdienst*. Reaching out early to either of the two is vital for a smooth permitting procedure, and the applicant can request a pre-application meeting (although it is not mandatory).

The six-month assessment period begins on the day when the authorities receive the application.[16] Exceptionally, they can extend the procedure by six more weeks.[17] However, the length of the procedure is prescriptive, and applicants/project developers cannot force the authorities to comply with the set terms.[18] Additionally, if a submitted application lacks the necessary documents, the authorities will pause the examination period and give the applicant time to submit the materials that are lacking.[19] However, in practice, delays can occur even with complete and correctly submitted applications, especially if an issue requiring additional investigation occurs at later stages of the application process. Whether a permit application will be assessed in a timely manner depends on the availability and the competence of the staff at the *Omgevingsdienst*.

[9] Art 4:13 General Administrative Law Act (*Algemene wet bestuursrecht*) of 4 June 1992; art 16.64 Environment and Planning Act.

[10] S 3.4 General Administrative Law Act.

[11] Art 5.7 Environment and Planning Act.

[12] ibid.

[13] This is because an MBA permit will require an extended procedure. See art 10.24(1)(b) Environment and Planning Decree (*Omgevingsbesluit*) of 3 July 2018. For more on an MBA permit, see subsection 3.4.

[14] Art 2.3(1) Environment and Planning Decree. Provincial government may also be the competent authority, see art 4.6(1).

[15] Omgevingsdienst NL, 'Omgevingsdiensten' (n.d.) <https://www.omgevingsdienst.nl/omgevingsdiensten> accessed 15 January 2025.

[16] Arts 16.61 and 16.64(1) Environment and Planning Act; art 14.1 Environment and Planning Decree.

[17] Art 4:14 General Administrative Law Act; arts 16.64(1) and 16.64(2) Environment and Planning Act.

[18] Although there is a possibility for an applicant (after the decision period has expired) to ask the court to order the competent authority to make a decision.

[19] Arts 4:5 and 4:15 General Administrative Law Act.

3. Specific Permits Applicable to Electrolysers

3.1 Planning Law

Perhaps the most important instrument introduced in the Ow is the so-called environmental plan (*omgevingsplan*).[20] From 1 January 2024 onwards, each Dutch municipality has an environmental plan that shall contain rules for all physical activities that might take place on its territory.[21] Since developing such detailed plans will take considerable time, the Ow envisages a transition period of eight years, from 2024 to 2032.[22] During this time, by operation of law (*ex lege*), environmental plans will consist of municipalities' old urban zoning plans and provisions that the government deemed necessary for each environmental plan on 1 January 2024.[23] However, by 2032 each municipality should have a complete environmental plan by including local provisions from local regulations that concern the physical living environment. With comprehensive requirements for all physical activities outlined in them, environmental plans will de facto form one of the relevant bases of municipalities' approaches to permitting procedures, including for electrolysers. Applicants can access relevant environmental plans for every address in the country by visiting the website of *Omgevingsloket* (the Environmental Desk).[24]

The first step an applicant should take is to check whether an environmental plan allows for the construction *and* operation of an electrolyser. This is likely to be the case in the so-called industrial areas (*bedrijventerreinen*), such as ports or industrial parks, which are sufficiently removed from residential and protected areas. Additionally, these areas are more likely to have the necessary infrastructure foundations in place. An environmental plan can allow for the construction and operation of an electrolyser without requiring a planning permit, in which case it will not be necessary to apply for one. Where an environmental plan allows the building and operating of an electrolyser but requires a permit to do so, an applicant will apply for the permit for a so-called [plan-consistent] environmental activity (*[binnenplanse] omgevingsplanactiviteit*; hereafter Opa).[25]

Where construction *and/or* operation of an electrolyser is not allowed, as is likely to be the case in the areas close to residential neighbourhoods and protected areas, the applicant will have to apply for the 'out-of-plan environmental activity' (*buitenplanse omgevingsplanactiviteit*; hereafter Bopa).[26] In themselves, both Opa and Bopa

[20] Art 4.2 Environment and Planning Act.
[21] ibid.
[22] ibid ch 22.
[23] ibid art 22.1.
[24] Omgevingsloket, 'Regels op de kaart' (n.d.) <https://omgevingswet.overheid.nl/regels-op-de-kaart/zoeken/locatie> accessed 30 January 2025.
[25] Art 5.1(1)(a) Environment and Planning Act.
[26] ibid, Appendix to art 1.1.

applications should be assessed by the relevant municipality within the eight weeks allocated by the regular procedure.[27]

It is also possible for the government to amend a given environmental plan in order to accommodate the construction of an electrolyser. Thus, Article 6.1 of the Energy Act introduces electrolysers with a certain minimum capacity—which is yet to be determined by a ministerial decision—into the scope of projects of national importance, for which the so-called project decision (*projectbesluit*) is mandatory.[28] *Projectbesluit* is a tool that the central government, provinces, or water authorities can use to streamline complex industrial projects.[29] The uniqueness of *projectbesluit* is that it can directly amend environmental plans to accommodate the project.[30] It can also contain all the necessary permits within it.[31] Because of such a 'unification' of permits, the *projectbesluit* procedure can be used to simplify the permitting process.

3.2 Building Law

Under the Ow, two types of permits are associated with building activities. The first one is the Opa permit itself. Since environmental plans will regulate *all* physical activities of a given municipality, including both the operation *and* construction of an electrolyser, an Opa permit can cover spatial planning requirements for the construction of an electrolyser.

The second one is the permit for 'building activity' (*omgevingsvergunning bouwactiviteit*).[32] It refers to the construction, renewal, alteration, or enlargement of a structure. Importantly, an electrolyser itself is not a structure but a machine. However, it can be placed into a structure. Additionally, accompanying structures for other electrolysis-related equipment (compressors, water purification plants) may be built. For structures with a roof, the criteria to decide whether a permit is required are given in Article 2.25 of the *Besluit bouwwerken leefomgeving* (Environmental Buildings Decree).[33] For structures without a roof, these feature in Article 2.26.[34] If any of the structures necessary for an electrolyser fall under the criteria of these two articles, then a permit for building activity is required. It is, therefore, advisable for applicants to consult the relevant municipality to establish whether this will be the case. It shall take no more than eight weeks to obtain a building activity permit from the municipality if applied individually.[35]

[27] The standard procedure is the norm under Environment and Planning Act unless the extended procedure is required.
[28] Art 6.1(1)(k) Energy Act.
[29] Art 5.44 Environment and Planning Act.
[30] ibid art 5.52(1).
[31] ibid art 5.52(2)(a).
[32] S 8.3 Environmental Quality Decree (*Besluit kwaliteit leefomgeving*) of 3 July 2018; para 7.2.2 Environmental Regulation (*Omgevingsregeling*) of 21 November 2019.
[33] Art 2.25 Environmental Buildings Decree (*Besluit bouwwerken leefomgeving*) of 3 July 2018.
[34] ibid art 2.26.
[35] The standard procedure is the norm under Environment and Planning Act unless the extended procedure is required.

Regardless of whether a permit for building activity will be needed, all construction activity will have to comply with the national rules for technical construction quality.[36]

3.3 Energy and Fuels Law

Energy law is an important domain for the operation of electrolysers in the Netherlands, with two main aspects at its core: adherence to the EU requirements for renewable electricity and the energy-saving requirements of domestic Dutch legislation.

Pursuant to the directly effective Delegated Acts 2023/1184 and 2023/1185 of the European Parliament and of the Council, hydrogen produced through electrolysis of water in the Netherlands is to be considered renewable if the process adheres to the requirements laid out in these Delegated Acts.[37] Hence, the origin of electricity used in the process must be strictly monitored.[38]

Next, there are domestic Dutch requirements for sustainable energy use. As long as water electrolysis is considered an MBA, electrolysers must adhere to the energy-saving requirements of Article 5.15 of the *Besluit activiteiten leefomgeving* (Environmental Activities Decree; hereafter Bal). Specifically, operators of electrolysers will have to adopt 'measures to make energy use more sustainable' if the energy consumption of an electrolyser exceeds 50,000 kWh of electricity in a calendar year.[39] Lists of known reduction measures feature in Annexes VII and XIV of *Omgevingsregeling* (the Environmental Regulation; hereafter Or).[40] Additionally, if energy consumption exceeds 10 million kWh—as was the case in one of the analysed permits[41]—research shall be conducted into all possible measures to make energy use more sustainable with a payback period of no more than five years.[42] However, these measures do not have to be complied with if all the electricity used is renewable *and* is produced directly on-site.[43]

[36] Ch 4 Environmental Buildings Decree.

[37] Commission Delegated Regulation (EU) 2023/1184 of 10 February 2023 supplementing Directive (EU) 2018/2001 of the European Parliament and of the Council by establishing a Union methodology setting out detailed rules for the production of renewable liquid and gaseous transport fuels of non-biological origin [2023] OJ L 157/11; Commission Delegated Regulation (EU) 2023/1185 of 10 February 2023 supplementing Directive (EU) 2018/2001 of the European Parliament and of the Council by establishing a minimum threshold for greenhouse gas emissions savings of recycled carbon fuels and by specifying a methodology for assessing greenhouse gas emissions savings from renewable liquid and gaseous transport fuels of non-biological origin and from recycled carbon fuels [2023] OJ L 157/20.

[38] For more information on the Delegated Acts, see Kim Talus, Jaqueline Pinto, and Francisca Gallego, 'Realism at the End of the Rainbow? An Argument Towards Diversifying Hydrogen in EU Regulation' (2024) 17(4) The Journal of World Energy Law & Business 217.

[39] Art 5.15 Environmental Activities Decree. The relevant measures include energy-saving measures, measures to produce renewable energy (up to the annual energy consumption of the business), and measures to replace an energy carrier that would lead to lower carbon dioxide emissions.

[40] Annexes VII and XIV Environmental Regulation.

[41] Permit Eemshaven 3.11.

[42] Art 5.15b Environmental Activities Decree outlines the requirements for such research. A consolidated version of requirements can be found at <https://iplo.nl/thema/energiebesparing/verduurzaming-energiegebruik/informatiebladen-toezicht-handhaving/toezicht-onderzoeksplicht/hulpmiddel-beoordelen-energiebesparingsonderzoek/opbouw-energiebesparingsrapport/> accessed 20 January 2025.

[43] Art 5.15(3)(c) Environmental Activities Decree.

Dutch law applies energy-saving requirements not only to MBAs but also to certain buildings that may house MBAs.[44] This means that the energy consumption of the building itself must be added to the energy consumption of an MBA.

The new Energy Act also regulates the ownership and control aspects of hydrogen production. Specifically, it forbids hydrogen-producing companies to be part of the same company group as transmission or distribution system operators (TSOs/DSOs) in the field of hydrogen, natural gas, or electricity, or for owners of hydrogen-producing companies to hold shares of the said TSOs/DSOs.[45] In the reverse, TSOs/DSOs (or groups associated therewith) cannot hold shares of or participate in companies that produce hydrogen. Finally, a natural or legal person exercising direct or indirect control over a hydrogen-producing company is not able at the same time to exercise direct or indirect control over the TSOs/DSOs (and vice versa: those exercising control over TSOs/DSOs cannot exercise control over hydrogen-producing companies).

However, following Article 3.21 of the Energy Act, a Dutch government minister is able to 'temporarily grant exemption' to one of the said TSOs/DSOs if the matter at hand will 'involve the holding of shares in a legal entity or participation in a company, which constructs, maintains and makes available to a third party a production facility for hydrogen.'[46] In practice, this exception would primarily allow large gas TSOs/DSOs to support the operation of their subsidiaries in the field of renewable hydrogen production.

3.4 Environmental Law

3.4.1 Permitting regime

The Ow defines MBA as 'an activity that may have adverse effects on the environment.'[47] Some—though not all—of the MBAs are designated in the Bal as MBAs that require an MBA permit (*vergunning milieubelastende activiteit*). Operating an electrolyser is an MBA that requires an MBA permit.[48] An MBA permit is separate from an Opa/Bopa permit, although they can be applied for at the same time.[49]

3.4.2 Environmental impact assessment

In addition to permit applications, constructing an electrolyser necessitates a decision by the competent authority on whether an environmental impact assessment (EIA) is required. To establish this, an authority will examine a so-called EIA-review (*Mer-beoordeling*), which will be prepared by the applicant (often a

[44] Art 3.84 Environmental Buildings Decree.
[45] Arts 3.10(1) to 3.10(4) Energy Act.
[46] ibid art 3.21(3)(a).
[47] Annex to art 1.1 Environment and Planning Act. Water discharge activities are excluded from the scope of MBA and form a separate type of activities.
[48] Art 3.73(1) in conjunction with art 3.72(1)(b) Environmental Activities Decree.
[49] Art 5.1(2)(b) Environment and Planning Act.

specialized company on an applicant's behalf).[50] Upon receiving an EIA-review, a municipality will have six weeks to decide whether an EIA is required.[51] If it decides the project will not cause significant environmental effects, it can proceed without an EIA. If it determines that significant environmental effects are not excluded, it can request that an EIA, which complies with the requirements of the EIA Directive, is carried out.[52]

An EIA was never required in the publicly available permits approved under the pre-2024 regulations. On the contrary, the most lenient form of EIA-review available at the time was found to be sufficient.[53] Under the old regime, the statutory threshold between an EIA and an EIA-review was indicatively set at the production level of 100,000 tonnes of hydrogen per year.[54] It is reasonable to assume that under the current regime, the practice will remain the same, and EIA-review will remain sufficient for electrolysers producing less than 100,000 tonnes of hydrogen per year.

An EIA-review can be free in form, but pursuant to the requirements of the EIA Directive it must include information on the project's characteristics and location.[55] Particular attention should be paid to the environmental vulnerability of areas likely to be affected by the project.[56] An EIA-review should also describe the project's potential effects, including the extent, duration, frequency, and reversibility of its impact.[57]

3.4.3 Emissions law

The key criterion for obtaining and maintaining an MBA permit is the adherence of electrolysers to BATs and BREFs, as introduced and mandated by the Industrial Emissions Directive (IED).[58] However, neither the EU nor the Netherlands has drafted BREFs specifically for hydrogen production through water electrolysis. This has two consequences. First, as confirmed by the examined permits, municipalities make use of those BATs and BREFs that are relevant to *some* aspects of water electrolysis, although they were not initially drafted for this process.[59] Second, where no relevant BATs or BREFs are available, municipalities can come to varying conclusions regarding emission regulations. Overall, Dutch Emissions Law aims to prevent or avoid

[50] This is mandated by Category F5 Annex V Environment and Planning Decree (*Omgevingsbesluit*) of 3 July 2018. This category stipulates that activities featuring 'treatment of intermediate products and manufactur[ing] of chemicals', of which water electrolysis is one, are subject to an EIA-review.

[51] Art 11.11 Environment and Planning Decree.

[52] ibid.

[53] Permit Eemshaven 2.10; Permit Farmsum 3.11; Permit Oosterwolde 3.11.

[54] Environmental Impact Assessment Decree (Besluit milieueffectrapportage) of 4 June 1994 (repealed on 1 January 2024), Annex I Category D 34.4.

[55] Annex III Directive 2014/52/EU of the European Parliament and of the Council of 16 April 2014 amending Directive 2011/92/EU on the assessment of the effects of certain public and private projects on the environment OJ L 124/1.

[56] ibid.

[57] ibid.

[58] Arts 11, 14, and 16 Industrial Emissions Directive; art 4.22(2)(c) Environment and Planning Act.

[59] The following BAT conclusions and BREFs were referenced in the examined permits: BAT conclusions for the production of chlor-alkali (2013); BAT conclusions for common waste water and waste gas treatment (2016); BAT conclusions for common waste gas management and treatment systems in the chemical sector (2022); BREF 'Industrial Cooling Systems' (2001).

noise, vibration, and light and odour pollution.[60] However, for example, while noise emissions requirements appear to be relatively uniform, this is not the case with light emissions.

As of now, substantive permitting requirements are imposed on electrolysers by virtue of being designated as IPPC installations. However, this will change. By 1 July 2026, the Netherlands will have to transpose Directive (EU) 2024/1785, which amends the IED (and turns it into IED 2.0).[61] This amendment introduces a critical update for the renewable hydrogen industry by excluding the production of hydrogen through electrolysis of water from its scope, as long as the production capacity of a given electrolyser does not exceed 50 tonnes per day.[62] This will mean that electrolysers below this threshold will not be considered IPPC installations under Dutch law. At 70–80% of electrolyser efficiency, this limit would translate into a required energy input between 86 MW and 99 MW, thus excluding most of the existing operational electrolysers in the EU from the IED scope.[63] *This will bring a substantive relief, and with it, a fundamental change to electrolysers permitting procedures.* The logical step for the Dutch authorities would now be to transpose the IED 2.0 and no longer require an MBA permit for an electrolyser.

3.4.3.1 Noise emissions

The Ow allows municipalities to introduce environmental values in their environmental plans.[64] For noise emissions, these values are measured in decibels (dB(A)). The level of noise emissions that is possible under law depends on whether the activity takes place in an industrial zone or a non-industrial zone. When it comes to industrial zones, municipalities are under an obligation to introduce noise production ceilings.[65]

Article 3.34 of the *Besluit kwaliteit leefomgeving* (Environmental Quality Decree; hereafter Bkl) contains standard *noise production ceilings* for industrial zones, which municipalities can transpose into their environmental plans. These are set at 50 dB(A) during the day and at 40 dB(A) during the night when measured over a long period of time.[66] In exceptional cases, these values can be exceeded, reaching the levels of 60 dB(A) and 50 dB(A), respectively.[67] To determine compliance with sound emission

[60] Art 2.2(1)(c)(5°) Environmental Activities Decree.

[61] Directive (EU) 2024/1785 of the European Parliament and of the Council of 24 April 2024 amending Directive 2010/75/EU of the European Parliament and of the Council on industrial emissions (integrated pollution prevention and control) and Council Directive 1999/31/EC on the landfill of waste OJ L 2024/1785.

[62] ibid Annex I (j).

[63] At the lower heating value, the energy density of hydrogen by weight is 33.3 kWh/kgH_2 (see Ludwig-Bölkow-Systemtechnik, 'Hydrogen Data' (n.d.) <http://www.h2data.de/> accessed 20 January 2025). This means that it will take a 100%-efficient electrolyser 33.3 MW to produce 1 tonne of hydrogen per hour, 24 tonnes of hydrogen per day. To produce 50 tonnes of hydrogen per day (2.08 tonnes per hour), a 100%-efficient electrolyser would need (33.3 MW * 2.08 = 69.4 MW of energy input. However, no electrolysers are 100% efficient. Thus, conventional alkaline electrolysers have an efficiency of 70–75%, in which case they would require more energy input to produce 50 tonnes per day, namely between 99 MW and 92 MW. Some PEM electrolysers can have 80% efficiency, in which case the necessary energy input is 86 MW. At 90% efficiency, an electrolyser would need 77 MW to produce 50 tonnes of hydrogen per day.

[64] Art 2.11 Environment and Planning Act.

[65] ibid art 2.11a.

[66] The exact measurement unit for noise production ceilings is L(den), which refers to dB(A) levels measured over time.

[67] Art 3.35 Environmental Quality Decree.

limits, noise levels must be tested at specific measuring points. Article 3.33 of the Bkl stipulates the location of such points, which will depend on the size of a given industrial zone.

Having discussed noise in industrial zones, we now turn to non-industrial zones. Article 5.65 of the Bkl contains *standard values* for non-industrial zones. Again, municipalities can introduce these into their environmental plans. These are set in the range between 40 dB(A) and 50 dB(A), with quieter limits for night and late evening. For moments of peak operation, the threshold is 65 dB(A) during the night and late evening and unlimited (at the municipality's discretion) for the day.

It is important to remember that while the Bkl provides standard noise thresholds, each municipality can introduce stricter limits into its environmental plan.[68] To achieve the necessary noise levels, applicants will have to consider using quieter (and often more expensive) equipment and sound isolation materials, as well as placing an electrolyser at a location that is farther removed from residential and protected areas.[69] This can be a costly endeavour but not a problematic one. For example, the noise levels of the loudest elements of the Eemshaven electrolyser—the pre-compressor units—reached 116 dB(A).[70] However, with proper isolation and distancing, the long-term noise level at the zone boundary did not exceed 18 dB(A).[71]

3.4.3.2 Light emissions

The Ow does not provide specific regulations for reducing light emissions from electrolysers.[72] Therefore, light nuisance prevention is the responsibility of local authorities and can be regulated in an environmental plan. In two of the reviewed permits that were approved under the pre-2024 regime, the reduction of light emissions was achieved with simple measures such as the choice of lighting equipment.[73] However, a third permit approached the issue in greater depth. Having considered municipal, provincial, and national policies on this matter, the *Omgevingsdienst Groningen* concluded that, according to the provincial policy, a 24/7 operation of an electrolyser ran the risk of a light nuisance.[74] The importance of darkness was recognized for the life cycles of humans and animals.[75] Light usage was therefore required to be brought to the necessary minimum,[76] and examples of suitable measures were given (eg installing more lamps but with lower power, ensuring lamps are facing downwards).[77] The applicant was also requested to draw up a lighting plan as a control obligation.[78]

68 Art 2.11 Environment and Planning Act.
69 Permit Farmsum 4.12.2; Permit Eemshaven 3.12.4.
70 Permit Eemshaven 3.12.2.
71 ibid 3.12.4.
72 Art 2.2(1)(c)(5°) Environmental Activities Decree. Nationally, only regulations for lighting in greenhouses and horticulture are provided in art 4.790 Environmental Activities Decree.
73 Permit Oosterwolde 4.13; Permit Farmsum 4.13.
74 Permit Eemshaven 3.13.3.
75 ibid 3.13.1.
76 ibid 3.13.5.
77 ibid 3.13.7.
78 ibid 3.13.8.

3.4.3.3 Odour emissions, emissions into the air, and soil testing

The Bal also aims to prevent odour emissions.[79] However, no specific rules exist for electrolysers, and odour was not a concern in any of the analysed permits since all substances present in an electrolyser are odourless (including elements of the aquatic solution in an alkaline electrolyser).[80] The same can be said about emissions into the air: while electrolysers can emit oxygen, this gas is not considered a pollutant under Dutch law and is not subject to emission regulations.[81] Finally, soil must be tested before an electrolyser is brought into operation[82] and after its decommissioning.[83] If changes occur during the operation period, soil quality must be compensated.[84] No concerns arose in the reviewed permits in these regards.

3.5 Water Management Law

Under Dutch law, water discharge is considered a specific 'discharge activity' (*lozingsactiviteit*).[85] In cases where discharged water has been previously employed in an MBA, the discharge activity requires a permit.[86] An application for such a permit will be assessed not by municipalities but by water boards (*waterschappen*), Dutch regional governing bodies charged with surface water management.[87] On its own, this permit application should be processed within eight weeks.[88]

Discharge water can be of concern for alkaline electrolysers, where particles that form part of aquatic solutions can escape filters and end up in the discharge water stream. It is also a point of attention for PEM (proton exchange membrane) electrolysers, which require water purification before it can be used in the machine, thus leaving brine as a byproduct to be discharged. For such cases, emission limit values have been established. For water discharge into open water, these are provided in Article 4.68 of the Bal, with calculation methods available in Article 4.69. For water discharge into sewage treatment plants, water boards will take the purification of water, which will happen at the plant, into account when calculating eventual emission limit values.[89] Among the three permits, only one featured an alkaline electrolyser, and the

[79] Art 2.2(1)(c)(5°) Environmental Activities Decree.
[80] Permit Eemshaven 3.14.2; Permit Oosterwolde 4.14.2; Permit Farmsum 4.14.2.
[81] Art 5.30 Environmental Activities Decree; para 2.2.1.1 Environmental Quality Decree.
[82] Para 5.2.2 Environmental Activities Decree.
[83] ibid para 5.2.1.
[84] ibid.
[85] Annex to art 1.1 Environment and Planning Act.
[86] Arts 3.1 and 3.3 Environmental Activities Decree.
[87] ibid art 2.4.
[88] The standard procedure is the norm under Environment and Planning Act unless the extended procedure is required.
[89] Art 8.26 Environmental Quality Decree.

discharge of its wastewater into open water was not a source of concern.[90] For a PEM electrolyser in Farmsum, discharge was organized through a salty water purification plant (*zout afvalwater zuiveringsinstallatie*) that had to be constructed next to the electrolyser site.[91]

Compared to alkaline and PEM electrolysers, which operate at temperatures below 100°C, solid oxide (SO) electrolysers can heat up to very high levels, reaching 700–850°C while operating, and thus require a significant amount of cooling water.[92] If this heated cooling water escapes an electrolyser, it can damage the environment around it. In such cases, the handling of cooling water has to be organized according to the BREF 'Industrial Cooling Systems',[93] as was the case in the Eemshaven permit.[94] In cases where electrolysis of water will no longer be considered an MBA that requires a permit, it is reasonable to assume that municipalities will continue to rely on this BREF.

3.6 Waste Law

Under Dutch law, waste is defined as 'any substance, mixtures or items which the owner discards, intends to discard or is required to discard'.[95] In principle, decommissioning the electrolyser itself at the end of its lifespan should be considered waste. However, this does not appear to be the case in the examined permits. Thus, no waste has been reported for all three electrolysers, except for the small amount of lubricant oil that can be released during maintenance.[96] An additional minor waste item for alkaline electrolysers was the alkaline electrolyte itself, which can be utilized accordingly upon replacement.[97] At the same time, all three permits mandate that upon electrolysers' decommissioning, 'all substances and materials present solely because' of the electrolysers' activities are to be removed 'in an environmentally hygienic manner in consultation with the competent authority'.[98] Still, such removal does not classify decommissioned electrolysers as waste, and it is unclear what will happen to the decommissioned (parts of) electrolysers upon their removal.

[90] Permit Oosterwolde 4.9.

[91] Permit Farmsum 4.9.

[92] Shiva Kumar and Hankwon Lim, 'An Overview of Water Electrolysis Technologies for Green Hydrogen Production' (2022) 8 Energy Reports 13797.

[93] European Bureau for Research on Industrial Transformation and Emissions (2001), 'Industrial Cooling Systems' (hereafter BREF Industrial Cooling Systems) <https://eippcb.jrc.ec.europa.eu/reference/industrial-cooling-systems> accessed 20 January 2025.

[94] Permit Eemshaven 3.9.

[95] Art 1.1 Environmental Management Act (*Wet milieubeheer*) of 13 June 1979 (partly repealed on 1 January 2024). Ch 10 outlines the rules for handling waste.

[96] Permit Farmsum 4.8.

[97] Permit Oosterwolde 4.8.

[98] Permit Eemshaven 1.3.1; Permit Farmsum 1.3.1; Permit Oosterwolde 1.10.1.

3.7 Nature Protection Law

Regarding nature protection, Natura 2000 areas must be protected from any significant effects of electrolysers' activities.[99] An assessment needs to be carried out to establish whether there is clarity on whether an electrolyser's operation could significantly affect a Natura 2000 site.[100] If there is no such clarity, then a special Natura 2000 permit will have to be requested from a provincial government under an extended procedure of six months.[101]

An assessment of a Natura 2000 activity must provide certainty that the activity will not affect the natural characteristics of the Natura 2000 area. If this condition is satisfied, a permit will be issued.[102] If the condition cannot be satisfied, an activity will only obtain approval if there are no real alternatives to it, there is an imperative reason for great public interest, and nature compensation will take place.[103] After the introduction of Regulation (EU) 2022/2577 in December 2022, the construction of an electrolyser—when it produces energy from renewable sources—can be presumed to be in the imperative public interest.[104]

Of the three analysed permits, none of the electrolysers were located near a Natura 2000 area. For permits issued in 2021 and 2023, nitrogen emissions (NO_x) were calculated under the guidelines provided in the governmental Nitrogen Approach Programme.[105] In both cases, the contributions to the closest Natura 2000 sites were found not to exceed 0.00 mol/ha/year.[106] In the Eemshaven permit, issued in 2024, no NO_x calculations were provided. In all three permits, the electrolysers were found not to cause significant effects on any of the nearby Natura 2000 areas.[107]

As long as electrolysers are installed in industrial zones removed from Natura 2000 areas, it is likely that no substantive examination of Natura 2000 activities will take place.

[99] Para 8.6.1 Environmental Quality Decree. Natura 2000 areas are protected zones that contain Europe's most precious and threatened species and habitats. These areas are designated under Council Directive 92/43/EEC of 21 May 1992 on the conservation of natural habitats and of wild fauna and flora (1992) OJ L 206/7 (hereafter Habitats Directive) and Directive 2009/147/EC of the European Parliament and of the Council of 30 November 2009 on the conservation of wild birds (2009) OJ L 20/7 (hereafter Birds Directive). It is not necessary for an activity to take place inside a Natura 2000 area to have an effect on it. Thus, emissions from an industrial installation located outside of a Natura 2000 area can affect the habitat inside the area. Possible effects might include, but are not limited to, the effects of emissions into the air, noise emissions, or vibrations.

[100] There is no definition of what constitutes a 'significant' effect in Environment and Planning Act, but there are pre-2024 guidelines for determining significance. See Steunpunt Natura 2000, 'Leidraad bepaling significantie' (2010) <https://www.commissiemer.nl/docs/mer/diversen/leidraad_bepaling_significantie27052010.pdf> accessed 20 January 2025.

[101] Art 10.24(1)(j) Environment and Planning Decree.

[102] Art 8.74b(1) Environmental Quality Decree.

[103] Art 8.74b(2) Environmental Quality Decree.

[104] Art 3 Regulation (EU) 2022/2577 of 22 December 2022 laying down a framework to accelerate the deployment of renewable energy OJ L 335/36.

[105] Permit Farmsum 3.7; Permit Oosterwolde 3.7.

[106] Permit Farmsum 3.7; Permit Oosterwolde 3.7 and 7.4.

[107] Permit Farmsum 3.7; Permit Oosterwolde 3.7 and 7.4; Permit Eemshaven 2.7.

3.8 Fire Prevention, Health and Safety Law

Given the high flammability of hydrogen in combination with oxygen, safety measures are of utmost importance for electrolysers. Under Dutch law, the two main concepts relevant to guaranteeing the safe operations of electrolysers are the so-called location-related risk (*plaatsgebonden risico*) and 'areas of concern' (*aandachtsgebieden*).[108]

'Location-related risks' should not increase the probability of one person out of 1 million dying in a year.[109] After being calculated, this risk is translated into distance from the source of the activity (in metres). Specific distances for various MBAs are given in Annex VII of the Bkl, but hydrogen production through water electrolysis is not among them.[110] The safety distance for hydrogen storage tanks—a measure that might be used as a reference for electrolysers—is set at 35 metres in category B5 of Annex VII of the Bkl. However, in the Oosterwolde permit, the final safety distance was set at 20 metres.[111]

For hydrogen, 'areas of concern' are areas with potential risks of fire or explosion. The risk calculations are based on the probability of the death of a group of ten or more people per year as a direct result of an unusual event caused by an activity onsite.[112] Annex VII of the Bkl provides a radius of 55 metres for hydrogen storage tanks.[113] However, since electrolysers are always located on designated territory where the presence of ten people simultaneously is unlikely, no 'areas of concern' were considered in any of the analysed permits.[114]

Specific rules begin to apply once the quantity of hydrogen or oxygen onsite increases beyond the thresholds set by the EU Seveso Directive.[115] The Seveso Directive introduces the so-called lower- and upper-tier thresholds. For hydrogen, the figures are 5 and 50 tonnes; for oxygen, these are 200 and 2,000 tonnes respectively. Since 2024, the Seveso Directive has been transposed into Dutch law by the *Omgevingswet* and through various provisions in the accompanying legislation. For lower-tier establishments,[116] calculations of the location-related risk and areas of concern become mandatory.[117] However, it is worth noting that although none of the analysed permits featured

[108] Para 5.1.2.2 Environmental Quality Decree.

[109] 'Location-related risk' is understood as the 'probability of death of an unprotected and continuously present person outside the boundary of the location where an activity is conducted as a direct result of an unusual occurrence caused by that activity'. See art 5.7(1) Environmental Quality Decree.

[110] Annex VII Environmental Quality Decree.

[111] Permit Oosterwolde 7.1.

[112] Art 5.15 Environmental Quality Decree.

[113] ibid Category B5 Annex VII.

[114] Permit Eemshaven 3.15.4; Permit Oosterwolde 4.15.4; Permit Farmsum 4.15.3.

[115] Directive 2012/18/EU of the European Parliament and of the Council of 4 July 2012 on the control of major-accident hazards involving dangerous substances, amending and subsequently repealing Council Directive 96/82/EC OJ L 197/1 (hereafter Seveso Directive).

[116] The term 'establishment' ('*inrichting*') is used in the Seveso Directive, where it means 'the whole location under the control of an operator where dangerous substances are present' (art 3(1)). This term was taken over by the new Dutch regime. For example, para 3.3.1 of Environmental Activities Decree refers to '*Seveso-inrichting*', and art 3.50 stipulates that Seveso establishments include an installation operating an MBA.

[117] Category E6 Annex VII Environmental Quality Decree.

an electrolyser that exceeded even the lower-tier threshold, location-related risks were calculated for all of them regardless. This was done because of the potential of 'unforeseen circumstances' associated with the use of hydrogen.[118] Such calculations were carried out within the Quantitative Risk Analysis (QRA) framework, an umbrella term for risk calculations.[119]

Additional safety regulations are provided by section 4.2 of the Bal, including measures necessary to protect employers, prevent major accidents, and limit their consequences.[120] More stringent requirements apply to the upper-tier establishments.[121]

Where electrolysers do not cross the lower-tier threshold, safe storage and handling of hydrogen and oxygen are organized by adhering to the so-called *Publicatiereeks Gevaarlijke Stoffen* (Dangerous Substances Publications; hereafter PGS), the national Dutch guidance documents for companies working with dangerous substances.[122] So far, no PGS has been devised specifically for electrolysers and the closest relevant PGSs are used. Thus, one analysed permit used PGS 15 (storage of packaged hazardous materials)[123] for hydrogen storage.[124] Another permit referred to PGS 35 (installations for delivery of hydrogen to road vehicles)[125] as a 'good starting point for the safe and environmentally responsible use of such installation [electrolysers] including storage'.[126] A third permit refers to both PGS 15 and PGS 35.[127] It is therefore advised that project applicants familiarize themselves with PGS 15 and PGS 35.

3.9 Archaeology Law

Under the Ow, municipalities are obliged to preserve cultural heritage, including of archaeological nature, and to devise rules to that effect.[128] The discovery of archaeological formations can postpone permitting and thus delay the construction of electrolysers. This was the case in one of the reviewed permits, where a late-stage re-examination of the site revealed that the area had to be studied further in light of cultural heritage preservation. According to a source who worked on this permit application, the subsequent research took six more months. In the end, specific

118 Permit Eemshaven 3.2.4; Permit Oosterwolde 4.15.2; Permit Farmsum 4.2.4.

119 For an example of a QRA, see AVIV, 'QRA Groene Waterstoffabriek VoltH2 Terneuzen' (29 July 2021) <https://repository.officiele-overheidspublicaties.nl/Bijlagen/TerInzageLegging/2022/til-2022-451/1/bijlage/QRA_20210729_D3_22.pdf> accessed 20 January 2025.

120 Arts 4.4 and 4.9 Environmental Activities Decree.

121 ibid art 4.14.

122 PGS Programmabureau 'Publicatiereeks Gevaarlijke Stoffen' (n.d.) <https://publicatiereeksgevaarlijkestoffen.nl/> accessed 20 January 2025.

123 Publicatiereeks Gevaarlijke Stoffen 15, 'Opslag van verpakte gevaarlijke stoffen' (2023) <https://publicatiereeksgevaarlijkestoffen.nl/publicaties/pgs15/> accessed 20 January 2025.

124 Permit Oosterwolde 1.8. Specifically, paras 7.4, 7.5, 7.6, 7.7, and 7.8 of PGS 15 are considered relevant.

125 Publicatiereeks Gevaarlijke Stoffen 35, 'Waterstofinstallaties voor het afleveren van waterstof aan voertuigen en werktuigen' (2021) <https://publicatiereeksgevaarlijkestoffen.nl/publicaties/pgs35/> accessed 20 January 2025.

126 Permit Farmsum 4.15.7.

127 Permit Eemshaven 3.15.8 and 3.15.9.

128 Art 2.12(3)(f) Environment and Planning Act; art 5.130 Environmental Quality Decree.

building rules had to be implemented by the builder, including creating a larger buffer zone between the foundation of the electrolyser and the archaeological layer and using piles for construction.[129] The excavation works had to be carried out under the supervision of an archaeological expert. These measures were selected by the municipality and were discretionary. While they were not too costly to implement, the extensive project delay was an issue of considerable concern for the applicants.

4. Recommendations to Improve the System

To improve and stabilize the Dutch permitting regime for electrolysers in times of rapid change, the following three key recommendations should be considered:

1. The minimum capacity threshold for electrolysers to fall into the *projectbesluit* frame has to be adopted with a thorough view of realistic forecasts for when electrolysers will become operational. It might be tempting to set the bar relatively high to avoid including too many electrolysers into the scope of *projectbesluit* and to incentivize large investments. However, the Minister should keep in mind that smaller projects hold the potential for a more steady rollout of electrolysers as they are faster and easier to build. We therefore suggest that the *projectbesluit* threshold is set at the production capacity of 50 tonnes of hydrogen per day, linking it to the regime of the IED 2.0. This will create a situation where all electrolysers below the threshold will benefit from the relaxation of the IED 2.0, while all those above it will benefit from the *projectbesluit*, effectively creating a lighter regime for *all* electrolysers in the country. We are mindful of the fact that this will have a centralizing effect that is not entirely in line with the framework of the Ow. However, if we are to prioritize the *realistic rollout* of (smaller) electrolysers, the *projectbesluit* threshold must not be too high.
2. A standardized guidance document for constructing and operating electrolysers in the Netherlands should be published. Such a guidance document should clearly differentiate between electrolysers exceeding the IED 2.0 50-tonnes-per-day production threshold and those that do not. A clear and comprehensive regime has to be developed for those not exceeding the threshold. For those exceeding the threshold, uniform emissions guidelines have to be provided (even with the view of the *projectbesluit* option). These guidelines would not prevent municipalities from introducing stricter emissions regulations, but developers could use them as a benchmark, thus finding certainty regarding basic emissions standards.

[129] Permit Farmsum 8.1.

3. A specific PGS for hydrogen production through water electrolysis has to be drafted. It should then be referenced in the relevant sections of the Ow.

5. Conclusion

The Dutch permitting regime for electrolysers is currently undergoing major changes, and at the moment of writing it remains too soon to judge whether the introduction of the Ow has been successful in simplifying the permitting procedure. Some of the significant current requirements—emission regulations, EIA review, and water discharge permits—are applicable because hydrogen production through water electrolysis is considered an MBA under Dutch law. On top of that, an electrolyser requires an MBA permit because it is an IPPC-installation. With the transposition of the IED 2.0, electrolysers—subject to the 50-tonnes-per-day limitation—will no longer be considered IPPC installations and will not require an MBA permit. This necessitates action on behalf of the authorities to close the regulatory gaps. This should be done in the spirit of simplifying the procedure, given the electrolysers' minimal environmental impact compared to other methods of hydrogen production.

While the development of uniform national guidelines would certainly be beneficial, Dutch municipalities have the power to take matters into their own (local) hands should this process take too long. Enacted on 1 January 2024, the Ow is based on the principle of subsidiarity, its motto being 'decentralized, unless …' (*decentraal, tenzij …*). The concept of an environmental plan, where municipalities can establish a wide array of rules for permitting procedures in their territory, clearly manifests this principle. In this light, the key advice to future project applicants is to reach out to the relevant municipality as soon as possible to learn about its rules for—and its experience with—electrolysers in its area of responsibility.

Appendix

Table II.1 List of Dutch environmental laws with English translations.

Dutch law	English translation
Omgevingswet (Ow)	Environment and Planning Act
Omgevingsbesluit (Ob)	Environment and Planning Decree
Besluit bouwwerken leefomgeving (Bbl)	Environmental Buildings Decree
Besluit kwaliteit leefomgeving (Bkl)	Environmental Quality Decree
Besluit activiteiten leefomgeving (Bal)	Environmental Activities Decree
Omgevingsregeling (Or)	Environmental Regulation

Table II.2 List of approved electrolyser permits analysed in this chapter.

Location	Approval date	Type of electrolyser
Oosterwolde	8 September 2021	1.3 MW alkaline electrolyser with storage and disposal facilities (tube trailers), which are discharged by third parties. The project's production capacity is 35 kg of hydrogen per hour, projected output approximately 300 tonnes per year. Production average of 0.84 tonnes per day.
Farmsum	4 October 2023	20 MW PEM electrolyser. The setup includes eight containers with electrolysis units, with electrical capacity of 2–2.5 MW each. The project's overall maximum production capacity is 360 kg of hydrogen per hour, projected output 3,139 tonnes per year. Production average of 8.8 tonnes per day.
Eemshaven	2 April 2024	The project includes two electrolysers: Three buildings with either alkaline or PEM electrolysers (100 + 100 + 150 MW) and an outdoor 20 MW solid oxide (SO) electrolyser. The choice between alkaline or PEM electrolysers has not been made in the permit (application). The expected combined production capacity is 7 tonnes of hydrogen per hour, with 4,500 full-load operation hours per year. Production average of 86 tonnes per day.

Further Reading

NL Hydrogen, *Handreiking vergunningverlening kleinschalig waterstofelektrolyse* (November 2023) https://nlhydrogen.nl/wp-content/uploads/2023/12/WP1-Handreiking-vergunningverlening-kleinschalige-waterstofelektrolyse.pdf accessed 12 February 2025.

NWP, *Hydrogen Roadmap for the Netherlands* (2021) https://nationaalwaterstofprogramma.nl/documenten/handlerdownloadfiles.ashx?idnv=2379389 accessed 12 February 2025.

Omgevingsloket, *Regels op de kaart* (n.d.) https://omgevingswet.overheid.nl/regels-op-de-kaart/zoeken/locatie accessed 12 February 2025.

Omgevingsdienst NL, *Omgevingsdiensten* (n.d.) https://www.omgevingsdienst.nl/omgevingsdiensten accessed 12 February 2025.

TNO, *Evaluation of the Levelised Cost of Hydrogen Based on Proposed Electrolyser Projects in the Netherlands* (13 May 2024) https://publications.tno.nl/publication/34642511/mzKCln/TNO-2024-R10766.pdf accessed 12 February 2025.

III

Denmark

Emilie Victoria Nørgaard Elkjær

1. Introduction

On a sunny day in October 2024, just outside Copenhagen, the future of the Danish hydrogen economy gathered at the World Hydrogen Week Conference.[1] The room was buzzing with voices and hope for the upcoming hydrogen sector. Hydrogen, in all its forms and with all its legal and financial challenges, was discussed by the many speakers and attendees. Despite the positive mindset at the event, one could not ignore the significant challenges that the hydrogen sector faces today. Amongst those are the slow roll out of electrolyser capacity despite national capacity goals, a lack of infrastructure, high costs, and complex permitting regimes.[2] The main aim of this chapter is to understand and examine, in particular, the latter challenge: namely, the Danish approach to the permitting regime for electrolysers.

The chapter is structured in the following way: initially, a brief introduction to the Danish regulatory landscape, with a particular view to electrolysers, is provided in the remainder of this introduction. Thereafter, the most important aspects of the actual permitting regime is examined in section 2. This is followed by section 3, which features a discussion of the advantages and disadvantages of the permitting regime, including suggestions for improvement. A conclusion is drawn at the end of the chapter.

[1] World Hydrogen Leaders, *World Hydrogen Week* https://www.worldhydrogenweek.com/event/249bfbeb-416c-4d31-9776-1b968ca70174/websitePage:7596864b-428a-4356-9b74-b01038494c2d accessed 5 October 2024.

[2] Thanh Tuan Le and others, 'Fueling the Future: A Comprehensive Review of Hydrogen Energy Systems and Their Challenges' (2024) 54 International Journal of Hydrogen Energy 791, 805 https://www.sciencedirect.com/science/article/abs/pii/S0360319923039988 accessed 5 October 2024.

The Danish energy sector is governed by a series of laws and regulations. Two significant pieces of legislation are the Law on Electricity Supply and the Law on Gas Supply, which establish the fundamental regulations for their respective sectors.[3] Hydrogen was formally incorporated into the Danish gas regulation in December 2022.[4] In addition, many political agreements have been concluded concerning hydrogen,[5] but a political agreement does not have any legal implications in the Danish legal system. The legal force of such an agreement is purely based on the actions taken by the law-makers afterwards.[6] With regard to the permitting regime, the Danish Law on Administration is a key legislative framework, outlining the procedures and rules that all Danish authorities must adhere to when processing cases.[7] Moreover, rules regulating the permitting regime for electrolysers are found in several specialized laws, such as environmental law.

In 2021, Denmark took a crucial step towards establishing its hydrogen sector with the creation of a 'Strategy for Power-to-X'.[8] This strategy defines that 'PtX covers a number of technologies, all of which are based on electricity being used to produce *hydrogen*', and further: '*The central technology in PtX is an electrolyser*, which uses electricity to split water into oxygen and hydrogen'.[9]
The strategy emphasizes the immense importance of Power-to-X (PtX) for the decarbonization of Denmark.[10] Crucially, it suggests that Denmark should aim for 4-6 GW electrolyser capacity for green hydrogen production by 2030.[11] To facilitate the development of electrolysers, the Danish Energy Agency (DEA) opened a hydrogen tender in April 2023.[12] Two key conditions in the tender were that the hydrogen produced was 'green' and generated via a 'water electrolyser'.[13] In October 2023, the DEA decided to provide grants to five developers of PtX projects in Denmark.[14] The winning

[3] The Ministry of Climate, Energy and Utilities, Law on Electricity Supply, LBK no 1248 of 24 October 2023 https://www.retsinformation.dk/eli/lta/2023/1248; Law on Gas Supply, LBK no 1100 of 16 August 2023 https://www.retsinformation.dk/eli/lta/2023/1100, both accessed 2 August 2024.

[4] The Ministry of Climate, Energy and Utilities, *Law amending the Gas Supply Law, the Act on Energinet and the Electricity Supply*, Law no 1594 of 28 December 2022, § 1 https://www.retsinformation.dk/eli/lta/2022/1594 accessed 2 August 2024.

[5] Political agreement between the Government (Socialdemokratiet, Venstre og Moderaterne), Socialistisk Folkeparti, Liberal Alliance, Det Konservative Folkeparti, Enhedslisten, Det Radikale Venstre, Dansk Folkeparti and Alternativet, *Economic framework conditions for hydrogen infrastructure part 2: Danish pipe-bound hydrogen infrastructure* (April 2024) https://www.kefm.dk/Media/638478420542283365/Økonomiske%20rammevilkår%20for%20brintinfrastruktur%20-2.%20delaftale%20om%20rørbunden%20brintinfrastruktur_april%202024.pdf accessed 29 December 2024.

[6] The Danish Parliament official webpage, 'What are the Implications of a Political Agreement?' https://www.ft.dk/da/ofte-stillede-spoergsmaal/lov_hvilken-betydning-har-en-politisk-aftale accessed 2 August 2024.

[7] The Ministry of Justice, Law on Administration, LBK no 433 of 22 April 2014, §§ 7, 8, 9, and 19 https://www.retsinformation.dk/eli/lta/2014/433 accessed 10 August 2024.

[8] The Ministry of Climate, Energy and Utilities and the Government, *Strategy for Power-to-X* (2021) https://kefm.dk/Media/637751860733099677/Regeringens%20strategi%20for%20Power-to-X.pdf accessed 2 August 2024.

[9] ibid 5; emphasis added.

[10] ibid 3.

[11] ibid 3.

[12] DEA, 'Tender for support for the production of Power-to-X' (Mercell, 19 April 2023) https://www.ethics.dk/ethics/eo#/2b3ea81c-1ca9-4d3d-b563-b87f629fb79c/homepage accessed 3 August 2024.

[13] DEA, 'Conditions for tender of State aid for the Production of Power-to-X in Denmark' (April 2023) s 5.5.

[14] DEA, 'Power-to-X tender' (The DEA official webpage) https://ens.dk/ansvarsomraader/power-x-og-groen-brint/power-x-udbud accessed 3 August 2023

developers will have a combined hydrogen production potential of 279 MW, significantly supporting the capacity goal of 4–6 GW electrolyser capacity by 2030.[15]

To assist the sector with upscaling, the Danish state is actively developing hydrogen infrastructure. For instance, political agreements have been concluded assigning responsibility for a future hydrogen grid,[16] as well as allowing for direct pipelines and geographically differentiated consumer tariffs for hydrogen.[17] Direct lines, defined as gas pipelines that complement the common grid, are ideal for companies that consume considerable amounts of energy as these reduce the need for grid expansions and ensure high energy security for the user.[18] A significant expansion of the electrolyser infrastructure was agreed upon in April 2024 via a political agreement that establishes a 'hydrogen backbone'—a pipeline connecting the Danish North Sea to Germany.[19] The idea is to exploit the vast amounts of offshore wind located in the Danish North Sea region to produce green hydrogen, and then transport this via the pipeline to Germany.[20] The project builds on the agreement between Denmark and Germany to develop hydrogen trade between the two countries.[21]

Despite the optimism and immense work done by the Danish state, it is important to note that, as of autumn 2024, some of the hydrogen momentum appears to be diminishing. For instance, the major Danish company Ørstad has stopped or postponed several of its electrolyser projects.[22] These cancellations are mainly driven by inadequate financing and the immaturity of the hydrogen market.[23] Furthermore, the establishment of the Danish hydrogen backbone has been pushed back to 2032 from the original date of 2028.[24] Due to these cancellations and postponements, the Danish Minister for Climate, Energy and Utilities said in October 2024 that it would be difficult to reach the hydrogen capacity goal that was set for 2030.[25]

[15] DEA, 'Fact sheet on the Power-to-X tender' 1 https://ens.dk/forsyning-og-forbrug/power-x-udbud accessed 4 August 2024.

[16] Political agreement between the Government (Socialdemokratiet, Venstre og Moderaterne), Socialistisk Folkeparti, Liberal Alliance, Det Konservative Folkeparti, Enhedslisten, Det Radikale Venstre, Dansk Folkeparti and Alternativet, 'The possibility of establishing a hydrogen infrastructure, part 1: Ownership and operation of the future Danish pipe-bound hydrogen infrastructure' (May 2023) 2 https://kefm.dk/Media/638204311368810699/Aftaletekst%20-%20mulighed%20for%20etablering%20af%20brintinfrastruktur.pdf accessed 3 August 2024.

[17] ibid 4.

[18] Law on Gas Supply (n 3) § 6(1)(4).

[19] 'The possibility of establishing a hydrogen infrastructure, part 1: Ownership and operation of the future Danish pipe-bound hydrogen infrastructure' (n 16) 2–3.

[20] ibid.

[21] Joint declaration of intent on the cooperation on green hydrogen and the realization of a land-based border crossing hydrogen pipeline between western Denmark and northern Germany (Denmark-Germany) (24 March 2023) https://www.kefm.dk/Media/638151855536501080/Joint%20Declaration%20Hydrogen%20DNK-DEU%20.pdf accessed 19 October 2024.

[22] Ritzau 'Ørsted har droppet over halvdelen af brintprojekter siden 2023' *Berlingske* (29 September 2024) <https://energiwatch.dk/Energinyt/Cleantech/article17355844.ece> accessed 14 October 2024.

[23] Cecilie Veile, 'For to år siden var det en vigtig satsning: Nu dropper Ørsted stort projekt' *Børsen* (15 August 2024) https://borsen.dk/nyheder/virksomheder/orsted-dropper-gront-braendstofprojekt-det-haenger-ikke-sammen accessed 5 October 2024.

[24] Maz Plechinger, 'Brintrøret forsinkes til efter 2030' *Energy Watch* (27 September 2024) https://energiwatch.dk/Energinyt/Cleantech/article17485924.ece accessed 1 November 2024.

[25] Cecilie Hänsch Emanuel, 'Rørforsinkelse er en bombe under brintmålsætningen' *Energy Watch* (15 October 2024) https://energiwatch.dk/article17539489.ece accessed 19 October 2024.

To sum up: hydrogen is still in an infant state in Denmark. However, many projects and law amendments are working towards creating a Danish hydrogen market and infrastructure, establishing a level playing field for possible developers and pushing investments in the hydrogen arena. Despite the great efforts, the Danish hydrogen dream seems to be facing difficulties for various reasons. A critical factor for the upscaling is without doubt smooth and fast permitting procedures.

2. General Observations on the Permitting Regime

This section examines the Danish hydrogen permitting regime. Subsection 2.1 reviews procedural initiatives to streamline the permitting procedures, while subsection 2.2 analyses the substantial requirements in the permitting regime relevant to a developer of electrolysers.

In Denmark, designated timeframes for the permitting of 'renewable energy facilities' have been implemented as a consequence of the recent changes to the Renewable Energy Directive (REDIII).[26] The Danish definition of a 'renewable energy facility' is the following: '*renewable energy* facilities established and operated for the purpose of *producing energy* from *renewable energy sources*'.[27] Hence there are two cumulative requirements: (i) the facility must produce energy and (ii) the energy source must be renewable. An electrolyser does not per se produce energy; instead it converts electricity into a new energy source. That being said, an electrolyser does produce hydrogen, which can, if the concepts are understood broadly, be classified as 'energy', fulfilling the first criterion. Furthermore, since the hydrogen discussed in this book is 'green', it is a precondition that the electricity used in the production comes from renewable energy sources, satisfying the second condition. Hence, the electrolyser is subject to the term 'renewable energy facility'.

If this conclusion is reached, the time frame for obtaining the relevant permits is two years.[28] If 'extraordinary circumstances' occur then this time limit may be exceptionally extended by six months, making the definite time limit two and a half years.[29] The establishment of a specific time frame is desirable as it enhances legal certainty for the developers and ensures that electrolysers will be put on the ground swiftly.

If an electrolyser is not considered a 'renewable energy facility', no specific time limit applies, as Denmark has no uniform deadlines for authorities when processing applications or permits.[30] Instead, all public bodies must act in line with the binding

[26] Directive (EU) 2023/2414 of the European Parliament and of the Council of 18 October 2023 on the promotion of energy from renewable sources [2023] OJ L [series] arts 16, 16a, and 16b.

[27] The Ministry of Climate, Energy and Utilities, Decree on contact point, the RE permit process and areas for the promotion of RE, BEK no 773 on 20 June 2024 §4(1) <https://www.retsinformation.dk/eli/lta/2024/773> accessed 12 August 2024; emphasis added.

[28] ibid §16(1).

[29] ibid §16(3).

[30] Guidance on the Public Administration Act. VEJ number 11740 on the 04th of December 1986. Point 205 <https://www.retsinformation.dk/eli/retsinfo/1986/11740> accessed 14 September 2025.

principle of *good administrative practice*, which requires that processing times be 'reasonable'.[31] What is 'reasonable' depends on the specific case, its material, and scope.[32]

The participation of the public in decision-making processes is crucial in a country like Denmark, where the Aarhus Convention has been signed.[33] Public participation is prescribed as a part of several steps of the permitting procedure for electrolysers, such as in the context of adopting a new local plan within planning law.[34] Despite the importance of public involvement in democratic processes, it has consequences for a timely permitting process as it extends case proceedings, ironically interfering with Danish and European goals for faster approvals of renewable energy projects. Public participation must therefore be taken into consideration when planning the permitting process for a specific PtX project in Denmark.

To install an electrolyser, applicants must engage with multiple authorities. To simplify this, the DEA serves as the primary guide for the permitting process, as a so-called contact point, and must also ensure adherence to the established time limits.[35] This system reflects recent updates to the REDIII which requires each Member State to designate a contact point for facilitation and coordination of renewable energy projects.[36] To comply with its contact point responsibilities, the DEA established a 'PtX Taskforce'. One of the taskforce's main aims is to '[c]ontribute to coordination across state and municipal authorities in relation to the PtX area with a particular focus on approval and permit procedures'.[37] The taskforce established an Authority Working Group (AWG) and a Stakeholder Forum (SF).[38] The AWG, composed of representatives from permitting authorities, coordinates efforts and shares knowledge to improve the quality and speed of permitting.[39] The SF, composed of state and market actors, fosters collaboration to address challenges, share best practices, and support the achievement of the hydrogen capacity goal.[40]

[31] The Danish Parliamentary Ombudsman official authority guides '#11 case processing time' section 3.1 <https:'//www.ombudsmanden.dk/find-viden/myndighedsguiden/generel-forvaltningsret/11-sagsbehandlingstid> accessed on 30th October; Law on The Parliamentary Ombudsman. LBK number 349 on the 22nd of March 2013 the principle of law derived from the laws §21 https://www.retsinformation.dk/eli/lta/2013/349 accessed 14 September 2025.

[32] ibid.

[33] Convention on Access to Information, Public Participation in Decision-Making and Access to Justice in Environmental Matters (adopted 25 June 1998, entered into force 30 October 2001) 2161 UNTS 447 (Aarhus Convention) https://treaties.un.org/Pages/ViewDetails.aspx?src=IND&mtdsg_no=XXVII-13&chapter=27#EndDec accessed 3 January 2025.

[34] The Ministry of City, Land and the Church, The Law on Planning, LBK no 572 of 29 May 2024 § 24 https://www.retsinformation.dk/eli/lta/2024/572 accessed 7 November 2024.

[35] Decree on contact point, the RE permit process and areas for the promotion of RE (n 27) § 5 and § 6(1) no 5.

[36] REDIII (n 26) art 16(3).

[37] The DEA 'Commissary for PtX taskforce' (September 2022) 1 <https://ens.dk/forsyning-og-forbrug/myndighedsarbejdsgruppe-og-interessentforum-ptx> accessed 5 August 2024.

[38] ibid.

[39] ibid 2–3.

[40] ibid 4–5.

3. Specific Permits Applicable to Electrolysers

3.1 Planning Law

3.1.1 Procedural aspects

The first step a developer of an electrolyser project in Denmark needs to take is to obtain permission to set up the PtX-facility, as required by planning law. The most relevant permits in this area can be found in the Law on Planning (Planning Law).[41] The municipality in which the PtX will be located is the competent authority within this legal field.[42]

3.1.2 Substantial aspects

The Danish territory is divided into three zones: urban zone, summerhouse zone, and rural zone.[43] The main purpose of the zones is to prevent arbitrary constructions in open land and thus to ensure a clear distinction between urban and rural areas.[44] The division of zones would normally follow that situation on the ground. Hence, an urban zone is where there is a city; a summerhouse zone is an area with summerhouses, where one may only stay continuously during the summer; and the rural zone encompasses land not covered by the two other categories.[45]

Furthermore, the land of the Danish municipalities is governed by (i) a municipal plan and (ii) a local plan.[46] The difference between the two is that a municipal plan is not binding upon citizens; it is an overarching strategy or vision for the land of the municipality that is valid for twelve years.[47] The local plan, on the other hand, is concerned with the planning of a specific location in the municipality. It is based on and cannot contradict the municipal plan, and it is binding upon citizens.[48] If a municipality has rural zones, planning in these areas is mainly governed by 'land zone permits', existing alongside the other plans.[49] In certain cases, a local plan can replace a land zone permit by containing a provision stipulating that the local plan also serves as such a permit ('local plan with bonus effect').[50]

The municipality shall develop a new local plan before 'major building or construction works' are initiated within its municipality.[51] There is no absolute and universal

[41] Law on Planning (n 34).
[42] ibid § 11(1) and § 13(1).
[43] ibid § 34.
[44] The Ministry of City, Land and the Church, Guidance on land zone administration, VEJ no 10076 on 5 June 2018 s 1.1. <https://www.retsinformation.dk/eli/retsinfo/2019/10076> accessed 29 December 2024.
[45] Law on Planning (n 34) § 34(1), (2), and (3), and § 40(1).
[46] ibid §11(1), § 11b(1).
[47] ibid § 11(1) and (2).
[48] ibid § 13(1) no 1.
[49] ibid § 35(1); DEA 'Establishment of PtX facilities on land' <https://veprojekter.dk/anlaeg/ptxanleag> accessed 14 January 2025.
[50] ibid § 15(4).
[51] ibid § 13(2).

understanding of what is covered by this wording, rather it is a judgment based on concrete cases in which an important factor seems to be whether the project significantly changes the physical environment.[52] Hence, depending on the size, capacity, and specific building situation, the electrolyser might fall within or outside the local plan requirement. One could, for instance, imagine that a small electrolyser serving only three or four houses falls outside the 'major building' wording. In this situation, the electrolyser might be constructed within the boundaries of an already existing local plan, which is also often the case for private solar panels on roofs.[53] As mentioned, if the electrolyser is placed in a rural zone, a 'land zone permit' is needed. The requirement of a land zone permit is simply that a 'new construction is built' in a rural zone.[54]

An interesting practical issue for electrolysers is that they would normally be classified as 'industrial facilities' which is typically placed within an urban zone.[55] Placement in this zone is also practically attractive because it ensures optimal access to crucial infrastructure, such as pipelines and water supply.[56] This is not always the case, however, as big electrolyser facilities could benefit from a placement close to a big renewable energy facility such as solar or wind parks, which are often located in rural zones. To mitigate this problem, urban zones can, in exceptional circumstances, be extended to an area in a rural zone.[57] However, this usually requires that the extension happens at the border of an already existing urban zone, also known as the 'inside out' principle, which significantly limits the possible extension of urban zones.[58] To diminish the practical problems of the 'inside out' principle', a new law on Energy Parks was implemented in July 2024, allowing for deviation from the principle.[59] The law is currently being used for the energy park 'Idomlund' in the municipality of Holstebro, which is designated for electrolysers.[60]

To sum up: to be in accordance with the Danish planning law one would need (i) a valid local plan, potentially with bonus effect, or in certain cases, a (ii) land zone permit.

[52] The Ministry of Environment and Equality, 'Guidance on local planning' (September 2009) s 1.3.2. <https://www.planinfo.dk/Media/637915963709392540/vejledning_om_lokalplanlaegning_hwu%20(1).pdf> accessed 3 November 2024.

[53] For the process of private solar planes see DEA 'Establishment and operation of solar cell systems on roofs' <https://veprojekter.dk/anlaeg/solcelleanlaegpaatage> accessed 3 November 2024.

[54] Law on Planning (n 34) § 35(1).

[55] The Ministry of City, Land and the Church, 'Guidance about the Law on Planning', VEJ no 187 on 14 November 1996, s F, subs 5 https://www.retsinformation.dk/eli/mt/1996/187 accessed 6 November 2024; Establishment of PtX facilities on land (n 49); The Ministry of Environment and Equality, 'Relation to planning law' https://miljogodkendelsesvejledningen.dk/opslag/51-forholdet-til-planomraadet accessed 5 November 2024.

[56] Establishment of PtX facilities on land (n 49).

[57] Law on Planning (n 34) § 15(2) no 1.

[58] ibid § 11a(8).

[59] The Ministry of City, Land and the Church, Law on Energy Parks, LAW no 614 on 11 June 2024 § 10 <https://www.retsinformation.dk/eli/lta/2024/614> accessed 11 November 2024.

[60] The Agency for Planning and Rural Development 'Draft order for an energy park at Idomlund in Holstebro Municipality' (Høring§Portalen, 1 October 2024) § 2 and § 3 <https://hoeringsportalen.dk/Hearing/Details/69103> accessed 11 November 2024.

3.2 Building Law

3.2.1 Procedural aspects

The primary law in relation to the actual construction of the electrolyser is the Law on Building (Building Law).[61] In this field of law, it is the municipalities that are the relevant authorities.[62] In the Building Law, there is no requirement for public participation. However, a practice of conducting 'neighbourhood hearings' has emerged, stemming from the administrative law's provision on consultation of affected parties.[63] The consultation, which might extend case process time, must be conducted if the building will result in 'concrete, substantial inconveniences' for the building's neighbours.[64]

3.2.2 Substantial aspects

A building permit is required when one is constructing a new building or making additions to already existing buildings.[65] The relevant question is therefore whether or not an electrolyser is a 'building'. In the Building Law, 'building' is defined as 'buildings and walls as well as *other fixed constructions and facilities*, when the application of the law to the constructions in question, is *justified by the considerations which the law intends to take care of*.'[66] Thus, there are two criteria that a construction would have to fulfil to be considered a building: (i) it must be covered by the 'building definition' and (ii) the Building Law's aims must justify the application of the law to a given building.

In relation to the first requirement, an electrolyser is covered by the definition of a fixed facility. An electrolyser will, usually, not be transportable and is thus 'fixed'. Further, it must be assumed that an electrolyser would be covered by the normal understanding of the term 'facility'. With regard to the second requirement, one of the aims of the law is 'to ensure that buildings and the property's outside areas are of a satisfactory quality, taking into account the intended use and that they are properly maintained'.[67] Setting up an electrolyser and ensuring its constructional safety is covered by the aim of securing the satisfactory quality of buildings. An electrolyser is an electrochemical facility which is also subject to many fire and security requirements. Due to this, it must be assumed that an electrolyser would be subject to the aim of securing its satisfactory quality, as the opposite (non-satisfactory quality) might be dangerous.

[61] The Ministry of Social Affairs and Housing, The Law on Building, LBK no 1178 on 23 September 2016 <https://www.retsinformation.dk/eli/lta/2016/1178> accessed 15 August 2024.

[62] ibid § 16.

[63] See the Law on Administration (n 7) § 19.

[64] The Danish Parliamentary Ombudsman official authority guides '#14 Consultation of neighbours in building cases' (The Danish Parliamentary Ombudsman official webpage, 27 March 2024) <https://www.ombudsmanden.dk/find-viden/myndighedsguiden/specifikke-sagsomraader/14-partshoering-af-naboer-i-byggesager> accessed 29 December 2024.

[65] Law on Building (n 61) § 2(1)(a), seen in conjunction with the laws §16.

[66] ibid § 2(2); emphasis added.

[67] ibid § 1.

Thus, the electrolyser satisfies the two requirements, and is covered by the term 'building', making it subject to the building permit.

To sum up: to be in accordance with Building Law, a developer would need a building permit.

3.3 Emissions and Environmental Law

3.3.1 Procedural aspects

In relation to Emissions and Environmental regulation the most important legal documents are the Law on Environmental Assessment (Law on EIA),[68] the Law on Environmental Protection,[69] and its related Decree number 1027 on the approval of List Activities (Decree on List Activities).[70] In the area of emissions and environmental law, EU plays an immense role. Two important EU acts impacting Danish environmental and emission law are the Industrial Emissions Directive and the Environmental Impact Assessment Directive.[71] The relevant authorities in this section are the municipalities.[72] As mentioned earlier in this chapter, some permits in accordance with environmental law stipulate public participation, affecting case processing time.[73]

3.3.2 Substantial aspects

To build a PtX facility, one may need a 'list activity permit'.[74] The permit has its name from a separate 'list' (Decree no 1027) to the Law on Environmental Protection stipulating activities that are 'especially polluting' and require a 'list activity permit' to be in accordance with environmental law.[75] In the Decree the following is mentioned in annex 1, section 4:

> *4.2. Production of inorganic chemicals such as:*
> *a) Gases such as:*
> …
> *(ii) hydrogen via an electrolyser….*

[68] Ministry of the Environment and Equality, Law on Environmental Assessment, LBK no 4 on 3 January 2023 <https://www.retsinformation.dk/eli/lta/2023/4> accessed 8 August 2024.

[69] Ministry of the Environment and Equality, Law on Environmental Protection, LBK no 1093 of 11 October 2023 https://www.retsinformation.dk/eli/lta/2023/1093 accessed 12 August 2024.

[70] Ministry of the Environment and Equality, Decree on the approval of List Activities, BEK no 1027 of 2 September 2024 https://www.retsinformation.dk/eli/lta/2024/1027 accessed 14 January 2025.

[71] Directive 2010/75/EU of the European Parliament and of the Council of 24 November 2010 on industrial emissions (integrated pollution prevention and control) [2010] OJ L 334/17 (Industrial Emissions Directive); Directive 2011/92/EU of the European Parliament and of the Council of 13 December 2011 on the assessment of the effects of certain public and private projects on the environment (codification) [2012] OJ L 26/1 (Environmental Impact Assessment Directive).

[72] Decree on the approval of List Activities (n 70) § 5(1); Law on EIA (n 68) § 17.

[73] Law on Environmental Protection (n 69) §§ 35–38.

[74] ibid § 33.

[75] ibid § 35 in conjunction with §33.

Thus, an electrolyser producing hydrogen is considered a list activity and requires a list activity permit to comply with emissions law.[76] This is, however, merely the case if the electrolyser is producing hydrogen at an 'industrial scale'.[77] In April 2024 the Industrial Emissions Directive, on which this requirement is based, was revised. The EU legislator implemented a new threshold for what is considered hydrogen production at an industrial scale for water electrolysers: production that exceeds 50 tons per day.[78] Hence, if the electrolyser reaches this threshold, it needs a list activity permit.

Furthermore, activities covered by Annex 1 to the Decree on List Activities must follow Best Available Techniques (BAT) requirements.[79] These are reports that identify the most economically and technically feasible techniques that deliver the highest level of environmental performance for a certain process or technology.[80] The BAT system stems from the Industrial Emissions Directive, and the BATs are developed at EU level by the Commission.[81] If a project is subject to Annex 1 to the Decree on List Activities, the municipality must scrutinize whether any relevant BATs have been properly implemented by the developer before giving the list activity permit.[82]

Additionally, a facility will be subject to an 'Environmental Impact Assessment' under Danish environmental law if the project's 'nature, dimensions, or location can be expected to have significant effects on the environment',[83] and:

- The developer has submitted an application and the project is subject to Annex 1 to the Law on EIA;[84] or
- The Municipality has decided that the project is subject to EIA, and the project is covered by Annex 2 to the Law on EIA;[85] or
- The project is subject to Annex 2 to the Law on EIA, and the developer has handed in an application for the project to be subject to an EIA.[86]

This system stems from the EU's Environmental Impact Assessment Directive, which has been transposed into Danish law.[87] Similar to EU law, the difference between Annex 1 and Annex 2 is that the projects in Annex 1 are always subject to an EIA. Meanwhile, projects in Annex 2 are only subject to an EIA if the authorities, based on a screening of the project, believed to have a significant impact on the environment.[88] In Annex 1, Section 6 the following is stipulated:

[76] ibid, seen in conjunction with Decree on approval of List Activities (n 70) § 3(1) and appendix 1, point 4.2(ii).
[77] Decree on approval of List Activities (n 70) Annex 1, point 4 introduction.
[78] Directive (EU) 2024/1785 of the European Parliament and of the Council of 24 April 2024 amending Directive 2010/75/EU on industrial emissions (integrated pollution prevention and control) and Council Directive 1999/31/EC on the landfill of waste [2024] OJ L, Annex 1 point 6.6.
[79] Decree on approval of List Activities (n 70) § 24(1).
[80] ibid § 2(1) no 3.
[81] ibid § 24(1).
[82] ibid § 18(1) no 1.
[83] Law on EIA (n 68) § 15(1) seen in conjunction with the laws §5(6)a.
[84] ibid § 15(1) no 1.
[85] ibid § 15(1) no 2 seen in conjunction with the laws §21.
[86] ibid § 15(1) no 3 seen in conjunction with the laws §19(4).
[87] Environmental Impact Assessment Directive (n 71) see especially art 4(1) and (2).
[88] Law on EIA (n 68) § 16; Establishment of PtX facilities on land (n 49).

Integrated chemical facilities, meaning plants for the production at an industrial scale of substances by chemical conversion, which are located side by side and functionally belong together, and which are:
(a) for the production of organic chemical elements
(b) for the production of basic inorganic chemical elements ....

This implies four requirements:

- the facility has to be integrated
- the production must be at an industrial scale
- production must occur via a chemical conversion
- the produced product has to be either organic or inorganic elements

Based on the wording of the article, the electrolyser is 'integrated' if it is connected to another component and these function together. It is assumed that an electrolyser will be connected to another infrastructure component via either the common grid or a direct line going, for example, to a fuelling station, making it subject to the phrase 'integrated'.

The law does not define what is considered 'industrial scale'. In the former guide to the law from 2009, the Environmental Ministry expanded the concept. The Ministry stated that production on an industrial scale is *not* dependent on a quantitative indication of the production since the production can vary in scale based on the product produced.[89] The current 2024 guide echoes this by underscoring that an EIA permit, in general, is highly concerned with the concrete, project-specific characteristics and their environmental impact, which is why fixed threshold values should be applied cautiously.[90] This seemingly excludes that the 50 tonne requirement introduced by the Industrial Emissions Directive is presumptively applied to the EIA. A rough estimate suggests that hydrogen production via an electrolyser for business purposes could be considered as falling within the meaning of 'industrial scale'. However, specific characteristics of the project can lead to the reverse conclusion.

Water electrolysers produce hydrogen through 'chemical reactions', fulfilling the third criterion.[91] Further, in the Decree on List Activities, hydrogen production via an electrolyser is categorized as production of 'inorganic chemicals', meanwhile hydrogen is one of the basic elements, meaning that the fourth condition is also met.[92]

[89] Ministry of the Environment and Equality, Guidance on Environmental Impact Assessment in the Planning Act, VEJ no 9339 of 12 March 2009, s 12(6) https://www.retsinformation.dk/eli/retsinfo/2009/9339 accessed 12 January 2025.

[90] Ministry of the Environment and Equality, Guidance on Environmental Impact Assessment, VEJ no 9093 of 21 February 2024, s 3.3 https://www.retsinformation.dk/eli/retsinfo/2024/9093 accessed 24 January 2025.

[91] Mostafa El-Shafie, 'Hydrogen Production by Water Electrolysis Technologies: A Review' (2023) 20 Engineering 101426 https://www.sciencedirect.com/science/article/pii/S2590123023005534 accessed 18 October 2023.

[92] Decree on the approval of List Activities 2024 (n 70) appendix 1, s 4.

Based on this short analysis, an electrolyser could potentially be subject to an EIA due to its coverage by Number 6 in Annex 1 to the Law on EIA. However, it depends on the specific project whether the electrolyser is producing at an 'industrial scale'.

Importantly, other environmental permits can replace an EIA permit for the 'project' itself.[93] The replacement is justified as the legislation on the basis of which the replacement permits are granted is deemed adequately to address the environmental considerations and trade-offs relevant to the specific project, as required by the EIA permit.[94] One of these permits is the list activity permit.[95] Hence, if a project is subject to a list activity permit, it will *not* be subject to an EIA.

Furthermore, if a PtX construction requires changes to a local plan, the municipality has, under certain circumstances, a duty to conduct a screening of how the new local plans affect the environment.[96] Such a screening has to be conducted for 'plans' related to 'spatial planning and land use' and if these plans are connected to 'future construction permits for the projects covered by Appendix 1 and 2 [to the Law on EIA]'.[97]

An electrolyser producing hydrogen would probably be subject to Annex 1 to the Law on EIA. A new local plan, stipulating where an electrolyser can be placed, would fall into the normal understanding of 'spatial planning and land use'. Based on this, it must be assumed that a newly adopted local plan would be subject to an environmental assessment insofar as the electrolyser itself is subject to either Annex 1 or 2.[98]

To sum up: for a PtX facility to be in accordance with the Danish emissions and environmental law, one would potentially need (i) a list activity permit, (ii) possibly an EIA, and (iii) an EIA on the changes to the local plan.

3.4 Water Management Law

3.4.1 Procedural aspects

Electrolysers need substantial amounts of water to function, making water management law relevant. The most important law is the Law on the Supply of Water (Water Supply Law).[99] It is the municipality that is the relevant authority in this section.[100]

[93] Minister for Green Tripartite, 'Decree on environmental assessment of plans and programmes and of specific projects' BEK no 1608 of 9 December 2024, §10 https://www.retsinformation.dk/eli/lta/2024/1608 accessed 14 January 2025, seen in conjunction with Law on Environmental Assessment (Law on EIA) (n 68) §§ 15 and 25.

[94] Guidance on EIA 2024 (n 90) s 2.2.

[95] Decree on environmental assessment of plans and programmes and of specific projects (n 93) § 10(1) no 2.

[96] Law on EIA (n 68) § 8.

[97] ibid § 8(1).

[98] ibid § 8(1).

[99] The Ministry of Environment and Equality, Law on the supply of water, LBK no 1149 on 28 October 2024 <https://www.retsinformation.dk/eli/lta/2024/1149> accessed 19 October 2024.

[100] ibid § 20(1) no 1.

3.4.2 Substantial aspects

Since an electrolyser requires clean water in the most common constellations, securing a water extraction permit is essential.[101] Importantly, electrolysers react to the purity of water. In particular, the energy efficiency and energy consumption of the PEM (proton exchange membrane) electrolysers are damaged when non-pure water is used, such as sea water.[102] This makes the need for an extraction permit significant from a financial point of view, since the cost of running an electrolyser rises when its efficiency is diminished.[103] It is however important to note that an electrolyser, in most instances, has an integrated or attached purification unit that purifies the water before usage to prevent damage to the electrolyser and enhance efficiency.[104]

A project developer can obtain a water extraction permit to utilize the Danish groundwater. The sole requirement is that the water is not used to water agricultural crops.[105] The yearly extraction is limited to 3,000 m^3.[106] Additionally, it is important to note that an electrolyser produces wastewater.

To sum up: to comply with water management law the developer would need a water extraction permit.

3.5 Waste Law

3.5.1 Procedural aspects

Waste governance in Denmark is subject to several laws. Most relevant in the context of electrolysers is the Law on Environmental Protection, also discussed in subsection 3.1.[107] Depending on the amount of sewage and whether the electrolyser is considered a 'list activity', it is either the municipality or the Ministry of Environment that is the relevant authority.[108]

3.5.2 Substantial aspects

In the event of a surplus of water, wastewater from the production of hydrogen, or wastewater resulting from the water purification process, the water must be led away, but no substance that might contaminate water may be discharged to streams, lakes, or the sea.[109] However, the municipality can, under 'special circumstances', issue a permit

[101] IRENA, *Green Hydrogen Cost Reduction: Scaling up Electrolysers to Meet the 1.5° Climate Goal* (2020) 40 <https://www.ourenergypolicy.org/resources/green-hydrogen-cost-reduction-scaling-up-renewables-to-meet-the-1-5-c-climate-goal/#:~:text=This%20report%20from%20the%20International%20Renewable%20Energy,from%20megawatt%20(MW)%20to%20multi%2Dgigawatt%20(GW)%20levels> accessed 11 January 2025.

[102] El-Shafie (n 91).

[103] ibid.

[104] EuroWater, 'Keeping the Water Ultrapure Inside Electrolyzers: Challenges and Solutions' (March 2024) https://hydrogentechworld.com/keeping-the-water-ultrapure-inside-electrolyzers-challenges-and-solutions accessed 13 January 2025.

[105] Law on the supply of water (n 99) § 20(1) no 1.

[106] ibid.

[107] Law on Environmental Protection (n 69) § 27(1).

[108] ibid § 28(1) and (2).

[109] ibid § 27(1).

to allow contaminated substances or sewage to enter streams, lakes, or the sea.[110] If the developer chooses not to obtain a permit to emit into streams, lakes, or the sea, the developer must be in possession of a permit to send water to the local wastewater treatment plant.[111]

To sum up: waste law requires a developer to either have a (i) permit to emit sewage into the public waterways or (ii) a permit to send wastewater to the local wastewater treatment plant.

3.6 Fire Prevention, Health and Safety Law

3.6.1 Procedural aspects

Denmark has considerable risk prevention laws, the most important being the Order on Control of the Risk of Major Accidents Involving Dangerous Substances (Control Order).[112] Fire prevention is primarily regulated in the Law on Emergency Prevention (Law on Emergency Prevention) and in the Order on technical regulations for gases.[113] Since hydrogen is a flammable substance posing an exploration risk, adherence to these laws is crucial for public safety.[114] The relevant authorities in this section are the municipalities, the National Safety Authority, and the Danish Emergency Management Agency.[115]

3.6.2 Substantial aspects

The Control Order governs risk and fire management for 'risk activities', defined as activities conducted at facilities containing dangerous substances.[116] These activities are classified into two categories - Category 2 and Category 3 - based on the quantity of dangerous substances present.[117] Category 2 covers facilities with small quantities, while Category 3 applies to large-scale storage. The classifications and thresholds are outlined in Annex 1, Part 2 of the Control Order, which lists hydrogen with thresholds of 5 tonnes for Category 2 and 50 tonnes for Category 3.[118] This system originates from the EU's Seveso Directive, designed to prevent major accidents involving hazardous

[110] ibid § 27(3) seen in conjunction with the laws § 27(1) for contaminated substances and § 28 for sewage.

[111] ibid § 28(3); For this specific permit it is always the municipality that is the relevant authority, see § 28(3).

[112] The Ministry of the Environment and Equality, Order on control of the risk of major accidents involving dangerous substances, BEK no 372 on 25 April 2016 (Control Order) <https://www.retsinformation.dk/eli/lta/2016/372> accessed 15 August 2024.

[113] Ministry of Defence, The Law on Emergency Prevention, LBK no 314 on 3 April 2017 <https://www.retsinformation.dk/eli/lta/2017/314> accessed 17 August 2024; Ministry of Defence, Order on technical regulations for gases, BEK no 1444 on the 15 December 2010 <https://www.retsinformation.dk/eli/lta/2010/1444> accessed 28 December 2023.

[114] Daniel A Crowl and Young-Do Jo, 'The Hazards and Risks of Hydrogen' (2007) 20 Journal of Loss Prevention in the Process Industries 158 https://www.sciencedirect.com/journal/journal-of-loss-prevention-in-the-process-industries/vol/20/issue/2 accessed 18 August 2024.

[115] Control Order (n 112) § 4(19)(a); Law on Emergency Prevention (n 113) § 33(1) no 1 seen in conjunction with the laws § 33a and § 34(1) and (2); Order on technical regulations for gases (n 113) Annex 1 s 1.3.5 seen in conjunction with the annex point 1.2.1.

[116] Control Order (n 112) § 4(1).

[117] ibid § 4(2) and (3).

[118] ibid Appendix 1, pt 2, point 15.

substances.[119] Depending on the quantity of hydrogen produced, an electrolyser may be subject to these risk prevention rules.

If an electrolyser is subject to the Control Order, due to the amount of hydrogen present or stored in the vicinity of the electrolyser, measures must be taken to prevent major accidents and minimize impacts on health and the environment.[120] To fulfil this duty, operators are required to prepare a prevention plan addressing potential accidents or risks.[121] Additionally, they must comply with Article 8 of the Control Order, which mandates including all information outlined in Articles 8(1) and 8(2) when applying for a list activity permit (see subsection 3.3.2). The owner of an electrolyser would furthermore have to inform the National Safety Authority of the existence of the electrolyser before establishing the facility.[122]

Additionally, projects posing a fire or explosion risk would normally need to obtain an emergency permit.[123] As mentioned hydrogen is a flammable substance posing a fire risk, making an electrolyser subject to this permit.[124] Lastly, facilities producing flammable and combustible gases need a fire prevention permit.[125]

To sum up: risk prevention rules require that an operator of an electrolyser has to (i) comply with the regime on the prevention of risks in the Control Order; (ii) the developer has to inform the National Safety Authority of the existence of the electrolyser; and an (iii) emergency permit. To comply with fire prevention law, an electrolyser would need to obtain a (i) fire prevention permit.

4. Recommendations to Improve the System

This section critically reviews the Danish permitting procedure, starting with its positive aspects, followed by suggestions for improvement to enhance the regime further.

On a positive note, Danish authorities make significant efforts to assist developers during the permitting process. The DEA has published a comprehensive and free guide on the permitting procedure for electrolysers on its official website.[126] Further support comes from the PtX taskforce and its associated AWG and SF, which coordinate the permitting process and foster market collaboration to address issues. A notable example is the March 2024 workshop held by the PtX taskforce, focusing on electrolyser development and permitting, with particular attention to planning and environmental law.[127]

[119] European Parliament and Council Directive 2012/18 of 4 July 2012 on the control of major-accident hazards involving dangerous substances, amending and subsequently repealing Council Directive 96/82/EC [2012] OJ L 197/1.

[120] Control Order (n 112) § 7(1).

[121] ibid § 7(1) no 1.

[122] Ministry for Business, Decree on safety for gas installations, BEK no 253 of 4 April 2018 § 5(1) https://www.retsinformation.dk/eli/lta/2018/253 accessed 17 August 2024.

[123] Law on Emergency Prevention (n 113) § 33(1) no 1 seen in conjunction with the laws § 34(2).

[124] Crowl and Jo (n 114).

[125] Order on Technical Regulations for Gases (n 113) Annex 1 s 1.3.5 seen in conjunction with the annex to point 1.2.1.

[126] Establishment of PtX facilities on land (n 49).

[127] DEA, 'Theme day on Power-to-X on 5 March 2024' <https://ens.dk/ansvarsomraader/power-x-og-groen-brint/temadag-om-power-x-den-5-marts-2024> accessed 28 August 2024.

Despite the positive aspects, Denmark should consider further simplifying the permitting process to address its current complexity. Developers must engage with multiple authorities and apply for various permits, with the DEA solely acting as an overreach guide to the process. This approach is inadequate. One solution could be extending the DEA's role to include a one-stop shop responsibility, consolidating the permit coordination under DEA as a single contact point - a model already used by the DEA for the wind sector.[128] Alternatively, an 'all-in-one permit' system could be introduced, managed either by the DEA or municipalities, as they are key permitting authorities. While this would streamline the process, it raises concerns about whether these entities have the expertise to assess permits currently handled by other authorities. Despite such challenges, Denmark should explore these centralized approaches to simplify permitting further.

The hydrogen market's current challenges also stem from insufficient financing. As noted earlier in this chapter, many projects have been delayed or cancelled due to funding shortages. In the 2023 hydrogen tender, the DEA received applications for aid totalling 4 billion DKK, far exceeding the available budget of 1.32 billion DKK.[129] This underscores the market's urgent need for financial support and its funding gap. To address this, the Danish government could consider launching a second hydrogen tender to aid the sector in upscaling.

Electrolysers offer a potential unexpected climate benefit: the reuse of surplus heat generated by certain PtX facilities.[130] The PEM electrolyser, for instance, produces significant heat, as much as 10–25% of the energy used in the electrolyser. This heat surplus could be utilized in the Danish district heating networks.[131] In Denmark, 70% of houses (1,982,623 houses in 2025) rely on district heating.[132] By reusing the heat surplus the CO_2 emissions from district heating systems could be reduced. Municipalities are responsible for planning and permitting district heating networks, giving them a key role in enabling such reuse.[133] Denmark could consider requiring developers to include a waste heat reuse plan as a condition for obtaining environmental permits, fostering more sustainable practices in PtX projects.

5. Conclusion

Denmark has made efforts to streamline the permitting process for PtX, including the creation of an online guide from the DEA and establishing a PtX Taskforce. However,

[128] DEA 'Procedures and Permits for Offshore Wind Parks <https://ens.dk/en/energy-sources/offshore-procedures-permits> accessed 14 January 2025.

[129] Fact sheet on the Power-to-X tender (n 15).

[130] PtX strategy (n 7).

[131] Els van der Roest and others, 'Utilization of Waste Heat from PEM Electrolysers Unlocking Local Optimisation' (2023) 48 International Journal of Hydrogen Energy 27872 <https://danskfjernvarme.dk/viden-vaerktoejer/udgivelser/power-to-x-og-fjernvarme> accessed 22 August 2024; Dansk Fjernvarme report 'Power-to-X og fjernvarme' (2022) <https://danskfjernvarme.dk/viden-vaerktoejer/udgivelser/power-to-x-og-fjernvarme > accessed 14 September 2025.

[132] Dansk Fjernvarme official webpage 'Facts about District Heating' <https://danskfjernvarme.dk/uk/english/statistics > accessed 24 August 2024.

[133] The Ministry of Climate, Energy and Utilities, Law on District Heating, LBK no 124 on 2 February 2024 § 3 and § 4 <https://www.retsinformation.dk/eli/lta/2024/124#P3> accessed 10 November 2024.

the system remains complex, requiring multiple permits from various authorities, underscoring the need for further simplification. Additionally, the market remains in an infant state, with flagship projects being cancelled or postponed, jeopardizing compliance with the 2030 capacity goal. Despite these flaws and immense challenges, Denmark has successfully expanded its electrolyser capacity, aided by the 2023 tender. Meanwhile, the Danish government and associated political parties have continually created political agreements and launched law amendments, facilitating a hydrogen economy and preparing the Danish grid and legal framework for the emerging hydrogen sector.

The focus for the upcoming years will be on the support of market development to ensure the successful scaling of the market. However, several barriers must be addressed for the industry to realize its potential in full. For instance, the sector could benefit from additional tenders or further simplification of the permitting process. While the initial steps in Denmark's hydrogen journey appear promising, the coming years will determine whether those early efforts have been truly worthwhile.

Further Reading

Danish law

The Ministry of City, Land and the Church, The Law on Planning, LBK no 572 on 29 May 2024 <https://www.retsinformation.dk/eli/lta/2024/572> accessed 7 November 2024.

The Ministry of Social affairs and Housing, The Law on building, LBK no 1178 on 23 September 2016 <https://www.retsinformation.dk/eli/lta/2016/1178> accessed 15 August 2024.

Ministry of the Environment and Equality, The Law on Environmental Protection, LBK no 1093 on 11 October 2024 nr. 1093 < https://www.retsinformation.dk/eli/lta/2024/1093> accessed 12 August 2024.

The Ministry of Environment and Equality, Law on the supply of water, LBK no 1149 on 28 October 2024 < https://www.retsinformation.dk/eli/lta/2024/1149> accessed 19 October 2024.

The Ministry of Defence, The Law on Emergency Prevention, LBK no 314 on 3 April 2017 <https://www.retsinformation.dk/eli/lta/2017/314> accessed 17 August 2024.

Strategy

The Ministry of Climate, Energy and Utilities and the Governments' 'Strategy for Power-to-X' (2021) <https://kefm.dk/Media/637751860733099677/Regeringens%20strategi%20for%20Power-to-X.pdf> accessed 2 August 2024.

Academic articles

Crowl, D, and Jo, Y. 'The Hazards and Risks of Hydrogen' (2007) 20 Journal of Loss Prevention in the Process Industries 158 <https://www.sciencedirect.com/journal/journal-of-loss-prevention-in-the-process-industries/vol/20/issue/2> accessed 28 December 2023.

Roest, E, and others. 'Utilization of Waste Heat from PEM Electrolysers: Unlocking Local Optimisation' (2023) 48 International Journal of Hydrogen Energy 27872 <https://www.sciencedirect.com/science/article/pii/S0360319923015410> accessed 22 August 2024.

IV

Germany

Ruven Fleming

1. Introduction

There currently is no clear and standardized procedure for the approval of electrolysers in Germany. The experience of plant manufacturers to date shows differences in the type and scope of the approval procedures applied, and experience in the approval of large plants (from > 10 MW up to > 100 MW) is currently limited on both the operator and authority sides. In addition, the amendment of the Fourth Ordinance on the Implementation of the Federal Emission Control Act (4th BImSchV) and the introduction of the Hydrogen Acceleration Act (WasserstoffBG) both changed the legal framework. This has led to uncertainties regarding the process and scope of approvals required to implement water electrolysis effectively in Germany in the short and medium term.

This chapter has two main objectives: first, the legal framework for the approval of electrolysis plants is explained in detail; thus the approval procedure for their construction and operation is presented as clearly as possible. The chapter is intended to serve as a quick guide for both operators and authorities to carry out the approval procedure.

Second, specific recommendations for the simplification and acceleration of the approval process are provided.

The analysis of the legal framework in this chapter takes a comprehensive look at the conditions for the approval of electrolysis plants. The section on the approval procedure focuses on larger electrolysis plants with a rated electrical output of 5 MW or more, as these are expected to be of considerable relevance in Germany.

To obtain approval for the construction and operation of an electrolysis plant, numerous laws, regulations, directives, technical standards, and rules must be observed. Which of these are actually relevant in individual cases depends on the specifics of the electrolysis plant: individual plant parameters and criteria have an impact on the classification of the plant.

At this point, it is important to mention that the authority conducting the procedure determines whether a specific law or approval procedure must be applied. For this reason, the information provided is an initial assessment based on both theoretical and practical experience with the permitting process in Germany. The concrete limit values, laws, regulations, and directives relevant to a particular case may be assessed differently by the competent authority in different cases.

2. General Observations on the Permitting Regime

For the applicant, it is practical to consider which approval procedure needs to be carried out on the basis of which law. In Germany, approval procedures of different levels of priority exist. In certain areas, a higher-ranking procedure includes approvals that are necessary under other areas of law (so-called concentration effect). Such a higher-ranking procedure can be the planning approval procedure, the emission control approval procedure under the Federal Emission Control Act (BImSchG), or the approval procedure under the Industrial Safety and Health Ordinance (BetrSichV).

By contrast, if only a building permit is required for the plant, this does not lead to a concentration effect and further permits must be obtained separately. Thus, the building permit is the last permit and is only included when it is part of a higher permit, such as those under planning law or emission control law. In other words, the permitting regime in Germany is partly an all-in-one permit regime, but only insofar as a Planning Approval Procedure, an Emission Control Procedure, or an Industrial Safety and Health Procedure is pursued. Only in these three circumstances is there the chance of obtaining an all-in-one permit. If none of these three procedures is necessary, there also is no all-in-one permit and individual permits need to be requested.

A very recent and fundamental change in the German permitting landscape for electrolysers has not yet been adopted at the time of writing, but it is currently being discussed in Parliament. Nonetheless, due to its fundamental nature, it will be mentioned here. This is the so-called Hydrogen Acceleration Act (WasserstoffBG), which was initiated by the Federal Government on 29 May 2024 to accelerate the production, storage, and import of hydrogen under planning and approval law. The WasserstoffBG will be implemented in conjunction with the amendment to the 4th BImSchV, which will bring far-reaching changes to the approval procedures for electrolysis plants in Germany, as it amends various existing laws.

3. Specific Permits Applicable to Electrolysers

3.1 Planning Law

The planning approval procedure is a comprehensive administrative process that regulates the permissibility of spatially significant projects, in particular large-scale infrastructure projects. It is typically used for projects such as the construction of federal roads, railway facilities, landfills, or high-voltage power lines. The procedure is characterized by the so-called concentration effect. It bundles and conclusively regulates all public law approvals required for the project in one procedure. The only exceptions to this concentration effect that may be relevant for hydrogen are the approval procedure under mining law (operating plans), the approval procedure under water law, and permits pursuant to Article 8 in conjunction with Article 10 of the Federal Water Act (WHG).

If planning approval is granted, Article 75 of the Administrative Procedure Act (VwVfG) establishes that all public law relationships between the project developer and the affected parties are made legally binding. Moreover, a planning approval procedure pursuant to Article 43(2) No 7 of the Energy Industry Act (EnWG) may be relevant for energy coupling plants. The term 'energy coupling plant' includes Power-to-X plants that convert electricity into other forms of energy such as heat, cold, or fuels. However, there is no general obligation to carry out a planning approval procedure for electrolysis plants. Rather, for electrolysers it is usually an optional procedure: both the project developer and the competent authority can decide whether this procedure is chosen.

Exceptions to this exist in some cases, where carrying out a planning approval procedure is actually obligatory. This particularly pertains to situations where larger supply lines for gas, electricity, or water are required. In those cases, an obligation to carry out a planning approval procedure might exist. However, this obligation usually applies to the operators of the relevant supply networks rather than to the operator of the electrolysis plant itself. If such pipelines are to be built at a scale that is already regulated by the planning approval procedure for the plant, it might make sense, for efficiency reasons, to integrate the electrolysis plant into the existing procedure.

In sum, however, the planning approval procedure will be of little relevance for most electrolysis plants, as they often do not have the scope or the spatially significant characteristics that would justify the mandatory implementation of this procedure. Instead, a permit in accordance with the Federal Emission Control Act (BImSchG) will be sufficient in most cases.

3.2 Federal Emission Control Act

Emission control law, anchored in the Federal Emission Control Act (BImSchG), regulates the approval requirement and the obligations of an operator for certain facilities resulting from a permit (Articles 4 and 22 BImSchG). For plants that are potentially harmful to the environment, an emission control permit is required, the granting of which depends on the eligibility for approval. Above a capacity threshold of 5 MW, electrolysis plants are subject to this approval requirement under emission control law.

According to Article 13 BImSchG, the Federal Emission Control Act, similar to the planning approval, features the concentration effect: it includes and replaces other permits under public law that would otherwise have to be obtained separately. The BImSchG approval requirements depend on the individual system components. Particularly relevant are the type of electrolysis used, the hydrogen (H_2) storage (if applicable), and the electrical substations (if applicable). Each of these plant components can be relevant for the BImSchG approval requirement. In the emission control approval procedure under the BImSchG, a distinction is made between the simplified procedure (V) and the formal procedure (G).

It should be noted that the strictest type of approval for a part of the plant determines the type of approval for the entire plant. Some parts of an electrolysis plant may require approval under the simplified procedure and others under the formal procedure. In such cases, the stricter procedure, namely the formal procedure (G), must be applied to the entire installation, even if parts of the installation would only require authorization under the simplified procedure (V). It should therefore be clarified that the electrolysis plant and its components are assessed as a single plant in the permit.

According to Article 4(1) sentence 3 BImSchG, the installations requiring approval are defined in more detail in a statutory ordinance. This has been implemented via Article 1 of the 4th BImSchV. That article then refers to Annex 1 of the 4th BImSchV for the list of installations requiring approval.

3.2.1 4th BImSchV

No 10.26 of Annex 1 of the 4th BImSchV is relevant for electrolysis plants, which, depending on the size of the plant, provides for a permit requirement for 'plants for the production of hydrogen by the electrolysis of water'. Whether a permit is required under emission control law and which procedure needs to be carried out—simplified procedure (V) or formal procedure (G)—is determined by the rated electrical output or production capacity of the electrolyser.

An electrolyser with a rated electrical power input of less than 5 MW does not require approval under emission control legislation. In this case, however, approvals may be necessary in accordance with other specialist legislation (in particular building regulations and water legislation).

Electrolysers with a rated electrical power input of 5 MW or more require approval in a simplified procedure in accordance with Article 19 BImSchG (without public participation). This is marked with a 'V' in the 'Type of procedure' column of Annex 1 of the 4th BImSchV.

If the rated electrical power is 68 MW and the production capacity is more than 50 tonnes of hydrogen per day, approval is required in a formal approval procedure with public participation in accordance with Article 10 BImSchG. This is marked with a 'G' in the 'Type of procedure according to BImSchG' column of Annex 1 of the 4th BImSchV. In addition, the requirements of the Industrial Emissions Directive (IED) apply to these electrolysers. These requirements are now discussed.

3.2.2 Initial Status Report and Industrial Emissions Directive IED (Directive 2024/1785/EU)

According to No 10.26.1 of Annex 1 of the 4th BImSchV, electrolysis plants with an electrical nominal input of 68 MW or more and a production capacity of more than 50 tonnes of hydrogen per day are classified as industrial emissions (IE) plants. These values are the German implementation of the new threshold values of Article 6.6 in Annex I to the Industrial Emissions Directive 2024 (2024/1785/EU). But they are not standalone requirements; in fact, the German Annex 1 features additional requirements for these larger IE plants:

- Submission of an initial status report (AZB) in accordance with Article 10(1a) BImSchG
- Special monitoring obligations of the authority according to Article 52a BImSchG
- Appointment of an emission control officer in accordance with Article 53(1) in conjunction with Article 1(1) 5th BImSchV
- Implementation of the best available techniques (BAT)[1]

According to Article 10(1a) BImSchG, an initial status report (AZB) must be prepared if relevant hazardous substances (rgS) are used, produced, or released to a significant extent in IE plants and could contaminate the soil and/or groundwater as a result. This report describes the condition of the soil and groundwater before the plant is commissioned and serves as a binding reference value.[2]

3.2.3 Storage and Hazardous Incident Ordinance (4th and 12th BImSchV)

Another important aspect of the permitting requirements under the Federal Emission Control Act concerns the storage and use of hydrogen on site. With regard to reaching quantity thresholds for storage, it is crucial to clarify that the term 'storage' in German environmental law already covers the mere presence of substances at the facility. The maximum possible total quantity that can be present in the entire facility/operating area must always be considered.

[1] The BAT reference documents can be downloaded from the website of the Federal Environment Agency.
[2] Art 5(4) BImSchG.

There are also more traditional storage activities that can take place at the site of an electrolyser and that are directly connected to it. LOHC (Liquid Organic Hydrogen Carrier) storage facilities as well as pressurized and solid storage facilities may fall under these regulations. Depending on the carrier material used, the Hazardous Substances Ordinance (ChemStoffV) and other regulations and building law may also become relevant.

The 4th and 12th BImSchV are particularly relevant here. The 4th BImSchV specifies which installations require a permit due to their potential pollutant emissions or their environmental impact. The 12th BImSchV (Hazardous Incident Ordinance) deals with installations in which hazardous substances are present in quantities that could potentially lead to serious accidents or incidents. These ordinances set out the requirements for hydrogen storage and related safety measures.

3.3 Building Law: Building Act (BauGB); State Building Regulations (LBO); Land Use Ordinance (BauNVO)

Electrolysers must comply with building regulations and, if necessary, obtain building permits. A separate building permit is not required in every case, as the concentration effect of higher-level approval procedures (such as the BImSchG procedure) often applies. For electrolysis plants with a rated electrical output of 5 MW or more, the building permit is examined as part of the higher-ranking procedure in accordance with Article 4 BImSchG, and the building permit is issued as part of that procedure.

The priority of other procedures and the associated concentration effect are regulated in Article 60(2) and (5) of the Model Building Act (MBO),[3] Article 75(1) of the Administrative Procedure Act (VwVfG), and Article 13 BImSchG.

3.3.1 Installations requiring a permit in accordance with building law

If a building is erected, modified, or removed, the building supervisory authority checks whether the building is compatible with the provisions of building regulations (Article 59(1) MBO).

It is important to mention that there are two different strands of building law in Germany: building planning law and building regulations law. Building regulations law is regulated at the state level and concerns the structural and technical requirements for a *specific building project*. Building regulations law is therefore *object related*. These regulations may differ in the sixteen federal states of Germany, and local municipal law may also be relevant. Due to the complexity and the large number of regulations, building regulations law is not examined in detail in this guide. Just to illustrate the complexities: the question of whether an electrolyser is actually a 'building' might be judged differently according to the applicable set of local laws.

[3] The Model Building Code (MBO) serves as a model for the building regulations of the individual federal states. There are often great similarities to and in the building regulations of the individual federal states (BMK, 2016).

Building planning law, on the other hand, is partly regulated at the federal level and partly set by the municipalities as part of *urban land-use planning*. It plays a decisive role in the choice of location for an electrolysis plant. The relevant regulations can be found in Articles 29 ff of the Building Code (BauGB) and the BauNVO.

Under building planning law, a distinction must be made between three constellations:

- **Planned inner area (Article 30 BauGB):** If there is a qualified or project-related development plan, the facility is located in the planned inner area. Approval is granted if the development complies with the provisions of the development plan in accordance with Article 9 BauGB and the development is secured (Article 30(1) BauGB).
- **Unplanned inner area (Article 34 BauGB):** If there is only a simple development plan or no development plan at all, the development may still be located in the unplanned inner area. Whether it is an inner or outer area can be questionable, particularly in outlying areas or larger open spaces within the municipality. The decisive factor is whether the project fits in with the nature and extent of existing building use in the immediate surroundings and whether the development is secured. The BauNVO is used to assess whether the project fits into the respective building area in line with the categories provided by Articles 2–9 BauNVO, which range from pure residential areas (Article 2) to recreation and special areas (Articles 10–11 BauNVO).

Typically, electrolysis plants are permitted in *industrial areas* (Article 9 BauNVO). There are certain restrictions in *commercial areas* (Article 8 BauNVO), as 'commercial enterprises of all kinds' can be located there only if they do not cause any significant nuisance that would make it necessary to locate them in an industrial area (Article 8(2) BauNVO). A significant nuisance is typically assumed if a formal approval procedure is required under Article 10 BImSchG. In a simplified approval procedure under Article 19 BImSchG, however, electrolysers may also be permitted in a commercial area.

Moreover, in *mixed-use areas* (Article 6 BauNVO), permissibility may be possible if the business does not significantly disturb residential areas. In core areas (Article 7 BauNVO), electrolysis plants are usually only permitted in exceptional cases.

- **Outdoor area (Article 35 and Article 249a BauGB):**
  If the first two constellations are not relevant, an electrolysis plant can also be approved in an outdoor area under certain circumstances. The outdoor area should be kept largely free of development to avoid urban sprawl. The core criterion for permissibility is privileged status. An electrolysis plant can be privileged in an outdoor area if it meets the requirements of Article 35 BauGB, in particular if it serves the use of renewable energies (Article 35(1) No 5 BauGB) or the public supply of gas (Article 35(1) No 3 BauGB). The system must be localized, which means that

it must be erected at this location due to geographical or technical characteristics. The location must be checked on a case-by-case basis.

The legislator provided certain privileges for hydrogen and electrolysis plants in Article 249a BauGB. According to Article 249a(1) BauGB, a 'project that serves the production or storage of hydrogen and is spatially and functionally connected to a plant for the research, development or use of wind energy in accordance with Article 35(1) No. 5 BauGB' is privileged. According to Article 249a(1) and (2) BauGB, electrolysis plants in outdoor areas are privileged if the electricity used for electrolysis comes exclusively from renewable sources and there is a spatial and functional connection to the renewable energy plants.

3.3.2 Installations not requiring a permit

According to Article 61(1) MBO, certain installations for hydrogen production are exempted from the procedure and do not require a building permit if they meet the specified conditions:

- Article 61(1) no 3 d MBO: Installations for hydrogen production, provided that the hydrogen produced is used exclusively for own consumption in the buildings for which they are erected
- Article 61(1) no 3 e MBO: Installations for the combined production and use of hydrogen and associated gas storage facilities, if the process steps are integrated in a factory-manufactured device and the storage quantity does not exceed 20 kg of hydrogen
- Article 61(1) no 2 MBO: Installations of technical building equipment, with the exception of free-standing flue gas systems with a height of more than 10 m
- Article 61(1) no 4 MBO: Supply and disposal installations for telecommunications, public supply of electricity, gas, oil, or heat with a height of up to 5 m and a gross floor area of up to 10 m^2

3.4 Energy Law: Energy Industry Act (EnWG) 2024 and Ordinances

The Energy Industry Act is the leading energy law in Germany. As it regulates both electricity and gas, it applies to electrolysis systems at various points.

If electricity is to be drawn from the electricity grid for use in an electrolysis system, either Article 17 EnWG (general grid connection) or, in special cases, Article 18 EnWG (general connection obligation) and Articles 20–28 EnWG on grid access apply. Grid connection can only be refused under very specific conditions, in particular if it is not possible or not reasonable for the grid operators to grant grid connection for operational, economic, or technical reasons, taking into account the purpose of Article 1 EnWG.

An electrolysis plant may be an energy plant pursuant to Article 3(15) EnWG and/or an energy storage plant pursuant to Article 3(15d) EnWG. Article 3(15d) also covers so-called sector coupling plants, in which the electricity is used 'as ... another energy source'. This means that the electricity is not converted back into electrical energy. This includes electrolysers and other Power-to-X plants without reconversion into electricity.[4]

In terms of the further use of hydrogen—for example, feeding it into a hydrogen grid or a natural gas grid—two different sets of rules must be considered. For access to the gas grids, these are Article 3 No 10c and Article 20 EnWG as well as ordinances like the Gas Network Access Regulation (GasNZV). For access to dedicated hydrogen grids, Articles 28j–28q EnWG and the Hydrogen Grid Charges Ordinance (WasserstoffNEV) are highly relevant. A more detailed examination, however, lies beyond the scope of this chapter, which is dedicated to the permitting procedure of the electrolyser itself.

3.5 Environmental Protection: Environmental Impact Assessment Act (UVPG)

The Environmental Impact Assessment Act (UVPG) is based on the well-known European law on Environmental Impact Assessment (EIA) and Strategic Environmental Assessment (SEA), which is constantly being updated. The aim of the German law is essentially to determine whether an environmental impact assessment must be carried out for certain facilities. This is decided on the basis of parameters such as storage volume or the length and diameter of pipelines leaving the plant site. The UVP serves to professionally record and assess the state of nature and the landscape as well as to prepare impact forecasts for planned projects, programmes, and plans with regard to the protected assets.[5]

According to Article 3 UVPG, a UVP comprises the identification, description, and assessment of significant impacts of a project, plan, or programme on specific protected assets. This already shows the decisive core criterion: whether or not electrolysis plants have a significant environmental impact. The procedure for carrying out the UVP as part of the emission control permitting procedure is regulated in detail in the 9th BImSchV. Articles 6–14 UVPG in conjunction with Article 1(2) sentence 1 of the 9th BImSchV list the plants that are subject to an obligatory UVP.

These plants can generally be grouped into two categories: those for which a general preliminary assessment is required and those for which a site-specific preliminary assessment is required. Depending on the rated electrical input of the electrolyser, a

[4] Lukas Assmann and Max Peiffer, *Energiewirtschaftsgesetz: EnWG* 11th edn (C.H.Beck, Muenchen 2024) art 3 no 15d marginal no 1, BT-Drs 19/27453, 88.

[5] Gerold Janssen and Juliane Albrecht, *Environmental Protection in Planning Law* (Federal Environment Agency 2008) 91 https://www.umweltbundesamt.de/sites/default/files/medien/publikation/long/3443.pdf accessed 25 September 2025.

general or a site-specific preliminary assessment of the individual case must be carried out.

The core criterion in a preliminary assessment is whether significant environmental impacts are to be expected. A preliminary assessment of the individual case may have to be carried out to determine whether significant adverse environmental impacts are to be expected.[6] Significant adverse effects would be, for example, environmental impacts on nature conservation or Fauna-Flora-Habitat (FFH) areas, emissions of substances of concern (TA Luft) or a complicated site location.

As opposed to this general assessment, the site-related preliminary assessment is carried out in two stages in accordance with Article 7(2) UVPG. In the first step, the local conditions are examined on the basis of the protection criteria listed in Annex 3 No 2.3 UVPG. Projects that could have a significant negative impact on a Natura 2000 site must be assessed for their compatibility with the conservation objectives of that site (Article 34(1) BNatSchG).

If the first assessment stage shows that there are no special local circumstances, there is no obligation to carry out a UVP. Otherwise, the general preliminary assessment is carried out in a second stage to decide whether or not a UVP obligation exists. In the general preliminary assessment, the authority determines whether a project requires a UVP due to its characteristics (eg size, accident risk), its location (eg protected areas, ecological sensitivity), or the severity, duration, and frequency of potential environmental impacts. The criteria for the general preliminary assessment of the individual case are listed in Annex 2 UVPG.

If the rated electrical output of the installation is at least 5 MW but less than 50 MW, a site-specific preliminary assessment of the individual case is required. At 50 MW or more, a general preliminary assessment must be carried out.

3.6 Nature Conservation: Federal Nature Conservation Act (BNatSchG)

According to Article 14(1) of the Federal Nature Conservation Act (BNatSchG), interventions in nature and the landscape must be avoided if they could significantly impair the form or use of land, the groundwater table, or the functionality of the ecosystem. Approval from the authority responsible for nature conservation and landscape management is required for an intervention that does not require official approval or notification under other legal provisions.

In principle, avoidable interventions in accordance with Article 15(1) BNatSchG must not be carried out. In the case of unavoidable interventions, approval must be applied for in writing. This approval must be granted if the requirements of Article 15(2) BNatSchG are met. For example, a plan for compensatory and replacement

[6] Art 7(1), (2), (4), (5) UVPG; art 8 UVPG; art 9(1)(2), (2)(2), (3) UVPG; art 11(2)(2) UVPG; art 12(1)(2) UVPG.

measures or compensation for interventions in nature must have been submitted. It should be noted that there may be different requirements in individual federal states.

Articles 31–36 of the Federal Nature Conservation Act (BNatSchG) stipulate in particular the protection of Natura 2000 sites under European law. In the site-related preliminary assessment for the UVP obligation, for example, nature conservation issues such as impacts on protected assets and FFH areas are examined. Projects must be checked for their compatibility with the conservation objectives of a nature conservation area (eg a Natura 2000 area) before they are approved or implemented, if they could cause significant adverse effects in that area (Article 34(1) BNatSchG).

Moreover, Article 37(1) No 1 BNatSchG requires species protection, including the protection of animals and plants of wild species from human interference and the guarantee of their other living conditions. In accordance with Article 44(1)(2)–(4) BNatSchG, it is prohibited to significantly disturb wild animals of strictly protected species and European bird species during certain periods of time. The authorities responsible for nature conservation and landscape management may grant exceptions to the prohibitions of Article 44 BNatSchG in individual cases in accordance with Article 45(7) BNatSchG.

3.7 Water Protection: Federal Water Act (WHG) and Ordinance on Installations for Handling Substances Hazardous to Water 1,2 (AwSV); State Water Acts (LWG)

Electrolysis for hydrogen production, and possibly also for cooling, requires a considerable amount of water. Environmentally sustainable water use is also becoming increasingly relevant in the context of hydrogen production. For this reason, the draft Hydrogen Acceleration Act (WasserstoffBG) contains various provisions relating to the Federal Water Act (WHG) (see at the end of this section).

If the water is not drawn from the public water supply but from surface water or groundwater, a separate permit is required in accordance with Articles 8(1) and 9(1) Nos 1 and 5 WHG. This permit under water law for water abstraction is not part of the permit under the Federal Emission Control Act (BImSchG) but must be applied for separately.

In addition to the WHG, the Wastewater Ordinance (AbwV) and the Ordinance on Installations Handling Substances Hazardous to Water (AwSV) are relevant for water law permits or approvals when it comes to water discharges. Annex 42 to the AbwV sets out various material requirements for the pollutant load of wastewater.

According to Article 55 WHG, wastewater from electrolysis plants must be disposed of properly. A discharge permit is required for electrolysis plants whose wastewater is discharged into existing public wastewater systems. The type of permit depends on whether there is *direct discharge of wastewater into bodies of water* (after treatment in an industrial wastewater treatment plant),[7] *indirect discharge of wastewater into public wastewater systems*,[8] or *discharge of wastewater into private wastewater facilities*.[9]

Electrolysis plants are likely to be mainly indirect dischargers; they discharge, for example, their wastewater into a public sewage treatment plant via the public sewer system. In this case, the drainage statutes of the municipality to which the wastewater treatment plant belongs must be observed.

3.8 Waste: Circular Economy Act (KrWG); State Circular Economy Acts (LKrWG)

Waste recycling and avoidance are often relevant issues for industrial plants. In principle, however, electrolysis plants should not produce problematic waste, other than the electrolysers themselves. The electrolysers themselves are not yet subject specifically to any German waste law. However, waste legislation could possibly become relevant if electrolysis plants are to be erected at landfills. In this case, Article 35(2) and (3) KrWG would have to be observed, as well as the relevant state recycling management laws (LKrWG). In such special cases, a planning approval procedure (Article 35(2) KrWG) or a planning permit procedure (Article 35(3) KrWG) would have to be carried out instead of an emission control procedure.

3.9 Occupational Health and Safety and Fire Protection: Occupational Health and Safety Act (ArbSchG); Workplace Ordinance (ArbStättV); Industrial Safety Ordinance (BetrSichV)

The general occupational health and safety requirements must also be observed for electrolysis systems. There are relatively few plant-specific features in this area. For this reason, we merely provide a list of potentially relevant occupational health and safety legislation. The BetrSichV is of particular relevance to electrolysis plants. The basis for occupational health and safety is the Occupational Health and Safety Act (ArbSchG), which transposes EU Directive 89/391/EEC into German law. According to Articles 18 and 19 ArbSchG, the federal government is authorized to prescribe by ordinance which measures are to be taken to fulfil the obligations of the ArbSchG. The most relevant ordinances include:

- Ordinance on Industrial Safety and Health (BetrSichV)
- Hazardous Substances Ordinance (GefStoffV)
- Ordinance on Biological Substances (BioStoffV)
- Workplace Ordinance (ArbStättV)

[7] Arts 8–10, 57 WHG.
[8] Art 58 WHG.
[9] Art 59 WHG.

- Noise and Vibration Occupational Health and Safety Ordinance (Lärm-VibrationsArbSchV)
- Ordinance on the Protection of Employees from the Dangers of Electromagnetic Fields (EMFV)

Please note finally that the first ordinance on the list (BetrSichV) is highly relevant to electrolysers but will be replaced in 2025 by the Ordinance on the Use of Work Equipment (AMBV) and the Ordinance on Installations Requiring Monitoring (ÜAnlV), which are currently being drafted.

3.10 Hydrogen Acceleration Act (WasserstoffBG)

As the name suggests, the Hydrogen Acceleration Act aims to accelerate, simplify, and digitalize relevant planning, approval, and award procedures. As it is not yet law at the time of writing (but is being discussed in Parliament), only its main contours are briefly mentioned here.[10]

The Act will bring about changes to environmental and public procurement law as well as accompanying amendments to the Energy Industry Act, the Highways Act, the Spatial Planning Act, and the Administrative Court Code. A central point of the WasserstoffBG is the stipulation that the construction or operation of electrolysers on land is to be regarded as a project of overriding public interest pursuant to Article 4(1) sentence 1 in conjunction with Article 2(1) of the Draft Hydrogen Acceleration Act. According to Article 2(1), this also includes the associated ancillary facilities for electrolysers. This legal attribution means that the approval authorities must generally give priority to the interest in the realization of an electrolysis project in relation to other affected interests and protected goods (eg monuments, landscape, and nature conservation). This is also the reason why the German law on monuments (Denkmalschutz) has not been discussed in this chapter. In the future, approval for a hydrogen project can only be refused in exceptional cases in Germany on the grounds that other interests and protected assets are affected.

An exception to Article 4(2) of the WasserstoffBG relates to water law approval procedures for water abstraction for electrolysers on land. The discussed prioritization of electrolysis plants is likely not to apply to these procedures if the public water supply or the water table balance may be significantly impaired by the water abstraction. A probable impairment is sufficient for this.

Another key point is the requirements for the digitalization of approval procedures. For example, Article 5(2), Article 6(3), Article 10(2), and Article 11(2) WasserstoffBG

[10] The progress of this law can be tracked via the Documentation and Information Service of the German Parliament at: Documentation and Information Service of the German Parliament, 'Gesetz zur Beschleunigung der Verfügbarkeit von Wasserstoff und zur Änderung ...' https://dip.bundestag.de/vorgang/gesetz-zur-beschleunigung-der-verf%C3%BCgbarkeit-von-wasserstoff-und-zur-%C3%A4nderung/312436 accessed 8 January 2025.

stipulate the mandatory digital submission of approval documents with the aim of reducing the time required and saving resources.

The draft Hydrogen Acceleration Act addresses important steps towards accelerating the approval of electrolysis plants. Provided that the prescribed digitalization is consistently implemented, this should result in an acceleration of approval procedures. Difficult and lengthy procedures can also be significantly shortened by prioritizing hydrogen projects in the balancing of interests by classifying them as an overriding public interest.

4. Recommendations to Improve the System

The following recommendations for action are a non-exhaustive list of possible measures to simplify and accelerate the authorization process for electrolysis plants. The recommendations focus primarily on improvements at the structural level and concern more efficient handling of existing requirements, given that many substantive improvements have already been proposed in the draft Hydrogen Acceleration Act.

- *Reduce the level of detail of documents to be submitted and streamline the review process.* The number of documents required and the level of detail demanded of the application documents by the enforcement authorities are often too high and do not correspond to the planning status of the project. A comparison with the Fee Structure for Architects (HOAI) shows that the level of detail in the required documents is more in line with implementation planning (HOAI Phase 5) than approval planning (HOAI Phase 4). In some cases, detailed mechanical engineering plans, specific health and safety concepts, or execution plans are required, which presupposes that the execution planning phase has already been completed. This leads to considerable time losses. The level of detail in the documents should only enable the enforcement authorities to examine and assess the likely environmental impacts. Instead of a comprehensive examination of each legal regulation on a case-by-case basis, only those aspects that are actually relevant for the assessment of environmental impacts should be recorded.
- *Accelerate planning and approval procedures through digitalization.* Full digitalization of administrative, planning, and approval procedures offers considerable potential for faster and more efficient processing of applications. Documents are still often requested in multiple copies and in paper form. Digitalizing the processes facilitates the workflows for both authorities and applicants as well as the involvement of those affected. However, the prerequisite for this is that the authorities are equipped with the necessary technical resources and that employees are trained accordingly. The development and use of the so-called ELiA software for the electronic application of authorizations under the emission law procedure is a good start and is currently in use in nine German federal states. But at present, ELiA applications cannot be transferred between federal states, as each state uses its own

version of the software (ELiA 2.8). ELiA 3.0 is currently under development and will be available as a nationwide web application. The entire connection process for all ELiA partner states is expected to be completed in 2025, starting with the first connections at the beginning of 2025.

- *Expertise and knowledge transfer through a national working group or specialist committee.* As the hydrogen industry is still developing, experience on the part of the authorities is often limited. Opportunities for further training and exchange should be utilized to strengthen the expertise of public authority employees. Clear guidelines and orientation aids are particularly necessary at lower administrative levels. Due to a lack of expertise and a lack of standardized guidelines, authorities regularly request documents that are not necessary for the approval of electrolysis plants.
- *Centralized information on competent authorities.* For operators, identifying the competent authorities at the state level for the authorization of electrolysers is often more difficult and time-consuming than necessary. The introduction of a centralized, nationwide, digital, and regularly updated register that lists the responsible authorities at the respective state level would considerably simplify the initial contact between operators and authorities.
- *Improve the resources of the competent authorities and reduce their workload.* The rapid processing of applications by the competent authorities is only possible with sufficient financial and human resources. Staff shortages are a major cause of delays. Improved funding and an increase in staffing levels at the responsible authorities would be of major benefit. Adequate planning and realization of the permits requires sufficiently staffed and well-trained authority teams.

In addition, the outsourcing of certain processes, such as the review of application documents and the coordination of authorization procedures, to external service providers should be used more regularly to reduce the workload. External service providers with specific expertise or appropriate accreditation can speed up the processes. From a legal point of view the use of external so-called project managers is possible since July 2024,[11] but authorities are still too hesitant to utilize this option, as a complex tendering process is required to appoint the project manager. To improve this, a pool of certified project managers should be developed.

5. Conclusion

The permitting system for plants like electrolysers is well established in Germany. What is needed now is the implementation of hydrogen-specific provisions, including certain privileges, into that system. With its partial all-in-one permitting regime and its Energy Industry Act that applies to both electricity and hydrogen, Germany is well on its way towards legal system integration in the field of electrolyser regulation.

[11] 9. BImSchV (Verordnung über genehmigungsbedürftige Anlagen) [9th Federal Emmission Control Ordinance] s 2b.

It remains to be seen what the new German government will do, but it seems unlikely that the chosen path of speeding up permitting procedures for hydrogen in Germany will be abandoned.

One major advantage of the German system is the dual consideration of hydrogen production facilities (such as electrolysers) and the necessary infrastructure for the transmission and distribution of hydrogen. At the transmission level, the German hydrogen core grid—which has just received approval by the German National Regulatory Agency (Bundesnetzagentur)—is rooted in Article 28r EnWG. At the distribution level, similar efforts to create regional hydrogen grids, like the Wasserstoffnetz Mitteldeutschland 2.0 initiative for central and east Germany, are creating momentum. Together, these efforts will serve as the future infrastructural backbone that enables the large-scale, decentralized hydrogen production via electrolysers in Germany. German law is already advanced and, after the expected reforms in 2025, is likely to become fully fit for purpose. Now it is a matter of getting the actual investments off the ground in Germany.

Appendix

Table IV.1 List of abbreviations and translations.

Abbreviation	German	English
Wastewater Ordinance	Abwasserverordnung	Waste Water Ordinance
AEG	Allgemeines Eisenbahngesetz	General Railway Act
AVBFernwärmeV	Verordnung über Allgemeine Bedingungen für die Versorgung mit Fernwärme	Ordinance on General Terms and Conditions for the Supply of District Heating
AwSV	Verordnung über Anlagen zum Umgang mit wassergefährdenden Stoffen	Ordinance on Installations for Handling Substances Hazardous to Water
AZB	Ausgangszustandsbericht	Initial status report
BauGB	Baugesetzbuch	Building Code
BauNVO	Baunutzungsverordnung	Land Use Ordinance
BauR	Baurecht	Building law
BbergG	Bundesberggesetz	Federal Mining Act
BBodSchG	Gesetz zum Schutz vor schädlichen Bodenveränderungen und zur Sanierung von Altlasten	Act on the Protection against Harmful Soil Changes and the Remediation of Contaminated Sites
BetrSichV	Betriebssicherheitsverordnung	Industrial Safety Ordinance
BImSchG	Bundes-Immissionsschutzgesetz	Federal Emission Control Act
BImSchV	Verordnung zum BImSchG	Ordinance to the BImSchG
BImSchVVwV	Allgemeine Verwaltungsvorschrift zur Durchführung der Verordnung über elektromagnetische Felder	General Administrative Regulation on the Implementation of the Ordinance on Electromagnetic Fields

(*continued*)

Table IV.1 Continued

Abbreviation	German	English
BNatSchG	Bundesnaturschutzgesetz	Federal Nature Conservation Act
BAT leaflet	Merkblatt zu den 'besten verfügbaren Techniken'	Fact sheet on the 'best available techniques'
Energy Industry Act	Energiewirtschaftsgesetz	Energy Industry Act
ERegG	Eisenbahnregulierungsgesetz	Railroad Regulation Act
DVGW	Deutscher Verein des Gas- und Wasserfaches	German Technical and Scientific Association for Gas and Water
FFH	Fauna-Flora-Habitat	Fauna-flora habitat
FFH Directive	Fauna-Flora-Habitat-Richtlinie	Fauna-Flora-Habitat Directive
GasHDrLtgV	Verordnung über Gashochdruckleitungen	Ordinance on high-pressure gas pipelines
GasNZV	Verordnung über den Zugang zu Gasversorgungsnetzen	Gas Network Access Regulation
IE system	Anlagen, die der IE-RL unterliegen	Installations subject to the IE Directive
IE-RL	Industrieemissionen-Richtlinie (2024/1785/EU)	Industrial Emissions Directive (2024/1785/EU)
i.V.m.	in Verbindung mit	in connection with
LAI	Bund/Länder-Arbeitsgemeinschaft Immissionsschutz	Federal/State Working Group on Emission Control
LBO	Landesbauordnung	State building regulations
MBO	Musterbauordnung	Model building regulations
ProdSG	Produktsicherheitsgesetz	Product Safety Act
RohrFLtgV	Verordnung über Rohrfernleitungsanlagen (Rohrfernleitungsverordnung)	Ordinance on Pipeline Installations (Pipeline Ordinance)
rgS	relevante gefährliche Stoffe	Relevant hazardous substances
Explosives Act	Gesetz über explosionsgefährliche Stoffe (Sprengstoffgesetz)	Act on Explosive Substances (Explosives Act)
MOT	Technischer Überwachungsverein	Technical Inspection Association
UVPG	Gesetz über die Umweltverträglichkeitsprüfung	Environmental Impact Assessment Act
RRP	Umweltverträglichkeitsprüfung	Environmental impact assessment
VwVfG	Verwaltungsverfahrensgesetz	Administrative Procedure Act
WasserstoffBG	Wasserstoffbeschleunigungsgesetz	Hydrogen acceleration law
WasserstoffNEV	Wasserstoffnetzentgeltverordnung	Hydrogen Network Charges Ordinance
WindSeeG	Windenergie-auf-See-Gesetz	Wind Energy at Sea Act
WHG	Wasserhaushaltsgesetz	Water Resources Act
ZÜS	Zugelassene Überwachungsstelle	Approved monitoring body

Further Reading

Josephine Glandien and others, 'Zur Entwicklung von Wasserstoff-Netzinfrastrukturen in Deutschland bis zum Jahr 2030' (2024) 75(3) EWP 60–66.

Cathérine Jansen, 'Accelerating Permission: Hydrogen Transport and Storage Regulation—A German Case Study' in Ruven Fleming (ed), *Cambridge Handbook of Hydrogen and the Law* (CUP 2024) 217–32 https://www.cambridge.org/core/books/cambridge-handbook-of-hydrogen-and-the-law/regulating-hydrogen-transport/5B1C65218B931C98A5D05528B03610EA accessed 9 January 2025.

Sabrina Jung and others, 'Wasserstoffelektrolyse im Gigawatt-Maßstab: Abbau von Innovationshürden' (2024) 75(9) EWP 20–25.

Gijs Kreeft, 'Legislative and Regulatory Framework for Power-to-Gas in Germany, Italy and Switzerland Deliverable 7.3' (STORE & GO Project, 2017) https://www.storeandgo.info/fileadmin/downloads/deliverables_2020/Update/20180430_STOREandGO_D7.3_RUG_accepted.pdf accessed 6 January 2025.

Florian Lehnert and others, 'Machbarkeitsstudie Wasserstoffnetz Mitteldeutschland 2.0' (2024) https://www.mitteldeutschland.com/wp-content/uploads/2024/07/240722_h2netzmd_kurzfassung_end.pdf accessed 9 January 2025.

Thorsten Müller, 'Beschleunigungsansätze im Zulassungsrecht für Elektrolyseure' (2024) NVwZ 791.

V

Poland

Maciej Owidzki

1. Introduction

Poland is currently the third largest hydrogen producer in the European Union (EU), responsible for meeting 14% of the European demand for the gas.[1] Although it is almost exclusively grey hydrogen, there are plans already in place to replace it with the blue and green kinds, as well as to drastically scale up hydrogen production, with targets reaching as high as producing 1 million tonnes annually by 2024, and 10 million tonnes by 2030. The Polish Hydrogen Strategy outlines a two-phase strategy for hydrogen integration: by 2025, the goals include a 1 MW power-to-gas (P2G) plant, hydrogen-natural gas blending, research and development for small-scale installations, hydrogen energy storage, and compact P2G/G2P (gas-to-power) systems. By 2030, the focus shifts to larger installations, hydrogen as energy storage, small-scale plants for various users, microgeneration for off-grid power, and adding electrolysers to solar plants.[2]

These plans seem far-fetched given that Polish targets in terms of green hydrogen targets for 2025 have already been missed.[3] However, given the pressing nature of facilitating the multi-sector green economy, the plan to create demand for renewables now and the supply later is not without merit. Polish coal-dependent electricity production is reminiscent of the times when solar or wind power were a novelty incapable

[1] Magdalena Skłodowska, 'Kto zarobi na polskim wodorze?' (4 November 2020) *Wysokie Napiecie* <https://wysokienapiecie.pl/32899-kto-zarobi-na-polskim-wodorze/> accessed 10 November 2024.

[2] Ministry of Climate and Environment, *Polska Strategia Wodorowa do roku 2030 z perspektywą do roku 2040* (Warsaw, October 2021)

[3] Ibid; Ellie Biddulph, 'Poland Renewable Energy Market: The Complete Guide' (12 August 2021) Greensolver https://greensolver.net/poland-renewable-energy-market-the-complete-guide/ accessed 10 November 2024.

of delivering cost-effective energy to a country with a robust mining industry. These times, as romanticized by some conservative-leaning politicians, are simply gone; the scientific and economic consensus today is that the most economical way of generating electricity today is solar, followed closely by other sustainable methods.[4] Although Poland was not spearheading the push for these in the past and can hardly claim credit for making these technologies cost-effective today, the significant decrease of fossil fuels in the country's energy mix is, at this point, just a matter of time and allowing the free market mechanisms to work.

Poland did miss the opportunity to be an early adopter of green electricity production methods, but today it stands before a chance to rectify this mistake and rehabilitate itself in the eyes of the world by being among the first to significantly stimulate the production of hydrogen using water electrolysis. The cost-effectiveness of this method of the gas production is questionable, but it could be decreased with some favourable regulatory and, importantly for this book, permitting arrangements.

The following chapter will serve as an overview of the perilous journey an investor must take to successfully obtain all the permits needed to erect an electrolyser. The Polish permitting regime is multi-tiered, consisting of a mix of rules both old and new; whereas the regulator has recently made some much-needed adjustments to the relevant legislation, it still has some significant shortcomings.

Following these introductory remarks, the chapter will move on to offering some general observations on the permitting regime, which provide a short overview of the structure of the Polish permitting regime. The heart of the analysis lies in section 2 where I dissect the multifaceted legal requirements across Planning, Building, Energy and Fuels, Environmental, Water Management, Waste, Nature Protection, and Fire Prevention, and Health and Safety Laws. Each subsection delves into the specific permits and assessments required, reflecting the intricate interplay between electrolysers and law. The narrative then transitions to section 4 which covers suggested reforms to streamline the permitting process, before concluding with a summary of the study's findings and the critical need for an efficient regulatory approach to support the adoption of a hydrogen economy.

2. General Observations on the Permitting Regime

Poland's administrative structure plays a significant role in the permitting process. The country is divided into *voivodships* (provinces), *powiats* (counties), and *gminas* (municipalities), each with its own level of authority and responsibility in the permitting process. The decentralization of spatial planning has shifted significant power to the regional and municipal levels, which means that investors must engage with local

[4] Christoph Kost, 'Study: Levelized Cost of Electricity—Renewable Energy Technologies' (2021) Fraunhofer Institute for Solar Energy Systems <https://www.ise.fraunhofer.de/en/publications/studies/cost-of-electricity.html> accessed 10 November 2024.

authorities to secure the necessary permits. This can lead to variations in the permitting process across different regions, as local policies and priorities come into play.

The permitting process for electrolysers typically follows a sequential order, starting with securing land rights and zoning compliance, followed by environmental and building permits, and concluding with operational permits such as fire safety and health regulations. Each step must be completed before moving on to the next, and delays or issues at any stage can impact the overall timeline for project completion.

The Integrated Environmental Permit is a key component of the Polish permitting regime, designed to consolidate various environmental requirements of some types of installations into a single permit. This approach may help to streamline the process for investors by reducing the number of individual permits needed. The Integrated Permit covers aspects such as water management, waste disposal, and emissions, ensuring that the electrolyser operates within the established environmental norms.

3. Specific Permits Applicable to Electrolysers

3.1 Planning Law

The first pillar of law relevant in the context of permits for electrolysers will be Polish spatial planning law. It governs, among others, the use of land, so it will directly determine where electrolysers can be placed. As navigating through Polish spatial planning law could prove difficult, in this chapter I focus on the issues relevant to a producer interested in investing in an electrolyser in Poland. The key issues would both be procedural as well as substantive in nature, describing the permitting path of an electrolyser and the requirements it needs to meet.

3.1.1 Procedural aspects

Recent reforms have decentralized spatial planning, replacing National Spatial Development Concept 2030, which used to have a major impact on the spatial policies in the entire country, with a medium-term national development strategy, reducing the national plan's significance and enhancing regional autonomy. This change affects investors, as there is no national spatial policy for electrolysers and compliance with the national development strategy is now the responsibility of lower tiers of government. On the one hand this change could have adversely affected investors looking to expand into the country on the basis of favourable long-term outlooks based on the national plan, but on the other it increased the autonomy of the lower tiers of government, who can now offer better conditions for investors and compete with each other on this field.

Voivodships, akin to 'provinces' or 'lands' in other jurisdictions, play a minor role in zoning for electrolysers, focusing mostly on landscape protection, broad regional development goals, and coordinating municipal spatial plans. New green hydrogen installations therefore need to pay most attention to spatial plans prepared by the municipalities. These are created with regard to the physical boundaries of the municipality, although there is no obligation to do so for all the territory within a municipality. It is therefore not obvious whether a land deemed economically desirable for an electrolyser actually has a plan that clearly allows for such an installation.

The municipal spatial plan is the very core of preparing the construction design and is a crucial prerequisite for a building permit, which needs to be in line with it. Basing activities in this scope on the municipal spatial plan is probably the most desirable method of development, as it minimizes the amount of red tape that the investor needs to go through. However, given that not all territory of a municipality needs to be or indeed is covered by the plan, it is possible that the plot chosen to be an electrolyser's site will not be covered by it—interested parties can then apply for a decision on construction conditions and land development that constitutes a formal basis for applying for a construction permit. This, however, cannot be done lightly, as there are specific substantive conditions which need to be first met.

3.1.2 Substantive aspects

As discussed, there are two ways of complying with the municipal spatial order—be in line with the spatial plan, in which case no additional activity is required, or apply and obtain a decision on construction conditions and land development. The most critical condition for this requires that at least one neighbouring plot, accessible by the same public road, is developed to a degree that establishes requirements for new buildings. This includes the continuation of functions, parameters, features, and development indicators, such as building dimensions, architectural form, development lines, and land use intensity.

This means that in principle, in case of a lack of a municipal spatial plan, water electrolysis plants can be built only in the direct vicinity of plants similar in nature. There are currently no guidelines as to what may constitute such a plant, which in practice makes it very difficult to develop an electrolyser on the basis of a decision on construction conditions. If the industry is therefore to develop, it is essential for the municipalities to take P2G into account in the zoning plans. Alternatively, water electrolysers could be granted a status similar to the facilities producing renewable electricity. Including them in the specialized legislation would then allow for an exemption, eliminating the need for a similar installation in the vicinity.

Of the two described options, the latter is clearly superior. The former would put too much responsibility on the municipalities as they are the ones solely responsible for their zoning plans. It is logical that not all municipalities will have enough professional staff available for carrying out the field operations and complex drafting which is involved in creating a comprehensive plan in a timeframe fully facilitating the goals of the Hydrogen Strategy. Therefore, it seems efficient to equate electrolysers with other Renewable Energy Sources (RES) facilities in the national legislation, without unnecessary alterations in municipal zoning laws.

The 2003 Spatial Planning Law also creates a special category for technologies or solutions that, despite their public utility, have not reached the level of maturity that would allow them to compete with established alternatives. For these projects a modified procedure and issuing a separate decision is intended—a decision on the location of a public purpose investment. There is a closed list of projects qualifying as such; these include particularly environmental projects, such as carbon capture and storage (CCS) facilities or offshore wind farms. There are again two routes to erect a public purpose investment: one on the basis of a local spatial plan and, in case of a lack thereof, a decision to determine the location of a public purpose investment. There are many ways in which it is more beneficial for the project to be qualified as a public purpose investment; financial penalties apply for public bodies' delay in granting a decision or generally streamlined proceedings. Such a decision also cannot be refused solely on the ground of not being compliant with a spatial order or with local sustainable development. Inclusion of electrolysers in the definition of a public purpose investment would therefore be a crucial element of streamlining the permitting procedure; it is certainly possible, given that inclusion of other climate-friendly installations happened in the past.

3.2 Building Law

3.2.1 Procedural aspects

Having dealt with the placement of a plant, one should now turn to the field crucial for actually *building* an electrolyser. Generally, before that could happen, a construction permit needs to be obtained, conditions for which are described in the substantive part of this section.[5]

In January 2025, Poland made a positive step in streamlining its permitting procedure by removing the need to obtain a building permit for electrolysers of up to 10 MW of installed capacity.[6] Instead they require a 'building notification' to be submitted to the municipality; it needs to include all the relevant permits described further in the chapter, right to build on the land, and the appropriate sketches or drawings.[7] It is a significant move towards deregulation and is sure it welcomed by the investors.

Apart from a potential need to obtain a construction permit, the *Building Law Act* also recognizes a separate permit, called a use permit, for certain types of buildings. These are listed in the Annex to the Act, and although this could depend on an individual facility, it is fair to assume that electrolysers constitute the following categories:

Category XVIII—industrial buildings, such as production and energy buildings,
Category XXX—facilities for the use of water resources, such as sea and inland water intakes

[5] Ustawa z dnia 7 lipca 1994 r. Prawo budowlane (consolidated text Dz U [Journal of Laws] 2021, item 2351, as amended) art 28(1).
[6] ibid art 29(1)(34).
[7] ibid art 30.

These categories do need the a use permit;[8] it is to be requested after the construction works have ceased[9] and is issued upon an inspection that checks whether the construction objects or parts thereof that are put into use can function independently as intended.[10] If this is deemed to be the case, the responsible authority may grant such permit even if not all construction is finalized—should this be the case, a date is set for when the work should be finalized.[11]

3.2.2 Substantive aspects

For a building permit to be issued, the following documents need to be included:

The site development project, which is a comprehensive plan that outlines the intended use of the land and the arrangement of the construction project within its boundaries. It includes details on the infrastructure, landscaping, access roads, parking spaces, and the location of the electrolyser and associated facilities.

The architectural and construction project, which is a detailed set of documents that provides a blueprint for the electrolyser's construction. It encompasses architectural drawings, structural designs, materials specifications, and technical descriptions. This project must be prepared by a licensed architect or engineer and comply with the Building Law, technical building codes, and safety standards.

Opinions, agreements, permits, and other documents required by specific laws. This category includes all additional documents that are mandated by various laws relevant to the specific characteristics of the construction project. For an electrolyser, a key document is the Integrated Environmental Permit, which ensures that the facility will operate within the environmental norms and standards. Additionally, a grid connection agreement with the Transmission System Operator (TSO) or the relevant Distribution System Operator (DSO) is necessary to secure access to the power grid for the electrolyser's energy supply. Other permits that constitute an element of this requirement will be described in the next parts of this chapter.

A declaration of the right to use the property for construction purposes. This is a legal statement confirming that the investor has the legal authority to undertake construction on the site. This could be in the form of ownership, perpetual usufruct, lease, or another legal title that grants the investor the right to develop the property.

A decision on building conditions and land development. As discussed in the previous section, decision on building conditions and land development is required when there is no local municipal development plan in place. This administrative decision sets out the conditions under which the construction can be carried out, including the building's purpose, height, building area, and its relation to the neighbouring properties and infrastructure. It is issued by the local planning authority and ensures that the

[8] ibid art 55(1)(1)(c).
[9] ibid art 57(3a).
[10] ibid art 59a(2).
[11] ibid art 59(3).

proposed construction aligns with the broader planning strategy for the area, even in the absence of a detailed local plan.[12]

When it comes to the use permit, a site needs to undergo *an inspection by the local supervision authority.* The inspection covers the building's conformity with the site development plan, key technical parameters, structural elements, roof geometry, building facilities, installations for intended use, and accessibility for disabled persons, including the elderly. It also verifies the use of construction products crucial for structural and fire safety, the fulfilment of demolition obligations for existing structures not intended for further use, and the proper organization of the construction site.[13]

3.3 Energy Law

Energy law in Poland is organized in the Energy Law Act of 10 April 1997.[14] This branch of law was, for a long time, a major roadblock in the development of the Polish hydrogen economy as it was entirely detached from the Polish ambitions as described in the Hydrogen Strategy. For example, it used to not even contain the definition of hydrogen, which meant that hydrogen was treated as a generic 'gaseous fuel', without any special dispositions and de facto putting it in the same basket as natural gas.

This situation changed when in December 2024, the President signed into law a comprehensive update to the Energy Law Act dedicated solely to hydrogen.[15] It now distinguishes between low-emissions hydrogen, hydrogen made using a renewable energy source, and a renewable fuel of non-biological origin (RFNBO) source, with the difference between the last two being that the 'renewable H_2' is a general term for any hydrogen produced with any renewable energy source, whereas 'RFNBO H_2' draws its definition from the relevant EU legislation.[16] The new Act also deals with how the hydrogen market is actually supposed to operate, how the ownership structure of the relevant infrastructure should be shaped, and how one is to actually enter this market.[17]

If one is to treat the permitting process as guiding an electrolyser plant from the proverbial A to Z, the most relevant change introduced to the Act would be the very last part of the Act: its grid connection rules, concession, and certification enabling market access. These will look different depending on the scope of activities that are planned by an undertaking, with some specific obligations placed on the hydrogen producer.

Interestingly, an undertaking which produces hydrogen does not need to apply for a concession, regardless of the size of the installation and type of hydrogen produced.

[12] ibid art 33.
[13] ibid art 59a.
[14] Ustawa z dnia 10 kwietnia 1997 r.—Prawo energetyczne (consolidated text Dz U 2021, item 716, as amended).
[15] 'Prezydent podpisał ustawę regulującą rynek wodoru w Polsce' (PAP biznes) <https://biznes.pap.pl/wiadomosci/firmy/prezydent-podpisal-ustawe-regulujaca-rynek-wodoru-w-polsce> accessed 23 December 2024.
[16] Art 3(3)(d) and (e), Ustawa z dnia 10 kwietnia 1997 r.—Prawo energetyczne (consolidated text Dz U 2021, poz. 716 z późn. zm.).
[17] 'Prezydent podpisał ustawę regulującą rynek wodoru w Polsce' (PAP biznes) https://biznes.pap.pl/wiadomosci/firmy/prezydent-podpisal-ustawe-regulujaca-rynek-wodoru-w-polsce accessed 23 December 2024.

Such a concession normally grants an entity the right to perform specific activities within the energy sector that would otherwise be prohibited without state authorization. This is a welcome development given that obtaining a concession usually requires a complex procedure which could considerably extend the investment process involving conditions around technical standards, environmental protection, and the security of energy supply.

Unless a producer decides to have a direct pipeline connecting it to a hydrogen consumer, such producer can be connected to either hydrogen DSO or TSO based on the third-part access (TPA) rules akin to those in the electricity or natural gas markets. To that end, there are three types of agreements that can be concluded:

- hydrogen sales agreements,
- hydrogen transmission or distribution services agreements,
- hydrogen storage services agreements.

If all three services are to be utilized, it is possible to conclude a so-called comprehensive hydrogen agreement. The regulator does not limit the contents of any of these—the parties are free to negotiate the specifics of each agreement, but these do have to include some minimal requirements such as the volume and price of hydrogen.

As far as the fees for connecting to the hydrogen network are concerned, they are to be equal to the actual costs incurred by the relevant distribution or transmission operator.[18] It is noteworthy that this has changed from the initial proposal of the Act's amendment, where the fee depended on the type of hydrogen-producing installation—low-emission hydrogen had a connection fee that would be half of the connection's actual costs; it would be one-fourth for green hydrogen.[19] The change in this regard seems premature, as one might assume that it would be the government's highest priority to enable new connections as cost-efficiently for the producers as possible, especially given that these costs are bound to be considerable for the early and may decrease in time as the industry and supply chains mature and the hydrogen grid develops.

The Energy Law Act also specifies the necessary elements of a Grid Connection Agreement between a hydrogen producer and hydrogen TSO/DSO,[20] but as they do not constitute a 'permit' per se, they remain outside the scope of this chapter.

3.4 Environmental Law

A branch of law perhaps most crucial for the development of a favourable permitting regime for new electrolysers in Poland is environmental law, if only by virtue of its complexity. In a somewhat paradoxical turn of events, the installations that are hoped to

[18] Art 7(8)(1)(b).

[19] Projekt ustawy o zmianie ustawy—Prawo energetyczne oraz niektórych innych ustaw UD382 (archived) https://legislacja.rcl.gov.pl/projekt/12365500 accessed 30 January 2025.

[20] Art 7(1)(2).

contribute to solving the environmental concerns of today's world are still subject to the substantive rules governing the limits of a project's environmental footprint. This subsection will determine whether the law in Poland will not hinder the erection of new electrolysers—in other words, we will examine whether Polish environmental law is truly a part of the solution, or part of the problem.

3.4.1 Permitting regime

The Polish environmental permitting regime is structured to ensure that any activity with potential environmental impact is conducted in a manner that is sustainable and minimizes harm to the environment. This framework is rooted in the principle of sustainable development and integrates environmental considerations into economic and social planning.

The issuance of environmental permits is administered by various authorities depending on the type and scale of the activity. For reasons described in detail in the subsequent parts of this chapter, electrolysers are equated with the most polluting facilities, and as such are required to obtain an Integrated Environmental Permit.

Conditions specified in the permits are legally enforceable, and failure to comply can lead to legal consequences, including financial penalties or the revocation of the permit. This enforcement mechanism is crucial to the effectiveness of the environmental permitting regime.

3.4.2 Environmental Impact Assessment

3.4.2.1 Procedural aspects

The way Environmental Impact Assessment (EIA), the prime instrument of environmental policy, is carried out in Poland is governed by a dedicated Act, which implements the Strategic Environmental Assessment (SEA), EIA, and Habitats Directives.[21] The body responsible for issuing an EIA is the regional director of environmental protection.[22] Given that electrolysers are producing an inorganic chemical product, they are listed as one of the installations which *must* undergo an impact assessment.[23] In principle, the assessment needs to be done before a building permit is issued and is hardly a one-stop-shop solution: there are six stages to the process, with different stakeholders responsible. These stages are as follows:

(1) qualification of the project for the EIA procedure (the so-called screening);
(2) determining the scope of analysis performed as part of the EIA (so-called scoping);

[21] Ustawa z dnia 3 października 2008 r. o udostępnianiu informacji o środowisku i jego ochronie, udziale społeczeństwa w ochronie środowiska oraz o ocenach oddziaływania na środowisko (u.i.o.ś) Dz.U. 2022, poz. 1029.

[22] Art 75(1) u.i.o.ś.

[23] Rozporządzenie Rady Ministrów z dnia 10 września 2019 r. w sprawie przedsięwzięć mogących znacząco oddziaływać na środowisko (Dz U 2019, poz. 1839 z późn. zm.) art 2(1)(1)(b).

(3) presenting, in the form of a report, the information on the environmental impact assessment evaluation to the competent authorities;
(4) verification of the report;
(5) consultations with the relevant environmental protection authorities and the public;
(6) issuing the Decision and making it publicly available.

The screening is an important part of the process and is required by the EIA Directive.[24] As previously mentioned, Article 4 of this Directive gives the Member States some leeway when it comes to the types of installations which need to be covered by the assessment; Member States may determine these on a case-by-case basis or based on published criteria.

In the case of Poland, streamlining green hydrogen plants by granting this exception may prove difficult, given that the definition of installations having a definite effect on the environment leaves little room for manoeuvre and electrolysers are almost certainly within the meaning of the provision, making it obligatory to apply for an EIA. No special designations were made for such plants; they must be therefore qualified as *installations for the production of basic products or intermediates of inorganic chemistry using chemical processes*,[25] meaning that they will always be required to undergo an environmental impact assessment. The document that qualifies them as such is, however, not an act of Parliament; it is a binding ordinance of the Cabinet which does not need to go through as lengthy a legislative procedure as an act. Indeed, it has been updated regularly since its first publication, which means that it could be updated again to accommodate electrolysers in a more sensible way, truly reflecting their limited impact on the environment.

The second stage of the EIA is scoping; it entails narrowing down the environmental effects covered by the assessment to solely the ones potentially caused by the installation in question.[26] The information is taken into account to determine the necessary scope includes the size and location of the installation, its technical capacity, and likely environmental impact.[27] This is therefore the stage where the special character of electrolysers can be considered; despite being technically a chemical plant, the pollution produced by these plants is relatively small—the whole idea behind electrolysers is, in the end, the production of a clean energy carrier. However, because the legislation regarding chemical plants is somewhat outdated and was made with more intrusive chemical industries in mind, the current permitting regime is not fully fit for installations as disruptive as electrolysers. Scoping therefore provides a way to rectify

[24] European Commission: Directorate-General for Environment, COWI, Milieu, McGuinn, J., Lukacova, Z. et al., *Environmental impact assessment of projects—Guidance on the preparation of the environmental impact assessment report (Directive 2011/92/EU as amended by 2014/52/EU)* (Publications Office 2017) https://data.europa.eu/doi/10.2779/41362 accessed 10 November 2024.

[25] Rozporządzenie Rady Ministrów z dnia 10 września 2019 r. w sprawie przedsięwzięć mogących znacząco oddziaływać na środowisko (Dz U 2019, poz. 1839 z późn. zm.) art 2(1)(1)(b).

[26] Art 67(1) u.i.o.ś.

[27] European Commission (n 24).

these legislative shortcomings and limit the administrative burden placed on the parties planning to install these P2G facilities. The Polish law says that the location, nature, and scale of the impact of the project can be taken into account to potentially limit the scope of the EIA—some lengthy processes such as an analysis of possible social conflicts related to the planned project can therefore be skipped entirely if a facility is of a small enough scale.[28] Although scoping does alleviate some burden and could shorten the time it takes to create a full assessment, it does not solve the fundamental problem of putting electrolysers on par with much more polluting installations.

The third step of the Polish EIA procedure is rather straightforward—the competent authority is presented with the necessary documentation by the applicant. These documents focus on the proposed actions aimed at identifying and then mitigating, reducing, or compensating for the impact on the environment. The data surrendered at this stage form the bulk of the documentation required in erecting a new electrolyser as a whole. They are listed in Article 66.1 of the 2008 Act.[29] Additionally, the applicant must include analyses of alternative solutions performed by an expert in the field in three variants: the one proposed by the applicant, a rational alternative variant, and the most favourable variant for the environment.[30]

Upon verification of the relevant documents in the next step, step 5 entails taking into account the opinion of relevant public bodies and public participation. The public is not officially a party to any permitting proceedings, but it must be given a *possibility* to voice concerns, for example via a dedicated website.[31] The administrative entities that are consulted at this stage include or may include: the Ministry for the Environment, the State Sanitary Inspection, the authority responsible for water management, and finally the body issuing the Integrated Environmental Permit.[32] Should, after 30 days, none of these bodies have any reservations regarding the assessment, the process can go through and further permits can be granted provided that they are in compliance with the assessment.[33]

3.4.2.2 Substantive aspects

The substantive aspects of the EIA process for electrolysers in Poland focus on the environmental considerations to which these installations must adhere. As classified installations for the production of basic inorganic chemical products, electrolysers are subject to a mandatory EIA due to their potential environmental impact, as defined by the Act. The assessment requires a detailed examination of the potential environmental impacts, including the size, location, technical capacity, and the nature of the electrolyser's operations. Despite being categorized with other chemical plants, electrolysers typically have a relatively low level of pollution, as their primary function

[28] Art 68(2)(1) u.i.o.ś.
[29] Art 66(1) u.i.o.ś.
[30] Art 66(1)(5) u.i.o.ś.
[31] Art 29 u.i.o.ś.
[32] Art 70 u.i.o.ś.
[33] Art 70.4 u.i.o.ś.

is to produce a clean energy carrier. This unique characteristic should be factored into the EIA process to ensure that the assessment is reflective of the actual environmental impact of the installation.

An essential element of the EIA is the analysis of alternative solutions, where the applicant must present an expert evaluation of the proposed project, a rational alternative, and the option most favourable to the environment. This analysis is crucial for determining the best approach to minimize environmental impact. Additionally, the EIA process involves consultations with relevant environmental protection authorities and the public, allowing for the incorporation of feedback and concerns into the decision-making process. Although the current EIA process aligns with more traditional chemical plant operations, if Poland is serious about kickstarting a hydrogen revolution, the hurdles of having to deal with a lengthy EIA do not work in its favour. A more comprehensive approach is needed, starting with recognizing that electrolysers are unlike some other chemical plants producing inorganic materials and their environmental impact is likely to be significantly lower.

3.4.3 Applicable environmental permits

Unlike many other jurisdictions, Poland uses an Integrated Environmental Permit which already consists of all the necessary permits; it is hardly a one-stop-shop solution, but it does allow the developers to minimize their potential workload.

3.5 Water Management Law

3.5.1 Procedural aspects

The next branch of law relevant for the erection of new electrolysers is water management law—this is because, after all, water is one of the only two feedstocks needed to produce hydrogen with electrolysis. Additionally, large quantities of water are used as a coolant in these types of plants. Todays, at least 9 kg of water are consumed to produce 1 kg of H_2, with that many times over needed to properly cool the device.[34] It is not impossible that future generations of the technology will use alternative cooling methods, but as of now it is clear that electrolysers need a steady water supply and a way to discharge the coolant after it has been used.[35] It is therefore clear that anyone interested in erecting an electrolyser in Poland needs to be aware of how water management works there.

In general, the Polish legal system recognizes a separate water permit that needs to be obtained by an economic entity that plans to make use of the country's water resources.[36] However, as the Integrated Permit covers the water management, no additional permits are required for the electrolysers given that they are subject to said

[34] Rebecca R Beswick, Alexandra M Oliveira, and Yushan Yan, 'Does the Green Hydrogen Economy Have a Water Problem?' (2021) 6(9) ACS Energy Letters 3167.

[35] ibid.

[36] Art 35 Ustawa z dnia 20 lipca 2017 r. Prawo wodne (t.j. Dz U z 2021 r. poz. 2233 z późn. zm.).

Integrated Permit.[37] Procedurally it certainly makes it easier to build a plant, but the substantive requirements are not very different—conditions constituting the proper way of utilizing the resource are still applicable.[38]

3.5.2 Substantive aspects

To obtain an Integrated Permit, one must fulfil the requirements of a water permit for water abstraction and a water permit for discharging sewage into waters or into the ground.[39] There is a limited number of grounds for refusal of such permits and do not adversely impact the aims of strategic documents for water management, wastewater treatment, drought, floods, and planning documents; to that end, an investor would usually receive an acceptable limit on the quantity of water to be used.[40] A party interested in erecting an electrolyser in Poland should be aware that the permit issued will regulate the use of the water in a strict way and will govern issues such as the amount of water abstracted; the amount of wastewater discharged into water or soil, or into sewage devices; timing of water collection and discharge as well as sewage discharge for plants with periodic or seasonally variable activity; detailing the parameters of water use in various periods of the plant's operation; sewage sampling site etc.[41] Additionally, an electrolyser should by its very nature include a device used for the intake of surface waters and/or groundwater—such a facility is recognized in Polish law as a water device.[42] It is required that the water intake of such a device be constantly monitored.[43]

Polish law recognizes cooling water as industrial sewage, which brings forth some consequences.[44] Its treatment might not be necessary, provided that clean water is used for the purposes of electrolysis, but this still means that its discharge into the ground of a body of water entails paying a special fee.[45] The fee will not be as large as it would have been in cases of any potentially harmful substances present in the water, as Polish law differentiates between various types of industrial sewage and modifies the fee payable accordingly. Its size will also depend on the water availability in the area, so the more strenuous an installation is on the local water resources, the higher the fee.[46]

The treatment and disposal of brine resulting from the ultra-purification of water for electrolysis must also be addressed—the production of hydrogen via electrolysis requires high-purity water, and the ultra-purification process generates brine as a by-product.[47] According to the Water Law, specifically in the context of waste management, brine is considered industrial wastewater.[48] Obtaining the necessary permits for

37 Art 182 Ustawa z dnia 27 kwietnia 2001 r. Prawo ochrony środowiska (t.j. Dz U z 2021 r. poz. 1973 z późn. zm.).
38 Art 211(1) Prawo ochrony środowiska.
39 ibid.
40 Art 399(1) Prawo ochrony środowiska in conjunction with art 396(1)(1) Prawo wodne.
41 Art 202(1) Prawo ochrony środowiska.
42 Art 16(65)(d) Prawo wodne.
43 ibid art 101(1).
44 ibid art 16(64).
45 Art 10(5) Rozporządzenie Rady Ministrów z dnia 22 grudnia 2017 r. w sprawie jednostkowych stawek opłat za usługi wodne (t.j. Dz U 2021, poz. 736 z późn. zm.).
46 ibid art 2.
47 Mostafa El-Shafie, 'Hydrogen Production by Water Electrolysis Technologies: A Review' (2023) 20 Results in Engineering 101426.
48 Art 13(73a) Prawo wodne.

wastewater discharge and adhering to the standards for the treatment and release of effluents into the environment is therefore necessary. The Integrated Environmental Permit, as discussed earlier, would encompass these requirements, ensuring that the disposal of brine does not adversely affect the environment and complies with the relevant legal provisions for waste management and water protection in Poland.

Electrolysers will undergo the same treatment as other industries or even households utilizing water resources; there is no urgent need to modify the law to accommodate hydrogen as it does not appear ill-suited for this purpose now. Having said that, a natural consequence of a further implementation of hydrogen into the Polish legal system should contain a definition of water electrolysis as a 'water service', as these constitute the legitimate uses of water resources. As of now, the Act includes a wide definition which includes the 'use of water for energy purposes',[49] a definition that suffices.

3.6 Waste Law

The basic legal act in the field of waste management is the Waste Act, the main purpose of which is to increase the degree of waste recovery and thus reduce the amount of waste deposited, while increasing the level of safety in waste disposal.

Alkaline water electrolysis is a technology which utilizes a liquid electrolyte, usually a solution of potassium hydroxide (KOH) or sodium hydroxide (NaOH), to extract hydrogen from water.[50] As the produced gas contains traces of the alkaline that need to be purified, the problematic chemical waste must be disposed of or neutralized onsite. The producer should prioritize the reuse of the waste, and only if this is not possible for technological reasons or it is not justified for ecological or economic reasons can the waste be dealt with in a different way.[51] Reuse is also desirable for economic reasons as it increases the efficiency of the process. Understandably, this is only applicable to plants with the production large enough to justify the investment in equipment capable of doing that—small-scale installations might decide to find an alternative solution. In these cases, chemical waste should ideally be processed onsite or, if this is not possible, they should be transferred to the nearest possible facility that is able to do that. It should not be mixed with other types of waste or diluted.[52]

The same considerations apply in cases of used-up electrodes necessary in the water electrolysis process. These could contain various hazardous substances such as fluoropolymer used in proton exchange membrane (PEM) electrolysers. They should be stored in a dedicated place without the risk of an unwanted reaction with other chemicals and be disposed of respecting the principles of waste hierarchy.

Overall, electrolysers do not pose any novel challenges to the Polish waste management regime as no new types of waste are created, nor are the quantities of waste likely

[49] ibid art 35(3)(6).
[50] El-Shafie (n 67).
[51] Art 17 Ustawa z dnia 14 grudnia 2012 r. o odpadach (t.j. Dz U z 2023 r. poz. 1587 z późn. zm.).
[52] ibid art 21(1).

to be overwhelming to the system. The current framework therefore does not need to be updated to accommodate the installations better.

3.7 Nature Protection Law

3.7.1 Procedural aspects

Nature protection law in Poland focuses on preserving biodiversity and managing natural resources sustainably. It is primarily governed by the Nature Conservation Act, which outlines the rules for safeguarding ecosystems, species, and landscapes.[53]

In Poland, obtaining a permit for tree removal is of particular importance; it is regulated under the Nature Conservation Act and is necessary for individuals or entities looking to remove trees or shrubs, whether on private or public property. The requirement for a permit is aimed at protecting the natural environment and ensuring that any tree removal is justified and conducted in a controlled manner.[54]

3.7.2 Substantive aspects

To obtain a tree removal permit, one must submit an application to the relevant local authority, which is typically the municipal office. The application must include the reasons for the tree removal, the number and type of trees or shrubs to be removed, and often a plan for compensatory planting. The authority will assess the application based on various criteria, including the tree's condition, its impact on the environment, and the public interest.[55] If granted, the permit may come with conditions, such as the requirement to plant new trees.[56] The decision can be appealed if the applicant or other stakeholders disagree with it.

Apart from the tree removal permit, there are other nature protection permits and approvals required for activities that may impact protected areas or species. For instance, activities within Natura 2000 sites, national parks, or nature reserves may require additional permits.[57] These permits ensure that any economic or development activities are compatible with the conservation objectives of these areas.

3.8 Fire Prevention, Health and Safety Law

The need to ensure the proper level of fire prevention is an important requirement in Polish law both before the plant's erection and during its operation. The Act that governs this branch of law delegates the establishment of the exact conditions to an Ordinance issued by the Ministry of Internal Affairs,[58] which is good news in and of

[53] Ustawa z dnia 16 kwietnia 2004 r. o ochronie przyrody (t.j. Dz U z 2024 r. poz. 1478 z późn. zm.).
[54] ibid art 83.
[55] ibid art 83b.
[56] ibid art 83c.
[57] ibid art 83b(1)(10).
[58] Art 13 Ustawa z dnia 24 sierpnia 1991 r. o ochronie przeciwpożarowej (t.j. Dz U z 2021 r. poz. 869 z późn. zm.).

itself—it means that whatever shortcomings are currently present in the law can be rectified easier than they would have if the amendment required a parliamentary vote.

3.8.1 Procedural aspects

Hydrogen is known to be a highly flammable material. Even when mixed with just a small amount of air, it poses a major threat which is further increased by the possibility of leaks resulting from the size of hydrogen molecules.[59] It is therefore recognized under Polish law as a 'fire-hazardous material'.[60]

The main way through which the safety of various industrial facilities is governed are the technical and construction regulations.[61] Polish law refers to hydrogen and health and safety mainly before commencing operation works in the area of hydrogen-cooled electric generators, at hydrogen tanks, water electrolysers, and hydrogen-filled cylinder storages. Measurements of the concentrations of gases present there are carried out and it is examined to ascertain whether the concentration of these gases reaches dangerous levels.[62] When assessing the risk of explosion, the most unfavourable situation, from the point of view of the possible effects of an explosion, should be considered, as prescribed via an Annex to the Building Law Act.[63]

The works may only commence after the risk of fire or explosion has been removed or minimized and the concentrations have been reduced to the values specified in the Annex and additional protective measures specified in the operating instructions have been applied.[64] The law also specifies the prescribed activities that are required to be carried out before commencing operational works.[65]

It is also critical to mention that the architectural and construction design projects, which are a necessary part of the building permit, require approval from a fire protection expert to ensure compliance with fire safety requirements.[66] Once the construction is completed and the need for a Use Permit materializes, the State Fire Service will need to be notified, after which it will check whether the installation meets the conditions of the construction project.[67]

[59] 'Lessons learned from a hydrogen explosion' (*Power Magazine*, 1 May 2009) https://www.powermag.com/lessons-learned-from-a-hydrogen-explosion/ accessed 10 November 2024.

[60] Art 2.1.1(a) Rozporządzenie Ministra Spraw Wewnętrznych i Administracji z dnia 7 czerwca 2010 r. w sprawie ochrony przeciwpożarowej budynków, innych obiektów budowlanych i terenów (Dz U nr 109, poz. 719 z późn. zm.).

[61] Art 7(3)(2) Prawo budowlane.

[62] Art 21 Rozporządzenie Ministra Energii z dnia 28 sierpnia 2019 r. w sprawie bezpieczeństwa i higieny pracy przy urządzeniach energetycznych (t.j. Dz U z 2021 r. poz. 1210).

[63] Annex I, art 1 Rozporządzenie Ministra Spraw Wewnętrznych i Administracji z dnia 7 czerwca 2010 r. w sprawie ochrony przeciwpożarowej budynków, innych obiektów budowlanych i terenów (Dz U nr 109, poz. 719 z późn. zm.).

[64] Maciej Ambroziewicz, 'BHP przy urządzeniach energetycznych cz. 2' (2020) LEX https://sip.lex.pl/#/publication/470129329/ambroziewicz-maciej-bhp-przy-urzadzeniach-energetycznych-cz-2?keyword=elektrolizer&cm=SREST accessed 10 November 2024.

[65] Art 22 Rozporządzenie Ministra Energii w sprawie bezpieczeństwa i higieny pracy przy urządzeniach energetycznych.

[66] Art 6b Ustawa z dnia 24 sierpnia 1991 r. o ochronie przeciwpożarowej (t.j. Dz U z 2024 r. poz. 275 z późn. zm.).

[67] Art 56 Prawo Budowlane.

3.8.2 Substantive aspects

There are some caveats to dealing with fire-hazardous material—it is reasonable that in the absence of specialized, sector-specific regulations, the default should be the widest possible standard of care. This unfortunately means that sectors in their infancy, such as hydrogen electrolysis, must comply with very strict rules. They must *maintain the amount of hazardous material at the workplace not greater than the daily demand or daily production, unless specific provisions provide otherwise*[68] in *a separate warehouse adapted for such purpose.*[69] As there are no specific provisions at the moment that would alter the contents of this article, it is apparent that the hydrogen producers must themselves get rid of the gas produced at a very fast pace, the logistics of which could prove problematic.

The placement of containers filled with hydrogen are also crucial: the law prescribes at least 50 centimetres of distance between these and any object or installation that can reach high temperatures.[70] A protective strip with a minimum width of 2 metres and a surface made of non-flammable materials or cleaned ground must be maintained.[71] Storage rooms intended for the storage of flammable gases or carbide must meet the requirements specified for rooms with a risk of explosion.[72] Additionally, electrolysis facilities are likely to have containers that are used to store oxygen, at least on a temporary basis. These tanks are required by law to be protected from all petroleum substances and oils.[73]

Overall, the current regime cannot be said to be tailored to the needs of the electrolysers. However, at the same time it does not impede their introduction in a very intrusive way—there are changes in the Polish law that are much more pressing.

4. Recommendations to Improve the System

Back when the Polish Hydrogen Strategy was announced, Poland set some ambitious goals for hydrogen production and consumption; as of early 2025, however, most of these goals have not been met. Serious steps in making Poland a more attractive market for electrolysers is therefore urgently needed, especially when it comes to permitting. In this part of the chapter, I identify three recommendations that might aid it in reaching this goal.

[68] Art 7(1)(3) Rozporządzenie Ministra Energii w sprawie bezpieczeństwa i higieny pracy przy urządzeniach energetycznych.
[69] ibid art 7(1)(4).
[70] ibid art 4(1)(8).
[71] ibid art 4(3).
[72] ibid art 12(1).
[73] Art 35 Rozporządzenie Ministra Gospodarki, Pracy i Polityki Społecznej z dnia 23 grudnia 2003 r. w sprawie bezpieczeństwa i higieny pracy przy produkcji i magazynowaniu gazów, napełnianiu zbiorników gazami oraz używaniu i magazynowaniu karbidu (Dz U 2004 nr 7, poz. 59).

4.1 Procedural Recommendations

The first and most obvious action would be decreasing the waiting time for each permit. This would not constitute a situation unheard of in the Polish legal system, as it was already done in the case of offshore windfarms in their dedicated Act.[74] There, if the relevant authority does not manage to issue a permit within a set deadline, it must submit the reason for its failure to do so to the Ministry of Climate and Environment, which may be a major deterrent.

Further, to accommodate bigger electrolysers that Poland needs to achieve its own ambitions, it might consider a dedicated legal act, just as was done with offshore wind. Such an act would comprise a single and comprehensive overview of all the procedural simplifications made available to green hydrogen producers. It could also, for example, mirror the solutions already used for some transmission lines by equating their status to *public purpose investments* and enabling issuing a Location Decision for a certain plot of land where an electrolyser is to be erected. Such a decision is binding on local authorities issuing zoning ordinances and is, in a way, 'reserved' for the installation in question.[75] The decision takes precedence over development plans for the location and when location decision proceedings are ongoing, all potential construction permits for the plot are suspended.[76]

4.2 Substantive Recommendations

Another shortcoming that can be easily addressed is the EIA procedure. Electrolysers, at least up to a certain capacity, should not always be required to undergo an EIA—as of now, these installations are in the same basket as other entities manufacturing products of inorganic chemistry. Onshore wind farms, for example, *must* go through an EIA only if their installed capacity exceeds 100 MW.[77] Given that electrolysers below 10 MW of power currently do not even need a construction permit, it would be consistent to also exclude them from the obligation of an EIA, at least up to a certain level of power.

5. Conclusion

The ambitious goals set forth by the Polish Hydrogen Strategy highlight Poland's commitment to becoming a leader in the hydrogen economy within the European

[74] Art 76 Ustawa o promowaniu wytwarzania energii elektrycznej w morskich farmach wiatrowych (Dz U 2024, poz. 182 t.j.).
[75] Art 11(2) Ustawa z dnia 24 lipca 2015 r. o przygotowaniu i realizacji strategicznych inwestycji w zakresie sieci przesyłowych (Dz U 2024, poz. 1199 t.j.).
[76] ibid art 7(2)(2).
[77] Art 2(5)(a) Rozporządzenie Rady Ministrów w sprawie przedsięwzięć mogących znacząco oddziaływać na środowisko.

Union. However, the current state of the permitting regime presents a complex and time-consuming challenge for investors looking to develop electrolyser projects in the country. While recent legislative updates have made strides in recognizing the unique nature of hydrogen production and streamlining certain aspects of the process, such as the removal of the need for a building permit for smaller electrolysers, there remains a significant need for further reform. The multi-tiered nature of the permitting process, from spatial planning to environmental impact assessments, requires careful navigation through various administrative levels and compliance with a multitude of regulations that may not fully reflect the low environmental impact of electrolysers.

To truly capitalize on the potential of hydrogen as a clean energy carrier and meet the targets it set for itself, Poland must consider a more comprehensive approach to reforming its permitting regime. This could involve simplifying the EIA process for electrolysers, particularly for smaller installations, and potentially creating a dedicated legal act that consolidates all procedural simplifications for green hydrogen producers. Such reforms would not only reduce the administrative burden on investors but also signal Poland's dedication to fostering a conducive environment for the growth of the hydrogen industry.

While Poland has taken important steps towards integrating hydrogen into its energy mix, the current permitting regime requires further refinement to ensure that it supports rather than hinders the growth of this emerging sector. By addressing the procedural complexities and aligning the substantive requirements more closely with the environmental benefits of electrolysers, Poland can enhance its attractiveness as a destination for hydrogen investment and move closer to achieving its vision of a robust and sustainable hydrogen economy.

Further Reading

Jerzy Korczak (ed), *Administracja publiczna wobec nowych technologii. W kierunku neutralności klimatycznej* (Warsaw 2024).

Michael Ball and Martin Wietschel (eds), *Hydrogen Economy: Opportunities and Challenges* (CUP 2010).

Agata Kosieradzka-Federczyk and Anna Fogel, *Prawo ochrony środowiska w procesie inwestycyjno-budowlanym* (WK 2015).

Piotr Jarzyński (ed), *Inwestycje budowlane w praktyce* (WKP 2022).

Anna Barczak, Maria M Kenig-Witkowska, and Marcin Stoczkiewicz (eds), *Współczesne wyzwania prawa ochrony klimatu* (WKP 2024).

Anna Hałdyj, 'Decyzja o środowiskowych uwarunkowaniach a pozwolenie emisyjne (analiza wzajemnych zależności)' (2022) 7 Państwo i Prawo 62.

VI
Spain

Íñigo del Guayo and Laura Bucher

1. Introduction[1]

The global transition towards low-carbon energy systems is accelerating, with hydrogen emerging as a cornerstone of this transformation. Spain, capitalizing on its abundant renewable resources and strategic location, is positioning itself as a leader in the green hydrogen economy.[2] To achieve this, the country has undertaken substantial policy and financial commitments,[3] including the allocation of up to €140 billion under the Recovery, Transformation, and Resilience Plan (2021–2026), supported by the European Union's 'Next Generation EU' initiative.[4] Central to this effort is the Renewable Hydrogen Roadmap, which prioritizes the development of 'hydrogen valleys'—integrated clusters for hydrogen production, transformation, and consumption, designed to achieve economies of scale and drive cross-sectoral innovation.[5]

[1] This chapter is based on a research paper authored by Laura Bucher, with input provided by Professor Del Guayo. The law is stated as to the 27 January 2025.

[2] Gobierno de España, *Hoja de Ruta del Hidrógeno: Una Apuesta por el Hidrógeno Renovable* (October 2020) https://www.miteco.gob.es/content/dam/miteco/es/ministerio/planes-estrategias/hidrogeno/hojarutahidrogenorenovable_tcm30-525000.PDF accessed 26 January 2025, 4.

[3] Real Decreto-ley 23/2020 de 23 de junio, por el que se aprueban medidas en materia de energía y en otros ámbitos para la reactivación económica, BOE núm. 175.

[4] Gobierno de España, *Plan de Recuperación, Transformación y Resiliencia* (16 June 2021) https://www.lamoncloa.gob.es/temas/fondos-recuperacion/Documents/160621-Plan_Recuperacion_Transformacion_Resiliencia.pdf accessed 26 January 2025, 4–10.

[5] Gobierno de España, *Hoja de Ruta del Hidrógeno* (n 1) 4.

Under the updated Integrated Energy and Climate Plan (PNIEC) 2023–2030,[6] which defines Spain's strategy for meeting the EU's climate and energy objectives, the country has significantly increased its electrolyser capacity target to 12 GW by 2030, tripling the original 4 GW goal set in the Renewable Hydrogen Roadmap.[7] This ambitious expansion reinforces Spain's commitment to positioning green hydrogen as a cornerstone of its decarbonization strategy. Furthermore, Spain has set a target for 74% of the hydrogen used in industrial applications to be renewable by 2030,[8] far exceeding the EU's target of 42% under the Renewable Energy Directive.[9] These objectives underscore the critical role of electrolysers in scaling up renewable hydrogen production and creating a sustainable, integrated energy system.

To achieve these ambitious hydrogen targets, Spain has attracted significant investments and launched key projects. For instance, Envision Group, in partnership with the Spanish government and European industry leaders, is investing US$1 billion to establish Europe's first integrated green hydrogen net-zero industrial park in Spain.[10] This park will design, research, and manufacture critical equipment for scalable green hydrogen and ammonia production, including high-capacity proton exchange membrane (PEM) electrolysers and both low-pressure and high-pressure alkaline electrolysers, contributing 5 GW to Spain's target.[11] Spain's advancements in PEM electrolyser technology are exemplified by Cummins' new PEM electrolyser manufacturing plant in Guadalajara, which commenced production in April 2024 with an initial capacity of 500 MW per year, scalable to over 1 GW.[12]

Additionally, Thyssenkrupp Nucera and Cepsa are contributing a 300 MW alkaline water electrolyser to the Andalusian Green Hydrogen Valley, a €3 billion initiative targeting 2 GW of electrolysis capacity and establishing Andalusia as a key hydrogen hub.[13] The Spanish government is supporting these efforts with €800 million in subsidies for hydrogen projects, aiming to unlock over €6 billion in private investments and cement Spain's leadership in green hydrogen production.[14]

[6] Ministerio para la Transición Ecológica y el Reto Demográfico (MITECO), *Plan Nacional Integrado de Energía y Clima Actualización 2023–2030* (2024), Royal Decree 986/2024 of 24 September, approving the revised PNIEC (accessed 26 January 2025).

[7] ibid 522.

[8] ibid 66–67.

[9] Directive (EU) 2023/2413 of the European Parliament and of the Council of 18 October 2023 amending Directive (EU) 2018/2001, Regulation (EU) 2018/1999 and Directive 98/70/EC as regards the promotion of energy from renewable sources, and repealing Council Directive (EU) 2015/652 [2023] OJ L256/1.

[10] Envision Group, 'Envision Energy Partners with Government of Spain and Industry Leaders to Develop Integrated Green Hydrogen Net Zero Industrial Park' (10 September 2024) https://www.envision-group.com/news-detail?id=66e05a837bdfae0a7fceb403&lang=en accessed 26 January 2025.

[11] ibid.

[12] Accelera™, 'Accelera Opens New Electrolyzer Factory in Spain, Enabling Europe's Energy Transition' (2024) https://www.accelerazero.com/es/news/accelera-opens-new-electrolyzer-factory-spain-enabling-europes-energy-transition accessed 26 January 2025.

[13] Thyssenkrupp, 'Cepsa Selects thyssenkrupp nucera as Preferred Supplier of a 300-MW Electrolyzer for Green Hydrogen Plant in Spain' (2023) <https://www.thyssenkrupp.com/en/newsroom/press-releases/pressdetailpage/cepsa-selects-thyssenkrupp-nucera-as-preferred-supplier-of-a-300-mw-electrolyzer-for-green-hydrogen-plant-in-spain-256577> accessed 26 January 2025.

[14] Europa Press, 'El Gobierno Reparte Ayudas de 794 Millones a Repsol, Iberdrola, EDP y Endesa para Impulsar el Hidrógeno Verde' (9 July 2024) <https://www.europapress.es/economia/energia-00341/noticia-gobierno-reparte-ayudas-794-millones-repsol-iberdrola-edp-endesa-impulsar-hidrogeno-verde-20240709131915.html> accessed 26 January 2025.

To incentivize renewable hydrogen production further, the government has introduced targeted fiscal measures. Royal Decree-Law 6/2022, as amended by Royal Decree-Law 18/2022, established key fiscal mechanisms aimed at stimulating investment in renewable energy, including biomethane and hydrogen (please note: all Spanish laws are cited in Table VI.2, along with their English translation). Among these measures is the introduction of freedom of amortization for renewable energy projects, allowing companies investing in hydrogen and biomethane facilities to reduce their taxable income during the early stages of development.[15] This provision alleviates the financial burden on developers and accelerates infrastructure growth.

All these investments are underpinned by the need for a stable regulatory framework for hydrogen, which is essential for fostering investor confidence and advancing the development of renewable hydrogen infrastructure. This chapter explores Spain's regulatory framework for electrolysers, providing an analysis of the permits and approvals required for their development and operation. It further examines the legislative landscape to identify the reforms needed for Spain to fully realize its potential as a European leader in the hydrogen economy.

Following this introduction, the chapter proceeds by presenting general observations on Spain's permitting regime, offering an overview of the broader regulatory context. It then highlights the key legal domains where permits are required, focusing on their implications for electrolysers. Each legal domain is addressed in two parts: the first considers its substantive applicability to electrolysers in Spain, while the second explores the procedural steps necessary to secure the relevant permits. The chapter concludes with recommendations for improving the permitting system and reflections on the challenges and opportunities within Spain's regulatory framework.

2. General Observations on the Permitting Regime

The 1978 Spanish Constitution abolished the centralized character of the Spanish state and recognized the right to autonomy of the regions and nationalities. As a result of the constitutional provisions on the territorial organization of the state, a number of Autonomous Communities were established, and the entire Spanish territory is now divided into seventeen Autonomous Communities, together with two Autonomous Towns in Africa (Ceuta and Melilla). The distribution of powers between the state and the Autonomous Communities is set out in the Constitution and in the seventeen autonomy statutes. Some powers are conferred exclusively by the Constitution on either the state (such as international relations) or the Autonomous Communities (such as

[15] Real Decreto-ley 18/2022, de 18 de octubre, por el que se aprueban medidas de refuerzo de la protección de los consumidores de energía y de contribución a la reducción del consumo de gas natural en aplicación del 'Plan + seguridad para tu energía (+SE)', así como medidas en materia de retribuciones del personal al servicio del sector público y de protección de las personas trabajadoras agrarias eventuales afectadas por la sequía, BOE núm. 251, art 22(6)(b) (Disposición adicional decimoséptima—Libertad de amortización en inversiones que utilicen energía procedente de fuentes renovables).

regional museums and libraries). However, many of the powers granted to the state by the Constitution are not absolutely exclusive but are limited to the basic or uniform aspects of a particular sector, meaning aspects that are to be enforced consistently throughout Spanish territory. These powers are typically shared with the Autonomous Communities. For instance, the state's competence includes laying down the basic legal framework for both environmental protection and energy/mines.

Conversely, those powers granted to the Autonomous Communities by the Constitution are, in many cases, not exclusive either but must be exercised within the general framework established by the state. Within that basic framework, it falls to the Autonomous Communities to develop the central statutory provisions.

Among the provisions of the Constitution, only one specifically addresses the powers of the state and the Autonomous Communities in relation to the energy sector.[16] However, other constitutional provisions are relevant to the energy sector insofar as they have an impact on it. These provisions include those that refer to the powers of the central state, such as the general planning of economic activities, and those that relate to the Autonomous Communities, such as regional and town planning and housing, or the execution of state environmental protection statutes. Competence in the energy sector is, therefore, shared in practice between the state and the Autonomous Communities, a division reflected in the statutes of the Autonomous Communities.

Since electrolysers are subject to an integrated environmental authorization (discussed in subsection 3.3), the relevant Autonomous Community is responsible for granting it, and the appropriate body within the Community will act as a 'one-stop shop'. This municipal participation within the procedure of the integrated environmental authorization ensures the compatibility of the installation with urban planning.

The Constitution guarantees a level of autonomy to municipalities, provinces, and islands under the supervisory powers of both the Autonomous Communities and the central government. There are over 8,000 municipalities, fifty provinces, and eleven main islands. The Local Organization Act 1985[17] addresses these local entities, as well as other territorial entities such as entities smaller than a municipality and associations of municipalities. The Act lists the competencies of municipal and provincial governments. While local entities do not possess specific competencies in the energy sector, there are various responsibilities with an indirect impact on energy matters. These include, in the case of municipalities, competencies in town planning, environmental protection, customer protection, street lighting, and the collection and treatment of waste. Consequently, municipalities play a crucial role in decisions concerning the location and timing of energy installations.

[16] The provision granting the central government the power to lay down the basic legal framework for energy and mines.

[17] Ley 7/1985, de 2 de abril, reguladora de las Bases de Régimen Local, BOE núm. 80 (consolidated by Real Decreto Legislativo 781/1986, de 18 de abril).

3. Specific Permits Applicable to Electrolysers

Spanish legislation does not specifically mention electrolysers but addresses them as installations with an intense demand for electricity. In particular, Spanish legislation refers to the product of an electrolyser—hydrogen—rather than to electrolysers themselves. An electrolyser is a general structure that must be built, requires water and electricity, and produces emissions and wastewater. Its location raises questions relating to planning and building requirements as well as considerations of monuments and/or nature protection areas. Accordingly, this chapter will examine each of these areas individually to assess whether the respective permits are necessary for electrolysers.

Electrolysers must adhere to various regulatory requirements to ensure compliance with planning, environmental, and safety standards. As outlined in subsection 3.1, planning and building laws must be satisfied, alongside regulations governing hydrogen as an energy carrier (subsection 3.2). Environmental permits addressing emissions and impacts are essential (subsection 3.5), as is compliance with water use, wastewater, and waste management regulations (subsections 3.6 and 3.7). The hydrogen industry's impact on protected natural areas (subsection 3.8) must also be considered. Industrial safety standards are critical due to hydrogen production's classification as an industrial activity (subsection 3.9),[18] and location requirements must respect monuments and historical sites (subsection 3.10).

3.1 Planning and Building Law

In accordance with Article 21 of Royal Legislative Decree 7/2015 of 30 October,[19] there are two basic categories of land: rural and urban. Rural land can, in turn, be subdivided further into rural land that is absolutely excluded from urban development and rural land that could be subjected to urban development. The Royal Decree of the Spanish Parliament establishes the basic conditions of equality in the exercise of the right to property. Property rights of owners depend on the location of their land. It is for the Autonomous Communities to pass the relevant urban and country planning Acts.[20] The Acts of the Autonomous Communities further develop these two basic categories but they are bound by the basic provisions of the 7/2015 Decree. Rural land can be developed (unless it is subject to special protection, for example, on environmental grounds) in accordance with those Acts and the urban plans of municipalities.[21]

[18] Ley 21/1992, de 16 de julio, de Industria (LI), BOE núm. 176.

[19] Real Decreto Legislativo 7/2015, de 30 de octubre, por el que se aprueba el texto refundido de la Ley de Suelo y Rehabilitación Urbana, BOE núm. 261.

[20] Constitución Española 1978, BOE núm. 311, art 148(1)(3).

[21] Real Decreto Legislativo 7/2015(n 18) art 13.

3.1.1 Substantive framework

To evaluate the possible implementation of hydrogen-related uses and facilities in a given territory, the provisions of the applicable land management or planning instruments—such as sectoral plans; management guidelines; general, partial, special, and natural resource management plans—must be considered. Regulations of the Autonomous Communities contain specific provisions, such as urban planning qualifications, actions of public interest, and special authorizations for evaluating and authorizing the establishment of uses other than those typical of rural land, such as agricultural, livestock, or hunting uses, on undeveloped land.

According to Article 13.1 of the 7/2015 Act on Land Planning,[22] the right of ownership of rural land includes the right to use, enjoy, and dispose of the land in accordance with its nature, subject to the limits established by land planning and town planning regulations. For electrolysers to be permitted on urban land, they must be classified as compatible with industrial activities in the General Plan of Urban Management (administered by the municipal authorities). This means electrolysers are not permitted in other areas of the municipality, such as residential zones. However, electrolysers can be located in rural land zones, subject to a specific procedure under the laws of the Autonomous Community, excluding any influence over protected land. An example of this can be seen in Article 22 of the Urban Act of the Autonomous Community of Andalusia,[23] which addresses extraordinary performances on rural land.

3.1.2 Procedural framework

Within this subsection, a distinction must be made between urban planning and urban licences.

The responsibility for approving urban planning lies with the municipal government, specifically the local council and its president, the Mayor. The government of the Autonomous Community also participates in the procedure to pass urban planning measures, which must be consistent with the broader territorial planning of the Autonomous Community.[24]

The issuance of construction licences is the responsibility of the municipal administration, and different rules apply depending on whether the land is classified as urban or rural.[25] Since the implementation, construction, and start-up of hydrogen-related facilities are subject to an integrated environmental authorization, the municipal licence is substituted by a report issued by the municipality aiming to verify that the proposed location of the electrolyser complies with urban planning requirements. According to Articles 12 and 15 of the IPPC (please note: all abbreviations and acronyms used in this chapter are covered in Table VI.1), the municipality in whose territory the facility is located must issue a report within a maximum period of thirty days. If this is not done, said report is supplemented with a copy of the application. If the regulated urban

[22] ibid.
[23] Ley 7/2021, de 1 de diciembre, de impulso para la sostenibilidad del territorio de Andalucía, BOE núm 303.
[24] Ley 7/1985 (n 16) art 25.
[25] ibid.

planning report is negative, provided that it was received in the autonomous community prior to the granting of the integrated environmental authorization, the competent body for granting said authorization will issue a reasoned resolution terminating the procedure and closing the proceedings.

3.2 Energy and Fuels Law

3.2.1 Substantive framework

The regulation of renewable gases, including biogas, biomethane, and renewable hydrogen, falls under the Hydrocarbon Sector Act (LSH).[26] The LSH addresses key aspects such as the production, storage, transportation, and distribution of gaseous fuels within the natural gas industry. The Act expressly states that it also covers biogas (a reference introduced into the Act by means of Royal Decree-Law 13/2012) and other synthetic gases.[27] Since 2022, several provisions have been added to the Act concerning renewable gases and renewable hydrogen.[28]

While the LSH primarily governs the renewable hydrogen industry, Spain's Act No 24/2013 on the Electricity Sector (LSE)[29] also plays a significant role. Although the LSE does not regulate hydrogen production directly, it is highly relevant due to the substantial amounts of renewable electricity required to produce green hydrogen. The LSE governs access to the electricity grid, an issue traditionally associated with renewable energy generation installations, such as solar or wind plants. However, with the rise of green hydrogen, grid access now also involves installations with intensive electricity consumption, such as electrolysers. Recent amendments to Spanish legislation have introduced a distinction between grid access for electricity generation (*acceso de la generación*) and electricity consumption (*acceso de la demanda*).

These points demonstrate that while the LSH remains the primary legislation regulating the renewable hydrogen industry, the LSE is crucial due to the fundamental role of electricity in the production of green hydrogen.

3.2.2 Procedural framework

The LSH has been amended several times since 2022 to extend natural gas regulations to renewable gases. Recent reforms in 2022, some of which were followed by secondary legislation issued by the Spanish National Markets and Competition Commission (CNMC), streamlined the regulation of renewable gas production, including renewable hydrogen.[30]

[26] Ley 34/1998 (LSH), de 7 de octubre, del Sector de Hidrocarburos, BOE núm 241.

[27] ibid art 54; modified by Real Decreto 13/2012, de 30 de marzo, por el que se transpone la Directiva 2009/73/CE del Parlamento Europeo y del Consejo, de 13 de julio de 2009, relativa a normas comunes para el mercado interior del gas natural, BOE núm 78 art 2.

[28] See LSH (n 25) art 55 and art 59.

[29] Ley 24/2013, de 26 de diciembre, del Sector Eléctrico (LSE), BOE núm. 310.

[30] Real Decreto-ley 14/2022, de 1 de agosto, de medidas de sostenibilidad económica en el ámbito del transporte, en materia de becas y ayudas al estudio, así como de medidas de ahorro, eficiencia energética y de reducción de la dependencia energética del gas natural, BOE núm. 184.

Article 56 of the LSH subjects the production of gases to prior authorization; however, Royal Decree-Act No 14/2022 of 1 August 2022 introduced a new provision (paragraph 4) within Article 56, which states: 'The provisions of Article 56 will not be applicable to production plants of renewable gases'. As a result, the production of renewable gases, including renewable hydrogen, now requires only environmental and other relevant permits, thereby bypassing the specific authorization previously mandated for the production of gases other than natural gas.

3.3 Guarantees of Origin

From a substantive point of view, and in accordance with Royal Decree 376/2022, renewable hydrogen is defined as hydrogen derived from renewable sources.[31]

From a procedural point of view, for hydrogen to be considered renewable, its producer must be registered in the register of production plants using gas from renewable sources.[32]

3.4 Grid Access and Connection Permits

As far as access to the grid is concerned, a distinction must be made between access for supply or generation—such as renewable electricity produced by solar or wind plants—and access for demand or consumption, for instance, plants producing renewable hydrogen, which require substantial quantities of renewable electricity.

3.4.1 Substantive framework

Access is governed by Royal Decree 1183/2020 of 29 December.[33] By means of Royal Decree 8/2023 of 16 May, specific regulations were introduced to streamline access to the grid for large renewable electricity-consuming projects, such as electrolysers, while discouraging speculative hoarding of permits. These regulations were followed by Circular[34] 1/2024 of 27 September, of the CNMC, which establishes the methodology and conditions for access and connection to the transmission and distribution networks of electricity demand facilities.

3.4.2 Procedural framework

A permit for access to the grid must be requested either from the transmission grid, granted by Red Eléctrica Española, or from the electricity distribution grid, granted by

[31] Real Decreto 376/2022 de 17 de mayo por el que se regulan los criterios de sostenibilidad y de reducción de las emisiones de gases de efecto invernadero de los biocarburantes, biolíquidos y combustibles de biomasa, así como el sistema de garantías de origen de los gases renovables, BOE núm. 118 art 2.22.

[32] ibid art 19.

[33] Real Decreto 1183/2020, de 29 de diciembre, de acceso y conexión a las redes de transporte y distribución de energía eléctrica, BOE núm. 340.

[34] A 'Circular' is a legal norm issued by the energy regulator.

the corresponding distribution grid operator in the area. The project owner is required to apply for a permit to connect the installation to the transmission or distribution networks within six months of obtaining the access permit report. This report provides information on availability and, where applicable, the conditions to which access would be subject.[35]

3.5 Environmental Law

The hydrogen industry is subject to environmental regulations concerning environmental liability and contaminated land, given its potential impacts. Article 12 of the Climate Change and Energy Transition Act 2021 requires the government to prioritize renewable hydrogen production from a sustainability perspective.[36] Four key environmental regulations relevant to electrolysers are discussed in the following subsections.

3.5.1 Environmental Impact Statement (DIA)

3.5.1.1 Substantive framework

The Environmental Impact Assessment (EIA) is a mandatory procedure for evaluating the environmental implications of plans, programmes, or projects prior to approval, ensuring compliance with environmental protection standards. The Environmental Impact Statement (DIA), issued as the final outcome of this process, determines a project's viability, specifies conditions for environmental protection—including mitigation measures—and ensures adherence to environmental standards.[37]

Act No 21/2013 on Environmental Assessment (LEA) consolidates the legal framework for evaluating plans, programmes, and projects, transposing EU Directive 2001/42/EC (Strategic Environmental Assessment) and EU Directive 2011/92/EU (Environmental Impact Assessment) into Spanish legislation. The Act unifies two previously separate pieces of legislation into one comprehensive framework.

Autonomous Communities may establish additional environmental protection rules, provided they align with the central government's basic legislation, as set out in Article 149.1.23 of the Spanish Constitution. While these regional regulations must adhere to the state's fundamental environmental standards, they allow for region-specific measures. Consequently, projects within these Communities must comply with both the state's basic environmental requirements and any supplementary regional regulations.[38]

Hydrogen-related activities, including the construction of electrolysers, fall under the scope of the LEA, which governs the environmental assessment of initiatives with significant environmental impacts.[39] Commercial hydrogen production typically

[35] Real Decreto 1183/2020 (n 32) art 10 and subsequent.

[36] Ley 7/2021, de 20 de mayo, de Cambio Climático y Transición Energética, BOE núm. 118.

[37] Ley 21/2013, de 9 de diciembre, de evaluación ambiental (LEA), BOE núm. 296.

[38] ibid, disposición final octava, títulos competenciales.

[39] ibid. See Annex I. Group 5: 'Installations for the production on an industrial scale of substances by chemical or biological transformation, of the following products or groups of products—2nd Inorganic chemical products: i) Gases and, in particular, ammonia, chlorine or hydrogen chloride, fluorine or hydrogen fluoride, carbon oxides, sulfur compounds, nitrogen oxides, hydrogen, sulfur dioxide, carbonyl dichloride'.

requires an ordinary EIA, irrespective of the project's size or technology, due to its substantial environmental effects.[40]

3.5.1.2 *Procedural framework*

Under the Spanish Constitution, hydrogen projects that extend beyond a single Autonomous Community are authorized at the central state level,[41] with the Secretary of State for Climate Change issuing the DIA pursuant to the LEA.[42] Projects confined to a single region fall under the competence of the respective Autonomous Community.[43]

The EIA process begins with the submission of an Environmental Impact Study by the project developer, outlining potential impacts and proposed mitigation strategies. Public consultations are then conducted by the substantive authority to gather input from affected administrations, organizations, and the public.[44]

The competent Environmental Authority, typically the relevant environmental department of the Autonomous Community, conducts a technical review of all submitted documents and input. Based on its evaluation, the DIA is ultimately issued, determining the project's environmental feasibility and specifying required protection measures.[45] If the DIA is not acted upon within two years of its publication in the *Official State Gazette* or the respective regional gazette, it becomes invalid.[46] Public disclosure of the DIA is mandatory, ensuring transparency and accountability.[47]

3.5.2 Integrated Environmental Authorization (AAI)

3.5.2.1 *Substantive framework*

The Integrated Environmental Authorization (AAI) permit, established under Royal Legislative Decree 1/2016 on Integrated Pollution Prevention and Control (IPPC),[48] which transposes the EU Industrial Emissions Directive[49] into Spanish legislation, is a mandatory requirement for the operation of industrial facilities, including electrolysers. Article 9 of the IPPC and Annex I specify that industrial-scale hydrogen production for commercial purposes requires an AAI, irrespective of the project's size or technology. The authorization ensures compliance with environmental standards during the operation. It applies to both public and private installations but excludes those used exclusively for research, development, or testing of new products.[50]

[40] ibid.
[41] Constitución Española 1978 (n 19) arts 148–149.
[42] LEA (n 36) art 1(1).
[43] Constitución Española (n 19) art 148; LEA (n 36) art 1(2).
[44] LEA (n 36) arts 17–23.
[45] ibid art 17 and art 24.
[46] ibid art 27.
[47] ibid art 26.
[48] Real Decreto Legislativo 1/2016, de 16 de diciembre, por el que se aprueba el texto refundido de la Ley de prevención y control integrados de la contaminación (IPPC), BOE núm. 316.
[49] Directive 2010/75/EU of the European Parliament and of the Council of 24 November 2010 on industrial emissions (integrated pollution prevention and control) [2010] OJ L 334/17.
[50] IPPC (n 47) preamble.

The AAI sets conditions to minimize environmental impacts and ensures alignment with the Best Available Techniques (BAT)[51] standards for the facility's primary activity. These authorizations must be reviewed and, if necessary, updated within four years following any revisions to the BAT conclusions.[52] Furthermore, the issuance of an AAI is contingent upon the prior approval of a DIA, which is required to establish the project's environmental feasibility before construction can commence. While the DIA addresses design and planning, the AAI ensures compliance with environmental standards during operation, including the management of emissions, waste, water, and energy.

The AAI consolidates all existing authorizations in the fields of emissions (subsection 3.5.4), waste discharge (subsection 3.6.2), waste (subsection 3.7), nature protection (subsection 3.8), safety and health (subsection 3.9.1) into a single administrative act, functioning as a 'one-stop-shop' and eliminating the need for separate applications. This streamlined approach allows facility operators to meet most regulatory requirements through a single permit.[53] Cooperation between public administrations ensures the seamless integration of these various permits.[54]

3.5.2.2 Procedural framework

To secure an AAI, the facility operator must submit an application to the competent environmental authority of the Autonomous Community where the facility is located.[55] This application must include detailed technical documentation describing the facility's activities, processes, and products, as well as data on emissions, energy use, waste management, and environmental control systems.[56] A preliminary report on soil and groundwater conditions at the site is also required, along with a report from the city council confirming urban compatibility and a non-technical summary. Additionally, the application must address contingency measures for managing non-standard operating conditions, such as leaks, malfunctions, or shutdowns.[57]

The competent authority of the Autonomous Community reviews the submitted documentation and issues the AAI, specifying the conditions under which the facility must operate. The authorization is subject to periodic reviews and may be updated or revoked as necessary to ensure continued compliance with environmental standards.[58]

[51] BAT: 'Best Available Techniques Conclusions': A European Commission decision containing the parts of a BAT reference document setting out the conclusions on best available techniques, their description, information for assessing their applicability, emission levels associated with the best available techniques, associated measurements, associated consumption levels, and, if appropriate, remediation measures for the site concerned. See ibid art 3(5).

[52] ibid art. 26.

[53] ibid art 11(1)(b), art 22(8)(b), and preamble.

[54] ibid art 6.

[55] ibid art 4.

[56] ibid art 12.

[57] ibid.

[58] ibid art 4.

3.5.3 Environmental liability

3.5.3.1 Substantive framework

Act No 26/2007 on Environmental Liability (LRM) transposes the EU Environmental Liability Directive 2004/35/EC into Spanish legislation, establishing operators' responsibilities to prevent, mitigate, and repair environmental damage. Article 24 and Annex III of the LRM require operators of activities subject to an AAI and Royal Decree 840/2015[59] to maintain a financial guarantee to cover the environmental liability inherent in their operations. Hydrogen production, as an activity subject to both an AAI[60] and Royal Decree 840/2015,[61] falls within this requirement.

The financial guarantee must specifically cover environmental liabilities arising from the operator's activities and must remain separate from any other civil, criminal, or administrative liability coverage.[62] The guarantee, capped at €20 million, ensures coverage of all potential environmental damage during the activity's operation.[63] Exemptions apply if repair costs are below €300,000 or up to €2 million for operators adhering to the Eco-Management and Audit Scheme (EMAS) or the environmental management system UNE-EN ISO 14001.[64]

3.5.3.2 Procedural framework

Operators planning to run an electrolyser must account for the financial implications of environmental liabilities and ensure they are financially capable of covering the associated costs once the plant is operational. To meet this obligation, operators may secure the financial guarantee in the form of insurance, a public-backed financial reserve, or a guarantee. Operators claiming exemption must notify the competent authority, providing proof of compliance with the exemption thresholds, which is subject to verification.[65] The financial guarantee process ensures operators can address potential environmental damage during operation while maintaining compliance with the regulatory framework.

3.5.4 Greenhouse gas emissions

3.5.4.1 Substantive framework

The 2024 revision of Directive 2024/1785 on Industrial Emissions introduces new requirements for hydrogen production facilities. Facilities producing more than 50 tonnes of hydrogen per day must obtain emission permits, while smaller operations are exempt.[66] According to the authors of this chapter, many electrolysers in Spain are expected to fall below this threshold.

[59] Real Decreto 840/2015, de 21 de septiembre, por el que se aprueban medidas de control de los riesgos inherentes a los accidentes graves en los que intervengan sustancias peligrosas, BOE núm. 251.

[60] IPPC (n 47) Annex I. 4(2)(a).

[61] Real Decreto 840/2015 (n 58) Part 2—Nominated Hazardous Substances—15.

[62] Ley 26/2007, de 23 de octubre, de Responsabilidad Medioambiental (LRM), BOE núm. 255 art 25.

[63] ibid art 26 and art 30.

[64] ibid art 28.

[65] ibid art 28.

[66] Directive (EU) 2024/1785 of the European Parliament and of the Council of 24 April 2024 amending Directive 2010/75/EU of the European Parliament and of the Council on industrial emissions (integrated

As this Directive has not yet been transposed into Spanish legislation, the provisions of Act No 1/2005 on Regulating the Greenhouse Gas Emission Allowance Trading Scheme (LCDEGEI) remain in force. Under the LCDEGEI, facilities producing hydrogen or synthesis gas in quantities exceeding 25 tonnes per day via reforming or partial oxidation must obtain a greenhouse gas emission permit.[67] They are also required to fulfil obligations such as emissions monitoring, reporting, and acquiring emission rights.[68]

3.5.4.2 *Procedural framework*

As outlined in subsection 3.3.2, obtaining an AAI automatically includes the permit required under the LCDEGEI. The substantive requirements of the LCDEGEI are internally verified by the competent authorities as part of the AAI process.[69]

3.6 Water Management Law

3.6.1 Water allocation

Water is essential for green hydrogen production, requiring approximately 9 litres of ultra-pure water per kilogram of hydrogen produced via electrolysis.[70] When evaporative cooling systems are included, total water demand increases to 60–95 litres per kg.[71] Extensive water treatment is necessary to meet the ultrapure water standards required for electrolysis, particularly for sources such as seawater or treated wastewater. These processes result in significant water losses, as desalination typically recovers only 40–50% of water, while recovery rates from treated wastewater and groundwater average 90–98%.[72]

Southern Spain's severe water crisis, exacerbated by droughts and climate change, further complicates the sustainability of hydrogen production, making the efficient use of water critically important.[73] Consequently, obtaining a water use permit is essential for the operation of an electrolyser.

pollution prevention and control) and Council Directive 1999/31/EC on the landfill of waste (text with EEA relevance) [2024] OJ L 2024/1785 Annex I (j)(6.6).

[67] Ley 1/2005, de 9 de marzo, por la que se regula el régimen de comercio de derechos de emisión de gases de efecto invernadero BOE núm. 59 Annex I (Actividades 24).

[68] ibid art 4.

[69] ibid first additional provision.

[70] Marcus Newborough and Graham Cooley, 'Green Hydrogen: Water Use Implications and Opportunities' (2021) 2021(7) Fuel Cells Bulletin <https://www.sciencedirect.com/science/article/abs/pii/S1464285921006581> accessed 26 January 2025; P Woods, H Bustamante, and KF Aguey-Zinsou, 'The Hydrogen Economy—Where Is the Water?' (2022) 7 Energy Nexus 100123 <https://www.sciencedirect.com/science/article/pii/S277242712200078X> accessed 26 January 2025; International Renewable Energy Agency, *Blue Risk: Water for Hydrogen Production* (Report, December 2023) <chrome-extension://efaidnbmnnnibpcajpcglclefindmkaj/https://www.irena.org/-/media/Files/IRENA/Agency/Publication/2023/Dec/IRENA_Bluerisk_Water_for_hydrogen_production_2023.pdf> accessed 26 January 2025.

[71] ibid.

[72] ibid.

[73] Joint Research Centre, 'Prolonged Drought and Record Temperatures Have Critical Impact on the Mediterranean' (2024) <https://joint-research-centre.ec.europa.eu/jrc-news-and-updates/prolonged-drought-and-record-temperatures-have-critical-impact-mediterranean-2024-02-20_en> accessed 26 January 2025.

3.6.1.1 *Substantive framework*

The legal framework for managing public water domains under state jurisdiction includes the Water Act (LA),[74] and the Regulations on the Public Water Domain (RDPH).[75] Article 149.1.22 of the Spanish Constitution grants the state exclusive jurisdiction over water legislation, management, and concessions when waters cross multiple Autonomous Communities.

With intra-community basins, regional regulations may apply.[76] For inter-community basins, Article 21 LA mandates the creation of basin organizations—Hydrographic Confederations (Water Board)—attached to the Ministry of Environment, which are responsible for basin management and administrative tasks.[77]

Under Article 59.1 of the LA, private water use requires an administrative concession from the Hydrographic Confederations, except for minimal use under Article 54. Minimal use refers to water consumption for domestic purposes or small-scale activities that does not exceed a total annual volume of 7,000 cubic metres. Electrolysers usually exceed these limits and therefore need a permit.

Administrative water concessions under the LA and RDPH must align with hydrological plans. The permits cannot exceed seventy-five years of duration and must serve the public interest.[78] Concessions are granted based on the priority order in the relevant river basin hydrological plan, with green hydrogen production ranked third, after water supply for populations and agricultural irrigation.[79] Permits include access to public water domain land as needed and specify the purpose, term, maximum flow rates (instantaneous, annual, and, if applicable, monthly).[80] Any modifications require prior authorization. Limits on water extraction are set on a case-by-case basis, taking into account specific circumstances.[81]

3.6.1.2 *Procedural framework*

Under Article 104 of the RDPH, obtaining a surface water concession requires the submission of an application to the relevant basin organization, which initiates the project competition process. The procedure concludes with an agreement on the permit terms between the applicant and the administration,[82] followed by registration in the Water Register.[83] Preference is given to projects that ensure more rational water use and better environmental protection.[84]

[74] Real Decreto Legislativo 1/2001, de 20 de julio, por el que se aprueba el texto refundido de la Ley de Aguas (LA), BOE núm. 176.

[75] Real Decreto 849/1986, de 11 de abril, por el que se aprueba el Reglamento del Dominio Público Hidráulico que desarrolla el título preliminar, I, IV, V, VI, VII y VIII del texto refundido de la Ley de Aguas, aprobado por el Real Decreto Legislativo 1/2001, de 20 de julio (RDPH), BOE núm. 103.

[76] LA (n 73) art 21.

[77] ibid art 22.

[78] ibid art 59(4); RDPH (n 74) art 93.

[79] LA (n 73) art 60(2); RDPH (n 74) art 98

[80] RDPH (n 74) arts 101–102.

[81] LA (n 73) art 64; RDPH (n 74) art 143.

[82] RDPH (n 74) art 116.

[83] ibid art 118.

[84] LA (n 73) art 79.

3.6.2 Water discharge

As discussed in subsection 3.6.1, producing 1 kg of hydrogen requires 9 litres of ultra-pure water, which may need 18–22.5 litres of source water due to pre-water treatment, resulting in 5–9 litres of waste reject. Including cooling system demands, total discharge can reach up to 50 litres per kg in inefficient systems.[85]

The river basin authority of the relevant Autonomous Community may issue a mandatory and binding report specifying discharge characteristics and corrective measures to ensure good ecological water status. The report must be issued within four months; if it is not provided within this period, the AAI may proceed with conditions aligned with sectoral legislation. However, if the report deems the discharge inadmissible, the AAI will be denied.[86] For electrolysers discharging into inter-community basins, the discharge authorization is integrated into the AAI.[87]

3.7 Waste Law

Act No 7/2022 on Waste and Contaminated Soil for a Circular Economy governs waste management and contaminated land, aiming to prevent waste generation, mitigate environmental and health impacts, and enhance resource efficiency.[88]

Electrolyser projects may be classified as potentially soil-polluting activities under Royal Decree 9/2005, which includes chemical industries and gas production.[89] In accordance with Articles 7 and 8 of Act No 7/2022, waste management must ensure no harm to health or the environment, align with climate change strategies, and adhere to the waste hierarchy. Furthermore, land used for electrolysers may fall under the contaminated land regime, necessitating decontamination and recovery measures if soil pollution risks are identified. The waste permit required under Law 7/2022 is integrated into the AAI and does not require a separate application.[90]

3.8 Nature Protection Law

The Natura 2000 Directive serves as a critical framework for biodiversity conservation in the European Union, focusing on maintaining or restoring habitats and species to favourable conservation status.[91] In Spain, its principles are implemented

[85] International Renewable Energy Agency (n 69).
[86] IPPC (n 47) art 19.
[87] LA (n 73) art additional provision ten.
[88] Ley 7/2022, de 8 de abril, de residuos y suelos contaminados para una economía circular, BOE núm. 85 art 1 and art 98(1).
[89] Real Decreto 9/2005, de 14 de enero, por el que se establece la relación de actividades potencialmente contaminantes del suelo y los criterios y estándares para la declaración de suelos contaminados, BOE núm. 15, Anexo I (20 y 35.21).
[90] Ley 7/2022 (n 87) art 33(9).
[91] Council Directive 92/43/EEC of 21 May 1992 on the conservation of natural habitats and of wild fauna and flora [1992] OJ L206/7.

through Act No 42/2007 on Natural Heritage and Biodiversity,[92] which integrates EU Directives into national legislation by designating protected areas. This Act mandates conservation plans, public participation, and measures to ensure ecological connectivity.[93] As outlined in subsection 3.3.2, a nature protection permit is integrated into the AAI, removing the need for separate permits related to nature or biodiversity protection.[94]

3.9 Fire Prevention, Health and Safety Law

Hydrogen production in Spain is classified as an industrial activity under Act No 21/1992 on Industry (LI), which governs industrial safety, quality standards, and permits applicable to chemical industry plants producing inorganic gases. The specific standards and permits required for electrolysers will be discussed now.

3.9.1 Health and safety law—risk control measures

3.9.1.1 Substantive framework

The AAI integrates the actions required under Royal Decree 840/2015 into its permitting process, which is facilitated by the Autonomous Communities without the need for additional permits.

Royal Decree 840/2015 governs hydrogen electrolysis facilities to prevent serious accidents and mitigate their impacts on human health, property, and the environment.[95] The regulation applies based on the quantity of hydrogen on-site, classifying facilities as either lower tier (5–50 tonnes) or higher tier (≥50 tonnes) establishments, which determines the scope of obligations.[96]

Hydrogen facilities must implement risk controls, including safety systems, a written prevention policy, and a safety management system.[97] Higher-tier facilities must also prepare safety reports and emergency plans.[98]

Procedural Framework

The AAI integrates the actions required under Royal Decree 840/2015 into its permitting process, which is facilitated by the Autonomous Communities without the need for additional permits.[99]

[92] Ley 42/2007, de 13 de diciembre, del Patrimonio Natural y de la Biodiversidad, BOE núm. 299.

[93] Ministerio para la Transición Ecológica y el Reto Demográfico, *Directrices para la Gestión de la Red Natura 2000* (Documento Oficial, 2019) <https://www.miteco.gob.es/content/dam/miteco/es/biodiversidad/temas/espacios-protegidos/rn2k/documentos/Directrices-N2000.pdf> accessed 26 January 2025.

[94] See also Ley 42/2007 (n 91) art sixth final provision.

[95] Real Decreto 840/2015 (n 58) Part 2—Nominated Hazardous Substances—15 and art 1.

[96] ibid.

[97] ibid arts 5–7.

[98] ibid arts 10–13.

[99] IPPC (n 47) art 11(5) and art 22(8)(b).

3.9.2 Fire prevention

3.9.2.1 Substantive framework

Hydrogen, known for its high flammability and combustibility, poses significant fire and explosion risks, potentially causing severe injuries and damage to property. To address these hazards, Royal Decree 2267/2004 establishes fire safety requirements for industrial establishments, including the prevention, containment, and mitigation of fires to protect people and property.[100] Given its properties, hydrogen is classified as a high-risk material under Royal Decree 2267/2004 when it comes to storage and/or presence at the production facility.[101] Here 'stored' does not exclusively refer to hydrogen held in tanks but includes the total amount of hydrogen present at the facility at any given time, consistent with interpretations across EU Member States.

3.9.2.2 Procedural framework

Therefore, presumably, an electrolyser facility does not require a separate fire safety permit, as the AAI process is designed to encompass all necessary safety authorizations for its construction and operation.

3.10 Laws on Monuments and Archaeology

When planning an electrolyser near a designated Historic Complex, Historic Site, or Archaeological Zone, compliance with Article 20 of Act No 16/1985 on Spanish Historical Heritage is essential. Protected areas are listed in official registers maintained by cultural heritage authorities or municipal urban planning departments.[102] Projects must align with a 'Special Protection Plan' that prioritizes conservation and outlines criteria for development.[103]

3.10.1 Substantive framework

The Special Protection Plan must specify permitted uses, conservation criteria, and rehabilitation measures for the area. Until the plan is approved, licences are suspended, and new alignments, changes in buildability, or subdivisions are prohibited. Projects must avoid adversely affecting monuments or protected surroundings.[104]

3.10.2 Procedural framework

Pending approval of the Special Protection Plan, any activity requires a 'favourable resolution' from the cultural protection authority.[105] After approval, municipalities may authorize works consistent with the plan for non-monument properties but must

[100] Real Decreto 2267/2004, de 3 de diciembre, por el que se aprueba el Reglamento de seguridad contra incendios en los establecimientos industriales, BOE núm. 303 art 1.

[101] ibid Annex I, Tables 1.2 and 1.3.

[102] Ley 16/1985, de 25 de junio, del Patrimonio Histórico Español, BOE núm. 155 art 15.

[103] ibid art 20(1).

[104] ibid arts 20(1)–20(3).

[105] ibid art 20(3).

notify the authority. Licences issued in contradiction with the plan are deemed invalid and may result in reconstruction or demolition orders. Early consultation with heritage authorities is crucial to ensure compliance and avoid delays or penalties.[106]

4. Recommendations to Improve the System

The development of Spain's renewable hydrogen industry is hindered by a fragmented legal framework that currently relies on scattered provisions within the LSH. While hydrogen production requires environmental and construction permits, investors seek a stable and predictable regulatory environment to provide greater security for long-term investments in the sector.

The AAI already offers a form of a 'one-stop shop' for permits. However, better co-ordination between the AAI process and regional and urban planning is essential, as municipal interventions may impede the coordinated development of renewable hydrogen projects.

Spain has also witnessed strong opposition from environmental groups against renewable energy installations, including biomethane plants and wind turbines. Similar resistance is likely to emerge against the renewable hydrogen industry, highlighting the need to balance the involvement of municipalities with granting the final decision-making authority to energy regulators.

To achieve a stable legal framework, more is required than merely an AAI. Spain should establish a cohesive legal system specifically tailored to renewable hydrogen. The hydrogen industry should be treated as an energy system or subsystem, akin to the electricity and natural gas systems. For this purpose, an 'industrial authorization' would be necessary, defining the rights and obligations of hydrogen producers, transporters, and suppliers. Such an authorization could be modelled on the provisions governing the electricity and natural gas industries, which require authorization for the transportation or distribution of natural gas or electricity.

One approach would be to integrate the proposed 'industrial authorization' into the existing procedure for obtaining an AAI, formalizing a prior authorization process for hydrogen production, transport, and/or supply. This should be implemented while respecting the powers of both the central government and the Autonomous Communities. Such an approach would provide investors with a clear, standardized approval pathway and reduce the uncertainty associated with the currently fragmented regulations.

Although the 1998 Hydrocarbons Act has been modified since 2022 to include renewable gases under its provisions, the entire Act requires further amendments to properly regulate the renewable gases industry.

Undoubtedly, a stable regulatory environment will be shaped by the recent decarbonization package at the EU level. There is now a key opportunity to strengthen

[106] ibid art 20(4).

Spain's legal framework by incorporating Directive (EU) 2024/1788 of the European Parliament and of the Council of 13 June 2024, which establishes common rules for the internal markets for renewable gas, natural gas, and hydrogen. This Directive also amends Directive (EU) 2023/1791 and repeals Directive 2009/73/EC. Additionally, Spain should amend its national legislation to align with Regulation (EU) 2024/1789, which modernizes the internal markets for renewable gas, natural gas, and hydrogen.

Finally, fiscal policies present a significant challenge to future investments in the renewable hydrogen industry. While fiscal advantages introduced in 2022 provided some incentives, the government's continued pursuit of the tax on 'windfall profits' has placed a substantial burden on companies expected to invest in this emerging sector. On 22 January 2025, Parliament rejected the government's proposal to maintain the tax, though efforts to gain a majority in favour of the tax are likely to continue. We recommend that this tax be abandoned to foster a more favourable investment climate.

5. Conclusion

Spain's progress in the hydrogen economy reflects a combination of ambition and complexity, positioning the country as a potential global leader while underscoring areas for strategic refinement. Spain stands at the intersection of opportunity and challenge, navigating legislative reforms and operational obstacles that will shape the trajectory of its green hydrogen ambitions.

A central question for Spain moving forward is how to reconcile centralized energy objectives with the decentralized decision-making powers of its Autonomous Communities. Striking this balance will require innovative governance models that facilitate meaningful local stakeholder participation while safeguarding broader national objectives.

Another pressing challenge is the regulation of water use for green hydrogen production, particularly in water-stressed regions. Spain must ensure that hydrogen development aligns with sustainable water management, balancing efficiency, equitable access, and environmental protection to secure hydrogen's role in its energy transition.

The legislative pipeline in Spain, including the incorporation of the EU's hydrogen and gas market regulations, presents a critical opportunity to redefine the country's energy framework. However, proactive measures are required to address the risks of overregulation and bureaucratic inefficiencies that could deter investment. Public engagement will also be pivotal, as growing opposition to renewable projects necessitates transparent communication about hydrogen's benefits and environmental safeguards to build societal consensus.

For other nations, Spain's approach offers both inspiration and caution. Its emphasis on renewable integration, ambitious electrolyser targets, and hydrogen valleys exemplifies the potential of forward-thinking national strategies. At the same time, Spain's experience highlights the importance of synchronizing fiscal, environmental, and industrial policies. Countries entering the hydrogen sector should prioritize adaptive regulatory frameworks that minimize friction across jurisdictional levels, ensuring a faster and more inclusive transition to clean energy systems.

Appendix

Table VI.1 List of Abbreviations

Abbreviation	Spanish	English
AAI	Autorización Ambiental Integrada	Integrated Environmental Authorization
BAT	Mejores Técnicas Disponibles	Best Available Techniques
CNMC	Comisión Nacional de los Mercados y la Competencia	The Spanish National Markets and Competition Commission
DIA	Declaración de Impacto Ambiental	Environmental Impact Statement
EIA	Evaluación de Impacto Ambiental	Environmental Impact Assessment
EMAS	Esquema de Gestión y Auditoría Medioambientales	Eco-Management and Audit Scheme
PEM	Electrolizadores de membrana de intercambio protónico	Proton exchange membrane electrolysers
PNIEC	Plan Nacional Integrado de Energía y Clima	Integrated Energy and Climate Plan
Water Board	Confederaciones Hidrográficas	Hydrographic Confederations
Abbreviation	**Law—Spanish**	**Law—English Translation**
RDPH	Real Decreto 849/1986 de 11 de abril por el que se aprueba el Reglamento del Dominio Público Hidráulico que desarrolla los títulos preliminar I, IV, V, VI, VII y VIII del texto refundido de la Ley de Aguas aprobado por el Real Decreto Legislativo 1/2001 de 20 de julio	Royal Decree 849/1986 of 11 April, Approving the Regulation on the Public Water Domain, Developing Preliminary Titles I, IV, V, VI, VII, and VIII of the Consolidated Water Law, Approved by Royal Legislative Decree 1/2001 of 20 July
LI	Ley 21/1992 de 16 de julio de Industria	Law 21/1992 of 16 July on Industry
LSH	Ley 34/1998 de 7 de octubre del sector de hidrocarburos	Law 34/1998 of 7 October on the Hydrocarbons Sector
LA	Real Decreto Legislativo 1/2001 de 20 de julio por el que se aprueba el texto refundido de la Ley de Aguas	Royal Legislative Decree 1/2001 of 20 July Approving the Consolidated Water Law
LCDEGEI	Ley 1/2005, de 9 de marzo, por la que se regula el régimen de comercio de derechos de emisión de gases de efecto invernadero	Law 1/2005 of 9 March 2005 regulating the greenhouse gas emission allowance trading scheme
LRM	Ley 26/2007 de 23 de octubre de Responsabilidad Medioambiental	Law 26/2007 of 23 October on Environmental Liability
LSE	Ley 24/2013 de 26 de diciembre del Sector Eléctrico	Law 24/2013 of 26 December on the Electricity Sector
IPPC	Real Decreto Legislativo 1/2016 de 16 de diciembre por el que se aprueba el texto refundido de la Ley de prevención y control integrados de la contaminación	Royal Legislative Decree 1/2016 of 16 December Approving the Consolidated Law on Integrated Pollution Prevention and Control

Table VI.2 List of Spanish Laws with English Translations

Law—Spanish	Law—English Translation
Constitución Española 1978	Spanish Constitution 1978
Real Decreto Legislativo 7/2015 de 30 de octubre por el que se aprueba el texto refundido de la Ley de Suelo y Rehabilitación Urbana	Royal Legislative Decree 7/2015 of 30 October 2015 approving the revised text of the Law on Land and Urban Rehabilitation
Ley 16/1985, de 25 de junio, del Patrimonio Histórico Español	Law 16/1985, of 25 June 1985, on Spanish Historical Heritage
Real Decreto 849/1986 de 11 de abril por el que se aprueba el Reglamento del Dominio Público Hidráulico que desarrolla los títulos preliminar I, IV, V, VI, VII y VIII del texto refundido de la Ley de Aguas aprobado por el Real Decreto Legislativo 1/2001 de 20 de julio	Royal Decree 849/1986 of 11 April, Approving the Regulation on the Public Water Domain, Developing Preliminary Titles I, IV, V, VI, VII, and VIII of the Consolidated Water Law, Approved by Royal Legislative Decree 1/2001 of 20 July
Ley 21/1992 de 16 de julio de Industria	Law 21/1992 of 16 July on Industry
Ley 34/1998 de 7 de octubre del sector de hidrocarburos	Law 34/1998 of 7 October on the Hydrocarbons Sector
Real Decreto Legislativo 1/2001 de 20 de julio por el que se aprueba el texto refundido de la Ley de Aguas	Royal Legislative Decree 1/2001 of 20 July Approving the Consolidated Water Law
Real Decreto 2267/2004 de 3 de diciembre por el que se aprueba el Reglamento de seguridad contra incendios en los establecimientos industriales	Royal Decree 2267/2004 of 3 December Approving the Fire Safety Regulation for Industrial Establishments
Ley 1/2005, de 9 de marzo, por la que se regula el régimen de comercio de derechos de emisión de gases de efecto invernadero	Law 1/2005 of 9 March 2005 regulating the greenhouse gas emission allowance trading scheme
Real Decreto 9/2005 de 14 de enero por el que se establece la relación de actividades potencialmente contaminantes del suelo y los criterios y estándares para la declaración de suelos contaminados	Royal Decree 9/2005 of 14 January Establishing the List of Potentially Soil-Polluting Activities and Criteria for Declaring Contaminated Soils
Ley 26/2007 de 23 de octubre de Responsabilidad Medioambiental	Law 26/2007 of 23 October on Environmental Liability
Ley 42/2007, de 13 de diciembre, del Patrimonio Natural y de la Biodiversidad	Law 42/2007 of 13 December on Natural Heritage and Biodiversity
Real Decreto 13/2012, de 30 de marzo, por el que se transpone la Directiva 2009/73/CE del Parlamento Europeo y del Consejo, de 13 de julio de 2009, relativa a normas comunes para el mercado interior del gas natural.	Royal Decree 13/2012 of 30 March 2012 transposing Directive 2009/73/EC of the European Parliament and of the Council of 13 July 2009 concerning common rules for the internal market in natural gas.
Real Decreto 815/2013 de 18 de octubre por el que se aprueba el Reglamento de emisiones industriales y de desarrollo de la Ley 16/2002 de 1 de julio de prevención y control integrados de la contaminación	Royal Decree 815/2013 of 18 October Approving the Regulation on Industrial Emissions and Developing Law 16/2002 of 1 July on Integrated Pollution Prevention and Control
Ley 24/2013 de 26 de diciembre del Sector Eléctrico	Law 24/2013 of 26 December on the Electricity Sector
Real Decreto 840/2015 de 21 de septiembre por el que se aprueban medidas de control de los riesgos inherentes a los accidentes graves en los que intervengan sustancias peligrosas	Royal Decree 840/2015 of 21 September Approving Measures for Controlling Risks of Serious Accidents Involving Dangerous Substances

(continued)

Table VI.2 Continued

Law—Spanish	Law—English Translation
Real Decreto Legislativo 7/2015 de 30 de octubre por el que se aprueba el texto refundido de la Ley de Suelo y Rehabilitación Urbana	Royal Legislative Decree 7/2015 of 30 October Approving the Consolidated Law on Land and Urban Rehabilitation
Real Decreto Legislativo 1/2016 de 16 de diciembre por el que se aprueba el texto refundido de la Ley de prevención y control integrados de la contaminación	Royal Legislative Decree 1/2016 of 16 December Approving the Consolidated Law on Integrated Pollution Prevention and Control
Real Decreto-ley 23/2020, de 23 de junio, por el que se aprueban medidas en materia de energía y en otros ámbitos para la reactivación económica	Royal Decree-Law 23/2020, of 23 June, approving energy and other measures for economic reactivation
Real Decreto 1183/2020 de 29 de diciembre de acceso y conexión a las redes de transporte y distribución de energía eléctrica	Royal Decree 1183/2020 of 29 December on Access and Connection to Electricity Transmission and Distribution Networks
Ley 7/2021, de 20 de mayo, de Cambio Climático y Transición Energética	Law 7/2021, of 20 May, on Climate Change and Energy Transition
Ley 7/2022 de 8 de abril de residuos y suelos contaminados para una economía circular	Law 7/2022 of 8 April on Waste and Contaminated Soil for a Circular Economy
Real Decreto 376/2022 de 17 de mayo por el que se regulan los criterios de sostenibilidad y de reducción de las emisiones de gases de efecto invernadero de los biocarburantes, biolíquidos y combustibles de biomasa, así como el sistema de garantías de origen de los gases renovables	Royal Decree 376/2022 of 17 May Regulating Sustainability Criteria, GHG Emission Reduction for Biofuels and Biomass Fuels, and Guarantees of Origin for Renewable Gases
Real Decreto-ley 6/2022 de 29 de marzo, medidas urgentes en el marco del Plan Nacional de Respuesta a las Consecuencias Económicas y Sociales de la Guerra en Ucrania	Royal Decree-Law 6/2022 of 29 March on Urgent Measures for the National Response Plan to the Economic and Social Consequences of the War in Ukraine
Real Decreto-ley 14/2022 de 1 de agosto, por el que se adoptan medidas en materia de energía	Royal Decree-Law 14/2022 of 1 August Adopting Measures on Energy
Real Decreto-ley 18/2022 de 18 de octubre, por el que se aprueban medidas de refuerzo de la protección de los consumidores de energía y de contribución a la reducción del consumo de gas natural en aplicación del 'Plan + seguridad para tu energía (+SE)', así como medidas en materia de retribuciones del personal al servicio del sector público y de protección de las personas trabajadoras agrarias eventuales afectadas por la sequía	Royal Decree-Law 18/2022 of 18 October, approving measures to reinforce the protection of energy consumers and to contribute to the reduction of natural gas consumption in application of the 'Plan + seguridad para tu energía (+SE)', as well as measures concerning the remuneration of public sector staff and the protection of temporary agricultural workers affected by the drought.

VII
Italy

Giovanni Volpi

1. Introduction

Italy's climate roadmap includes a target of 5 GW of hydrogen electrolysis capacity by 2030. This goal is part of two key strategies—the National Integrated Plan for Energy and Climate (PNIEC)[1] and the National Recovery and Resilience Plan (PNRR).[2] Together, these plans set out Italy's path towards a sustainable energy transition. The recently adopted Italian National Hydrogen Strategy[3] similarly highlights hydrogen as a key solution for achieving decarbonization goals. However, an increasingly complex legal framework only allows for slow progress, highlighting the need for streamlined implementation.[4]

Hydrogen is pivotal to both plans, to enhancing energy system flexibility, to decarbonizing transport, and to addressing 'hard to abate' industrial sectors.[5] In particular, electrolysers, which split water into hydrogen and oxygen using electricity, play a key

[1] Ministry of Economic Development, Ministry of the Environment and Protection of Land and Sea, and Ministry of Infrastructure and Transport, *Integrated National Energy and Climate Plan 2030* (December 2019) https://www.mase.gov.it/sites/default/files/archivio/pniec_finale_17012020.pdf accessed 21 June 2024.

[2] Italian Government, 'National Recovery and Resilience Plan (PNRR)' (April 2021) <https://www.governo.it/sites/governo.it/files/PNRR.pdf> accessed 21 June 2024.

[3] MASE, *'Idrogeno: presentata la Strategia Nazionale, più scenari per la sua diffusione'* (Ministero dell'Ambiente e della Sicurezza Energetica, 26 November 2024) https://www.mase.gov.it/comunicati/idrogeno-presentata-la-strategia-nazionale-piu-scenari-la-sua-diffusione accessed 26 November 2024.

[4] Viviana Cigolotti, Stephen J McPhail, and Maria Cristina Tommasino, *La regolamentazione del settore idrogeno e delle sue applicazioni in Italia* (HyLAW, 2019) https://www.h2it.it/wp-content/uploads/2019/07/HyLAW_National-policy-Paper-IT_ita.pdf accessed 25 March 2024.

[5] Information can be found on pp 9–10 PNIEC and pp 129–42 PNRR.

role in advancing Italy's renewable energy goals.[6] By converting excess renewable electricity into hydrogen they allow for effective storage and integration of renewables into the grid. The PNIEC highlights the need for continued research to enhance electrolyser performance, a priority also reflected in the PNRR's emphasis on innovation in hydrogen technology.

A significant recent change has been introduced regarding the permitting procedure for electrolysers through the Renewable Energy Consolidated Act.[7] This reform has consolidated into a single text what was previously governed by a range of separate legislative acts. Other relevant laws include:

- The general rules on the administrative procedure Law No 241 of 7 August 1990.[8]
- Environmental provisions of Legislative Decree No 152 of 3 April 2006.[9]
- The Cultural Heritage and Landscape Code outlined in Legislative Decree No 42 of 22 January 2004.[10]

This chapter will analyse these key laws and the permitting process for water electrolysers itself, which in Italy mainly come in three designs: PEM, alkaline, and solid oxide.[11] Whether these different designs influence the regulatory framework will be discussed in the respective sections.

Electrolysers generally resemble shipping containers from the outside. This is important for the permitting procedure, especially concerning landscape preservation.

This chapter starts with an overview of the permitting regime in Italy. It then identifies the key legal areas where permits are required. Each area is discussed in two parts: a substantial discussion of its applicability to electrolysers in Italy, followed by procedural remarks on how to obtain the necessary permits. The chapter concludes with recommendations for improving the permitting procedure for electrolysers in Italy, followed by reflections and conclusions.

2. General Observations on the Permitting Regime

The Italian permitting procedure enables authorities to evaluate projects, ensuring environmental and health impacts are identified and mitigated. The Renewable Energy

[6] MASE (n 3).

[7] Decreto Legislativo 25 novembre 2024, n 190, *Disciplina dei regimi amministrativi per la produzione di energia da fonti rinnovabili, in attuazione dell'articolo 26, commi 4 e 5, lettera b) e d), della legge 5 agosto 2022, n. 118*, Gazzetta Ufficiale della Repubblica Italiana, Serie Generale.

[8] Legge 7 agosto 1990, n 241, *Nuove norme in materia di procedimento amministrativo e di diritto di accesso ai documenti amministrativi*, Gazzetta Ufficiale della Repubblica Italiana, Serie Generale.

[9] Decreto legislativo 3 aprile 2006, n 152, *Norme in materia ambientale* (Environmental Code), Gazzetta Ufficiale della Repubblica Italiana, Serie Generale n. 88 del 14 aprile 2006.

[10] Decreto legislativo 22 gennaio 2004, n 42, Codice dei beni culturali e del paesaggio, ai sensi dell'articolo 10 della legge 6 luglio 2002, n 137.

[11] S Sebbahi and others, 'A comprehensive review of recent advances in alkaline water electrolysis for hydrogen production' (2024) 82 International Journal of Hydrogen Energy 583–99 https://www.sciencedirect.com/science/article/pii/S0360319924031161 accessed 27 August 2024.

Consolidated Act repealed the provisions set out in Article 38 of Legislative Decree No 199 of 8 November 2021,[12] for electrolysers installed after 30 December 2024, the date on which the Consolidated Act came into force. Regional and local authorities will have 180 days from the date of enactment to comply with the provisions of the Consolidated Act.

Although classified as industrial chemical plants under the Environmental Code, electrolysers are included in the annexes of the Consolidated Act. However, the scope of application of the Consolidated Act in relation to electrolysers might have been delineated with greater clarity, as it appears to address primarly facilities producing energy from renewable sources or related infrastructure. Electrolysers do not come under the first category, as hydrogen is not considered renewable energy under Italian legislation. While they could be seen as associated infrastructure for renewable energy facilities, serving as storage units, Article 12 of the Consolidated Act distinguishes between storage facilities and associated infrastructure, excluding electrolysers from the latter category. Electrolysers may be considered hybrid plants, which combine different renewable energy sources,[13] but only if they integrate two energy sources, such as wind and solar. Since electrolysers do not clearly fall into these categories, their inclusion in the annexes raises further questions about the scope of the Consolidated Act.

The Renewable Energy Consolidated Act establishes the Single Desk for Renewable Energies (SUER), a unique digital platform for managing applications related to the plants regulated by the Consolidated Act, providing guidance and support throughout the entire administrative procedure. The competent authorities differ depending on the applicable procedure: the relevant municipality handles the Simplified Authorization Procedure (PAS), while the Ministry of the Environment, the relevant region, or the delegated province is responsible for the Single Authorization (AU) procedure.

When it is necessary to obtain understanding or consent from several public administrations, the proceeding administration convenes a services conference. The services conference, introduced by Article 14 of Law 241/90, streamlines the permitting procedure by coordinating several administrations. In this way, all the necessary documents and decisions are consolidated in a single procedure, which is concluded within forty-five or ninety days.[14] The decision made by the services conference supersedes all individual permits. A ruling from the State Council confirmed that all administrations involved in a project must attend the conference and provide their opinions.[15]

While procedural acceleration mechanisms, such as services conference and the principle of silent consent,[16] are in place, delays often arise, particularly at the environmental

[12] Decreto Legislativo 8 novembre 2021, n 199, Attuazione della direttiva (UE) 2018/2001 sulla promozione dell'uso dell'energia da fonti rinnovabili (Italy).

[13] Decreto Legislativo 25 novembre 2024, n 190, art 4(f) (Italy).

[14] Legge 7 agosto 1990, n 241, art 14-ter (Italy).

[15] Consiglio di Stato, Sezione IV, n 4818, 29 May 2024 (Italy).

[16] In the PAS, the silent consent mechanism expedites authorization by finalizing it if the municipality or relevant authorities fail to respond within a specified time.

impact assessment stage.[17] Furthermore, limited information, changes introduced in the Consolidated Act, and uncertainty around the regulatory definition of electrolysers could challenge competent authorities, delaying permitting and project implementation.

The construction of electrolysers is also subject to a detailed regulatory framework shaped by EU law. To establish an electrolyser facility, developers must secure several key permits, including:

- Permit for construction and operation
- Environmental authorizations
- Safety-related permits
- Other permits (such as landscape authorization)

3. Specific Permits Applicable to Electrolysers

3.1 Planning Law

3.1.1 Substantive framework

The initial step in the construction process for a developer of electrolysis projects is to identify suitable locations. This requires an analysis of Italy's complex legal framework for spatial planning, which involves multiple levels of governance.[18] Although Italy is a unitary state, its land-use planning resembles that of a federal system, as legislative and administrative authority is largely delegated to the regions.[19] National laws serve primarily as a framework, providing guidelines for regional legislation. Despite this decentralized approach, regional planning across Italy remains relatively harmonized through various coordination mechanisms, such as the services conference, where multiple administrative levels convene to make decisions on permits.[20]

Italy's land-use planning operates at four levels of governance:[21]

(1) *State Level*: Focuses on establishing principles, guidelines, and the conservation of heritage sites and natural landscapes.[22] The key law here is the Basic Urban Planning Law of 1942 (Law No 1150).[23]
(2) *Regional Level*: Regions are responsible for creating regional spatial coordination plans, which set development priorities and objectives, although

[17] Angelo Mastrandrea, 'Ci vuole troppo tempo per fare un grande impianto fotovoltaico in Italia' *Il Post* (8 April 2023) https://www.ilpost.it/2023/04/08/fotovoltaico-tempi-approvazione-impianti/ accessed 20 September 2024.

[18] OECD, *Land-use Planning Systems in the OECD: Country Fact Sheets, The Governance of Land Use Country Fact Sheet: Italy* (OECD Publishing 2017).

[19] ibid.

[20] ibid.

[21] Antonio Cappuccitti, 'Pianificazione territoriale e urbanistica' in Claudia Mattogno (ed), *Ventuno parole per l'urbanistica* (Aracne 2008) 199–218 https://digilander.libero.it/urbanistica.ing/Documenti/Mattogno/Pianificazione%20territoriale%20e%20urbanistica.pdf accessed 13 April 2024.

[22] OECD (n 18).

[23] Legge 17 agosto 1942, n 1150, Legge urbanistica (Italy).

these plans address general governance rather than specific land-use regulations.[24]

(3) *Provincial Level*: Provinces develop territorial coordination plans, aimed at aligning municipal land-use decisions and overseeing major infrastructure projects.[25]

(4) *Municipal Level*: Municipalities play a central role in spatial planning, drafting General Land Use Plans that determine specific land-use decisions.[26]

The General Land Use Plan is crucial for organizing and guiding the development of municipal territory. This plan is designed following L.1150/1942, which requires key components to be included. These are the zoning of the municipal territory, identification of public spaces, areas designated for public buildings, and constraints for historically, environmentally, or culturally significant areas. It also sets guidelines for preserving historical, environmental, and landscape features, and outlines the rules for implementing these plans.

The zoning regulations, which are influenced by national, regional, and provincial planning objectives, detail how different areas of the municipality are designated for specific uses.[27] According to the Interministerial Decree No 1444 of 2 April 1968,[28] the land is categorized into different types, with Category D specifically designated for industrial activities and similar facilities. In Italy, hydrogen production is classified as an industrial activity regardless of the production method used. Therefore, electrolysers could be built in areas designated under Category D. However, under certain circumstances, electrolysers could also be built outside industrial areas, in particular in areas defined as expansion areas, classified under Category C. The detailed circumstances depend on the general land use plan of each municipality.

To give an example of what that can mean in individual cases: a planning officer from Verona's urban development department confirmed that municipalities have some discretion in zoning decisions, potentially permitting electrolysers in Category C Zones. However, these decisions must align with higher-level regulations, such as in Verona the provincial rule requiring industrial facilities to be at least 500 metres from residential zones, as well as the specific requirements of the zoning area.

3.1.2 Procedural framework

To ensure compliance with General Land Use Plans, developers must work closely with municipalities to determine where electrolysers can be constructed. Each municipality may have distinct requirements, as illustrated in the case of Verona. Fortunately, the SUER will simplify this coordination, guiding developers efficiently through the permitting procedure.

[24] OECD (n 18).

[25] ibid.

[26] ibid.

[27] Cappuccitti (n 21).

[28] Decreto del 2 aprile 1968, n. 1444, Decreto interministeriale sui limiti non negoziabili di densità edilizia, altezza, distanza tra gli edifici e rapporti massimi tra spazi per insediamenti residenziali e produttivi e attività pubbliche o collettive, aree verdi o parcheggi, da osservare per la formazione di nuovi strumenti urbanistici o la revisione di quelli esistenti, ai sensi dell'articolo 17 della legge n. 765 del 1967.

3.2 Building Law

3.2.1 Substantive framework

The primary law governing building activities in Italy is DPR 2001, No 380,[29] which encompasses the general principles and the provisions for the regulation of building activities. A crucial question is whether electrolysers are classified as 'buildings'. This distinction is more than just a matter of terminology; it has significant implications for the permitting procedure and applicable regulations. It is unlikely that an electrolyser falls under the definition of a building as outlined in Annex A No 32 of the Standard National Building Regulation,[30] as it also requires the element of accessibility for people. Instead, electrolysers are more appropriately classified under the category of 'Structures/Constructions/Facilities'—above-ground structures that are solid, stable, and immovable.[31] Under DPR No 380, Article 10, electrolysers likely qualify as 'new constructions', thus requiring a building permit. This classification is based on Article 3(e), which defines new constructions as above-ground or underground structures.

3.2.2 Procedural framework

The construction of electrolysers is governed by specific procedures aimed at simplifying administrative obligations, in accordance with EU requirements. The Renewable Energy Consolidated Act has streamlined procedures for the development of electrolysers by consolidating all provisions into a single, cohesive document. This reform solves the complexity of the previous system, characterized by frequent references to external provisions while introducing certain changes in the procedures, which will be discussed further.

The permitting procedures set out in the Consolidated Act are threefold:

- Free building activity for electrolysers up to 10 MW (Article 7)
- Simplified authorization procedure (PAS) for electrolysers in industrial areas (Article 8)
- Single Authorization (AU) for stand-alone electrolysers (Article 9)

3.2.2.1 Free building regime

The Free building regime is the most straightforward procedure and applies to the categories of projects listed in Annex A, including electrolysers with a capacity of up to 10 MW, as specified in letter u). For this category, the developer is not prescribed

[29] Decreto del Presidente della Repubblica 6 giugno 2001, n 380, Testo unico delle disposizioni legislative e regolamentari in materia edilizia (Italy).

[30] Intesa ai sensi dell'articolo 8(6) della legge 5 giugno 2003, n 131, tra il Governo, le Regioni e i Comuni concernente l'adozione del regolamento edilizio-tipo di cui all'articolo 4(1-sexies) del Decreto del Presidente della Repubblica 6 giugno 2001, n 380 (Rep. Atti n 125/CU) (Italy).

[31] Corte di Cassazione Civile, sentenza n 18500, 4 September 2020 (Italy).

to obtain authorizations. However, a preliminary communication through the single form referred to in Article 7 of Consolidated Act is required. In any case, the works must be compatible with urban planning and the applicable building regulations. Furthermore, the developer must have legal possession of the land before starting the works.

If the project involves protected areas under the Cultural Heritage and Landscape Code, protected areas, Natura 2000 sites, or areas subject to the constraints set out in Article 20, paragraph 4 of Law 241/90, the PAS regime will apply. For projects on properties or areas of significant public interest, consent from the competent landscape authority will be required.

Lastly, if the electrolyser is constructed in non-urbanized areas, the developer must provide a deposit as a guarantee for the restoration of the land.

3.2.2.2 Simplified authorization procedure

For electrolysers with a capacity exceeding 10 MW located in industrial areas, the PAS applies. The applicant must submit the request to the relevant municipality via the SUER platform, attaching the documentation specified in paragraph 4. The new regulation removes the requirement to submit the PAS at least thirty days before the start of the works.

If the municipality is not responsible for the necessary authorizations, it must convene a service conference. The PAS is characterized by its speed, which is guaranteed by the principle of silent consent. If no negative decision or reasoned objection is communicated by the competent authorities in environmental, landscape, cultural, health, or safety matters within sixty days of the project's submission, the authorization is automatically considered granted.

To access the procedure, the applicant must have control of the land, and ensure the compatibility of the works with the existing urban planning regulation. If this condition is not met, the AU Article 9 will apply.

Moreover, a new provision states that the authorization will expire if work does not begin within a year of the PAS conclusion or is not completed within three years from the start, ensuring definite timelines for the completion of the works.

3.2.2.3 Single authorization

The last permitting procedure discussed in this section applies to electrolysers listed in Annex C of the Consolidate Act, specifically stand-alone electrolysers connected to energy plants under regional (Section I of the annex) or national (Section II of the annex) jurisdiction, subject to the AU.

The AU includes various provisions, such as the Environmental Impact Assessment (in Italian 'VIA') and any other necessary authorizations for the execution of the project. The application must be submitted via the SUER platform to the competent authority, which is the region for projects in Section I, and the Ministry for the

Environment and Energy Security for projects in Section II, along with the documentation specified in paragraph 3 of Article 9.

If the project is not subject to a VIA, the competent authority will convene a service conference within ten days of verifying the completeness of the information or after a request for additional details. In the case of a VIA, the timeline will be extended to include the public consultation process. After this phase, the service conference will be convened, and the outcome will constitute the AU.

For projects within regional competence, the regional single authorization procedure (PAUR) applies, unless the regions opt to adopt the AU.

3.3 Energy and Fuels Law

3.3.1 Substantive framework

Electrolysers convert electricity into H_2, which can then be stored and later converted into electricity, heat, or gas, demonstrating their versatility in the energy sector.[32]

However, the versatile applications complicate their energy law classification as they can be deployed across diverse scenarios with overlapping legal frameworks in the electricity and gas sectors.[33] There is no standardized legal definition for electrolysers, necessitating their classification under traditional legal definitions within the energy sector.[34] Electrolysers can be classified as storage units, as defined in Article 3(6) of Legislative Decree 210/2021.[35] Although there is no specific regulation for gas produced by electrolysers in Italy, the interpretation of the regulatory framework could suggest that electrolysers fall also under the category of production units.[36] Additionally, storage systems are included within the definition of 'final consumer' as outlined in Article 34 of Legislative Decree 93/2011.[37] Classifying an electrolyser under the storage or final consumer group could have significant consequences, as electrolysers are subject to double taxation: the first at the time of energy storage and the second at the time of actual usage.[38] To address the issue, new incentives have been introduced:[39] one exempts facilities that convert hydrogen into electricity from network services and

[32] Nathan Giovannini, 'Analisi della regolazione a livello nazionale ed europeo sull'idrogeno: dal power-to-gas agli utilizzi finali' (2023) https://www.rse-web.it/wp-content/uploads/2024/09/Analisi-della-regolazione-a-livello-nazionale-ed-europeo-sullidrogeno-dal-power-to-gas-agli-utilizzi-finali.pdf accessed 10 November 2024.

[33] Giovannini (n 32).

[34] ibid.

[35] Decreto Legislativo 8 novembre 2021, n 210, Attuazione della direttiva UE 2019/944 del Parlamento europeo e del Consiglio, del 5 giugno 2019, relativa a norme comuni per il mercato interno dell'energia elettrica e che modifica la direttiva 2012/27/UE, nonché recante disposizioni per l'adeguamento della normativa nazionale alle disposizioni del regolamento UE 943/2019 sul mercato interno dell'energia elettrica e del regolamento UE 941/2019 sulla preparazione ai rischi nel settore dell'energia elettrica e che abroga la direttiva 2005/89/CE (Italy).

[36] Giovannini (n 32).

[37] Decreto Legislativo 1 giugno 2011, n 93, Attuazione delle direttive 2009/72/CE, 2009/73/CE e 2008/92/CE relative a norme comuni per il mercato interno dell'energia elettrica, del gas naturale e ad una procedura comunitaria sulla trasparenza dei prezzi al consumatore finale industriale di gas e di energia elettrica, nonché abrogazione delle direttive 2003/54/CE e 2003/55/CE (Italy).

[38] Giovannini (n 32).

[39] ibid.

fees,[40] while the other exempts from network fees only electrolysers powered by renewable energy.[41] Due to unbundling rules, national gas and electricity operators, TERNA and SNAM, are prohibited from constructing and operating electrolysers.[42]

3.3.2 Procedural framework

The Ministerial Decree of 3 June 2022[43] set an initial limit of 2% for the injection of hydrogen into the national gas network, with the aim of gradually integrating this energy source into transport and distribution infrastructures.

This measure was adopted to foster innovation in the sector while ensuring the highest standards of safety for users, the public, and the environment.[44] For access procedures and technical requirements, the principal reference document is the SNAM Network Code.[45]

3.4 Environmental Law

3.4.1 Substantive framework

Legislative Decree No 152 of 3 April 2006, known as the Environmental Code, is fundamental to environmental regulation in Italy. It incorporates key principles from Constitutional and European law which shape national environmental policies. Article 3-quater establishes the principle of sustainable development, as defined in the Brundtland Report, while paragraph 2 ensures that actions taken by public administrations align with this principle.[46] The practical implementation includes specific procedures provided in Part II of the Environmental Code.[47] Among these are the Strategic Environmental Assessment (VAS), the Environmental Impact Assessment (VIA), and the Integrated Environmental Authorization (AIA). In addition to these, DPR No 59 of 13 March 2013 also introduced the Single Environmental Authorization (AUA).[48]

These instruments form the core of environmental protection procedures, ensuring that administrative and project-related decisions are compatible with environmental conservation.[49]

[40] ARERA, Delibera 574/2014/R/eel, Disposizioni relative all'integrazione dei sistemi di accumulo di energia elettrica nel sistema elettrico nazionale (21 November 2014).

[41] Ministero della Transizione Ecologica, Decreto ministeriale 21 settembre 2022 (Italy).

[42] ibid.

[43] Decreto 3 giugno 2022, Aggiornamento al decreto del Ministro dello sviluppo economico 18 maggio 2018, recante 'Regola tecnica sulle caratteristiche chimico-fisiche e sulla presenza di altri componenti nel gas combustibile' (Italy).

[44] Giovannini (n 32).

[45] SNAM Rete Gas, Network Code https://www.snam.it/en/our-businesses/transportation/network-code-tariffs-committee-area-and-consultations/network-code.html accessed 26 January 2025.

[46] Marco Luigi Antonioli, 'La sostenibilità dello sviluppo nelle fonti del diritto' in Procedimenti Europei—European Procedures (ed), *Sostenibilità dello sviluppo e governance ambientale* (G Giappichelli Editore 2017) 40.

[47] ibid.

[48] Decreto del Presidente della Repubblica 13 marzo 2013, n 59, Regolamento recante la disciplina dell'autorizzazione unica ambientale e la semplificazione di adempimenti amministrativi in materia ambientale gravanti sulle piccole e medie imprese e sugli impianti non soggetti ad autorizzazione integrata ambientale, a norma dell'articolo 23 del decreto-legge 9 febbraio 2012, n 5, convertito, con modificazioni, dalla legge 4 aprile 2012, n 35 (Italy).

[49] ibid.

Under the Environmental Code, electrolysers are categorized as chemical plants. Article 6 of Annex II of the Environmental Code refers to integrated chemical plants as industrial-scale facilities that use chemical transformation processes, with multiple production units that are functionally interconnected. Article 6-bis provides a similar definition but applies to chemical plants that produce only green hydrogen. Both types of plants fall under state jurisdiction for the VIA. However, non-green hydrogen plants are subject to this only if their production exceeds 100 million kilograms annually.

Regarding multiple production units, it has been clarified that physical proximity is not required.[50] The definitions of integrated chemical plants and industrial scale are more nuanced. The concept of 'integration' requires multiple production units working together as a single entity, with functional connections between them;[51] for example an electrolyser and a methanation unit.

A single electrolyser, even powered by renewable energy, isn't considered to be an integrated chemical plant, as the renewable source is merely an auxiliary service. Meanwhile 'industrial scale' has no universal thresholds and must be assessed on a case-by-case basis.[52]

Both Articles 6 and 6-bis of Annex II set the same four criteria: the plant must be integrated, on an industrial scale, involve chemical transformation, and have multiple production units. Only if all these criteria are met do electrolysers require a VIA.

3.4.2 Procedural framework

VIA, VAS, AIA, and any other necessary environmental authorizations can be applied for in the simplified procedure PAUR.

Notably, pilot projects focused exclusively on developing and testing new methods or products, with a duration of no more than two years. They are subject to VIA only if a preliminary assessment deems it necessary.[53] Additionally, these pilot projects are exempted from AIA requirements. The regions are the competent authority for conducting the assessment. Furthermore, the Renewable Energy Consolidated Act exempted projects in Annex B and C, thus electrolysers under 10 MW and those located in industrial areas, from being subjected to the VIA.

With regard to VAS and VIA, Italian regulations can be considered a direct 'copy and paste' of the European SEA and EIA directives. Both aim to protect environmental interests, but they differ in terms of scope and timing. VAS intervene at an earlier stage, focusing on the environmental assessment of plans and programmes, while VIAs concentrate on the specific effects of individual projects.[54]

VAS is required for plans likely to impact the environment or cultural heritage significantly. Plans and programmes regarding hydrogen have to be subjected to VAS, a

[50] Ministero dell'Ambiente e della Sicurezza Energetica (MASE), 'Risposta prot. 124801' (28 July 2023) (Italy).
[51] ibid.
[52] Ministero dell'Ambiente e della Sicurezza Energetica (MASE), 'Risposta prot. 23713' (7 February 2024) (Italy).
[53] Environmental Code art 6(6)(a) (Italy).
[54] Barbara Giuliani, 'Valutazione ambientale strategica, valutazione d'impatto ambientale e autorizzazione integrata ambientale' in Allena and others (eds), *Trattato di diritto del territorio* (Giappichelli 2018) 1067.

requirement coming directly from a ruling of the Constitutional Court.[55] VAS is conducted by the Ministry of Environment or regional authorities.

VIA, on the other hand, focuses on the environmental impacts of individual projects. Project location and viability are determined during the prior planning phase, with broader considerations addressed through VAS.[56] VIAs assess specific projects and impacts, with the responsible authority determined by the project's production capacity at either the state or regional level.

To accelerate the approval and implementation of PNRR and PNIEC projects, Article 8, paragraph 2-bis, of the Environmental Code, establish a fast track for the VIAs of PNRR projects, prioritizing green hydrogen plants. This provision reduces the processing time of VIAs to thirty days after public consultation or 130 days from the documentation's publication.

What then happens to electrolysers that do not meet the four criteria mentioned in Article 6 and Article 6-bis of the environmental code? Such projects are categorized as 'chemical installations' under Annex XII of Part Two of the Environmental Code and are directly subjected to the AIA.[57] The AIA is the final overarching permit required for all chemical industrial installations, regardless of whether or not they are subject to the VIA.[58] Unlike the VIA, the AIA focuses on the operational aspects of the plants, consolidating all necessary permits into a single authorization.[59] The relevant permits covered under the AIA include:

- Atmospheric Emission Authorization
- Discharge authorization
- Single permit for waste disposal and recovery facilities

The Council of State clarified the relationship between AIA and VIA. While the VIA is a mandatory prerequisite for the AIA, a positive VIA does not automatically guarantee that the AIA will be approved.[60]

The AIA's comprehensive nature streamlines the process, reduces bureaucracy, and provides administrations with an overview of the plant's activities.[61] The required authorizations are granted through the services conference and require the use of the Best Available Techniques (BAT) standards.[62] BAT standards are a fundamental aspect of the AIA and serve as technical reference points for both the competent authority

[55] Corte Costituzionale, sentenza n 258, 3 November 2020 (Italy).
[56] ibid.
[57] MASE (n 50).
[58] ibid.
[59] TAR Lazio (Roma), sentenza n 4830, 20 March 2023 (Italy).
[60] ibid.
[61] Altalex, 'Autorizzazione integrata ambientale: la guida completa: oggetto, competenze, procedura, durata, controlli e ispezioni' (Altalex, 6 May 2020) https://www.altalex.com/guide/autorizzazione-integrata-ambientale accessed 19 September 2024.
[62] ibid.

and operators in the issuance of permits.[63] BAT can be found in the reference documents BREFS.

Whether the AIA is issued by the Ministry of Environment or regional authorities depends on the thresholds outlined in Annex XII of the Environmental Code. Electrolysers exceeding the threshold in Annex XII of the Environmental Code are subject to the AIA under state jurisdiction, while those below the threshold are under regional authority. For regional projects, no specific threshold is set for the AIA, but production must be on an industrial scale, with the competent authority assessing this. Electrolysers not exceeding the threshold nor meeting the industrial scale requirement require an AUA, a simplified permitting procedure that, similar to AIA, consolidates various authorizations. The AUA application must be submitted to the competent SUAP (One-Stop Shop for Productive Activities), which forwards it to the relevant authorities.

3.5 Emission Law

3.5.1 Substantive framework

The Environmental Code is the primary legislation in Italy governing industrial emissions, including those into the atmosphere, water, and soil. The code aligns closely with the European Union's Industrial Emissions Directive,[64] which sets comprehensive standards for reducing the environmental impact of industrial activities. Emissions into the atmosphere are classified as pollutants that can harm air quality, human health, or the environment.[65] While electrolysis is CO_2-neutral, indirect emissions may result from the use of non-renewable energy sources. Its main by-product, oxygen, is not considered a pollutant.[66]

Moreover, noise during electrolysis can be problematic.[67] Noise is not directly regulated under the Environmental Code. The reference law is Law No 47 of 26 October 1995,[68] while limit values were set by the DPCM of 14 November 1997.[69] Assessments and authorizations related to noise are regulated under the AIA and AUA.[70]

Directive 2024/1785 recently updated the IED.[71] With this reform, the European Union aims to take another crucial step toward its net zero ambitions. Electrolysers

[63] Attilio Balestrieri, 'I procedimenti di autorizzazione ambientale e di VIA' (2024) 10 *Ambiente & Sicurezza*, Suppl 1 (Guida all'Ambiente) 10.

[64] Directive 2010/75/EU of the European Parliament and of the Council of 24 November 2010 on industrial emissions (integrated pollution prevention and control) (recast) (Text with EEA relevance) [2010] OJ L 334/17.

[65] Environmental Code art 268(1)(a-b) (Italy).

[66] Vurimindi Himabindu and S Shiva Kumar, 'Hydrogen production by PEM water electrolysis—A review' (2019) 2(3) Materials Science for Energy Technologies 442–45 https://www.sciencedirect.com/science/article/pii/S2589299119300035 accessed 26 August 2024.

[67] European Industrial Gases Association Aisbl, *Environmental Impacts of Hydrogen Plants* Doc 122/18 (EIGA 2018) https://www.eiga.eu/uploads/documents/DOC122.pdf accessed 8 September 2024.

[68] Legge 26 ottobre 1995, n 447, Legge quadro sull'inquinamento acustico (Italy).

[69] Decreto del Presidente del Consiglio dei Ministri 14 novembre 1997, Determinazione dei valori limite delle sorgenti sonore (Italy).

[70] Maddalena Orcali, 'Le altre forme di inquinamento' (2024) 10 Ambiente & Sicurezza, Suppl 1 (Guida all'Ambiente) 192.

[71] Directive (EU) 2024/1785 of the European Parliament and of the Council of 24 April 2024 amending Directive 2010/75/EU on industrial emissions and Council Directive 1999/31/EC on the landfill of waste [2024] OJ L 47/1.

for hydrogen production will only require an emission permit if their capacity exceeds 50 tonnes per day. The recently adopted directive must be implemented by Member States, and while details remain unclear, it is expected to simplify the process. Many electrolysers are likely to fall below this threshold, corresponding to a plant size of approximately 100 MW. However, at the time of writing, Italy has not yet transposed the Directive into national law.

3.5.2 Procedural framework

Installations emitting into the atmosphere require a permit.[72] Under Article 267, activities subject to the AIA are exempt from a separate emission permit. Annex VIII classifies hydrogen production under the category 'Chemical Industry', requiring an AIA authorization. The permitting procedure is overseen by the Ministry of Environment or regional authorities and the AIA must be renewed every ten years. Moreover, the authorization for atmospheric emissions is included among the permits replaced by the AUA. Unlike the AIA, the AUA has a longer validity period of fifteen years.

3.6 Water Management Law

3.6.1 Substantive framework

This chapter analyses water electrolysers, making water procurement regulation in Italy central. The primary legal frameworks governing water in Italy are the Royal Decree No 1775[73] and the Environmental Code. The Environmental Code states that all surface and groundwater are publicly owned. The intention here is not to grant the state unlimited control but to entrust public authorities with safeguarding water resources.[74] Article 144, paragraph 2 of the Environmental Code reinforces sustainable water use, respecting future generations' rights to an intact environmental heritage.

3.6.2 Procedural framework

The use of water as a public resource, requiring a permit from the appropriate authority, is not regulated by the AIA or AUA. Large extractions are managed by the regional authority, while smaller ones are handled by the municipality or province.[75] Electrolysers, classified as chemical industrial plants, are subject to Article 6, letter e of the Royal Decree, which distinguishes between small and large industrial derivations, setting the limit at 100 litres per second. Permits specify both the methods and duration

[72] Environmental Code art 269 (Italy).

[73] Regio Decreto 11 dicembre 1933, n 1775, Approvazione del testo unificato delle disposizioni di legge sulle installazioni idriche ed elettriche (Italy).

[74] Emanuele Boscolo, 'Water Resources Management in Italy: Institutions, Laws, and Approaches' in *Water Law, Policy and Economics in Italy* (Springer 2021) 105–33.

[75] ibid.

of use. Moreover, the Royal Decree stipulates that all water derivation concessions are temporary, with a maximum duration of thirty years. For large industrial derivations, the limit is reduced to fifteen years. Additionally, such concessions may require water-saving measures, including recycling or reuse.

3.7 Waste Law

3.7.1 Substantive framework

The by-products of electrolysis are oxygen, which can be safely released into the atmosphere, and wastewater. Developers must address waste management requirements under the Environmental Code. Specific regulations for wastewater management are outlined in Part 3, Section 2 of that Code. Since hydrogen production is considered an industrial activity, wastewater that has been generated by electrolysers is classified as industrial wastewater. This refers to wastewater that is discharged from buildings or facilities engaged in commercial or goods-producing activities, excluding domestic wastewater and stormwater runoff.[76]

3.7.2 Procedural framework

Article 124 of the Environmental Code requires that all discharges be subject to authorization. Authorizations for discharges are included within those granted under both AIA and AUA. Unless otherwise specified by regional legislation, the application for authorization is submitted to the province or the governing body of the area if the discharge is into the public sewer system.[77] Direct discharge into the soil and subsoil is prohibited. Discharges into surface waters are regulated by Article 105 and must comply with the standards set out in Article 101 of the Environmental Code. Meanwhile, Article 107 regulates discharge into the sewage network. Moreover, particularly relevant is Article 125, which outlines the information the applicant must provide in the authorization request for the discharge of industrial wastewater.

Although no explicit order of preference exists, a systematic reading reveals that priority is given to wastewater reuse, followed by discharge into sewage systems, and only when neither possible nor appropriate, into surface watercourses.[78]

Notably, alkaline electrolysers use substances like potassium hydroxide (KOH) or sodium hydroxide (NaOH), which can alter wastewater ph. Therefore, compliance with pH limits in Table 3/A of Annex 5 to Part Three of the Environmental Code is essential.

[76] Environmental Code art 74(1)(h) (Italy).

[77] ibid art 124(7) (Italy).

[78] Carlotta Casagrande, 'La gestione delle acque e del servizio idrico' (2024) 10 Ambiente & Sicurezza, Suppl 1 (Guida all'Ambiente) 56.

3.8 Nature Protection Law

3.8.1 Substantive framework

Italy, with its diverse morphological and climatic features, boasts an extraordinary richness of animal and plant species. According to Legambiente,[79] the country is home to over 67,000 species, nearly 43% of those in Europe. This exceptional biodiversity is recognized in the Italian legal framework, where nature and biodiversity protection are a constitutional value under Article 9.

Moreover, Article 117 (2) of the Constitution assigns to the state the exclusive authority to legislate on environmental and ecosystem protection. The primary reference law is Law 394/91,[80] which divides the territory into national and regional parks, reserves, and marine protected areas.

National protected areas are divided into zones with varying protection levels. Article 12.2(d) designates areas for economic and social promotion, allowing activities that align with park objectives to enhance local life and visitor experiences. These are outlined in the multi-year economic and social plan. In regional protected areas, the regulatory framework is less strict. On regional protected areas, Article 25 of Law 394/91 states that parks aim to promote the economic, social, and cultural development of local communities.

Furthermore, Natura 2000 sites, established under EU-derived legislation via DPR 8 September 1997, No 357,[81] are designed to conserve habitats, flora, and fauna of Community interest.

3.8.2 Procedural framework

Execution of works or constructions within protected areas requires the issuance of three specific permits: the building permit, the landscape authorization, and, where applicable, the approval of the Park Authority. The approval from the Park Authority differs from the landscape authorization. It is an intra-procedural step that precedes the landscape authorization and ensures the intervention complies with the plan and regulations governing the protected area. This approval must be issued within sixty days; if no response is given, it is considered granted.[82]

Plans and projects that may significantly affect a Natura 2000 site are required to undergo an appropriate assessment (VIncA),[83] integrated into the VIA and VAS procedures.[84]

[79] Anna Gaggino, 'Storie di biodiversità in cammino' (Parco del Monviso, 14 May 2024) https://www.parcomonviso.eu/attivita/i-monitoraggi-scientifici/storie-di-biodiversita-in-cammino#:~:text=In%20Italia%20si%20stima%20ci,in%20termini%20di%20abbondanza%202.059. accessed 11 September 2024.

[80] Legge 6 dicembre 1991, n 394, Legge quadro sulle aree protette (Italy).

[81] Decreto del Presidente della Repubblica 8 settembre 1997, n 357, Regolamento recante attuazione della direttiva 92/43/CEE relativa alla conservazione degli habitat naturali e seminaturali, nonché della flora e della fauna selvatiche (Italy).

[82] Corte di Cassazione Penale, Sez III, sentenza n 20721, 13 July 2020 (Italy).

[83] Decreto del Presidente della Repubblica 8 settembre 1997, n 357, art 5 (Italy).

[84] Environmental Code art 10(3) (Italy).

3.9 Fire Prevention, Health, and Safety Law

3.9.1 Substantive framework

Hydrogen's properties, such as low ignition energy, high flame velocity, and low flame visibility, pose significant safety risks.[85] To address these, operators must comply with Legislative Decree No 105 of 26 June 2015,[86] which aims to prevent major accidents involving hazardous substances and minimize their impact on health and the environment. Hydrogen is listed in Annex I of the decree, imposing responsibilities on electrolyser operators that vary by the quantity of hydrogen stored on-site, with thresholds at 5 and 50 tonnes. 'Stored' does not necessarily imply that the hydrogen is contained in a tank but rather that it is present at the facility at a single point in time.

Regarding fire prevention, Italy introduced Decree 7 July 2023[87] specifically addressing hydrogen production plants using electrolysis.

This applies to new and modified plants while existing facilities must comply only if major changes occur. Regarding fire prevention, Articles 5 and 6 of Decree 7 July 2023 set fire prevention requirements, covering construction standards and fire protection products.[88] Adherence to Annex I's technical standards is also required.

Moreover, the Technical Standards for Construction (NTC)[89] address aspects related to the structural safety of infrastructures.

3.9.2 Procedural framework

Article 12 of Legislative Decree No 105 requires operators to take all necessary steps to prevent major accidents and mitigate their consequences. Article 14 mandates operators to establish a policy for preventing major accidents, targeting events posing serious, immediate, or delayed threats. Plants storing over 50 tonnes of hydrogen must also submit a detailed safety report and implement an internal emergency plan. All plants, regardless of size, must adopt an external emergency plan managed by public authorities.

The decree encourages public participation, allowing citizens sixty days to submit comments, which must be considered before permits are granted. Safety inspections,

[85] Daniel A Crowl and Young-Do Jo, 'The hazards and risks of hydrogen' (2007) 20 Journal of Loss Prevention in the Process Industries 158 https://www.sciencedirect.com/journal/journal-of-loss-prevention-in-the-process-industries/vol/20/issue/2 accessed 28 December 2023.

[86] Decreto Legislativo 26 giugno 2015, n 105, Attuazione della direttiva 2012/18/UE relativa al controllo del pericolo di incidenti rilevanti connessi con sostanze pericolose (Italy).

[87] Decreto 7 luglio 2023, Regola tecnica di prevenzione incendi per l'individuazione delle metodologie per l'analisi del rischio e delle misure di sicurezza antincendio da adottare per la progettazione, la realizzazione e l'esercizio di impianti di produzione di idrogeno mediante elettrolisi e relativi sistemi di stoccaggio (Italy).

[88] L Montemezzo and E Bonifacio, 'Prevenzione incendi negli elettrolizzatori e relativi sistemi di stoccaggio' (18 January 2024) *Sicurezza, Salute Ambiente e molto altro*, Anno VI, no 26 https://www.aias-sicurezza.it/userfiles/Contenuto/534/allegati/MONTEMEZZO_BONIFACIO_from_aiasmag_26_web_1.pdf accessed 15 October 2024.

[89] Decreto 17 gennaio 2018, Aggiornamento delle 'Norme tecniche per le costruzioni' (Gazzetta Ufficiale, 20 February 2018, n 42).

investigations, and enforcement fall under the regional technical committee, as per Article 10.

Electrolyser operators must also consider Decree No 151 of 2011.[90] In terms of fire protection, Hydrogen production plants are not explicitly listed in Annex I of Decree No 151 and are thus not automatically supervised by the Fire Department. However, designers must verify if plant activities fall under Annex I. Notably, Annex I, point 6 of the 7 July 2023 decree specifies electrolysers fall under activity no 1 of Decree No 151/2011 when:[91]

- The total flammable gas volume exceeds 25 normal cubic metres per hour (Nm^3/h).
- Storage activities involve significant quantities of flammable gases.

Furthermore, according to Article 94 of DPR 380/2001, in seismic areas, excluding those classified as low seismicity, construction works require prior authorization from the regional technical office.

3.10 Law on Monuments and Archaeology

3.10.1 Substantive framework

Italy is home to the largest number of UNESCO World Heritage sites, a testament to its extraordinary cultural richness.[92] The importance of preserving this heritage is so profound that it is enshrined in the Constitution. Article 9 commits the Republic to promoting culture, scientific research, and protecting the nation's landscape and historical heritage.

Given the importance of protecting Italy's cultural heritage, anyone looking to develop electrolysers must understand and comply with the relevant legal requirements. The key legal reference here is the Cultural Heritage Code, which distinguishes between two main categories: 'cultural heritage', as defined in Article 10, paragraph 1, and 'landscape heritage', as defined in Article 131, paragraph 1. Any work involving assets in these categories requires specific authorization.

3.10.2 Procedural framework

The landscape authorization is typically issued by the Region, though this responsibility can be delegated to Municipalities or Provinces. In practice, Municipalities usually handle the process. The competent authority must obtain the Superintendent's

[90] DPR 1 August 2011, n 151, *Regolamento recante semplificazione della disciplina dei procedimenti relativi alla prevenzione degli incendi, a norma dell'art 49, comma 4-quater, del decreto-legge 31 maggio 2010, n 78, convertito, con modificazioni, dalla legge 30 luglio 2010, n 122* (Gazzetta Ufficiale, 22 September 2011, n 221).

[91] Montemezzo and Bonifacio (n 88).

[92] UNESCO, 'World Heritage List Statistics' (UNESCO World Heritage Convention, 2024) https://whc.unesco.org/en/list/stat/ accessed 21 September 2024.

opinion, a peripheral body of the Ministry of Culture. Depending on Article 146, this opinion may be binding or non-binding.

There are two types of landscape authorization: ordinary and simplified. The simplified procedure applies to 'minor impact' projects. Electrolysers, being container-like structures, generally have a relatively small landscape impact. However, connected infrastructure, such as storage units or energy plants, must also be considered, meaning project specifics largely determine the procedure.

Landscape authorization is processed within the services conference. The maximum timeframe is 120 days, though extensions may occur if the Superintendent requests additional details from the project designer, suspending procedural deadlines.[93] Consultations with experts suggest that this provision could cause significant delays as authorities often adopt a meticulous approach, even for minor projects like building renovations, potentially affecting electrolyser approval timelines.

If construction affects areas subject to cultural heritage constraints, prior authorization must be obtained from the territorially competent Superintendent. Such opinion shall also be issued within the framework of the conference of service. Under no circumstances may the following be authorized: the destruction of the area; any damage to it; or use that is incompatible with its historical and artistic character or that may compromise its preservation.

4. Recommendations to Improve the System

This section will examine certain shortcomings in the permitting procedures under review and will propose recommendations for improvement.

4.1 Substantive framework

From a substantive point of view, the regulatory uncertainty surrounding the definition and categorization of electrolysers needs to be addressed. As a versatile technology with various applications, solving this issue is complex. However, the lack of clarity creates ambiguities and hinders the widespread adoption of the technology.

Unfortunately, the Renewable Energy Consolidated Act failed to clarify their legal definition. This was a missed opportunity, as the previous version of the Act submitted for parliamentary review included a clear reference to storage systems.[94] In the final text, electrolysers are listed in annexes without further details in the main body regarding their nature. This choice has practical implications, particularly regarding the applicability of certain provisions that could offer significant advantages. One example is Article 2, which allows facilities under Article 1(1) to be located in agricultural areas.

[93] Legge 7 August 1990, n 241, art 2(7).
[94] Senato della Repubblica, *Atto del Governo* n 187, XIX Legislatura (12 August 2024).

In the coming months, it will be crucial to clarify whether electrolysers fall under the categories of projects outlined in Article 1(1) or if a reference to storage systems should be included.

This is particularly relevant, as a 2019 report highlighted the shortage of suitable areas as one of the main barriers to their development.[95] Little has changed in the past five years: electrolysers are still limited to industrial areas and, in some cases, within areas classified as C zones. Clarification is essential to determine if the placement of electrolysers is influenced by factors such as the type of energy source used or the intended purpose of the hydrogen (eg industrial use or commercial activities). Additionally, clarifying whether smaller electrolysers, such as those under 10 MW, qualify as industrial plants—as was done with photovoltaic plants—could facilitate small-scale deployment, helping Italy in achieving its hydrogen objectives.

Moreover, a clearer legal definition is necessary to address the issue of taxation and network charges. Electrolysers are considered both storage units and end-users, leading to double taxation: once during storage and again upon final use. Although the incentive mechanisms, outlined in Section 3.3 of this chapter, provide support, their implementation remains unclear.[96] Exemptions from general charges and network service fees currently apply only to facilities reconverting hydrogen into electricity, while for electrolysers producing hydrogen as an energy carrier only general charges are exempt. Extending exemptions for network service fees also to these facilities could encourage a wider adoption. This objective highlights the importance of establishing a clearer legal definition for electrolysers, ideally excluding them from the classification of final consumers.

4.2 Procedural framework

Given the complexity and relative novelty of the current shape of the permitting procedures, developers should not be left without support, particularly in 'free building' activities where only a preliminary communication is required. Drafting national guidelines on necessary permits and compliance requirements would help to address this gap, especially for small operators in the private sector who may lack the expertise to navigate the permitting process. Therefore, comprehensive and detailed guidelines for the permitting procedures of electrolysers are essential to ensure clarity and consistency. In this context, particular importance should be given to the recognition outlined in the recent Italian National Hydrogen Strategy, which emphasizes, among its priorities, the need to simplify the permitting procedure. To this end, the adoption of guidelines and explanatory circulars to support local authorities is recommended as a key measure.

[95] Cigolotti, McPhail, and Tommasino (n 4).
[96] Giovannini (n 32).

The Italian legislator has sought to simplify regulations for renewable energy installations by consolidating procedures into a single text, in line with the Commission's recommendations.[97] However, concerns remain about the extent of the promised simplification. A key criticism is the potential for ambiguity between the new provisions and the transitional rules for procedures already underway, which could complicate the work of administrations.[98] ITALIA SOLARE warns that ongoing procedures risk falling under new authorization regimes due to public administration delays. With some procedures shifting from the ministry to regional authorities, operators could lose substantial work already completed. ITALIA SOLARE insists that such delays must not disadvantage operators.[99] Moreover, administrations may lack the necessary knowledge and expertise to manage permitting procedures effectively. A critical yet missing element is the provision of technical support to administrations, which could be achieved, for example, through an interpretative notice. Such measures are essential to ensure the effective implementation of the permitting procedure.[100]

5. Conclusion

This chapter examined the procedures for constructing electrolysers in Italy, analysing various legal aspects, from planning to waste management and risk mitigation. The permitting procedure has seen improvements, notably the services conference mechanism and expedited environmental impact assessment procedure for green or renewable hydrogen production, which could serve as a reference model for other legal systems. Recent reforms, such as unifying the procedures for the construction and operation of electrolysers into a single text appear promising, though significant room for improvement remains. Recommendations include greater procedural clarity and expanding suitable installation areas. However, above all, persistent uncertainties, particularly regarding the legal definition of electrolysers, highlight the need for further research and legal clarification at both the Italian and EU levels. Addressing these issues through case law and evaluations could enhance legal certainty and create a more favourable framework for the construction of electrolysers.

[97] European Commission, COM(2023) 612 final, 24 May 2023.

[98] Wolters Kluwer Redazione, 'Il Testo Unico per l'energia rinnovabile è stato approvato' (Teknoring, 26 November 2024) https://www.teknoring.com/news/energie-rinnovabili/approvato-testo-unico-2024-semplificazione-normativa-produzione-fonti-verdi/ accessed 22 January 2025.

[99] Italia Solare, 'Testo unico rinnovabili: per ITALIA SOLARE è "assolutamente deludente"' (Press Release, Italia Solare, 23 December 2024) https://www.italiasolare.eu/comunicati-stampa/testo-unico-rinnovabili-per-italia-solare-e-assolutamente-deludente/ accessed 28 January 2025.

[100] ibid.

Further Reading

V Cigolotti, Stephen J McPhail, and Maria Cristina Tommasino, *La Regolamentazione del settore Idrogeno e delle sue applicazioni in Italia* (HyLAW 2019) https://www.h2it.it/wp-content/uploads/2019/07/HyLAW_National-policy-Paper-IT_ita.pdf accessed 25 March 2024.

N Giovannini, 'Analisi della regolazione a livello nazionale ed europeo sull'idrogeno: dal power-to-gas agli utilizzi finali' (Ricerca sul Sistema Energetico-RSE SpA 2023) https://www.rse-web.it/wp-content/uploads/2024/09/Analisi-della-regolazione-a-livello-nazionale-ed-europeo-sullidrogeno-dal-power-to-gas-agli-utilizzi-finali.pdf accessed 10 November 2024.

MASE 'Idrogeno: presentata la Strategia Nazionale, più scenari per la sua diffusione' (Ministero dell'Ambiente e della Sicurezza Energetica) https://www.mase.gov.it/comunicati/idrogeno-presentata-la-strategia-nazionale-piu-scenari-la-sua-diffusione accessed 26 November 2024.

Wolters Kluwer Redazione, 'Il Testo Unico per l'energia rinnovabile è stato approvato' (Teknoring, 26 November 2024) https://www.teknoring.com/news/energie-rinnovabili/approvato-testo-unico-2024-semplificazione-normativa-produzione-fonti-verdi/ accessed 22 January 2025.

VIII
Greece

Konstantinos Kounelis and Dimitra Douka

1. Introduction

Dimitris, an engineer, stood on the rugged hills overlooking the Aegean Sea. He was not there to enjoy the view but stood amidst a wind farm, holding a blueprint that could transform his business and Greece's energy future. For months, Dimitris had been planning something extraordinary: building the country's first large-scale electrolyser facility for green hydrogen. Despite Greece's ambitious climate goals—including scaling up electrolyser capacity to 231 MW by 2030 and producing 1.2 TWh of hydrogen annually—only two small research units and a pilot facility for electrolytic hydrogen production have been established to date.[1] The hydrogen produced is primarily intended for the production of synthetic kerosene and synthetic methanol, contributing to the decarbonization of heavy road transport and the maritime and aviation sectors.[2] Dimitris had already faced technical hurdles, financial uncertainties, and, perhaps most challenging, the permitting process. Sitting with his team one afternoon, he said, 'We need to understand this step by step. We cannot just build the electrolyser—we have to get through the labyrinth of permits'. The term 'labyrinth' was no exaggeration. Despite its abundant wind and solar resources, Greece has long lacked a comprehensive national hydrogen strategy, and the absence of a clear legislative framework has hindered progress. Encouragingly, recent developments signal a shift: the country's

[1] European Commission, 'Greece—Final updated NECP 2021–2030 (submitted in 2025)' <https://commission.europa.eu/publications/greece-final-updated-necp-2021-2030-submitted-2025_en> accessed 4 February 2025.

[2] ibid.

first dedicated hydrogen law is now in place, providing an initial regulatory foundation for Greece's emerging hydrogen sector. This chapter aims to guide readers through the complex regulatory landscape for permitting electrolysers in Greece.

The chapter proceeds as follows. First, an exploration into Greece's broader permitting landscape, encompassing environmental and energy permits, is undertaken to comprehend the regulatory framework within which electrolysers operate. Any distinctions in the permitting regime between different types of electrolysers will be highlighted. Second, a descriptive overview of the pertinent laws and permits is provided, delineating and then analysing the legal prerequisites for the deployment of electrolysers. This section addresses various categories of laws, including planning, environmental, energy, water management, waste, building, emissions, nature protection, safety, fire prevention, and monument laws. The necessary permits obtained based on these categories serve as a structural foundation, facilitating step-by-step navigation of the permits and requirements for deploying electrolysers in Greece. The final section entails an analytical examination, culminating in recommendations aimed at enhancing Greece's permitting system concerning electrolysers. By identifying areas for improvement and making practical suggestions, this section strives to contribute to the streamlining of regulatory processes and the promotion of sustainable hydrogen production practices.

2. General Observations on the Permitting Regime

As with the permitting regime for any industrial plant in Greece, the regime for hydrogen production is also complex. Law 5215/2025, which partially transposes the Hydrogen and Gas Decarbonisation Package, establishes the foundation rules for the organization of the hydrogen market.[3] Notably, it introduces a maximum duration of two years for completing the permitting process.[4] The law also designates the Department of Renewable Energy Sources, Transport and Alternative Fuels, operating under the Ministry of Environment and Energy, as the central contact point for the permitting coordination.[5] In parallel, a multitude of laws come into play, each with its own set of provisions relevant to hydrogen. Many of these provisions are further specified by Ministerial or Presidential decrees, adding layers of complexity to the framework.[6] Bureaucratic delays and the involvement of multiple authorities further complicate the permitting process, posing significant challenges for stakeholders.

[3] N 5215/2025, 'Framework for the promotion of biomethane production, rules for the organization of the hydrogen production market and geographically limited hydrogen networks—Partial transposition of Directive (EU) 2024/1788 and other provisions for environmental protection', FEK A 116/04 July 2025; Directive 2024/1788/EU of the European Parliament and of the Council of 13 June 2024 on common rules for the internal markets for renewable gas, natural gas and hydrogen (recast) (Text with EEA relevance) [2024] OJ L 1788/1.

[4] ibid art 26(1).

[5] ibid art 26(2).

[6] According to para 2 of art 43 of the Greek Constitution, legislative authorization is permitted for the issuance of regulatory acts by other bodies of the Administration, only for the regulation of specific matters or matters of local interest or of a technical or detailed nature. This category includes Ministerial Decisions.

Despite these efforts, the broader permitting landscape remains intricate. A multitude of legal instruments continue to apply, each bringing its own set of requirements for hydrogen-related projects. These are often further elaborated through Ministerial or Presidential decrees, adding additional regulatory layers. Bureaucratic inefficiencies and the involvement of numerous authorities exacerbate the complexity of the process, creating significant hurdles for stakeholders and project developers alike.

The permitting process involves various levels of government, each with distinct responsibilities:

1. The *National government* has significant responsibilities in spatial planning, environmental protection, and regional development. It enacts framework laws and approves the majority of spatial plans, including by-laws governing the planning process.
2. *Decentralized Administrative Units*: Greece has seven Decentralized Administrative Units (Decentralized Administrations), established under the 2011 Kallikratis reform, to represent the state at a regional level.[7] They share responsibilities with the national government and municipalities for spatial planning, permits (eg electrolysers), and oversee areas as diverse as urban planning, environment, energy, forestry, migration, and citizenship.[8] Governed by a government-appointed secretary general and supported by an advisory council, these seven units operate with administrative and financial autonomy, bridging local and national governance.
3. *Regions*: The thirteen regions in Greece have limited responsibilities regarding land use. They primarily have advisory roles in the creation of certain spatial plans.
4. *Municipalities*: They have a crucial role in approving local spatial plans and issuing land-use certificates.

In the Greek jurisdiction, the requirements from various *legal frameworks have been consolidated into four so-called umbrella permits*, which will be listed next. While this approach integrates multiple requirements into a more cohesive framework, the process remains complex for project developers. At the heart of the new permitting regime lies the Hydrogen Producer Certificate (HPC), which serves as the primary legal requirement for any prospective investor seeking to develop a hydrogen production facility in Greece. Further recommendations for streamlining the process are provided at the end of this chapter.

In essence, the initial step for a project promoter is to obtain the HPC, followed by the acquisition of the four umbrella permits, namely:

[7] OECD, 'Decentralization in Greece' in OECD (ed), *Working Together for Local Integration of Migrants and Refugees in Athens* (OECD Publishing 2018) 63.

[8] N 3852/2010, 'New Architecture of Local Government and Decentralized Administration—Kallikratis Program', FEK A 87/7 June 2010.

Environmental Terms Approval (based on the Environmental Impact Assessment (EIA))
Building Permit
Approval of Establishment
Operational Permit

From legislation, it is evident that some permits are required first in order to obtain the next permits. However, it is important to note that before initiating the permitting process, developers must first take a *preliminary step*, a fifth step in the process, namely ensure compliance with planning law, which is not a permit but a prerequisite for proceeding further. This will now briefly be discussed.

3. Specific Permits Applicable to Electrolysers

3.1 Planning Law

Before applying for any permits, the first step for the developer of an electrolyser is to check the compatibility of the nature and size of the planned activity with the designated land use of the site. This preliminary check is crucial as it determines whether the project can proceed to the permitting stage. When the land use is compatible with the activity planned, the building department of the municipality in which the site is located issues a land use certificate. The production of hydrogen is categorized as an industrial land use of a medium or low nuisance.[9] Electrolysers with a to-be-installed capacity exceeding 500 kW are classified as medium nuisance activities, whereas those with an installed capacity below 500 kW are classified as low nuisance activities.[10]

3.2 Hydrogen Producer's Certificate

Hydrogen production is permitted only for entities holding a valid Hydrogen Producer's Certificate, making it a prerequisite for commencing the permitting process.[11] The application for a Hydrogen Producer's Certificate is submitted to the Electronic Registry, as provided in Article 29 of Law 5215/2025. This certificate specifies the installed capacity, maximum production capacity, and maximum hourly hydrogen production capacity (in kWhth), the installation site, the validity period of the certificate, and the origin of the electricity supply, whether through a direct line or from the grid.[12] The

[9] YA 3137/191/Φ. 15/2012 Annex 1 (87), FEK 1048/B, 4 April 2012.
[10] ibid.
[11] N 5215/2025 (n 3) art 27(1).
[12] ibid art 27 (7).

Hydrogen Producer's Certificate is granted for a period of up to twenty-five years and may be renewed for an equal period.[13]

3.3 Environmental Aspects

Following the issuance of the Producer's Certificate, the developer must initiate the procedure for complying with the environmental legislation.[14] The construction and operation of an electrolyser might bring about environmental concerns. It is therefore important to adhere to environmental legislation, which mandates the completion of an EIA, conducted by the project developer and the attainment of Environmental Terms Approval issued by the relevant public authority. The process of assessing the potential effects on the environment from the implementation of projects and activities aims to evaluate them as early as possible and integrate the environmental dimension into the decision-making process.[15]

3.3.1 Environmental impact assessment/law on the monuments

The Greek legislature is unique in combining the procedures for environmental protection and the protection of the monuments into the same permit, with the aim of decreasing the number of authorizations that the project developer requires. Therefore, both will be examined and discussed within this subsection.

Compliance with Greek environmental legislation requires the developer to obtain an Environmental Terms Approval, which sets conditions, restrictions, and specifications for the realization of the project. These include the position, size, type, applied technology, and general technical characteristics of the electrolyser project, as well as corrective or preventive measures and monitoring actions for environmental media and parameters. The approval process, which may also mandate compensatory measures, or environmental restoration, is contingent upon the completion of an EIA for the electrolyser. Thus, an electrolyser needs to be examined according to the EIA rules, set in Law 4014/2011, which is the national law transposing Directive 2011/92/EU.[16] Law 4014/2011 aligns with the provisions of the EIA Directive. Having said that, it also includes certain specifications not covered by EU law, requiring the project developer to pay attention to the details of national law and that will be discussed later.

The starting point, however, is, Article 1 of Law 4014/2011, which is a direct transposition of the EU EIA Directive. It classifies projects and activities of the public and

[13] ibid art 28 (1).

[14] ibid art 30(1α).

[15] Ministry of Environment and Energy, 'Environmental Licensing' (Ministry of Environment and Energy) <https://ypen.gov.gr/perivallon/perivallontiki-adeiodotisi/> accessed 19 January 2024.

[16] N 4014/2011, 'Environmental licensing of projects and activities, regulation of arbitrary in connection with the creation of an environmental balance and other provisions of the competence of the Ministry of Environment', FEK A 209/21 September 2011; Directive 2011/92/EU of the European Parliament and of the Council of 13 December 2011 on the assessment of the effects of certain public and private projects on the environment [2011] OJ L 26/8.

private sector, the construction or operation of which may have an impact on the environment, into two categories (A and B).[17] The first category (A) includes projects that may have a significant impact on the environment and for which an EIA is required. Category A projects and activities are further classified under Greek law into (i) those likely to cause very significant impacts on the environment and constitute sub-category A1, and (ii) those likely to cause significant impacts to the environment and constitute sub-category A2. For reasons of legal certainty, Joint Ministerial Decision n. 92108/1045/Φ.15 has been issued, which clusters (among category A1, A2, or B), the various projects, based on their technical characteristics.[18] Electrolysers are classified in sub-category A2 of the 9th Group, 'Industrial and related activities facilities';[19] specifically in n. 92: Production of chemical substances and products, 'Production of industrial and medical gases' (production either by chemical conversion through chemical process or by biological process).[20] All types of electrolysers likely to be used in Greece for the foreseeable future produce hydrogen from water and electricity through chemical reactions. For this reason, they meet the criteria of category A, for which an EIA is required, and the competent environmental authority for the environmental licensing of the projects and activities of subcategory A2 is the relevant decentralized administration.[21]

When it comes to the relevant provisions of the Law on Monuments, an opinion from the Ministry of Culture is required on whether the area where the electrolyser is located is of archaeological interest.[22] Monuments and sites of archaeological significance are of great importance in Greece. This importance is underscored by the necessity to obtain a positive opinion from the competent authority of the Ministry of Culture in the permitting process. Such an opinion is likely to serve as a decisive factor in ensuring that proposed projects do not compromise or adversely impact culturally significant sites or artefacts.

According to the Law on Monuments, permits for the establishment or operation of an industrial, craft, or commercial enterprise, as well as building activity, such as an electrolyser, near an ancient site are only possible after approval by the Minister of Culture, a permit that is issued after the opinion of the Council (Central Archaeological Council or the Central Council for Modern Monuments).[23] Approval is granted if the distance from, or relationship to, an immovable monument is such that there is no risk of direct or indirect damage to it due to the nature of the project, business, or work.[24] This assessment is included in the Environmental Terms Approval requirements, serving the broader aim of safeguarding Antiquities and Cultural Heritage.[25]

[17] N 4014/2011 (n 16) art 1(1).
[18] KYA 92108/1045/Φ.15/2020, FEK B 3833/9 September 2020.
[19] ibid Annex I.
[20] ibid Annex I (92).
[21] N 4014/2011 (n 16) art 4(1).
[22] ibid art 2(4).
[23] N 3028/2002 art 10 (3), 'For the protection of Antiquities and Cultural Heritage in general', FEK 153 A/28 June 2002; Council refers to the Central Archaeological Council or the Central Council for Modern Monuments, depending on the type of the monument.
[24] ibid.
[25] N 4014/2011 (n 16).

The opinion of the archaeological service is not required for projects that are situated in their entirety in areas within a city plan or within the boundaries of settlements, except in the cases expressly provided for by the relevant legislation.[26] The opinion of the forestry service is required only for projects located in forests, forested and reforested areas, woodlands, parks, and generally in areas outside approved urban plans.[27]

The following steps outline the process that the project developer must initiate to obtain the Environmental Terms Approval.

1. Submission of an EIA: The applicant submits an EIA file, accompanied by the necessary documentation and plans, to the Competent Authority.
2. Review and Response: The project developer may respond to any feedback or issues raised during the consultation process, ensuring the documentation complies with the relevant requirements.
3. Final Decision: Once the evaluation is complete, the project developer receives the decision on the Environmental Terms Approval, which either approves or rejects the project's proposed environmental terms.[28]

The next section will discuss the actual, substantive requirements, following the procedural steps discussed above. All substantive requirements that follow must be met for obtaining an Environmental Terms Approval when an electrolyser is located in a protected area, if it falls under emissions law, and if it produces waste. These will be discussed in the following three sections. Cumulatively these will outline the steps a project developer must follow in order to be granted approval.

3.4 Nature Protection Law

Special environmental studies, management plans, and determination of land use take place for protected areas in Greece. Therefore, it is crucial for developers of electrolysers to become acquainted with the specific laws and regulations governing these protected areas. Construction and operation of an electrolyser may be prohibited in these areas to ensure their preservation and conservation. Hence, developers must carefully assess and adhere to the legal requirements and environmental regulations associated with protected areas to avoid any potential restrictions or prohibitions on their projects.

Biodiversity protection areas encompass terrestrial, aquatic, marine, or mixed regions with natural habitats and species of international, EU, or national importance requiring conservation.[29] These areas include sites listed in the National List of the European Ecological Network Natura 2000.[30]

[26] ibid art 4(2).
[27] ibid art 2(5).
[28] ibid art 4(3).
[29] N 1650/1986 art 19(1), 'For the Protection of the Environment', FEK A 160/16 October 1986.
[30] ibid; 'Natura 2000 is a network of protected areas covering Europe's most valuable and threatened species and habitats. It is the largest coordinated network of protected areas in the world, extending across all 27 EU

For all the protected areas, one or more protection zones are defined by the Presidential Decree under paragraph 4 of Article 21 of the Law 1650/1986.[31] These zones can be the following:

- Zone of absolute protection of nature,
- Nature protection zone,
- Habitat and species conservation zone,
- Zone of sustainable management of natural resources[32]

Installing an electrolyser is not permissible in an absolute protection zone, a nature protection zone, or a habitat and species conservation zone; Article 19(4) of Law 1650/1986, in conjunction with Presidential Decree No 59/2018, specifies the types of installations potentially allowed in these zones, which do not include electrolysers. However, in the sustainable management of natural resources zones, installing an electrolyser appears to be permissible. In these zones the law explicitly prohibits high-nuisance industrial and manufacturing facilities, while hydrogen production is classified as a low- or medium-nuisance industrial activity, as explained earlier in this chapter.[33] Nevertheless, the permissibility of installing an electrolyser will be determined for each zone of sustainable natural resource management following the publication of Presidential Decrees that will define the land uses in each specific zone.[34]

If an electrolyser project falls within a protected area of the Natura 2000 Network that is not characterized as an absolute protection zone, nature protection zone, or habitat and species conservation zone, a Special Ecological Assessment (SEA) must be included as part of the EIA submitted to the competent authority.[35] The SEA evaluates the consequences of the project on the area based on its conservation objectives.[36] The significance of the impacts is assessed in relation to the specific characteristics and environmental conditions prevailing in the protected area affected by the project, taking into particular account the conservation objectives of the area.[37]

Based on the conclusions of the SEA and the EIA, the competent authority may approve of the project or activity only after ensuring it will not harm the integrity of the specific area.[38] This includes examining potential impact mitigation measures and alternative solutions to demonstrate that the project or activity will not compromise the

Member States, both on land and at sea. The sites within Natura 2000 are designated under the Birds and the Habitats Directives'; European Environment Agency, 'The Natura 2000 protected areas network' (European Environment Agency, 28 February 2023) <https://www.eea.europa.eu/themes/biodiversity/natura-2000> accessed 10 December 2023.

[31] N 1650/1986 (n 29) art 19(4).
[32] ibid.
[33] PD 59/2018 art 14 (δ), FEK A 114/29 June 2018.
[34] N 1650/1986 (n 29) art 21.
[35] N 4014/2011 (n 16) art 10 (1).
[36] ibid art 10(2).
[37] ibid.
[38] ibid.

area's ecological functions.[39] The decision should focus on and be limited to the conservation objectives of the area.[40]

The importance of nature protection law and the SEA is underscored by the fact that nearly half of Greece is under protection. For this reason, it is critical for electrolyser developers to verify the permissibility of their activities at a specific site. Beyond the provisions of environmental and nature protection law, developers must also meet specific requirements to obtain the Environmental Terms Approval. In this context, the provisions of the law on industrial emissions will be discussed further, as hydrogen production falls within its scope.

3.5 Law on Industrial Emissions

In relation to the regulation of industrial emissions the most important legal document is the Ministerial Decision No 36060/1155 /E.103.[41] This decision is the transposition of the Industrial Emissions Directive into Greek law.[42] Furthermore, Law 4014/2011 empowers the Minister of the Environment and Energy to establish procedures and criteria for the issuing of Environmental Terms Approval of projects and activities, including those related to hydrogen production.[43] For an electrolyser, obtaining an Environmental Terms Approval is contingent upon full compliance with Greek emissions law. This compliance is both crucial and paramount, as an Environmental Terms Approval cannot be issued without it. Notably, the Ministerial decision establishes specific provisions and criteria for the Environmental Terms Approval of the activities listed in its Annex I.[44]

According to Annex I hydrogen is included in the following way:

4.2. Production of inorganic chemicals, such as: a) gases, such as … hydrogen …

This means that the developer of such an activity has to comply with the provisions of the Articles 8–23 of the Ministerial Decision. Specifically project developers shall take the necessary measures to provide that installations are operated in accordance with the following principles:

(a) all the appropriate preventive measures are taken against pollution;

[39] ibid.

[40] ibid.

[41] ΥΑ 36060/1155 /Ε.103/2013, ΦΕΚ 1450/Β 14 June 2013.

[42] Directive 2010/75/EU of the European Parliament and of the Council of 24 November 2010 on industrial emissions (integrated pollution prevention and control) (recast) (Text with EEA relevance) [2010] OJ L 3334/17; The main tool for the incorporation of Directives remains Law 1338/1983, which provides for the use of existing or current authorizations of national legislation as well as autonomous authorizations, in order to issue ministerial decisions and presidential decrees; Eleni Martsoukou and Nikos Trantas, *EU Law in Greece—Handbook of Harmonization* (Online) (1st edn, General Secretariat of the Government 2013) 13. https://gslegal.gov.gr/wp-content/uploads/2013/10/versionA.pdf accessed 22 September 2025.

[43] N 4014/2011 (n 16) art 2(13).

[44] ΥΑ 36060/1155 /Ε.103/2013 (n 41) art 8.

Directly applicable, as electrolysers must ensure that hydrogen production does not release pollutants into the environment.

(b) the best available techniques (BAT) are applied;
Crucial for electrolysers, as BAT ensures energy efficiency and minimises emissions, particularly in large-scale hydrogen production.

(c) no significant pollution is caused;
Largely applicable, though the electrolysis process itself generates minimal pollution when powered by renewable energy and clean water sources.

(d) the generation of waste is prevented in accordance with Section B of Law 4042/2012;
Directly relevant, as any waste, such as auxiliary materials, must be managed under strict waste prevention rules.

(e) where waste is generated, it is prepared for re-use, recycled, recovered or, where that is technically and economically impossible, it is disposed of while avoiding or reducing any impact on the environment;
Applicable, particularly to water used in electrolysis, which should be treated or recycled to avoid environmental harm.

(f) energy is used efficiently;
Highly pertinent, as energy efficiency is fundamental to the economic and environmental viability of electrolysers, especially given their reliance on electricity from renewable sources.

(g) the necessary measures are taken to prevent accidents and limit their consequences;
Crucial for hydrogen facilities, as hydrogen is flammable, necessitating robust safety protocols and emergency measures.

(h) the necessary measures are taken upon definitive cessation of activities to avoid any risk of pollution and return the site of operation to the satisfactory state defined in accordance with Article 18.
Directly applicable, as decommissioning electrolysers involves ensuring the site is free of contamination and adheres to restoration requirements under Article 18.

To facilitate the implementation of these measures, additional requirements are established through the EIA process. More specifically, the production of hydrogen has to be done in line with BAT.[45] BAT are identified for each type of activity in the 'Best Available Techniques Reference Documents' (BREFs), which delineate the optimal techniques for managing emissions at an industrial scale. This system is derived from the Industrial Emissions Directive, and BREF reports are developed at the EU level.[46] However, currently there are no existing BREFs or guidance specifically covering the production of hydrogen. Where BAT for an activity is not covered by an existing BREF report, the regulator must adhere to Article 11(5) of the Ministerial Decision. In such

[45] ibid art 11(1).
[46] European Parliament and Council Directive 2010/75/EU of 24 November 2010 on industrial emissions (integrated pollution prevention and control) (recast) [2010] OJ L 334/17 (IED Directive).

cases, the competent authority, after consulting with the operator, sets permit conditions on the basis of the best available techniques that it has determined for the activities or processes concerned, considering the criteria outlined in Annex III of the Ministerial Decision.[47] Hence, before issuing the Environmental Terms Approval, the competent authority must scrutinize whether BATs have been implemented.[48]

Hydrogen production is also subjected to other regulations such as Waste Gas Management (WGC) and Common Wastewater and Waste Gas Treatment/ Management Systems in the Chemical Sector (CWW).[49] Consequently, developers of electrolysis projects must adhere to the techniques outlined in the corresponding BREF reports to ensure compliance with these regulations. Beyond complying with legal provisions on industrial emissions, developers must also ensure proper waste management, as Environmental Terms Approval cannot be issued without it. The next subsection will explore this in greater detail.

3.6 Waste Law

An important part of the environmental permitting process is the waste management aspect of a project. Law 4819/2021, which implements three EU Directives on waste, is the main regulation governing waste management in Greece.[50] While Article 2 of this law excludes wastewater from its scope when other European or national laws regulate its management, no specific Greek law currently addresses wastewater directly.[51] As a result, wastewater from electrolysers falls under the provisions of waste law.

Speaking of wastewater, the type and composition of wastewater in particular can vary depending on the type of electrolysis used, such as proton exchange membrane (PEM), alkaline electrolysis, or high-temperature electrolysis. Each method generates different by-products and waste streams that may impact the permitting process. For instance, PEM electrolysis produces oxygen and relatively clean water as a by-product, Alkaline electrolysis may generate wastewater containing trace amounts of potassium hydroxide or other chemicals used in the electrolyte solution. According to Annex II of

[47] YA 36060/1155 /E.103/2013 (n 41) art 11(5).

[48] ibid art 11(1); BAT Conclusions: Document containing the sections of the BAT reference document that include conclusions regarding BAT, their description, information for assessing their applicability, emission levels associated with BAT, relevant monitoring, corresponding consumption levels, and, where applicable, related measures for site restoration.

[49] Commission implementing decision (EU) 2016/902 of 30 May 2016, establishing best available techniques (BAT) conclusions, under Directive 2010/75/EU of the European Parliament and of the Council, for common waste water and waste gas treatment/management systems in the chemical sector, OJ L152/23; Commission implementing decision (EU) 2022/2427 of 6 December 2022, establishing the best available techniques (BAT) conclusions, under Directive 2010/75/EU of the European Parliament and of the Council on industrial emissions, for common waste gas management and treatment systems in the chemical sector, OJ L 318/157.

[50] N 4819/2021, 'Integrated framework for waste management—Integration of Directives 2018/851 and 2018/852 of the European Parliament and of the Council 30 May 2018 amending Directive 2008/98/EC on waste and Directive 94/62/EC on packaging and packaging waste, framework for the organisation of the Hellenic Recycling Organisation, provisions on plastic products and the protection of the natural environment, spatial planning—urban planning, energy and related urgent regulations', FEK A 129/23 July 2021.

[51] ibid art 2(2)a.

Law 4014/2011, the EIA must encompass the description, evaluation, and analysis of the potential significant impacts that the proposed project or activity may pose to the environment through waste disposal.[52] Thus, the Environmental Terms Approval includes the terms and methods of waste disposal.

This means that waste producers, including operators of electrolysers, must comply with the general waste management requirements of Article 35 of Law 4819/2021, which mandate the safe disposal of waste to protect human health and the environment, in particular:[53]

(a) *without risk to water, air, soil, plants or animals;*
(b) *without causing a nuisance through noise or odours; and*
(c) *without adversely affecting the countryside or places of special interest.*[54]

Moreover, the original waste producers are responsible for either treating the waste themselves or outsourcing the treatment to a licensed dealer, organization, or entity conducting waste treatment operations.[55] This can also be arranged through an agreement with a public or private waste collection entity.[56] Consequently, the wastewater generated after electrolysis must undergo treatment before disposal.

Additionally, waste produced during the pre-electrolysis stage, particularly from water purification, which often generates brine, also requires proper management to ensure compliance with environmental standards and to minimize ecological impact. In conclusion, effective waste management is a crucial element of the permitting process for electrolysers. Developers must either implement a customized waste management system or entrust the treatment to specialized, licensed entities. This concludes the substantive requirements for obtaining an Environmental Terms Approval to operate an electrolyser in the Greek system. As the first of four umbrella permits that must be obtained, we now turn to the second: the building permit.

3.7 Building Permit

3.7.1 Initial requirements of the Building Permit

The building code serves as a crucial law in Greece, governing various aspects of construction activity across the country.[57] Typically, it applies to all developments unless specific rules have been established by a particular plan for the area. The building permit is a mandatory requirement for any structural activity in Greece. The relevant question is whether an electrolyser qualifies as a 'building' under this code. According

[52] N 4014/2011 (n 16) Annex II (5).
[53] N 4819/2021 (n 50) arts 34 and 35; art 34 is direct implementation of art 12 of Directive 2008/98/EC, as amended by para 14 of art 1 of Directive (EU) 2018/851.
[54] ibid art 35; art 35 is direct implementation of art 13 of Directive 2008/98/EC.
[55] ibid art 41 (1); art 41 is direct implementation of art 15 of Directive 2008/98/EC.
[56] ibid.
[57] N 4067/2012, 'New Building Regulation', FEK A 79/09 April 2012.

to the building code, 'a structure is any kind of construction, regardless of materials or construction method, that is firmly attached to the ground, is not motorised, and cannot be towed'.[58] Electrolysers meet this definition as they are commonly fixed installations connected to permanent infrastructure such as water and electricity, designed for long-term operation, and not intended for temporary use or relocation. Furthermore, the code defines a 'building' as a structure consisting of rooms and facilities, intended for the temporary or permanent residence of users.[59] While electrolysers are not designed for residence, the code also identifies 'special buildings' as those where more than 50% of the total floor area is used for non-residential purposes.[60] Thus, an electrolyser qualifies as a 'special building' because it is a structure that contains facilities and is primarily used for industrial purposes, not residence. These definitions collectively establish that for the installation of an electrolyser, regardless of the technology it uses, a building permit is required.[61]

In Greece, building permits are regulated mainly by Law 4495/2017.[62] According to Law 4495/2017, the building permit is defined as the administrative act that allows the execution of any construction work, and that is issued by the competent building service of the municipality.[63] The process of submission, control, and issuance of the building permit is carried out exclusively via an electronic platform.[64]

The application is carried out by the so-called administrator, who could be one of the engineers of the project or a technical company who is assigned by the project developer to submit the required supporting documents and data for the issuance of the administrative act.[65] The administrator of the application submits the required supporting documents to the information system, under their own responsibility.[66]

Contrary to the usual procedure, in which the permit is issued automatically after the submission of the documents, electrolysers require pre-approval as they are considered projects of particular environmental and residential importance.[67] Projects related to hydrogen are considered to be of environmental significance for the following reasons. On the one hand, hydrogen is classified as a dangerous substance, as it is included in a Joint Ministerial Decision describing (among other things) what constitutes dangerous substances, and on the other hand because an EIA is required.[68] This means that all the submitted documents will be thoroughly checked and approved by the competent construction authority. The building permit is valid for four years from its issuance.[69]

[58] ibid art 2(16).
[59] ibid art 2(42).
[60] ibid art 2(21).
[61] N 4495/2017 art 29(1), 'Control and protection of the Built Environment and other provisions', FEK A 167/03 November 2017.
[62] ibid.
[63] ibid art 28(a).
[64] ibid art 33(1).
[65] YA ΥΠΕΝ/ΥΠΡΓ/48123/6983/2018 art 2(1), FEK B, 3136/31 July 2018.
[66] ibid.
[67] N 4495/2017 (n 61) art 35(2γ).
[68] KYA 172058/2016 Part 2 of Annex I, FEK 354/B 17 February 2016.
[69] N 4495/2017 (n 61) art 42(2).

The process is twofold, divided into a pre-approval check and the usual procedure that has been discussed previously. The required documentation for both processes differs. The required documents for a pre-approval check for a building permit application are as follows: a topographic diagram, a building coverage diagram, the property ownership document, and a technical report accurately describing the project, the size, and use.[70] After the pre-approval check is completed, the administrator will follow the aforementioned usual procedure, and the permit will be issued automatically. The required documentation for the building permit, except the ones that were already submitted during the pre-approval, are as follows: architectural study (which includes the study of passive fire protection); static study/study of structural adequacy; study of plumbing and drainage systems; electrical and mechanical building installation study; waste management plan; active fire protection study (according to the existing provisions on fire protection, which is drawn up based on the passive fire protection study to be discussed below); and, an explanatory statement of section 1 of Article 3 of Law 1577/1985, as well as approvals of other services and administrative bodies, where required.[71] The process necessitates the submission and review of numerous documents, which can potentially delay approval. Nevertheless, these requirements are essential for electrolyser installations because they ensure compliance with safety and structural standards.

3.7.2 Fire protection requirements as additional prerequisites for the Building Permit

As part of the broader safety requirements for building permits, fire protection plays a key role in ensuring the safe operation of facilities like electrolysers. Fire Protection approval, as mentioned earlier, is inherently important and required as part of the application for a building permit. This brings us to both the Active and Passive Fire Protection Assessments.

The significance of these assessments for electrolysers lies in hydrogen's flammability, more specifically the wide concentration range of 4% to 75% in air, which surpasses that of other common fuels.[72] Both Passive and Active Fire Protection Assessments are integral to the building permit application process, requiring developers to address specific risks associated with electrolysers.

3.7.2.1 Passive fire protection assessment

Passive fire protection focuses on designing and constructing facilities to minimize the impact of potential fire outbreaks. For electrolysers, this involves:

[70] ibid art 35(5).

[71] ibid art 40(1); the above mentioned are required in the majority of cases and are considered basic. However, supporting documents may be required—approvals from various municipal services (Forestry Service, Archaeologies).

[72] Hydrogen Tools, 'Hydrogen Flames' (Hydrogen Tools) <https://h2tools.org/bestpractices/laboratory-safety/laboratory-operations/hydrogen-hazards/hydrogen-flames> accessed 22 June 2024.

- Fire compartments: dividing the facility into fire-resistant compartments to delay the spread of fire.
- Structural adequacy: ensuring the load-bearing elements maintain stability during a fire.

According to Law 4495/2017, the passive fire protection assessment is included in the architectural study and must be approved by the municipal Building Service, during the building permit application process.[73] The passive fire protection assessment seems to be particularly crucial for electrolysers because they mitigate the risks of fire escalation in facilities handling flammable substances like hydrogen.

3.7.2.2 Active fire protection

Active fire protection involves suppressive measures and systems that become activated in response to a fire. For electrolysers the relevance of these systems lies in mitigating risks associated with hydrogen—a flammable substance. Effective fire protection ensures the safety of personnel, equipment, and surrounding infrastructure while minimizing operational downtime. Key components of active fire protection in electrolysers include permanent systems, such as alarms, sprinklers, and foaming systems integrated into the facility's infrastructure, and semi-permanent solutions, such as portable foam generators and containers. Legislation for fire protection systems depends on the building use and permit date. Compliance requires not only adherence to technical specifications but also regular maintenance, including visual inspections and pressure gauge checks. This ensures systems remain functional and responsive in case of emergencies.

For project developers, the focus should be on integrating fire safety considerations early into the planning and design phases. The following elements are particularly significant for electrolysers:

1. *Hydrogen-specific risks*: Hydrogen's flammability and potential for rapid escalation make detection and suppression systems critical. Developers must prioritize systems that can detect leaks and suppress fires effectively, such as gas detectors integrated with automated foam or sprinkler systems.
2. *Accessibility and maintenance*: Given the complexity of electrolyser facilities, ensuring accessibility for inspections and maintenance is vital.

The fire safety offices of the competent Fire Service are responsible for the control, approval of studies, and the granting of active fire protection certificates.

The regulatory requirements for the building permit, including fire protection assessments, ensure the safe design and operation of electrolysers. They serve as the

[73] N 4495/2017 (n 61) art 40(1ε); The architectural study includes the study of passive fire protection, static study/study of structural adequacy, study of plumbing and drainage systems, electrical and mechanical building installation study.

second of the four umbrella permits in the Greek system and are necessary as precursor to obtaining the Approval of Establishment mandated under the SEVESO Directive for projects involving hazardous substances like hydrogen, which is discussed in the following subsection.

3.8 Approval of Establishment

In line with the overarching framework for manufacturing activities in Greece, the establishment and operation of hydrogen production facilities are governed by Articles 17 to 40 of Law 3982/2011, subject, however, to the specific provisions introduced by the most recent hydrogen legislation.[74] Facilities handling hydrogen which is classified as a dangerous substance under the SEVESO Directive (implemented through Joint Ministerial Decision 172058/2016), require an Approval of Establishment.[75] An Approval of Establishment is a mandatory permit for facilities engaging in potentially hazardous activities. This stage is perhaps the most critical during the authorization process as it verifies that the planned activity aligns with local regulations, land use requirements, and safety standards. Crucially this Approval of Establishment always addresses the operator or future operator of the electrolyser and not necessarily the project developer, if these should be two different entities. It is therefore instrumental for the operation stage, not only for the planning stage. The Directorate of Regional Unity Development at the project's location is the competent authority for issuing the Approval of Establishment.[76] In cases of hydrogen facilities that are to be connected to the National Natural Gas System, the Hydrogen System, the Natural Gas Distribution Network, or the Hydrogen Transmission or Distribution Network, the Approval of Establishment is granted only after the connection offer from the relevant system operator has been issued and accepted by the applicant in accordance with the applicable Network Management Code.[77]

Hydrogen's inclusion in the SEVESO framework requires project operators to submit a *Notification File* or *Safety Report*,[78] which must detail:

- The amount of hydrogen present or expected.
- Whether the facility qualifies as a lower-tier or upper-tier establishment according to Annex I (for hydrogen production the lower tier threshold is 5 tonnes/day, and the higher tier threshold is 50 tonnes/day).[79]

[74] N 5215/2025 (n 3) art 34(1).

[75] N 3982/2011, 'Simplification of the licensing of technical professional and manufacturing activities and business parks and other provisions', FEK A 143/17 June 2011; KYA 172058/2016 (n 68); Directive 2012/18/EU of the European Parliament and of the Council 4 July 2012 on the control of major-accident hazards involving dangerous substances, amending and subsequently repealing Council Directive 96/82/EC Text with EEA relevance [2012] OJ L 197/1 (SEVESO-III Directive).

[76] N 3982/2011 (n 75) art 17(14); the Directorate of Regional Unity Development is a public authority and operates under the jurisdiction of the relevant Region.

[77] N 5215/2025 (n 3) art 30(3).

[78] YA 64618/856/Φ15/2018 art 1(2γ), FEK 2278/B 15 June 2018; KYA 172058/2016 (n 68).

[79] KYA 172058/2016 (n 68) Annex 1 Part II (15).

Project operators may consult the General Chemical State Laboratory for clarification on substance classification.[80]

The Notification File, submitted by the operator of the establishment regardless of whether it is a higher or lower-tier facility, is evaluated by the competent authority to ensure it contains all necessary information.[81] It must include a *Major-Accident Prevention Policy Report* (MAPPR), outlining:

- The operator's safety objectives;
- Risk control measures;
- Commitment to ongoing safety improvements.[82]

Following the submission, an on-site inspection is conducted, and the Approval of Establishment is issued.

In addition to the Notification File, operators of upper-tier establishments must submit a comprehensive Safety Report with their application.[83] The Safety Report is reviewed at least every five years or after a major accident.[84] Its registration, alongside the Approval of the Notification File, is required for both the Approval of Establishment and Operational Permit, incorporating any additional conditions or restrictions identified during the evaluation. Following the Safety Report's approval and an on-site inspection, the Approval of Establishment is issued. This is the third of the four umbrella permits required. The chapter will now turn to the last of the four required umbrella permits, the Operational Permit.

3.9 Operational Permit

3.9.1 Initial requirements of the Operational Permit

Following the granting of the Approval of Establishment, which entails the evaluation and authorization of the plans for an electrolyser facility, the next pivotal stage is the

[80] ibid art 5(B).

[81] The Notification File must include the following:

Maps and topographic diagrams at a scale of 1:5000, showing various useful elements with coordinates, if available from the relevant authorities.
Complete topographic map.
List of dangerous substances if no prior opinion as provided for in paragraph B of Article 5 has been obtained. A template of this list is included in Annex VIII.
Description of the activity that is carried out and is expected to be carried out in the facility or in the storage area.
Summary of non-technical content in plain and understandable language to facilitate the provision of understandable information to the public by the licensing authority; KYA 172058/2016 (n 68) art 6.

[82] ibid art 7.

[83] ibid art 9(A)1. The report must include:

Data and information from Annexes I and III, identifying contributors.
Risk analysis and accident scenarios (Annex IX).
An internal emergency plan.
Scientific documentation supporting the findings.

[84] ibid art 9(Δ).

acquisition of an Operational Permit. This marks a crucial milestone in the regulatory process, signifying the transition from planning to operational readiness. While the Approval of Establishment ensures that the plans comply with safety, land use, and environmental regulations, the Operational Permit validates that the facility has been constructed in accordance with the approved specifications and that all operational conditions have been met.

This transition from the approval of plans to operational readiness is particularly significant for hydrogen-related facilities, given the complexities and inherent risks associated with hydrogen, a substance classified as dangerous under the SEVESO Directive.[85] Law 5215/2025 further clarifies that once the Approval of Establishment is granted and the installation of the unit and any required connection works are completed, the hydrogen producer must apply to the competent System Operator for the start of trial operation.[86] The trial operation may last up to six months.[87] Upon successful completion, the System Operator issues a Trial Operation Completion Certificate, which must be submitted along with other documentation to the competent authority in order to obtain the Operational Permit.[88] The Operational Permit, issued by the Development Directorate of the relevant Regional Unit, acts as the final safeguard, confirming that all infrastructure, safety measures, and environmental protections are fully in place.[89] To secure the permit, project developers must submit the requisite documentation, as stipulated in Article 5 of Ministerial Decision 64618/856/Φ.15/2018, thereby completing the permitting process prior to the commencement of operations.[90] These documents are scrutinized to ensure compliance with regulatory standards, facilitating the granting of the Operational Permit. In case that the project is categorized as an upper-tier establishment, the registration of the Safety Report and the Approval of the Notification File constitute a necessary condition, also for the issuance of the Operation Approval.[91] Any additional terms, measures, and restrictions that arose during the evaluation process of the Safety Report will be included.[92] After the examination and approval of the submitted documents, an on-site inspection is performed and the Operational Permit is issued. Following this, the Water Use Permit will be analysed, as it is a document that must be submitted to the relevant public authority to obtain an Operational Permit.

[85] SEVESO-III Directive, Annex I Part 2(15).
[86] N 5215/2025 (n 3) art 34(2).
[87] ibid.
[88] ibid art 34(3).
[89] N 3982/2011 (n 75) art 17(14).
[90] YA 64618/856/Φ.15/2018 (n 78); General documentation requirements include: (i) a summary technical description of the establishment, signed by a legally authorized engineer, which must include a topographic diagram showing building facilities, necessary signage, and traffic regulations within the premises; a description of the activity (eg production process, types of raw materials and products, and a flowchart of tasks performed); and a site plan indicating the placement of machinery along with a list of machinery specifying their power ratings; (ii) an affidavit from the authorized engineer certifying the structural adequacy and industrial-technical suitability of the building; (iii) the Environmental Terms Approval; (iv) a Building Permit; and (v) a water use permit.
[91] KYA 172058/2016 (n 68) art 9(Γ)4.
[92] ibid.

3.9.2 Water management requirements as additional prerequisites for the Operational Permit

Water is a crucial element for the production of hydrogen via water electrolysis. In Greece water management is regulated under Law 3199/2003 'Water protection and Management'. In particular, water use is divided into water supply, irrigation, industrial use, energy use, and recreational use.[93] The process of categorizing water use is outlined in Annex I of Joint Ministerial Decision No. 146896/2014.[94] In conjunction with Ministerial Decision No 36060/1155/E.103, which designates the electrolyser as an industrial activity, it is likely that water use associated with this activity will be classified as industrial use. While there are no differences in the permitting process between different uses, water use may relate to surface water or groundwater, either as basic use or in the context of a water resources utilization project.[95]

According to Law 3199/2003, '[a]ny legal or natural person can use water or carry out water resource utilisation projects to satisfy their actual needs. It can also carry out water resource utilisation projects for needs beyond its own or independently of them, as long as they serve the common good'.[96]

For permits regarding water supply and water use, the interested party must apply for a Water Use Permit to the regional authority of the location of the project.[97] The permit is issued after a proposal from the competent Water Department of the Decentralised Administration.[98] The availability of the quantities of water to be utilized must be documented, as well as the feasibility of its issuance in accordance with the relevant Management Plan and the measures determined by the Program of Measures.[99] At the discretion of the Secretary General of the Decentralised Administration, and following endorsement by the Special Secretariat for Water, additional or more specific conditions may be imposed during the permitting process.[100] These may include further assessments to address the requirements of a particular water use or project category.[101] Additionally, the possibility to impose restrictive measures on the uses and operation of projects exists, especially when coupled with unique circumstances. Water resource utilization projects, including groundwater extraction and surface water extraction from lakes, require an Environmental Permit, which includes the submission of an EIA.[102] This requirement is incorporated into the project's Environmental Terms Approval. For additional information, please consult Joint Ministerial Decision 1958/2012, which categorizes each water resource utilization project into categories A and B, as well as Law 4014/2011.[103]

[93] N 3199/2003 art 10(1), 'Protection and management of water resources—Harmonisation with Directive 2000/60/EC of the European Parliament and the Council of 23 October 2000', FEK A 280/9 December 2003.
[94] KYA 146896/2014 Annex I, FEK 2878/B 27 October 2014.
[95] ibid art 2(1).
[96] N 3199/2003 (n 93) art 11(1).
[97] ibid art 11(2).
[98] ibid.
[99] ibid.
[100] ibid art 11(3).
[101] ibid.
[102] KYA 146896/2014 (n 94) art 2.
[103] YA 1958/2012, FEK B 21/13 January 2012; N 4014/2011 (n 16).

4. Recommendations to Improve the System

When examining the permitting regime for operating an electrolyser, it becomes evident that the process is lengthy and requires project developers and operators to secure four different umbrella permits. This requires engagement with multiple authorities and the acquisition of numerous documents, significantly extending the time needed for permitting. Such delays increase the cost of essential projects, and jeopardize the timely achievement of climate targets. Resulting from this as well as the analysis in this chapter substantive as well as procedural challenges have been identified that will now be discussed. The substantive requirements of the permitting process involve securing permits that address various legal and environmental considerations. The Greek regime deserves recognition for its integrated permit approach into the four umbrella permits, which aims to streamline the process in certain aspects. Specifically, the Environmental Terms Approval covers areas such as waste management, industrial emissions, and nature protection laws. The comprehensive nature of this permit enables the competent authority to evaluate environmental, conservation, and industrial aspects within a single framework.

However, certain aspects of the permitting regime lead to inefficiencies. Notably, several permits or documents must be submitted multiple times throughout the process. For example, the Environmental Terms Approval is required for both the Approval of Establishment and the Operational Permit. This redundancy creates inefficiency, as the same documents are reviewed multiple times. Implementing a one-stop-shop approach could mitigate this issue, by designating a single competent authority with which developers would engage and that coordinates the authorities. This would reduce the time required for the permitting process and provide better guidance, as developers would have only one contact point for information.

Additionally, the legal framework itself is notably complex. With multiple ministerial decisions and fragmented laws, assessing the requirements becomes a daunting task, requiring developers to make considerable efforts to identify and comply with applicable rules. Furthermore, the need to engage with various authorities throughout the process complicates coordination and increases the likelihood of delays. To address these issues, enhancing guidance and transparency by publishing detailed instructions on the permitting process, including step-by-step guidelines, on official government websites would help developers to understand and fulfil requirements.

5. Conclusion

Looking ahead, Greece is well positioned to become a key player in the European hydrogen economy, especially as the country continues to pursue its decarbonization goals. The development of a national hydrogen strategy is anticipated in the near future, which will provide a clearer roadmap for the integration of hydrogen into Greece's energy mix. With its strategic location in the Mediterranean and access to abundant renewable energy resources, particularly solar and wind power, Greece has the potential to become a hub for green hydrogen production.

Electrolysers will play a critical role in various applications across Greece's industrial, transportation, and energy sectors. In the industrial sector, hydrogen could be utilized for steel production, refining, and chemical industries, while the transport sector is likely to see hydrogen adoption in heavy-duty vehicles, buses, and possibly even aircraft. Furthermore, Greece's commitment to renewable energy growth, particularly wind and solar, coupled with ongoing efforts to improve its regulatory and policy framework, positions the country as a leading market for electrolyser technology. However, the permitting regime for hydrogen production remains complex. It is encouraging that the Greek government has taken an important first step with the adoption of Law 5215/2025, and it appears likely that by the end of 2025 a clearer regulatory framework will be in place to support the sector's growth. If the permitting process can be streamlined, Greece could emerge as a major hub for hydrogen production, not only to meet domestic energy needs but also in view of exporting hydrogen to neighbouring countries.

Further Reading

Primary Sources

Legislation

N 5215/2025, *Framework for the promotion of biomethane production, rules for the organization of the hydrogen production market and geographically limited hydrogen networks—Partial transposition of Directive (EU) 2024/1788 and other provisions for environmental protection*, FEK A 116/04.07.2025.

N 4014/2011, *Environmental Licensing of Projects and Activities, Regulation of Arbitrary Constructions in Connection with the Creation of an Environmental Balance, and Other Provisions within the Competence of the Ministry of the Environment*, FEK A 209/2011.

Policy Documents

Ministry of Environment and Energy, 'National Energy and Climate Plan' (December 2019) https://energy.ec.europa.eu/system/files/2020-01/el_final_necp_main_el_0.pdf accessed 10 November 2023.

Ministry of Environment and Energy, 'National Energy and Climate Plan Revised Edition' (August 2024) <https://commission.europa.eu/document/download/b2fbbef4-ee32-44fc-acce-49737bf492c8_en?filename=EL%20%E2%80%93%20FINAL%20UPDATED%20NECP%202021-2030%20%28English%29.pdf> accessed 1 February 2025.

Secondary Sources

Books

T Fortsakis and A Iliadou, *Δίκαιο της Ενέργειας* (3rd edn, Νομική Βιβλιοθήκη 2023).

I Kokkoris, *Το νέο μοντέλο λειτουργίας της ελληνικής ενεργειακής αγοράς: Από το μοντέλο κοινοπραξίας στο μοντέλο στόχος* (Νομική Βιβλιοθήκη 2023).

Online sources

Ministry of Environment and Energy, 'Natura 2000 Network' (Ministry of Environment and Energy) <https://ypen.gov.gr/perivallon/viopoikilotita/diktyo-natura-2000/> accessed 19 February 2024.

IX
United Kingdom—England and Wales

Silke Goldberg and Martyn Jarvis

1. Introduction

This chapter explores the planning and permitting regime for hydrogen electrolysers in the context of the wider UK decarbonization strategy.

For the purposes of this chapter, planning and permitting is understood in the narrow sense as the regulatory framework pertaining to the development of hydrogen electrolyser projects only. The evolving nature of the economic regulation of the British hydrogen sector such as the hydrogen business model is therefore out of scope of this chapter.[1]

Planning in the United Kingdom is the process by which projects obtain the fundamental permissions required to be constructed and operated. Without a planning consent of some form, the delivery of a project would be unlawful. Planning is a public or state function which is closely linked to and carried out in the context of the constitutional and public law frameworks and competencies of different institutions and levels

[1] For a general discussion on the evolving UK hydrogen sector, please see: Eadson, William, Phil Northall, and Hywel Jones, 'The UK Hydrogen Economy: A Review of Global, National and Regional Policy' (Sheffield Hallam University, Centre for Regional and Economic Research 2022) https://www.shu.ac.uk/-/media/home/research/cresr/reports/u/uk-hydrogen-economy.pdf accessed 22 May 2025; Rahmatallah Poudineh, 'Can UK Green Hydrogen Contract for Difference (CfD) Match the Cost-Saving Success of Renewable Electricity?' (Oxford Institute for Energy Studies Paper: ET 39, 2024) https://www.oxfordenergy.org/wpcms/wp-content/uploads/2024/10/ET39-Can-UK-green-hydrogen-contract-for-difference-CfD-match-the-cost-saving-success-of-renewable-electricity-final.pdf accessed 22 May 2025.

of the state as a whole.[2] As such, planning law is inherently shaped by constitutional and administrative law.[3]

This is also true for the UK,[4] whose complex constitutional and legislative landscape makes it necessary to clarify the geographical scope of this chapter. It has been said that '[t]he UK is characterized by asymmetrical devolution in which different territories are accorded different powers, but in each case land-use planning has been an important devolved power'.[5]

The Scotland Act of 1998 bestowed full responsibility for spatial planning and related issues to the Scottish Parliament; in Wales, planning competences were devolved to the Welsh Assembly Government under the Government of Wales Act 2006, which contained a specific duty to promote sustainable development as part of planning policy. In Northern Ireland, the relevant devolved powers of the Northern Ireland Assembly and the minister for the department of infrastructure are set out in the Northern Ireland Act 1998.

There is therefore an inherent tension between the formulation of energy policy as set by Westminster for the UK and the devolved nature of the planning regimes in the countries constituting the UK. Against this background, the geographical scope of this chapter is, in as far as energy policy is concerned, Great Britain, and, in as far as planning laws are concerned, England and Wales.

After this brief introduction, section 2 provides an overview of the role of hydrogen in the UK decarbonization strategy. Section 3 discusses the different available routes to obtain planning consent in England pursuant to the Town and Country Planning Act 1990 and the Planning Act 2008, whereas section 4 analyses the role of Environmental Impact Assessments (EIAs) in the context of the available routes to obtain planning consent pursuant to the aforementioned planning acts. Section 5 sets out some alternative planning consenting routes and section 6 summarizes further permits and authorizations outside the planning regime that will be required for hydrogen projects. Section 7 concludes with an evaluation of the current regime in the context of the UK government's ambitious hydrogen plans in the context of Clean Power 2030.

2. The Role of Hydrogen in the UK Decarbonization Strategy

Hydrogen has been a key part of the decarbonization strategy of two successive UK governments. The UK Government is subject to a legal requirement to ensure the UK carbon account for the year 2050 is at least 100% lower than the net UK emissions of

[2] J Tomaney and C Colomb, 'Devolution and Planning' in J Ferm and J Tomaney (eds), *Planning Practice: Critical Perspectives from the UK* (Routledge 2018) 20.

[3] On the concept of administrative law as ordo-political normative idea, see eg E Schmidt-Aßmann, *Das allgemeine Verwaltungsrecht als Ordnungsidee* (Berlin 2006).

[4] The United Kingdom comprises Scotland, England, Wales, and Northern Ireland. In turn, Scotland, England, and Wales constitute Great Britain (GB). When used as an adjective, 'UK' or 'British' are used as synonyms in this chapter.

[5] Tomaney and Colomb, (n 2) 20–35.

carbon dioxide in 1990 (Net Zero).[6] To evidence how this is to be achieved over time, Government is also subject to a legal requirement to set carbon budgets for each five-year period beginning 2008–2012.[7] The UK Government must also ensure that the net UK carbon account for each five-year period does not exceed the carbon budget relating to it.

In August 2021, the then UK Government published the UK Hydrogen Strategy[8] which identified that low carbon hydrogen will be essential for achieving Net Zero and meeting targets to reduce emissions ahead of 2050. That analysis by the Department of Energy and Industrial Strategy for the sixth carbon budget (for the period 2033–2037) suggests that 250–460 TWh of hydrogen could be needed in 2050, with between 5% and 50% of that amount to be produced by electrolysis.[9]

The UK Hydrogen Strategy envisaged the development of a hydrogen business model and small-scale production from the early 2020s onwards, increasing in scale and range of production, and culminating in regional or national networks with large-scale storage from the mid-2030s onwards.[10]

Subsequently and as part of the British Energy Security Strategy, the UK Government set its ambition of up to 10 GW of low carbon hydrogen production capacity by 2030, subject to affordability and value for money, with at least half of this coming from electrolytic hydrogen.[11]

After winning the July 2024 election, the new Labour government presented a detailed plan for the decarbonization of the energy system in Great Britain (GB), Clean Power 2030 (CP 2030). CP 2030 envisages '43–50 GW of offshore wind, 27–29 GW of onshore wind, and 45–47 GW of solar power [... as well as ...] flexible capacity, including 23–27 GW of battery capacity, 4–6 GW of long-duration energy storage, and development of flexibility technologies including gas carbon capture utilization & storage, hydrogen, and substantial opportunity for consumer-led flexibility'.[12] It set the aim of clean energy sources producing 'at least as much power as Great Britain consumes in total over the whole year, and at least 95% of Great Britain's generation'.[13]

In relation to hydrogen, CP2030 builds on the previous government's strategy and acknowledges that hydrogen to power (H2P) can play a key role within the GB electricity system. H2P faces several primary deployment barriers, including (i) investment risk arising from it being a first-of-a-kind technology; (ii) exposure to cross-chain risks from reliance on a nascent hydrogen value chain; and (iii) dependence on access to grid-scale hydrogen infrastructure, such as new transport pipelines and storage

[6] Climate Change Act 2008 s 1.
[7] ibid s 4.
[8] HM Government, UK Hydrogen Strategy (August 2021).
[9] Department for Business, Energy and Industrial Strategy, 'Impact Assessment for the Sixth Carbon Budget' (April 2021), (Table 6: Modelled sustainable energy carriers in 2050 (in TWh)).
[10] Global Hydrogen Council, 'United Kingdom' https://gh2.org/countries/united-kingdom accessed 22 May 2025.
[11] HM Government, British Energy Security Strategy (April 2022).
[12] HM Government, Clean Power 2030 Action Plan: A New Era of Clean Electricity—Main Report (13 December 2024) https://www.gov.uk/government/publications/clean-power-2030-action-plan/242aa00e-a82e-4f29-a785-9d7d690a1230#fn:2 accessed 22 May 2025.
[13] ibid.

facilities, all of which have long lead-in times and are in turn subject to their own regulatory and planning risks.

CP2030 intends to de-risk investment and bring forward H2P capacity at an accelerated rate. To support this, an updated version of the UK Hydrogen Strategy together with the relevant business models for revenue support for H2P projects has been announced as intended to be published by Government later in 2025 within CP2030.[14]

Accordingly, low carbon hydrogen production, including by electrolysis, is identified to be a vital competent of the UK's future decarbonized energy mix, and electrolytic hydrogen production facilities will need to be delivered at pace to contribute to meeting the UK's legal commitments in respect of Net Zero and pledges in relation to the decarbonization of its electricity system.

A variety of planning and other regulatory approvals are currently required to authorize the construction and use of hydrogen production facilities in the UK, and in this chapter we consider the permitting regime for electrolytic hydrogen production facilities in England and Wales, including the infrastructure and activities which are required to support their function. We consider whether the existing regulatory regimes and systems in place to administer those are capable of facilitating the delivery and operation of the necessary infrastructure at the pace required.

3. Planning Permission and Development Consent

In England and Wales, there is no dedicated regime for the permitting of hydrogen projects. Such projects must achieve consents, permits, and licence authorizations pursuant to multiple different regulations.

One of the most fundamental consents that must be obtained for any hydrogen production facility is the authorization to construct and use a development, which can be obtained in the form of a planning permission or, in certain circumstances, a development consent. This section provides an overview of the two main routes to obtaining the authorization to construct and use development under the Town And Country Planning Act 1990 (subsection 3.1) and the Planning Act 2008 (subsection 3.2), respectively.

3.1 Planning Permission and the Town and Country Planning Act 1990

The primary planning permitting route for electrolytic hydrogen production facilities in England and Wales is the Town and Country Planning Act 1990 (the 1990 Act).

Section 57 of the 1990 Act provides that planning permission is required for development, and section 55 of the 1990 Act defines development as 'the carrying out of

[14] See ibid.

building, engineering, mining or other operations in, on, over or under land, or the making of any material change in the use of any buildings or other land'.

Applications for planning permission are determined by the local planning authority for the area in which the development is proposed, save for in circumstances where they are called in[15] for determination by the Secretary of State or the Mayor of London, or are the subject of an appeal (where an appointed inspector will take the decision on behalf of the Secretary of State). There are 337 local planning authorities in England, and there are twenty-two in Wales.

The statutory timescale for an application for planning permission to be decided following submission is thirteen weeks,[16] or sixteen weeks where the development is a category of development for which an EIA is required (discussed further below).[17] However, whilst this is the statutory timescale, in practice local planning authorities will require more time to consider applications. Consultation with stakeholders and the surrounding community will also be undertaken in advance of any application being submitted.

Accordingly, the application process for major developments would rarely be less than twelve months at the current time, and in practice this may span across several years for larger hydrogen production facilities.

The planning system in England and Wales is plan-led at a local level, and for each local planning authority there is a development plan which contains policies in respect of what development can be built and where this can be located within the local authority area. The development plan comprises local plans, neighbourhood plans, and in some instances spatial development strategies.

Local plans are prepared by local planning authorities and set out their vision and framework for the future development and use of land in their area. Broadly they identify what development is needed, where it should be located, and areas of land which are protected from future development.[18]

Neighbourhood plans are a further tier of planning policy relating to defined areas of land within a local planning authority area, which are prepared by parish or town councils or local groups. Neighbourhood plans can contain policies which further identify the development to be located in and the infrastructure which should be provided in the defined neighbourhood area.[19]

Spatial development strategies are also made in some areas with elected mayors or combined authorities, for example in Greater London. A spatial development strategy contains strategic policies for the development and use of land in the area they cover. The Planning and Infrastructure Bill[20] will enable the government to introduce a system of strategic planning across England.

[15] Town and Country Planning Act 1990, s 77.

[16] The Town and Country Planning (Development Management Procedure) (England) Order 2015 art 34(2)(a).

[17] The Town and Country Planning (Environmental Impact Assessment) Regulations 2017, reg 68(2).

[18] The Town and Country Planning (Local Planning) (England) Regulations 2012, reg 5.

[19] Planning and Compulsory Purchase Act 2004, s 38A.

[20] UK Parliament, Planning and Infrastructure Bill https://bills.parliament.uk/bills/3946 accessed on 22 September 2025.

In addition, the National Planning Policy Framework (NPPF)[21] sets out the UK Government's planning policies for England and how those should be applied. The NPPF provides policies in respect of plan-making and decision-taking. All development plan documents are required to be prepared in accordance with the NPPF, and whilst the NPPF does not form part of the development plan it is a material consideration for the purpose of decisions on whether to grant planning permission. The NPPF applies to England only, and in Wales the equivalent policy documents are Future Wales—the National Plan 2040[22] and Planning Policy Wales.[23]

In addition, and as discussed further below, national planning policy for Nationally Significant Infrastructure Projects (NSIPs) contains some support for low carbon hydrogen projects on a general basis, and this policy will be a material consideration for the purpose of decision on whether to grant planning permission.[24]

Applications for planning permission are required to be determined in accordance with the development plan applicable to the area in which the proposed development is located unless material considerations indicate otherwise.[25]

Despite this, there are no express planning policies which relate to hydrogen production facilities within the NPPF (or the equivalent Welsh documents). Instead, there is general support for renewable and low carbon energy infrastructure in the NPPF, and it is stated that development plans should contain policies which provide for the delivery of such infrastructure.

Given the nascence of hydrogen production technology and the processes for the production on local plans, which more recently has arguably stalled in light of wider reforms to the planning system for England,[26] it is rare that a local plan would contain specific policies in respect of hydrogen production facilities or identify sites where such facilities are most appropriate to be located.

Accordingly, whilst support for hydrogen production facilities can be gained from policies which support the increase of the use and supply of renewable and low carbon energy more generally, and the likelihood of obtaining consent will be more likely where they are located in areas which are of a nature which more appropriately accommodates them, low carbon hydrogen production development proposals will often be speculative in principle and in terms of their proposed location. Consequently it is likely that additional pre-application engagement will be required with the relevant local planning authority and other stakeholders to confirm

[21] HM Government, Ministry of Housing, Communities and Local Government, National Planning Policy Framework (December 2024).

[22] The Welsh Government, Future Wales—The National Plan 2040 (February 2021).

[23] The Welsh Government, Planning Policy Wales, 12th edn (February 2024).

[24] HM Government, Department for Energy Security & Net Zero, Overarching National Policy Statement for Energy (EN-1) (November 2023) para 1.2.2.

[25] Town and Country Planning Act 1990 s 70(2), and Planning and Compulsory Purchase Act 2004 s 38A.

[26] HM Government, 'Proposed Reforms to the National Planning Policy Framework and Other Changes to the Planning System: Outcome of Consultation' (February 2025) https://www.gov.uk/government/consultations/proposed-reforms-to-the-national-planning-policy-framework-and-other-changes-to-the-planning-system/proposed-reforms-to-the-national-planning-policy-framework-and-other-changes-to-the-planning-system accessed 22 May 2025.

the appropriateness of proposals before submission, further lengthening the overall consenting timescales.

It is also arguable that the existing plan-led system in England and Wales is a fragmented policy framework where policies must be read across multiple documents which are not always consistent with one another, and where other material planning considerations can lead to outcomes which are not consistent with development plan policies. As a result, it is a system which lacks the clarity and certainty required to guarantee the grant of planning permission for hydrogen production facilities in appropriate locations. This is even more problematic when seeking to rely on policies which are not specifically focused on the type of development for which planning permission is sought, and where it can be necessary to shoehorn the assessment of a development against policies which are not directly applicable. Moreover, in the face of rapid innovation, planning policies within development plan documents are often not sufficiently up to date to provide the support needed to facilitate the delivery of planning permissions for emerging technologies.

The lack of certainty of outcomes which is inherent in the England and Wales plan-led system as a result can be seen as a significant failing of the planning system for England and Wales, which is adversely impacting the delivery of development and which deters investment.[27] This is the case for many types of development, and it can be seen how this is likely to be an issue for hydrogen production facilities until a more certain planning policy framework is provided.

Moreover, because of the nascent nature of hydrogen production technology in England and Wales and without a clear and robust approach to the location of such infrastructure and requirements for policies in respect of the same, it will often be the case that local planning authorities will require additional time to understand the proposed development and its potential impacts, which can delay the granting of planning permissions and the delivery of such infrastructure.

A chronic shortage of resources within local planning authorities coupled with the general ever-increasing demand on their services in the current economic and social climate within the UK is also unarguably a contributing factor to the delay of planning permissions for all types of development, including hydrogen production facilities.

Accordingly, whilst obtaining planning permission is the primary consenting route for electrolytic hydrogen production facilities, it is evident how that consenting regime has not yet established a clear and robust consenting process for such facilities in which developers and investors can have confidence.

[27] On the impact of planning law and its application, see Confederation of British Industry, 'Plan for Growth by Turning Unfit Planning System into a Magnet for Investment' (30 August 2024) https://www.cbi.org.uk/media-centre/articles/plan-for-growth-by-turning-unfit-planning-system-into-a-magnet-for-investment accessed 22 May 2025. Alex Irwin-Hunt, 'Why the UK's Planning System is Hindering Investment' (FDI Intelligence, 27 June 2024) https://www.fdiintelligence.com/content/f93f7d2a-0952-5eec-a03b-4052a09c028c accessed 22 May 2025.

3.2 Development Consent and the Planning Act 2008

Within England and Wales, there is a further planning consenting regime in respect of infrastructure which is deemed to be nationally significant by virtue of being major projects relating to energy, transport, water, and waste, established by the Planning Act 2008 (the 2008 Act) and known as the NSIP regime. This regime applies to major infrastructure in England and in Wales, albeit to differing extents.

The 2008 Act establishes the types of projects which may be NSIPs and the thresholds above which projects are NSIPs. Where an infrastructure project is an NSIP, development consent will be required, which must be obtained from the relevant Secretary of State. Hydrogen production facilities will *prima facie* not be NSIPs as they are not a type of development stated to be such. However, that does not mean that these projects cannot find themselves within the scope of the NSIP regime, and there may be merit in them being brought into this regime, particularly where they are part of a hydrogen system with elements which are otherwise defined as an NSIP.

Development consent is obtained via the making of a Development Consent Order (DCO), which is a statutory instrument made by Parliament and which in addition to granting development consent may contain several other necessary authorizations, such as compulsory purchase powers for land and to undertake works required to highways. To this end, a DCO is the England and Wales equivalent of the one-stop-shop planning consent for major infrastructure.

Section 14 of the 2008 Act establishes the projects which are nationally significant infrastructure projects, subject to the meeting of relevant thresholds stated in later provisions of the 2008 Act.[28]

This includes the following elements of relevance to low carbon hydrogen systems:

(1) the construction or extension of an electricity generating station—within England with a generating capacity of more than 50 MW onshore and 100 MW offshore, and in Wales more than 350 MW;[29]
(2) the installation of an electric line above ground—with a nominal voltage of 132 kV or higher and with a length of two kilometres or more;[30]
(3) development relating to underground gas storage facilities—with a capacity of at least 43 million standard cubic metres or a flow rate of at least 4.5 million standard cubic metres per day;[31] and
(4) the construction of a pipeline by a gas transporter—where the pipeline is wholly or partly in England (and only to such part as is within England), the pipeline is more than 800 millimetres in diameter and more than 40 kilometres in length

[28] Planning Act 2008, ss 15–30A.
[29] ibid s 15.
[30] ibid s 16.
[31] ibid s 17.

and the gas conveyed for supply is to at least 50,000 customers, or potential customers, of one or more gas suppliers.[32]

Should any hydrogen production facility be related to any NSIP development, including for example where a renewable generating station with a capacity of more than 50 MW is to be delivered to power it, it may be necessary to consider the merits of it being consented pursuant to the same NSIP regime. This is the case because of the difference in process that is required, including in particular timescales, and what could be the benefit of an integrated hydrogen system being consented wholly by a DCO and able to benefit from the broader consenting scope which this provides for (eg powers to acquire land and rights over land).

To be consented via a DCO an applicant would need to identify why that hydrogen production facility is an associated development,[33] for example by virtue of how it will support the operation of the principal NSIP development (such as its connection to the generating station or storage facilities which it will supply), or a direction may be sought from the Secretary of State to direct that the production facility development requires a DCO on the basis that it is or forms part of a project in the field of energy. The Secretary of State also needs to consider if the project (or proposed project) is of national significance, either by itself or when considered with one or more other energy projects (or proposed projects).[34]

It should be noted that in Wales a direction that development should be consented via a DCO is not able to be sought, and the scope of what may be associated development is also much more limited and would not include a hydrogen production facility. Accordingly in Wales a planning permission must be obtained for any electrolytic hydrogen production facilities.

The process to obtain a DCO is more prescriptive than the process to obtain a planning permission, involving a more intensive and defined pre-application consultation, application examination and decision-making process reflecting the requirements for the consenting of major infrastructure.

It is also inherently longer than the planning permission process. Typically, based on experience, an applicant would require around four years to navigate the NSIP process from project inception to the granting of development consent by the Secretary of State, and the process will often take longer than this, particularly where the project is considered to be controversial (which major infrastructure often can be) or where there is a need to consult on proposals more than once.

The NSIP regime is also one where decisions are to be taken in accordance with planning policy unless other considerations indicate otherwise,[35] with such planning policy being contained in National Policy Statements (NPSs) made by the Secretary of State which relate to specific types of NSIP. The most recent version of the Overarching

[32] ibid s 20.
[33] ibid s 115(2).
[34] ibid s 35.
[35] ibid s 104.

Energy NPS EN-1,[36] which sets out the government's policy for delivery of major energy infrastructure, was adopted in November 2023 and it has specific regard to and provides planning policies in respect of the role of low carbon hydrogen infrastructure.

This NPS confirms the content of the UK Hydrogen Strategy and the ambition for up to 10 GW of low carbon hydrogen production capacity by 2030.[37] It establishes that there is an urgent need for all types of low carbon hydrogen infrastructure to allow hydrogen to play its role in the transition to Net Zero.[38] The NPS also considers the current and future role of and need for low carbon hydrogen infrastructure, including that applicants will be expected to consider foreseeable future demand when considering the size and route of their investments.

As such, the overarching Energy NPS EN-1 provides general support for hydrogen production facilities and, moreover, low carbon hydrogen infrastructure, and is of assistance to facilitate the delivery of such infrastructure in appropriate locations.

Whilst that is the case, it is also clear that the consenting of any low carbon hydrogen infrastructure through the NSIP regime would be inherently time consuming and resource intensive. Whilst this may not impact the bringing to market of electrolytic hydrogen production facilities (where those are consented under the 1990 Act), it will inevitably impact on timescales for the delivery of the low carbon hydrogen systems which they must form a part of so as to meaningfully support electricity system decarbonization and the transition to Net Zero.

Accordingly, the NSIP regime is not particularly well suited to consenting electrolytic hydrogen production facilities of the scale currently envisaged in England and at the required pace, and it can be seen how the mandatory application of the NSIP regime to other hydrogen system components could delay decisions being taken on the delivery of electrolytic hydrogen production facilities which would be connected to them.

4. Environmental Impact Assessment

This section sets out the requirements for EIAs in the context of planning applications for hydrogen projects. EIA does not of itself comprise a separate consent from a planning permission or development consent; rather the findings of an EIA are required to be considered as an integrated part of the decision on whether to grant planning permission or development consent. Nonetheless, the need to undertake an EIA and for this to be considered by the relevant decision-maker will inevitably add to the process to produce an application and to obtain the relevant planning permit.

[36] HM Government, Department for Energy Security & Net Zero, Overarching National Policy Statement for Energy (EN-1), November 2023.
[37] ibid para 3.3.49.
[38] ibid para 3.4.12.

Within the UK, the requirements of the EU's Environmental Impact Assessment (EIA) Directive (2011/92/EU[39] as amended by 2014/52/EU[40]) is transposed into UK regulation by the Town and Country (Environmental Impact Assessment) Regulations 2017 in relation to planning permissions and the Infrastructure Planning (Environmental Impact Assessment) Regulations 2017 in relation to applications for a DCO.

The relevant EIA regulations detail the types of development which are EIA development, which includes schedule 1 development and schedule 2 development where such developments are likely to have significant effects on the environment by virtue of factors such as its nature, size, or location.

Hydrogen production facilities are not classified as schedule 1 developments. They could however constitute schedule 2 development depending on the characteristics of the relevant development and the likelihood of such characteristics giving rise to significant effects on the environment. Should the area of the development exceed more than 5 hectares, the relevant development will meet the threshold to be subject to an EIA as an industrial estate development project,[41] subject to the consideration of the other relevant factors.

Judgments of the European Court of Justice (ECJ) continue to provide relevant guidance post-Brexit in relation to the interpretation of the EIA Directive. Pursuant to case law, it is necessary to take a broad approach so that projects which are likely to have significant effects on the environment by virtue of factors such as its nature, size or location do not avoid assessment.

In C-72/95 *Kraaijeveld and others v Gedeputeerde staten van Zuid-Holland* (colloquially known as the Dutch Dykes case), the ECJ considered the scope of the expression 'canalisation and flood-relief works' in point 10(e) of Annex II to the EIA Directive to determine whether this would encapsulate works to reinforce dykes. In that case the ECJ held that '[t]he wording of the directive indicates that it has a wide scope and a broad purpose'[42] and concluded that point 10(e) encompassed 'all works for retaining water and preventing floods—and therefore the dyke works—even if not all the linguistic versions are so precise'.[43]

Accordingly, it could be argued that whilst not expressly referred to, production installations may need to be subject to EIA in the same manner as an industrial installation for the production of electricity, steam, and hot water,[44] where the applicable threshold is set at a much lower site area of 0.5 hectares. This is particularly the case in circumstances where the EIA Directive and UK regulations were made at a time before hydrogen production was an established technology.

[39] Directive 2011/92/EU of the European Parliament and of the Council of 13 December 2011 on the assessment of the effects of certain public and private projects on the environment [2011] OJ L 26/1.

[40] Directive 2014/52/EU of the European Parliament and of the Council of 16 April 2014 amending Directive 2011/92/EU on the assessment of the effects of certain public and private projects on the environment [2014] OJ L 124/1.

[41] The Town and Country Planning (Environmental Impact Assessment) Regulations 2017, SI 2017/571, sch 2 para 10(a).

[42] Case C-72/95 *Kraaijeveld and others v Gedeputeerde staten van Zuid-Holland* [1996] I-05403, para 31.

[43] ibid.

[44] The Town and Country Planning (Environmental Impact Assessment) Regulations 2017, sch 2 para 3(a).

Moreover, the UK Government's Planning Practice Guidance also confirms that it should not be presumed that developments above the indicative thresholds should always be subject to assessment, or those falling below those thresholds could never give rise to significant effects, especially where the development is in an environmentally sensitive location, and that each development will need to be considered on its merits.[45] This legal position further adds to the uncertainty and is likely to encourage a cautious approach to confirming whether an EIA is required.

There may also be instances where a hydrogen production facility is properly considered to form part of a wider project for which an EIA is required, having regard to factors including common ownership, simultaneous determinations of other elements, functional interdependence with other elements, and whether projects can properly be said to be stand-alone or not.[46] Where a decision-maker determines that a hydrogen production facility does form part of a wider project for which an EIA is required, an EIA will be required in relation to it.[47]

Taking this into account, there can often be uncertainty as to the need for an environmental impact assessment for electrolytic hydrogen production facilities, and in those circumstances a prudent course of action is to seek a screening decision from the local planning authority or Secretary of State (as is relevant) to confirm whether or not an EIA is required,[48] having regard to the characteristics of the production facility and where relevant any hydrogen system-related elements. Such a screening decision would then determine for the purpose of the relevant regulations whether development is or is not EIA development for which an assessment must be undertaken, and that decision would only be capable of legal challenge on public law grounds.

It is however unsatisfactory that it can be alleged that there is uncertainty regarding whether hydrogen production facilities are EIA development or not which may be considered to necessitate the seeking of screening decisions, and this is a matter that could be addressed as part of any future reforms to streamline the planning consenting processes for low carbon hydrogen production projects, by way of updates to the relevant regulations.

5. Other Planning Consenting Routes—Development Orders

For completeness with respect to planning consenting, this sections briefly discusses the granting of planning permission by way of a different consenting route, a development order, as an alternative to the planning routes explored in section 3 of this chapter together with the limitations of this route for hydrogen projects.

[45] HM Government, Ministry of Housing and Local Government, Planning Practice Guidance, Environmental Impact Assessment, March 2014 (last updated May 2020), para 018 Reference ID: 4-018-20170728.
[46] *R (on the application of Wingfield) v Canterbury City Council* [2020] EWHC 1975 (Admin).
[47] ibid.
[48] The Town and Country Planning (Environmental Impact Assessment) Regulations 2017, reg 6.

Development orders can be general orders which are applicable to all land, or a special order, which is applicable to such land as may be specified in the relevant development order, which are made by the Secretary of State.

The most well-known general order is the Town and Country Planning (General Permitted Development) (England) Order 2015 (the GPDO), which grants planning permission for certain types of development. The types of development the GPDO grants planning permission for is broad and varied, including certain changes of use of land, certain renewable energy developments and development by electricity and gas undertakers in connection with their licensed undertakings.

This GPDO does not permit any development which is development requiring an EIA, and the development authorized is subject to other limitations which must be complied with for that development to be lawful. However, whilst this is the case, the GPDO can be relied upon to authorize substantial developments. At the current time, GPDO does not permit any hydrogen production facilities, however there is no reason that it could not do so in the future to assist with the delivery of such facilities at greater pace.

Special orders can be made to provide planning permission for certain development on defined areas of land, again subject to relevant conditions and limitations. Special development orders will be more strategic in their nature and will often be sought by the developers and landowners with an ability to develop certain areas of land. Whilst there could be some benefit in such an order including hydrogen production facilities as part of a wider scheme of development which they are authorizing, they are unlikely to be appropriate to permit individual hydrogen production facilities given the processes for them to be made. Seeking a planning permission would remain preferable, or for very significant capacity installations the seeking of development consent.

In addition to the development orders which may be made by the Secretary of State, a local planning authority may also make a local development order which grants planning permission for development specified in the order, and subject to undertaking the necessary processes this may include EIA development.[49]

Local development orders must follow a defined process, including requirements in respect of consultation, and they will seldom be quick to make. Much like special development orders referred to above, they are therefore unlikely to be appropriate to permit individual hydrogen production facilities.

6. Other Permits and Authorizations

Once planning consent has been obtained in relation to a hydrogen project, further permits and authorizations are likely to be required prior to the commissioning of the relevant project. This section provides a brief overview of these additional

[49] Town and Country Planning Act 1990, s 61A and sch 4; The Town and Country Planning (Environmental Impact Assessment) Regulations 2017, reg 32.

permits: subsection 6.1 discusses authorizations in relation to land acquisition and highways; subsection 6.2 sets out any environmental permits that might be required (in addition to the EIA discussed in section 4 above), whereas subsection 6.3 summarizes potential licensing requirements pursuant to the Gas Act 1986.[50] Subsection 6.4 discusses consent requirements in relation to hazardous substances; subsection 6.5 provides an overview of the relevant provisions pertaining to the Control of Major Accident Hazards (COMAH) Regulations 2015;[51] and subsection 6.6 provides a brief overview of relevant construction law.

6.1 Land Acquisition and Highways

Assuming planning consent is obtained by way of a planning permission, it may also be necessary for an electrolytic production facility to avail itself of powers to acquire land and rights over land and to obtain authorizations to undertake works to public highways which are required in connection with the delivery and use of the proposals.

With respect to the acquisition of land and rights over land not already owned and not able to be acquired by private treaty, it would be necessary to obtain compulsory purchase powers by way of a compulsory purchase order.[52] Certain persons benefit from statutory rights to make such orders and to have them confirmed by the Secretary of State, which includes licensed electricity undertakings and gas transporters. However, a licence is not required to produce hydrogen under the Gas Act 1986 where unbundled from the transport and supply of the gas, and an operator of an electrolytic hydrogen production facility would *prima facie* not be able to benefit from such powers.

Instead, it would be necessary for such an operator to petition the local planning authority to make the necessary compulsory purchase order to facilitate the development, and for such an order to be confirmed by the Secretary of State.[53]

Following this process would add additional time and uncertainty to the delivery of the facility, with the compulsory purchase order in all likelihood being required to be confirmed before the development commences. Based on recent practical experience with this process, it could be anticipated that the making and confirmation process for a compulsory purchase order would be between twelve to eighteen months.

[50] Gas Act 1986, 1986 ch 44.

[51] The Control of Major Accident Hazards Regulations 2015, 2015 No 483.

[52] A compulsory purchase order (CPO) is a mechanism by which land can be acquired without the consent of the owner. CPOs are a complex area of law and a detailed discussion of the same is outside the scope of this chapter. For a more detailed discussion of CPOs, see eg Edward Mitchell, 'Compulsory Purchase and the State Redistribution of Land: A Study of Local Authority—Private Developer Contractual Behaviour' (2021) 13(1) Journal of Property, Planning and Environmental Law 1–16.

[53] Town and Country Planning Act 1990, s 226.

Highways authorizations should, however, be more certain, and less time-consuming to obtain. Conventionally where a planning permission has been granted for a development in respect of which works are required to highways, the local highway authority will not be able to refuse to enter into the relevant agreements to authorize such works,[54] though it will need to be satisfied with the design of the works.

6.2 Environmental Permits

In addition to obtaining planning permission, it will also be necessary to obtain an environmental permit for the operation of an electrolytic hydrogen production facility. Within England the relevant regulator with powers to grant environmental permits is the Environment Agency, and in Wales this is Natural Resources Wales.[55]

In March 2024, the Environment Agency published guidance on the emerging techniques for the production of hydrogen from water using electrolysis[56] to assist businesses to design and develop industrial facilities for the production of green hydrogen in accordance with environmental permitting requirements.

The guidance confirms that an electrolytic hydrogen production plant is an inorganic chemicals activity in England and Wales[57] for which an environmental permit is required. The Guidance explains the factors that must be considered in relation to plant design and operation, including those in connection with energy efficiency and supply, water efficiency and supply, emissions to air and water, effluent and waste products, the risk of accidents and noise.[58]

Given how those matters will relate fundamentally to the design of the hydrogen production facility for which a planning consent is sought and how it will operate, it will be essential for the Environment Agency (taking England as the example) to be engaged with when seeking the relevant planning consents, including at the pre-application stage, so that the plant can be designed and consented to in a form which will be likely to achieve the grant of an environmental permit and so as to avoid the need to seek variations to the authorizing planning permission (or development consent) at a later date.

Whilst that is the theory for how the planning consenting and environmental consenting processes should be aligned, it is the case that the Environment Agency, like many Government agencies, are significantly resource strained, and obtaining access to the right expertise can at times be difficult. The need to wait for Environment Agency engagement can therefore further slow the related planning process and roll back the date of such facilities being delivered and operational.

[54] Highways Act 1980, s 278.
[55] The Environmental Permitting (England and Wales) Regulations 2016, reg 32(1).
[56] Environment Agency, Hydrogen Production by Electrolysis of Water: Emerging Techniques (March 2024) Hydrogen production by electrolysis of water: emerging techniques - GOV.UK accessed 22 May 2025.
[57] Environmental Permitting (England and Wales) Regulations 2016, part A (1) 4.2(a)(i).
[58] ibid.

6.3 Licensing under the Gas Act 1986

Depending on the role a developer of a hydrogen project will play in relation to the same at commissioning, they may require a licence pursuant to the Gas Act 1986 (as amended by the Energy Act 2023).[59]

The Energy Act 2023 introduced a range of measures relevant to hydrogen, such as:

- The regulatory framework for the support regime for hydrogen production;
- The framework for the hydrogen business models authorizing funds to be allocated to production, transport, and storage projects; and
- The necessary powers to appoint a hydrogen levy administrator in charge of raising funds to support the hydrogen business models.

The Gas Act 1986 defines hydrogen as a gas so no structural changes to the existing licensing regime were required.[60] The Energy Act 2023 clarified the licensing position by formally extending the licensing regime of the Gas Act 1986 to expressly cover hydrogen related licensable activities.[61]

This means that:

(1) Owners and operators of pipelines for the transport of hydrogen will need to obtain gas transporter licences for the transmission and distribution of hydrogen; and
(2) Persons arranging with a hydrogen transporter for hydrogen to be introduced into, conveyed by means of, or taken out of, a pipeline system operated by the relevant transporter, require a gas shipper licence; and
(3) Anyone engaging in the supply of hydrogen will require a gas supply licence.

The stand-alone production of hydrogen (unless tied to supply or transportation of the same) is not a licensable activity pursuant to the Gas Act 1986.

The relevant licences are available from Ofgem, the energy market regulatory authority for Great Britain, on application and subject to the applicable procedures.[62] For gas transporter licence applications, Ofgem has to publish a notice of intention to grant a licence setting out their relevant reasons for such a grant. Applicants for gas transporter licences will also be subject to the full ownership unbundling regime; they cannot concurrently hold a gas supply licence or an electricity generation or electricity supply licence.[63]

[59] The Energy Act 2023 is available here: https://www.legislation.gov.uk/ukpga/2023/52/contents accessed 3 June 2025.

[60] s 48, Gas Act 1986.

[61] s 134, Energy Act 2023.

[62] Ofgem, 'Applying for a Gas or Electricity Licence' (1 August 2024) https://www.ofgem.gov.uk/sites/default/files/2022-03/Applying%20for%20a%20gas%20or%20electricity%20licence.pdf accessed 22 May 2025.

[63] s 7A, Gas Act 1986.

6.4 Hazardous Substances Consents

In addition to planning permission and an environmental permit to construct and operate an electrolytic hydrogen production facility, a consent will be required under the Planning (Hazardous Substances) Regulations 2015 to authorize the storage of 2 tonnes or more of hydrogen[64] where required in connection with the operation of the production facility.

The purpose of such a hazardous substances consent is to regulate the storage and use of substances which may be hazardous to the public, and such a consent may be granted subject to conditions to regulate such storage and use and ensure the protection of the public.[65] Such a consent must be obtained from the relevant hazardous substances' authority, which in practice will be the same entity as the local planning authority. The statutory timescale for the determination of an application for a hazardous substances consent is eight weeks,[66] but as with applications for planning permission the determination timescale will often be longer.

6.5 Control of Major Accident Hazards

In addition to the need for an operator to have obtained a hazardous substances consent where 2 tonnes or more of hydrogen are to be stored in connection with a production facility, a production facility which will involve the presence of more than 5 tonnes of hydrogen will be within the scope of the Control of Major Accident Hazards (COMAH) Regulations 2015 and is subject to regulatory requirements in that respect.

Where the quantity of hydrogen present is five tonnes or more but less than 50 tonnes the production facility will be subject to the lower tier requirements, and where it is 50 tonnes or more the production facility will be subject to upper tier requirements.[67] Duties for lower-tier operators are the requirement to produce a major accident prevention policy and implement this via a safety management system,[68] and upper-tier operators must in addition include the preparation of safety reports[69] and internal emergency plans.[70] Such policies and plans would need to be produced, and in respect of safety plans approved (by the Health and Safety Executive), prior to the operation of any production facility which is within the scope of the COMAH Regulations. Operators will also be subject to requirements to provide information to local authorities[71] and the public[72] regarding the facility.

64 Planning (Hazardous Substances) Regulations 2015, s 3 and sched 1 pt 2.
65 GOV.UK, 'Hazardous Substances' https://www.gov.uk/guidance/hazardous-substances accessed 22 May 2025.
66 Planning (Hazardous Substances) Regulations 2015, s 11(3) and (4).
67 The Control of Major Accident Hazards Regulations 2015, reg 2 (1) and pt 2 of sched 1.
68 ibid reg 7.
69 ibid pt 3 and sched 3.
70 ibid pt 4 and sched 4.
71 ibid reg 13.
72 ibid reg 17.

6.6 Construction Law

In England and Wales, construction law is not a stand-alone area of law.[73] Instead, it draws on general contract and tort law, insurance law, landlord and tenant law, and, in relation to contentious matters, the law pertaining to restitution and breach of restitution as well as, in certain circumstances, criminal law (in case of acts and omissions pertaining to construction activities which carry a criminal sanction under English law).[74]

The authority to construct a hydrogen or electrolyser project is contained in the planning consent granted in relation to the relevant project pursuant to either the Planning Act 2008 or the Town and Country Planning Act 1990.

There is no hydrogen- or electrolyser-specific construction law as such in England and Wales. Nonetheless, certain construction specific legislation will need to be considered in the context of hydrogen or electrolyser projects.

Construction related legislation in England and Wales is generally focused on health and safety of the relevant construction sites as well as the relevant building itself: For instance, the Building Act 1984[75] can be seen as a cornerstone of construction legislation and focusses on the health, safety, welfare, and convenience of individuals in and around buildings. A number of Statutory Instruments (ie secondary legislation such as the Building Regulations 2010)[76] specify additional detail on requirements for the construction of buildings (eg in relation to structural integrity to fire safety measures and energy efficiency standards).[77] The Construction (Design and Management) Regulations 2015[78] are another example of statutory instruments for the construction industry; they are applicable to all construction projects in the UK and specify the roles and responsibilities of various stakeholders, including designers, and contractors, in health and safety management.

7. Conclusion

The UK Government is pursuing an ambitious decarbonization policy and hydrogen is intended to play a key role in its Clean Power 2030 agenda. In order to deliver this agenda, significant investment in hydrogen projects and related infrastructure is required.

[73] Vivian Ramsey, 'Construction Law: The English Route to Modern Construction Law' (2022) 75 Arkansas Law Review 251.

[74] A detailed discussion of English construction law is outside the scope of this chapter. For a general introduction, see Stephen Emmitt, *Barry's Introduction to construction of Buildings* (John Wiley & Sons 2023).

[75] Building Act 1984, ch 55 1984.

[76] The Building Regulations 2010, Statutory Instrument 2241 of 2010.

[77] The Building Regulations 2010; An overview of the Building Regulations can be found here: HM Government: 'Manual to the Building Regulations: A Code of Practice for Use in England', July 2020.

[78] The Construction (Design and Management) Regulations 2015, Statutory Instrument 51 No 51 of 2015.

However, there is no dedicated consenting regime for hydrogen projects at present. Instead, hydrogen projects must navigate a complex landscape of existing regulations and consents, which were originally designed for other industries like chemical processing, gas, and power generation.

The 1990 Act provides the primary planning permitting route for electrolytic hydrogen production facilities in England and Wales, however the absence of clear and consistent planning policy support for hydrogen production facilities and the wider systems that they form part of results in a consenting process which lacks the clarity and certainty to reasonably guarantee the grant of planning permission for hydrogen production facilities in appropriate locations. Arguably local planning authorities are also not sufficiently resourced to process applications for hydrogen production facilities, given the nascence of the technology, and the need for local planning authorities to understand the projects and their impacts with confidence for the purpose of decision-making. The more general resource constraints to which they are subject also affect their capability to do so.

The introduction of plans and policies that provide clear policy support for hydrogen production facilities of the capacity required and the identification of the locations which will be appropriate to be considered for their location would represent a significant step to addressing the current issues with obtaining planning permission for hydrogen production facilities.

By contrast, the NSIP regime, whilst providing a more holistic approach to the consenting of major infrastructure projects, is arguably not suitable to facilitate the delivery of low carbon hydrogen infrastructure at the pace required as the associated procedures are inherently time-consuming and resource intensive. The NSIP process also suffers from a lack of post-consent flexibility which would allow for unexpected issues during the development stage, which are more likely to be encountered for such 'first of a kind projects' than for more established technologies.

The UK Government has recently focused on how it can accelerate and improve the consenting process for major infrastructure projects, including by introducing a fast-track route to consent.[79] However this has arguably increased pre-application requirements and limited design flexibility in proposals to achieve a quicker examination and decision process following submission. It therefore has not addressed the timely and expensive procedures inherent in this NSIP process, and further reform is needed to streamline the pre-application requirements, allow for greater project design flexibility, and/or to provide a more proportionate procedure to authorize amendments to proposals. Further streamlining of the NSIP process, including the removal of statutory pre-application consultation and its replacement with non-statutory consultation, is proposed within the Planning and Infrastructure Bill.[80]

[79] GOV.UK, 'Planning Act 2008: Fast Track Process for Nationally Significant Infrastructure Projects' https://www.gov.uk/guidance/planning-act-2008-fast-track-process-for-nationally-significant-infrastructure-projects accessed 22 May 2025.

[80] GOV.UK, 'Consultation on streamlining infrastructure planning' https://www.gov.uk/government/consultations/consultation-on-streamlining-infrastructure-planning/consultation-on-streamlining-infrastructure-planning#scope-of-the-consultation accessed 22 September 2025.

The uncertainty as to whether hydrogen production facilities are required to be subject to EIAs, an issue which impacts on both above planning consenting regimes, is also unsatisfactory. To avoid the risk of legal challenge at later stages, this results in projects seeking screening decisions, and without a clear position on whether such projects require EIA there will be an inconsistency in the screening decisions which are issued. Updates to the EIA regulations and/or the issuing of clear guidance on whether and when such projects should be subject to EIA would resolve the current uncertainty and issues it gives rise to.

There is also a need for hydrogen projects to obtain a range of other consents and licences once planning permission or, to a lesser degree, once development consent has been obtained. Those can often only be obtained following the planning stage being complete, increasing the time it takes to authorize projects and deliver them.

This current consenting and authoring framework results in a fragmented and time-consuming process, not least as hydrogen projects are currently 'first of a kind' which might encounter more unexpected difficulties in the development stage compared to more established technologies. This is a relevant consideration for the significant investment decisions required to be taken in respect of hydrogen production facilities and low carbon hydrogen facilities more generally, and the lack of a clear pathway for delivery to the market will adversely impact on those. The consenting and licensing regime in England and Wales currently presents significant barriers and uncertainties for developers of low carbon hydrogen systems which will impact upon the realization of Government's ambitious Clean Power 2030 agenda. To create the conditions for delivery at scale the current uncertainty and friction of the planning system must be removed and the process to obtain consent must be streamlined.

The UK planning regime needs to evolve to create an appropriate delivery pathway for hydrogen projects for them to be delivered at scale and at pace. Whilst Government seems to be committed to addressing these issues, it is slow in implementing the necessary change and in some instances could be seen to not be willing to go far enough to do so, even though the success of CP2030 might well depend on a coherent fit-for purpose planning regime that recognizes the challenges for hydrogen projects and related infrastructure.

Further Reading

Town and Country Planning Act 1990.
Climate Change Act 2008.
Planning Act 2008.
Energy Act 2023.
HM Government, Clean Power 2030 Action Plan: A New Era of Clean Electricity (December 2024).
HM Government, UK Hydrogen Strategy 2021.
HM Government: Hydrogen Projects: Planning Barriers and Solutions: Research Findings, December 2023.

Ernesto Bonafé, Marco Conte, and Katharina Bouchaar, 'Hydrogen Valleys: Assessing the EU Legal and Financial Frameworks that Enable the Hydrogen Economy' (2023) 4(1-2) Global Energy Law and Sustainability 96.

Kevin Dillman and Jukka Heinonen, 'A "Just" Hydrogen Economy: A Normative Energy Justice Assessment of the Hydrogen Economy' (2022) 167 Renewable and Sustainable Energy Reviews 112648.

Will Eadson, Phil Northall, and Hywel Jones (2022), 'The UK Hydrogen Economy: A Review of Global, National and Regional Policy'. Sheffield Hallam University, Centre for Regional and Economic Research 2022) https://www.shu.ac.uk/-/media/home/research/cresr/reports/u/uk-hydrogen-economy.pdf accessed 22 May 2025.

Stephen Emmitt, *Barry's Introduction to Construction of Buildings* (John Wiley & Sons 2023).

KC Humphries, *National Infrastructure Planning Handbook* (4th edn, Bloomsbury Professional 2022).

Genaro Longoria and others, *The Impact of Planning and Regulatory Delays for Major Energy Infrastructure* (ESRI Working Paper No 725, 2022).

William Walton, 'Can Zero-Carbon Development be Delivered through the Existing English Legal and Policy Planning Framework?' (2025) 51(1) Built Environment 132–146.

PART 2
HYDROGEN DOWNSTREAM
Key Regulatory Issues

X

Repurposing Offshore Oil and Gas Infrastructure for Hydrogen Production

Diomidis Afentoulis, Torhild Nordtveidt, and Ignacio Herrera Anchustegui

1. Introduction

The energy transition facilitates the integration of different energy solutions, enabling the interaction of both new and old technologies and regulatory frameworks. Hydrogen production is a prime example. Hydrogen can be produced by electrolysers installed on the topsides of former hydrocarbon platforms, as discussed in section 3. Existing natural gas pipelines connected to the platform may also be used to transport the produced hydrogen, blended or in pure form, provided these are retrofitted. This creates opportunities for repurposing existing energy installations and offers more circular solutions to traditional decommissioning practices that involve removing the infrastructure, while also contributing to cost savings. However, such repurposing operations introduce a series of technical and legal challenges.

This chapter discusses the legal barriers to repurposing petroleum infrastructure for hydrogen production and transportation. It analyses the legal implications of producing hydrogen offshore using electrolysers installed on repurposed petroleum installations and transporting that hydrogen in pipelines originally laid for natural gas.

Our analysis uses Norway as a case study to discuss the barriers and avenues regulators and energy companies will need to address if they opt for this modality. We examine the extent to which Norwegian legislation allows for the repurposing of petroleum installations and gas pipelines for offshore hydrogen production and transport, as well as the licensing procedure associated with such projects.

This chapter is structured as follows. Section 2 discusses hydrogen's role in Norway's energy and climate policy. Section 3 covers the types of infrastructure that can be reused for offshore hydrogen production and transport, along with their economic and environmental benefits. Section 4 clarifies the permissibility of reusing offshore hydrocarbon infrastructure under Public International Law. Sections 5 examines the legal challenges within the Norwegian licensing framework for reusing hydrocarbon infrastructure on the NCS. Section 6 concludes by summarizing the key findings, highlighting the regulatory gaps, and proposing recommendations for facilitating the transition to offshore hydrogen production and transport.

2. The Norwegian Offshore Energy Landscape: Between Oil and Gas and Hydrogen

In 2024, Norway produced about 240.2 million standard cubic metres of oil equivalents (crude, natural gas liquids, and condensate), increasing its production compared to 2023.[1] Almost all of this production is exported, making Norway the fourth-largest natural gas exporter in the world in 2023.[2] Petroleum production takes place offshore. Vast infrastructure has been built to extract oil and natural gas and transport them to onshore terminals in Germany, Belgium, France, and the United Kingdom.[3]

The oil and gas installations on the Norwegian Continental Shelf (NCS) are aging.[4] This includes twelve concrete facilities, sixty-four fixed steel facilities, twenty floating steel facilities, and about 500 subsea installations across ninety-four productive fields.[5] While some fields are no longer operational, it is expected that in the next decade many others will be decommissioned as they become depleted or commercially unviable. Other mature oil and gas jurisdictions, notably the United Kingdom,[6] face similar situations.

Decommissioning offshore oil and gas installations, including their various parts, is mandated by the United Nations Convention on the Law of the Sea, along with North Sea regional and national legislation. These instruments generally require this

[1] All websites referred to in this chapter were last visited on 22 May 2025. Norwegian Petroleum, 'Historical Production' https://www.norskpetroleum.no/en/facts/historical-production/.

[2] Norwegian Petroleum, 'Exports of Oil and Gas' https://www.norskpetroleum.no/en/production-and-exports/exports-of-oil-and-gas/.

[3] Norwegian Petroleum, 'The Oil and Gas Pipeline System' https://www.norskpetroleum.no/en/production-and-exports/exports-of-oil-and-gas.

[4] Norwegian Petroleum, *Fields*, https://www.norskpetroleum.no/en/facts/field.

[5] Norwegian Petroleum, 'Cessation and Decommissioning' https://www.norskpetroleum.no/en/developments-and-operations/cessation-and-decommissioning/.

[6] North Sea Transition Authority (formerly UK Oil and Gas Authority), *Decommissioning Strategy* (2021).

infrastructure (rigs or platforms, including their topsides, concrete, and steel fixed facilities such as jackets or tension leg platforms, in addition to components and machinery to operate the infrastructure), to be removed unless exceptions apply, as discussed in section 4. Pipelines used for transporting oil and gas typically need not be removed and may stay in place. However, they must be cleansed, filled with water, and would no longer be in use.

Decommissioning operations are expensive. In the United Kingdom alone, it is estimated that a total expenditure exceeding £23 billion between 2023 and 2032.[7] Decommission operations also impact the ecosystem. An alternative to removing the infrastructure is repurposing it for different uses, such as producing and transporting hydrogen. This would allow the infrastructure to remain in place, be productive, reduce costs, and support the energy transition.

These synergies between existing offshore oil and gas installations and hydrogen as an energy carrier have not gone unnoticed in Norwegian energy policy. Norway's government aims to scale up hydrogen production, focusing on low-carbon variants such as 'blue' or 'green' hydrogen, as part of its pledge to become a low-carbon society by 2050 and diversify its energy exports.[8]

The 2020 Norwegian Government's *Hydrogen Strategy* highlights two key comparative advantages for Norway as a hydrogen producer.[9] First, the capacity to produce low-carbon hydrogen; second, the possibility of *using part of the existing oil and gas infrastructure for such production and transport*.[10] However, the strategy remains silent on how this is both technically feasible and legally permissible under the current offshore regulatory regime. As discussed in the following sections, combining offshore oil and gas infrastructure for hydrogen production and transport is technically and legally challenging.

3. What Do We Mean by Reusing Offshore Hydrocarbon Infrastructure for Hydrogen Development?

3.1 What Can be Repurposed to Produce and Transport Hydrogen?

Petroleum infrastructure, including platforms, rigs, topsides, pipelines, and abandoned oil and gas fields, can be repurposed for both the production and transport of hydrogen.[11] Depleted offshore hydrocarbon fields may be repurposed to store

[7] North Sea Transition Authority, *UKCS Decommissioning Cost and Performance Update* (2024).

[8] 'The target is to achieve reductions of greenhouse gas emissions of the order of 90–95 % by 2050 from the level in the reference year 1990'. Lov om klimamål (klimaloven—Climate Law), LOV-2017-06-16-60, s 4 (own translation).

[9] Norwegian Ministry of Petroleum and Energy and Norwegian Ministry of Climate and Environment, *The Norwegian Government's Hydrogen Strategy Towards a Low Emission Society* (2020).

[10] ibid 48–49.

[11] L B Wilcox and others, 'Repurposing an Offshore Oil and Gas Platform for Green Hydrogen Production: A North Sea Case Study' Paper presented at the SPE Europe Energy Conference and Exhibition, Turin, Italy, June 2024 https://doi.org/10.2118/220114-MS. Vysus Group, *Feasibility Study on Repurpose of Oil and Gas Infrastructure for Offshore Hydrogen Generation* (Vysus Group 2021). Siemens-Energy, 'Can Gas Lines

the greenhouse gases associated with the reaction between natural gas and steam to produce hydrogen.[12] For production, infrastructure may be linked to thermochemical reactions such as steam reforming, auto-thermal reforming, and gasification. Topsides may be also repurposed to host electrolysers so hydrogen can be produced with electricity, which is the focus of our paper.

Hydrogen production through electrolysis using oil and gas components (topsides or floating platforms to host an electrolyser) is an alternative in current development.[13] The electrolyser produces hydrogen by separating hydrogen and oxygen from demineralized seawater.[14] The electricity used to separate the molecules may come from the onshore grid (renewable or not) or an offshore (renewable) electricity facility, such as an offshore wind park. Producing hydrogen through electrolysis on a no-longer active oil and gas platform may be suitable for installations on the NCS. More than 40% of Norwegian petroleum platforms are already electrified from both onshore and offshore produced electricity.[15]

Recent studies highlight the potential to install electrolysers on a repurposed platform with a production capacity of 100–700 MW,[16] or even up to 1 GW, as highlighted by the Scottish Hydrogen Offshore Production Project HOP2 report from 2024.[17] These figures should be taken with caution when compared to current and planned onshore production capacity, especially considering the space needed to install large electrolysers. Some testing is underway. Pilot projects have shown modest results but offer hope for this combined technology. The PosHYdon project, which has already assessed its production onshore, is expected to start hydrogen generation on a repurposed gas platform 13 km from the Hague coastline in the Dutch North Sea.[18] The hydrogen will be transported to shore through an existing pipeline to users in Rotterdam. In June 2023, the Sealhyfe project, 20 km off the western French coast produced offshore hydrogen using a 1 MW electrolyser installed on a re-engineered floating

and Other Existing Infrastructure Handle Hydrogen?' (Siemens-Energy 11 September 2020). Kornél Telessy and others, 'Repurposing Natural Gas Pipelines for Hydrogen: Limits and Options from a Case Study in Germany' (2024) 80 International Journal of Hydrogen Energy 821–31.

[12] UK Oil and Gas Authority (now North Sea Transition Authority), *UKCS Energy Integration* (2019) 18–20.

[13] Wilcox and others (n 11); TKI Offshore Energy—Topsector Energie, *State of Art in Offshore Hydrogen Production* (2024) 9.

[14] ibid 6.

[15] In 2020, the Norwegian Offshore Directorate estimated that in this decade, more than 50% of the Norwegian petroleum production would be electrified from the shore: Norwegian Offshore Directorate, 'Almost Half of Norwegian Petroleum Production Will Soon Be Run on Power from Shore' (2020) https://www.sodir.no/en/whats-new/news/general-news/2020/almost-half-of-norwegian-petroleum-production-will-soon-be-run-on-power-from-shore/. For legal discussions around (offshore wind) electrification of oil and gas fields see *inter alia* Ignacio Herrera Anchustegui and Rudiger Tscherning, 'Offshore Oil and Gas Infrastructure Electrification and Offshore Wind: A Legal Exploration' (2024) 17(1) The Journal of World Energy Law & Business 35–53 https://doi.org/10.1093/jwelb/jwad035; Siv Elén Årskog Vedvik, 'Hurtigløp for Elektrifisering av Sokkelen med Havvind? Moglegheiter og Hindringar i Dagens Regelverk' (2024) Karnov Forlag 1; Ignacio Herrera Anchustegui and Aleksander Glapiak, 'Wind of Change: A Scandinavian Perspective on Energy Transition and the "Greenification" of the Oil and Gas Sector' in Katarzyna Gromek-Broc (ed), *Regional Approaches to the Energy Transition: A Multidisciplinary Perspective* (Springer 2023) 49–74.

[16] TKI Offshore Energy (n 13) 11.

[17] Net Zero Technology Centre, *Basis of Study Report: Hydrogen Offshore Production Project HOP2* (2024) 3.

[18] PosHYdon, 'Onshore Test Kicks off Successfully' (8 May 2024) https://poshydon.com/en/poshydon-onshore-test-kicks-off-successfully/.

platform.[19] However, commercial production of hydrogen on a repurposed oil and gas installation has not yet been achieved.

Pipelines transporting natural gas may generally be used for hydrogen transport, subject to repurposing and recertification processes.[20] First, hydrogen-associated risks to the infrastructure itself need to be addressed (leakage, pipeline embrittlement, or pipeline cracks). Second, technical modifications will depend on the type of hydrogen transported, whether it will be *pure* hydrogen, or *blended* with natural gas,[21] and/or compressed, or converted into liquid form,[22] or transformed into ammonia or methanol.[23]

Studies have been conducted on the feasibility of repurposing over 8,800 kilometres of Norwegian natural gas pipelines. The 2023 German-Norwegian Energy Cooperation Joint Feasibility Study indicates that modifications are technically possible, but there is a significant lack of regulatory requirements to implement such changes.[24]

3.2 Associate Benefits to Repurposing

Repurposing offshore petroleum assets for hydrogen production could offer significant synergies leading to business opportunities. Norway is well suited to explore such practices due to its existing (but aging) offshore infrastructure and capacity to produce electricity onshore and offshore.

Using existing infrastructure would reduce capital expenditures. Concerning rigs or platforms, two comparative scenarios have been assessed: (i) the production of hydrogen on a repurposed platform versus a new dedicated platform;[25] (ii) the cost difference between a full removal decommissioning of a North Sea field and repurposing it for hydrogen production with an electrolyser.[26] Cost savings are also significant for pipelines. In 2023, DNV estimated that repurposing would cost 10–35% when compared to building new hydrogen-dedicated pipelines, potentially leading to about half of the world's pipelines being repurposed.[27] Less optimistic is the 2021 Re-Stream

[19] Lhyfe, 'Lhyfe Announces that Sealhyfe, the World's First Offshore Hydrogen Production Pilot, Produces Its First Kilos of Green Hydrogen in the Atlantic Ocean' (27 June 2023) https://www.lhyfe.com/press/lhyfe-announces-that-sealhyfe-the-worlds-first-offshore-hydrogen-production-pilot-produces-its-first-kilos-of-green-hydrogen-in-the-atlantic-ocean/.

[20] Vysus Group (n 11); Siemens-Energy (n 11); Telessy and others (n 11); DNV, *Repurposing Onshore Pipelines for Hydrogen* (2024); Alex Procyk, 'Repurposed Gas Reservoirs, Pipelines Increase Hydrogen Applications' (2024) 14 Oil & Gas Journal https://www.ogj.com/energy-transition/article/14305668/repurposed-gas-reservoirs-pipelines-increase-hydrogen-applications.

[21] Carbon Limits and DNV, *Re-stream—Study on the Reuse of Oil and Gas Infrastructure for Hydrogen and CCS in Europe* (Carbon Limits and DNV 2021).

[22] Aliaksei Patonia and Rahmatallah Poudineh *Global Trade of Hydrogen: What is the Best Way to Transfer Hydrogen Over Long Distances?* (Oxford Institute for Energy Studies 2022) 1.

[23] ibid 3; LLF Group, *Hydrogen—An Overview of the Issues Associated with its Production, Storage and Transportation* (5 April 2022) https://www.lffgroup.com/posts/hydrogen-an-overview-of-the-issues-associated-with-its-production-storage-and-transportation.

[24] Gassco, Deutsche Energie-Agentur GmbH (dena—German Energy Agency), *German-Norwegian Energy Cooperation Joint Feasibility Study—Hydrogen Value Chain Summary Report* (2023), 12.

[25] Net Zero Technology Centre, *Basis of Study Report: Hydrogen Offshore Production Project HOP2* (2024).

[26] Wilcox and others (n 11).

[27] DNV (n 20) 4.

report, which estimated that only between 2% and 25% of EU/EEA offshore-located pipelines can be effectively and commercially repurposed (onshore, the percentage is 20–30%).[28]

Extending these assets' lifetime and giving them new functions is highlighted in policy documents by the Norwegian and UK governments and regulators.[29] By prolonging their useful life, decommissioning operations are delayed, positively affecting costs and benefiting taxpayers, as these costs are often deducted by oil and gas companies. Additionally, developing new functions for these assets leads to new business opportunities and revalorizes the asset,[30] especially if the field were to be abandoned.

Repurposing assets instead of decommissioning and disposing them offers a more circular approach to material utilization from a waste hierarchy perspective.[31] Instead of recycling most of these materials,[32] they are given a new life in a different but related energy activity. Concurrently, opportunities related to hydrogen production and transport may promote the cessation of petroleum activities, offering new business pathways to petroleum companies. Lastly, repurposing assets may have a positive environmental impact compared to installing new facilities dedicated to hydrogen production.

4. Supranational Challenges in Reusing Hydrocarbon Infrastructure for Offshore Hydrogen Production

4.1 Public International Law

The legal permissibility of reusing offshore petroleum infrastructure for hydrogen production is linked to the right of states to exploit natural resources and install infrastructure in their marine spaces. This matter is regulated by international conventions, to which Norway is a contracting party,[33] and is relatively settled in the literature.[34] It is

[28] Carbon Limits and DNV (n 21) vii.

[29] North Sea Transition Authority, *UKCS Decommissioning Cost and Performance Update* (n 7).; Norwegian Ministry of Petroleum and Energy and Norwegian Ministry of Climate and Environment (n 9).

[30] TKI Offshore Energy (n 11) 35.

[31] The waste hierarchy applies as a priority order in waste prevention and management legislation and policy to minimize the impact of generation and management of waste and improve resource efficiency, see Directive 2008/98/EC on waste (2008) OJ L 312/3.

[32] The recycling rate in terms of weight can be very high, up to 98% in one of the latest decommissioning operations in Norway. See Aker Solutions, 'Aker Solutions to Sort, Recycle 18,000t Topside' (23 October 2023) <https://www.akersolutions.com/news/news-archive/2023/aker-solutions-to-sort-recycle-18000-t-topside/>.

[33] 'United Nations Convention on the Law of the Sea' (10 December 1982) https://treaties.un.org/pages/ViewDetailsIII.aspx?src=TREATY&mtdsg_no=XXI-6&chapter=21&Temp=mtdsg3&clang=_en; OSPAR Commission, 'Contracting Parties' https://www.ospar.org/organisation/contracting-parties#:~:text=The%20Contracting%20Parties%20are%20Belgium,together%20with%20the%20European%20Union.

[34] Liv Malin Andreasson and Martha M Roggenkamp, 'NSE III Deliverable 2.2, 2.3—Regulatory Framework: Legal Challenges and Incentives for Developing Hydrogen Offshore' (2020) 14–21 Deliverable 2.2, 2.3 – Regulatory Framework: Legal Challenges and Incentives for Developing Hydrogen Offshore – the University of Groningen research portal; Martha M Roggenkamp and Dinant Drankier, 'Chapter XIV—The Regulation of Decommissioning in the Netherlands: From Removal to Re-Use' in Martha M Roggenkamp and Catherine Banet (eds), *European Energy Law Report* (Intersentia, CUP 2020); Ignacio Herrera Anchustegui, Gunnar S Eskeland, and Frode Skjeret, 'Understanding Decommissioning of Offshore Infrastructures: A Legal and Economic Appetizer' [2022] SNF Report No 07/21, 36–45.

generally agreed that even though the removal of offshore hydrocarbon infrastructure is the norm, the repurposing or reutilization of infrastructure at sea is legally permissible. Utilization of parts of hydrocarbon infrastructure—including but not limited to platforms, topsides, and pipelines—to be decommissioned for a new purpose, such as offshore hydrogen production and/or transport is legally uncontroversial.

4.2 EU EEA Relevant Law

The interaction of EU law with Norway is a complex issue, particularly concerning energy. Norway is a member of the EU Single Market through the EEA Agreement.[35] The EEA Agreement provides for the integration of EU law on the free movement of goods, capital services, and people in the Norwegian legal system.[36] Article 24 of the EEA Agreement confirms that EEA energy law is covered in Annex IV of the EEA Agreement. Due to the dualistic doctrine of Norwegian law,[37] as cemented in the Norwegian Constitution[38] and the EEA Agreement,[39] EU law needs to be incorporated into the EEA Agreement by a decision of the EEA Joint Committee and then be made part of the national legal order.

At the time of writing, Norway has not adopted the latest 2024 EU legislation on gas and hydrogen markets,[40] nor the 2018–2019 and 2024 electricity and renewable energy-related legislative packages. Furthermore, the applicability of EU EEA law on the NCS is heavily debated at academic[41] and political[42] levels. For these reasons, and because the reuse of hydrocarbon infrastructure for offshore hydrogen production is covered by the Norwegian licensing framework, the potential implications of future EU EEA law are not assessed here.

[35] Agreement on the European Economic Area [1994] OJ L 1/3.

[36] ibid art 1(2).

[37] For a comprehensive analysis of monistic and dualistic theories see Peter Malanczuk, *Akehurst's Modern Introduction to International Law* (Routledge 1997) 63–71.

[38] *The Constitution of the Kingdom of Norway* (Kongeriket Noregs grunnlov) [1814] https://lovdata.no/dokument/NL/lov/1814-05-17-nn.

[39] Agreement on the European Economic Area (n 35) art 7.

[40] Directive 2024/1788/EU of the European Parliament and of the Council of 13 June 2024 on common rules for the internal markets for renewable gas, natural gas and hydrogen (recast) [2024].; Regulation (EU) 2024/1789 of the European Parliament and of the Council of 13 June 2024 on the internal markets for renewable gas, natural gas and hydrogen (recast) [2024].

[41] Christian Franklin and Halvard Haukeland Fredriksen, 'Of Pragmatism and Principles: The EEA Agreement 20 Years On' (2015) 52 Common Market Law Review 655, 656; Knut Almestad, 'The Notion of Opting Out' in Carl Baudenbacher (ed), *The Handbook of EEA Law* (Springer 2016) 90, 91. Finn Arnesen, 'Article 126 Territorial Application of the EEA Agreement' in Arnesen and others (eds), *Agreement on the European Economic Area: A Commentary* (1st edn, Nomos 2018) 945, 953; Finn Arnesen, *Kontinentalsoklene og EØS—Replikk til Andenæs og Bekkedal* (Universitetsforlaget 2024) S 503–12 (Lov og rett: 7/2024). Tina Soliman Hunter and Ignacio Herrera Anchustegui, 'Ernst, Are You Kidding Me? Reflections About Norwegian Energy Law by Non-Norwegian Energy Lawyers' in Konow and others (eds), *Fakultetsbyggjar, Vestlending og Verdsborgar: Festskrift til Ernst Nordtveit 70 År* (Cappelen Damm 2023).

[42] Ministry of Foreign Affairs, *The EEA Agreement and Norway's Other Agreements with the EU* [2012-2023] ('EØS-avtalen og Norges Øvrige Avtaler med EU') https://www.regjeringen.no/en/dokumenter/meld.-st.-5-2012-2013/id704518.

5. Norwegian Legal Challenges When Reusing Infrastructure for Hydrogen Production

5.1 Introduction

Activities on the NCS are regulated by national Norwegian law. The Norwegian offshore energy legislation is based on the Petroleum Act (PA)[43] and the Offshore Energy Act (OEA).[44] These acts were adopted in 1996 and 2010, respectively. Hydrogen has only recently emerged as an alternative energy carrier, and the existing legislation was not drafted with hydrogen activities in mind. This background highlights the potential lack of sufficient rules concerning hydrogen, which is analysed in this section.

Norwegian legislative techniques, methodology and legal argumentation techniques differ from Continental law traditions. Belonging to the Nordic Scandinavian Legal Realist tradition, its standards of interpretation can be compared to those of the Court of Justice of the European Union in that case law has a strong standing, although it is limited by statutes. However, concepts, theories, and principles have a low standing. Instead, the function of law in society is at its centre. Law is understood on a case-by-case basis and legal interpretation is pragmatic. Although the legal system seeks harmony between statutes, they do not necessarily have a binding effect on each other; for example, one term can be defined differently in different statutes. Lack of clarity regarding the scope of an act in many cases can and will be solved by way of interpretation following Norwegian standards.

Regarding the repurposing of offshore petroleum infrastructure for hydrogen production and transportation, it is important to note that Norwegian law has traditionally been based on a principle of free access. If something at sea is not explicitly regulated as belonging to someone, it is an 'open resource' that can be exploited by anyone. The Norwegian legislator has not established property law for areas at sea where Norway has exclusive rights. Instead, certain resources, such as petroleum, minerals on the seabed, and renewable energy, are deemed to belong to the state.[45]

This section assesses the legal challenges arising from the Norwegian licensing framework pertaining to the reuse of petroleum installations and pipelines for hydrogen production and transport on the NCS. The analysis focuses on repurposing this infrastructure as an alternative to decommissioning, not as a parallel to hydrocarbon production, therefore the production of hydrogen at an oil and gas installation

[43] *Act of 29 November 1996 No 72 relating to Petroleum Activities* (Petroleum Act, hereinafter PA) ('Lov om petroleumsvirksomhet', 'petroleumsloven') https://lovdata.no/dokument/NL/lov/1996-11-29-72.

Norwegian Offshore Directorate, *Act 29 November 1996 No 72 Relating to Petroleum Activities* https://www.sodir.no/en/regulations/acts/act-29-november-1996-no2.-72-relating-to-petroleum-activities/.

[44] *Act of 4 June 2010 No 21 on Offshore Renewable Energy Production at Sea* (Offshore Energy Act) ('Lov om fornybar energiproduksjon til havs', 'havenergilova') https://lovdata.no/dokument/NL/lov/2010-06-04-21 (hereinafter OEA).

[45] Ernst Nordtveit, 'Konsesjonsordningar og kvotesystem som regulering av tilgang til opne ressursar—privatisering eller regulering?' in Inge Lorange Backer, Ole Kristian Fauchald, and Christina Voigt (eds), *Pro natura: Festskrift til Hans Christian Bugge på 70-årsdagen* (Universitetsforlaget 2012).

that has not ceased production is not examined. However, the situation where some remaining hydrocarbon installations and a repurposed hydrogen installation share a pipeline will be addressed. In this scenario, both hydrogen and petroleum will be transported through the same pipeline simultaneously. Further, the licensing regime for installing electrolysers on new artificial islands is not reviewed.

Lastly, the framework for offshore cable connections between wind farms and oil and gas installations has been extensively reviewed in the context of electrification.[46] As the provision of electricity in these scenarios is not hydrogen-specific, the relevant licensing framework is not analysed. However, it is assumed that the energy used for electrolysis comes from a renewable source, or that emissions from the energy production are captured and stored (CCS).

5.2 Repurposing for Hydrogen Production

5.2.1 Introduction

Subsection 5.2 addresses the repurposing of offshore petroleum infrastructure for hydrogen production, that is the fitting of electrolysers. Currently, there are no specific rules for hydrogen activities on the NCS. Therefore, it is necessary to analyse statutes and regulations in related areas of law to determine their applicability to offshore hydrogen production.

5.2.2 Petroleum Act

In Norwegian law, the decommissioning of hydrocarbon installations is regulated under Chapter 5 of the PA and Sections 43–45 of the PA's Regulations.[47] PA Section 5-1 stipulates that the operator of the installation must submit a decommissioning plan to the Ministry of Energy (ME) no later than two years before the planned cessation of production or end of licence.[48] The plan shall 'include proposals for continued production or shutdown of production and disposal of facilities'.[49] Such disposal 'may include, *amongst others*, continued use in the petroleum activities, *other use*, full or partial removal or abandonment'.[50]

PA Section 5-3 does not specify what can be considered a final disposal of a petroleum installation.[51] The preparatory works point to the ME's decision in this respect, stating that the disposal in accordance with the PA is completed when the approved

[46] On the (offshore wind) electrification of oil and gas fields see *inter alia* Anchustegui and Tscherning (n 15); Vedvik (n 15).

[47] *Regulations of 27 June 1997 No 653 to the Petroleum Act* (hereinafter Regulations to the PA) ('Forskrift til lov om petroleumsvirksomhet') https://lovdata.no/dokument/SF/forskrift/1997-06-27-653.

Norwegian Offshore Directorate, 'Regulations to Act Relating to Petroleum Activities' (27 June 2024) https://www.sodir.no/en/regulations/regulations/petroleum-activities.

[48] PA s 5-1(2) sentence 1.

[49] ibid sentence 2.

[50] PA s 5-1(1) sentence 3 (emphasis added).

[51] Ulf Hammer and others, *Petroleumsloven* (Universitetsforlaget 2009) 433.

plan has been fulfilled.[52] If the ME's decision allows for repurposing, the disposal will be completed when the necessary adaptations have been made, and the new user has taken over control of the installation, a critical step concerning our study. At this point, the installation is *no longer be a petroleum installation*, and the PA, which applies to 'petroleum activities' only,[53] will in principle not apply to the installation. However, the PA's decommissioning rules may still apply in part when the other use ends, as the petroleum licensee typically remains liable for the decommissioning of the installation alongside the new operator.[54]

Despite the reference to *other use* of the petroleum installation in its preparatory works,[55] the PA does not regulate the repurposing of the installation as a part of the decommissioning plan. It is likely that a new energy actor, not the holder of the hydrocarbon's extraction licence, will be interested in reusing the installation for hydrogen production. Considering the perpetual or residual liability regime established in the PA,[56] the PA licensee will be jointly and severally liable for decommissioning alongside the owner of the installation, and the new user planning to produce hydrogen.[57] Additionally, in the case of a new user, it is not clear who, amongst the PA licensee and the new user, has the responsibility for the maintenance of the platform until it is repurposed for a new use. The infrastructure is left in place (not removed) waiting for its new function to be permitted and to start. This is a rather complex process connected to the licensing of the new activity granted on a disused petroleum installation and needs to be clarified by the legislator or practice.

In conclusion, while Section 5-1 of the PA enables the ME to accept reuse as a means of disposing of an offshore installation that is going out of use in the petroleum industry, it does not offer a basis for providing licences for the new activity and leaves repurposing as part of decommissioning unregulated.

5.2.3 Pollution Control Act

The Pollution Control Act (PCA)[58] aims to prevent and reduce pollution and waste.[59] Activities that fall within the scope of the act may only be performed with a licence.[60] If offshore hydrogen production is covered by the act, a licence to pollute will also be a

[52] Official Norwegian reports/Norges offentlige utredninger (NOU) 1993:25, Avslutning av petroleumsproduksjon—fremtidig disponering av innretninger 23.
[53] PA s 1-4(1) sentence 1.
[54] PA s 5-3(5), (NOU 1993: 25, s 4.4.2), cf OEA s 6-1.
[55] PA s 5-3.
[56] ibid. For more on the residual liability concept see: Foroogh Torabi and Seyed Mohammad Tababaye Nejad, 'Legal Regime of Residual Liability in Decommissioning: The Importance of Role of States' (2021) 133 Marine Policy 1–8.
Hanne Storstein and Guro Kristoffersen Lysnes, 'Liability for Decommissioning of Oil and Gas Installations on the Norwegian Continental Shelf: Norwegian Public and Private Law Perspectives' (2022) University of Bergen.
[57] PA s 5-3(5), 5-4(1)(3); OEA s 6-1(2) sentence 1, 1-4(4).
[58] *Act of 13 March 1981 No 6 on the Protection Against Pollution and Waste* (Pollution Control Act, hereinafter PCA) ('Lov om vern mot forurensninger og om avfall', 'forurensningsloven') https://lovdata.no/dokument/NL/lov/1981-03-13-6.
[59] PCA s 1(1).
[60] ibid s 11.

prerequisite for that activity. It must be noted that a licence to pollute does not equate to a licence for any other activities. If the activities that lead to pollution require a licence, the initiator must also obtain such a licence.

Section 3(2) number 3 first sentence of the PCA stipulates that it applies on pollution on the Exclusive Economic Zone (EEZ) 'if the source of pollution is a Norwegian vessel or facility, or otherwise to the extent the King determines'.[61] No regulations have been adopted to extend the scope of the PCA based on Section 3(2) number 3. The term 'facility' is not defined by the PCA. It must therefore be interpreted according to its literal meaning, covering any construction not classified as a 'vessel'.[62]

The material scope of the PCA is limited to 'pollution and waste', Section 3(1). Section 6(1) of the PCA defines pollution as, amongst other things, '1. the introduction of a solid, liquid or gas into the air, water or ground, 2. noise and vibrations'.[63] The other parts of the definition are irrelevant to this discussion.

Electrolysis powered by renewable energy does not produce direct emissions. However, if the electricity comes from fossil fuels, there can be associated Scope 2 carbon emissions, even if mitigating sources such as CCS are used. Such emissions would call for an application for a licence under the PCA to produce such electricity. Obtaining such licence is beyond the scope of this chapter, and it is unlikely for Norway, a nation with over 98% of its electricity production carbon-emissions free.[64]

It is unclear whether the PCA's material scope covers electrolysis powered by renewable energy. Technical research has shown that, during the construction phase, cable laying for the provision of electricity to the electrolyser can negatively impact nature and underwater sound.[65] The wording of PCA's Section 6(1) number 2 ('noise and vibrations') requires a licence. The PCA does not define 'noise' nor do the preparatory works. Some guidance could be found in the Act on Neighbours but there will be no neighbours in the EEZ. It is of greater relevance that the Pollution Control Regulations (PCR) chapter 5 regulates noise mapping, action planning, and limits. Section 5-13 stipulates that outdoors noise levels shall be calculated in accordance with Directive 2002/49/EC with amendments. The regulations seem to be mainly focused on avoiding human health hazards, whereas construction works may affect life in the sea. An extensive interpretation of 'noise' to also protect life in the sea is however not ruled out. In light of Norway's obligations under the Convention on Biological Diversity and the precautionary principle, it is not unlikely that noise from the fitting and use of an electrolyser offshore would be considered 'noise' under the PCA if it is established that the sound emissions would reach a level that could be harmful to life in the sea. If so, electrolyser operators would have to apply for a pollution permit under the PCA also when

[61] ibid s 3(2) no 3 first sentence.
[62] Ot.prp. no 11 (1979–1980), 90.
[63] PCA s 6(1).
[64] Energy Facts Norway, *Electricity Production* (last updated in late 2023) https://energifaktanorge.no/en/norsk-energiforsyning/kraftproduksjon/.
[65] Sytske Stuij and Suzan Tack, 'NSE II Deliverable D.2—Strategic Assessment of Environmental Impacts of Offshore System Integration Options' (North Sea Energy 2018) 44.

electrolysis is powered by renewable energy. The application for a permit is stipulated in Section 36-2 of the PCR.[66]

Further, during the operational phase, by-products of hydrogen production through electrolysis such as natrium chloride (salt) and waste (organisms) are produced and likely discharged into the sea. Technical research on the impact of introducing these elements into seawater is limited.[67] Whether the disposal of these elements into seawater is considered pollution under the PCA should be evaluated on a case-by-case basis, considering the precautionary principle and the aim of the PCA to reduce and prevent pollution.

Conclusively, it is unclear whether hydrogen production via electrolysis is covered by the PCA as a 'source of pollution'. We maintain that the ME should clarify whether the PCA applies to electrolysers by specifying what is meant by 'noise', particularly outside Norwegian territory. Nevertheless, we assert that hydrogen development through electrolysis should not be subject to detailed licensing processes which currently apply only to highly polluting energy carriers.[68]

5.2.4 Offshore Energy Act

5.2.4.1 Scope of the Act

The OEA was adopted to regulate renewable energy production on the NCS. The establishment of this legal framework was driven by a political decision to create a national strategy for offshore renewable energy production.[69]

The OEA's scope covers 'renewable energy production and the transformations and transferal of electrical energy at sea'.[70] The wording of this provision is inaccurate as energy cannot be produced, only transformed from one form to another. Like hydrogen, electricity is an energy carrier, not a specific form of energy. Both electricity and hydrogen production result in an energy carrier but not in new energy.

In OEA's Section 1-4 (1) 'renewable energy production' is defined as 'the production of electrical energy through the utilization of renewable energy resources, for example wind, waves and tides'. The definition seems to identify renewable energy production as electrical energy production, which contradicts the wording of Section 1-2 (1).[71] A strictly literal reading of the definition in Section 1-4 (1) would rule out hydrogen production from the scope of the OEA.

However, in the interpretation, the preparatory works must also be considered. In its proposition for the OEA to the Parliament, the ME alternates in terminology between 'energy' and 'electricity', and even uses 'energy carrier', a term fitting for hydrogen.[72]

[66] *Regulations of 1 June 2004 No 931 on the Limitation of Pollution* (Pollution Control Regulations, hereinafter PCR) ('forurensningsforskriften') https://lovdata.no/dokument/SF/forskrift/2004-06-01-931.

[67] Stuij and Tack (n 65) 45.

[68] PCR s 36-1(2).

[69] Ot.prp. no 107 (2008–2009), 5.

[70] OEA s 1-2(1).

[71] This has become even more true since 2016, with market shares for electric vehicles surging to reach 25% in 2024. More than 80% of new vehicles sold in Norway are now fully electric.

[72] Ot.prp. no 107 (2008-2009) 5, and Ot.prp. no 107 (2008-2009) 79, respectively.

Furthermore, the Act is said to cover '*energy* production from *all renewable energy carriers* within the geographical scope [of the Act]'.[73] If 'energy production' refers to the process of transferring energy from one energy carrier to another, it would include both transferring energy from wind to electricity and from wind to hydrogen.

There appears to be a discrepancy between what the ME seems to have intended to regulate, and what it thought it intended to regulate. The confusion between 'energy' and 'electricity' is unsurprising, as electricity has been the main energy source in Norwegian homes (and partly industry) for decades. When the OEA was drafted, offshore wind energy was the primary focus, whilst hydrogen was not yet considered an important part of the future energy mix. This suggests that the apparent exclusion of hydrogen from the scope of the OEA is an *incuria*. In such cases, the Norwegian Supreme Court is likely to interpret the wording in an extensive manner to align with the intended meaning (ie cover hydrogen production as it is an energy carrier),[74] provided the Supreme Court found sufficient legal grounds for such extensive interpretation.

In this sense, when interpreting the OEA, both the various wordings and the expressions in the preparatory works, as well as so-called real considerations (*reelle hensyn*) must be considered. The latter covers a balancing of interests,[75] such as political support.[76] A narrow interpretation of the OEA's scope would leave offshore hydrogen production unregulated, as no other legal rules cover it. As noted, following the Norwegian legal method, it is likely that the Supreme Court would favour an extensive interpretation of scope provisions if necessary to ensure that legal regulation covers important societal aspects, particularly in relation to safety and environmental protection.[77]

As discussed in subsection 4.2, the applicability of EU EEA Law on the NCS is debated, and therefore, the EU definition of renewable energy will not affect the interpretation of 'renewable' in the OEA. The EU definition comes into relevance when hydrogen is sold to the EU market.

In conclusion, it is likely that the Supreme Court would emphasize the production of energy carriers without emissions. This means that offshore hydrogen production using an electrolyser would fall within the scope of the Act.

[73] Ot.prp. no 107 (2008-2009) 79–80. Note that the wording of s 1-2 and 1-4(1) have not been changed since the proposal.

[74] Inge Lorange Backer, 'Samspillet mellom Lovgiverne og Høyesterett' in Gunnar Bergby and others (eds), *LOV SANNHET RETT—Jubileumsskrift til Norges Høyesterett 200 år* (Universitetsforlaget 2015) 108, see references in (n 24) concerning *incuria*. Concerning lack of adaptation, see *inter alia* Rt. 1979 p 1079 (right of appeal for the mentally ill) and Rt. 1977 p 1035 (doctor's journal). A further large number of examples in Supreme Court case law could be mentioned.

[75] Hammer and others (n 51) s 1-4.

[76] See *inter alia Norwegian Ministry of Climate and Environment and Ministry of Petroleum and Energy, The Norwegian Government's Hydrogen Strategy* (3 June 2020) https://www.regjeringen.no/en/dokumenter/the-norwegian-governments-hydrogen-strategy/id2704860/. This document continues the work of the previous government, proving that the development of a hydrogen industry finds support across political division lines, as it did in Rt. 1979 p 1079.

[77] Hammer and others (n 51) s 1-4.

5.2.4.2 The licensing procedure

Under the OEA, the first step to produce hydrogen offshore production (or any other project) is the opening of an area for 'renewable energy' production by the King in Council.[78] Before opening an area, the ME shall conduct an impact assessment of the environmental and socioeconomic consequences of renewable energy production.[79] The proposal for the renewable energy production area and the impact assessment shall be put out for public consultation.[80] The ME may decide to allocate the area by auction, or assess the applicants, or combine the two processes.[81] The assessment shall be based on 'objective and non-discriminatory conditions'.[82]

Subsequently, the operator of the electrolyser should apply for a production licence,[83] to be granted by the ME.[84] The production licence application should include a detailed plan addressing technical, safety, and environmental considerations,[85] a project-specific impact assessment[86] and a processing fee.[87] The production licence can have a duration of up to thirty years from the time the facility starts operating.[88] To be eligible to apply for a licence, an entity must be established under Norwegian law.[89]

In conclusion, the OEA´s scope and definitions are vague. Further, there is uncertainty whether offshore hydrogen production via electrolysers falls under OEA's scope. To facilitate offshore hydrogen production, as a future Norwegian industry, it is important to clarify that alternative energy carriers, such as hydrogen produced by electrolysis, are covered by the OEA.

5.3 Repurposing for Hydrogen Transport

In this subsection, we discuss the relevant legal regulations and their effect for repurposing of oil and gas pipelines into hydrogen pipelines. The aim could be complete repurposing, resulting in the pipeline being used for transporting hydrogen only, or semi-repurposing, resulting in the pipeline being used for transporting both hydrogen and natural gas, as discussed in subsection 3.1.

Hydrogen activities on the NCS fall within the scope of the OEA, suggesting that hydrogen transportation should be covered by this Act. However, transportation does

78 OEA s 2-2(1).
79 ibid s 2-2(2).
80 ibid s 2-2 (3).
81 ibid s 2-3(2).
82 OEA s 2-3(2).
83 *Regulations of 12 June 2020 No 1192 to the Offshore Energy Act* (hereinafter Regulations to the OEA) ('Forskrift til havenergilova') https://lovdata.no/dokument/LTI/forskrift/2020-06-12-1192, s 7.
84 OEA s 3-1(1).
85 ibid s 3-1(2).
86 ibid s 3-1(3); Regulations to the OEA, ss 2 lit. a, 3, 4, and 6.
87 Regulations to the OEA s 5,
88 ibid s 3-5(2).
89 ibid s 3-5(1).

not constitute exploitation of a renewable energy source, which is what the OEA regulates. The alternative would be to apply the pipeline transportation rules of the PA by way of analogous interpretation.

The OEA does contain provisions on transportation of electricity, which suggests that the transportation of energy carriers may fall within its scope.[90] In principle, hydrogen transportation in pipelines could be regulated through OEA Section 3-2, which grants the ME the authority to issue licences for offshore electricity grid networks, and Sections 3-3 to 3-5, which outline general procedural rules for the application process, the decision to grant a licence, and any limits or legal prerequisites for the award. Section 3-2 applies to 'network facilities', defined in Section 1-4 (3) as 'electrical equipment and associated building engineering constructions for the conversion and transmission of electrical energy'. The strict delimitation of the scope of this provision to 'electrical' equipment can be an *incuria*. A benefit of using the rules of the OEA is that it would ensure that all aspects of hydrogen activity fall within a single regulatory framework.

However, there is a significant difference between transporting respectively charged ions and hydrogen. Hydrogen is a gas and therefore resembles natural gases more than electricity. This suggests that analogies from the PA's rules on pipelines for transportation of petroleum would be more appropriate, in our view. This would also align with a literal interpretation of the OEA, as it explicitly speaks of the transmission of electrical energy. Several reasons support such an analogical interpretation of the PA. Although the transportation of hydrogen is not petroleum activity and therefore falls outside of the scope of the PA, the PA seems to offer the most suitable existing rules for the transportation of a gas. The PA maintains high safety standards and sets detailed rules on licences in that more regulations, circulars, and decisions have been passed than in relation to the OEA. Nevertheless, it is essential to consider the physical differences between hydrogen and natural gas, as these might hinder the applicability of petroleum rules for hydrogen, especially regarding safety. Another argument for using the PA and its regulations is that the OEA is drafted in a very general manner, lacking sufficiently specific rules. It would also be beneficial if both transportation of natural gas and transportation of hydrogen were regulated the same way and within the same legal framework, as dual-purpose pipelines will have to fulfil the demands for transporting both gases.

To conclude, provisions in the PA and its regulations, or parts thereof, should apply to hydrogen transportation when suitable, although hydrogen activities offshore are regulated by the OEA. However, there is a lack of hydrogen-specific rules addressing the unique characteristics of hydrogen. The Norwegian legislator should therefore seek to establish regulations specifically for hydrogen transportation.

[90] ibid s 3-2 in particular, cf s 1-2(1).

6. Conclusion

The repurposing of offshore petroleum infrastructure for hydrogen production and transportation presents a promising avenue for advancing Norway's energy transition. It can give a competitive advantage to the production of transport of hydrogen, reduce oil and gas decommissioning costs for infrastructure owners and the state, as well as promote more circular uses and practices in the energy sector. However, our analysis highlights several regulatory shortcomings that must be addressed to facilitate this transition effectively.

First, the current Norwegian legal framework, primarily the PA and the OEA, does not explicitly cover hydrogen production and transportation. Both hydrogen production and transport are omitted from their wording and their application relies on legal analogy and an expansive interpretation. This regulatory gap creates uncertainty for stakeholders and regulators alike and may hinder the development of offshore hydrogen projects. The PA, while allowing for the reuse of petroleum installations, does not provide a clear basis for licensing new hydrogen activities using these infrastructures. Similarly, the OEA's scope, which focuses on offshore renewable energy production, does not explicitly include hydrogen, leading to ambiguity in its application, and being an instrument draft with electricity production and transport in mind. Additionally, both instruments are rather vague and open-ended.

Second, the PCA raises questions about the environmental licensing requirements for hydrogen production via electrolysis. The PCA's definitions of pollution and noise are not clearly applicable to hydrogen production by electrolysis. This lack of clarity necessitates further guidance from the Ministry of Energy to ensure that hydrogen production and its associated pollution risks are appropriately regulated without imposing undue burdens on developers.

Third, it is not clear what is the applicable regime for the transportation of hydrogen through repurposed pipelines, either in pure or blended form. Both the OEA and the PA could be applicable. Concerning the OEA, its provisions seem better suited to the transportation of electricity (as it is the energy carrier explicitly addressed). On the other hand, the PA's provisions on pipeline transportation are tailored to natural gas and petroleum, and it is unclear whether these rules can be extended to cover hydrogen, at least without a regulatory reform. The potential for pipeline embrittlement and other technical challenges associated with hydrogen transport further complicate the regulatory landscape.

From this stems the fact that hydrogen production offshore is in and of itself scarcely regulated in Norway. Repurposing existing oil and gas infrastructure adds to the complexity and brings about further uncertainty for project developers, limiting this Norwegian comparative advantage. To address these challenges, the Norwegian legislator must provide clear and comprehensive regulations tailored to the unique requirements of offshore hydrogen production and transportation. Additionally, administrative practices concerning the current petroleum decommissioning framework, ought to be reviewed to incentivize and/or require circular practices beyond recycling. By addressing these legal challenges, Norway can leverage its existing offshore infrastructure to become a leader in hydrogen production, contributing to its climate goals and energy security. The transition to a hydrogen economy requires not only technological advancements but also a robust and adaptive legal framework that supports innovation while safeguarding environmental and public interests.

Acknowledgements

This chapter has been possible thanks to two research grant for the projects: 'Legal-by-design Digital Disruption in the Circular Economy: An Exploratory Research Project' by the Iceland Lichtenstein and Norway Grants (EEA Grants), project coordinated by the University of Minho, Portugal (Bilateral Initiative No. FBR_OC2_58); Norwegian Centre for Hydrogen Value Chain Research (HyValue), funded by the Research Council of Norway (project 333151).

Further Reading

L M Andreasson, 'Offshore Production and Transport of Green Hydrogen: A Case Study on Denmark and the Netherlands' in R Fleming (ed), *The Cambridge Handbook of Hydrogen and the Law* (CUP 2024) 173–188.

D Drankier and others, *North Sea Energy Deliverable B.1—Regulatory Framework: Barriers or Drivers for Offshore System Integration* (North Sea Energy 2018).

R Fleming, *The Cambridge Handbook of Hydrogen and the Law* (CUP 2024).

I Herrera Anchustegui and others (eds), *Offshore Energy Law: Challenges and Opportunities for Renewables and Hydrocarbons* (Hart-Bloomsbury 2025).

S Kumar and others, 'Synergy of Green Hydrogen Sector with Offshore Industries: Opportunities and Challenges for a Safe and Sustainable Hydrogen Economy' (2023) Journal of Cleaner Production 384.

EG Pereira and others (eds), *The Regulation of Decommissioning, Abandonment and Reuse Initiatives in the Oil and Gas Industry: From Obligation to Opportunities* (Kluwer Law International BV 2020).

R Peters and others, 'Offshore Hydrogen Production in the North Sea Enables Far Offshore Wind Development' (2020) *Offshore Technology Conference.*

L van Nieuwkoop and M Roggenkamp, 'Legal Challenges for Offshore System Integration in Energy Hubs: North Sea Energy 2020-2022' (North Sea Energy 2022).

XI

Decarbonizing Gas Infrastructure with Hydrogen

Overview of the Permitting Regime for Hydrogen Pipelines in Poland

Monika Radomska

1. Introduction

The energy transition is a global endeavour that requires, *inter alia*, both the repurposing of existing fossil fuel infrastructure and building of new infrastructure to produce or distribute 'clean' energy.[1] In recent years, Poland has made significant progress towards energy transition and improved the security and sustainability of its energy system, despite its heavy reliance on coal.[2] The country's energy policy focuses

[1] Suriya Evans-Pritchard Jayanti, 'Repurposing Pipelines for Hydrogen: Legal and Policy Considerations' (2022) 8 Energy Reports 815, 816; Ankica Kovač, Matej Paranos, and Doria Marciuš, 'Hydrogen in Energy Transition: A Review' (2021) 46(16) International Journal of Hydrogen Energy 10016, 10021.

[2] Ewelina Kochanek, 'Evaluation of Energy Transition Scenarios in Poland' (2021) 14(6058) Energies 1, 1; International Energy Agency, *Poland 2022 Energy Policy Review* (International Energy Agency 2022) 11 https://iea.blob.core.windows.net/assets/b9ea5a7d-3e41-4318-a69e-f7d456ebb118/Poland2022.pdf accessed 20 August 2024.

on decarbonizing energy supply by, *inter alia*, increased use of renewable energy, introducing nuclear energy, and enhancing energy efficiency.[3] Consequently, decarbonizing the energy sector has become a key objective in Poland's efforts to achieve climate change mitigation goals.[4]

Hydrogen-based technologies are instrumental for the acceleration of Poland's decarbonization process, particularly by leveraging the country's existing gas infrastructure.[5] Hydrogen can be obtained from fossil sources, such as natural gas, oil, or coal ('grey' hydrogen), or from renewable sources by electrolysis ('green hydrogen').[6] By repurposing and upgrading its gas infrastructure, Poland can establish hydrogen pipelines to transport hydrogen as a low-carbon energy carrier for various applications, such as power generation, heating, and transportation.[7] Poland is already one of the largest producers of hydrogen in the European Union, ranking third in 2018 with over 1 million tonnes of hydrogen produced.[8] It needs to be emphasized that the majority of this hydrogen production has been 'grey' hydrogen.[9]

1.1 Overview of the Polish Hydrogen Strategy

In recent years, Poland established ambitious objectives for the development of hydrogen.[10] These objectives and means of achieving them were outlined in the 'Polish Hydrogen Strategy 2030 with the prospects to 2040'—a strategic document officially adopted by the Polish government in November 2021.[11] More recently, the 'Act amending the Energy Act and certain other acts' (Amendment) has been adopted by Sejm and published in the Journal of Laws, but at the time of writing this chapter has not yet entered into force.[12] This Amendment enables the implementation of the Polish Hydrogen Strategy into law, specifically one of the strategy's goals, the 'creation of a stable regulatory environment', by providing a legal basis for the operation of hydrogen infrastructure.[13]

[3] International Energy Agency (n 2) 12.

[4] ibid.

[5] ibid 30 and 139; Resolution No 149 of the Council of Ministers of 2 November 2021 on the Adoption of the 'Polish Hydrogen Strategy until 2030 with an Outlook until 2040' (Polish Monitor—Official Journal of the Republic of Poland, Warsaw 7 December 2021 item 1138) [*Uchwała numer 149 Rady Ministrów z dnia 2 listopada 2021 roku w sprawie przyjęcia 'Polskiej strategii wodorowej do roku 2030 z perspektywą do 2040 roku'* (*Monitor Polski—Dziennik Urzędowy Rzeczypospolitej Polskiej, Warszawa dnia 7 grudnia 2021 roku pozycja 1138*)] (Polish Hydrogen Strategy) 20.

[6] Fernando Moreno-Brieva, José Guimón, and Juan Carlos Salazar-Elena, 'From Grey to Green and from West to East: The Geography and Innovation Trajectories of Hydrogen Fuel Technologies' (2023) 101 Energy Research & Social Science 1, 2.

[7] International Energy Agency (n 2) 30.

[8] ibid 29.

[9] Lidia Gawlik and Eugeniusz Mokrzycki, 'Analysis of the Polish Hydrogen Strategy in the Context of the EU's Strategic Documents on Hydrogen' (2021) 14(6383) Energies 1, 11.

[10] ibid.

[11] Polish Hydrogen Strategy (n 5).

[12] Act of 21 November 2024 Amending the Energy Act and Certain Other Acts (Journal of Laws 2024, item 1881) [*Ustawa z dnia 21 listopada 2024 roku o zmianie ustawy—Prawo energetyczne oraz niektórych innych ustaw (Dz U 2024 poz 1881)*].

[13] Polish Hydrogen Strategy (n 5) 23.

The strategy is a response to changes in the European and global energy environments, resulting in a shift from conventional fuels to low-carbon solutions.[14] It emphasizes the critical role hydrogen can play in achieving climate neutrality, particularly through decarbonization efforts.[15] Additionally, the strategy addresses hydrogen transport methods, including using the existing natural gas pipelines.[16] It suggests that introducing a 5% hydrogen admixture into the natural gas transmission network would significantly increase the hydrogen demand and reduce the costs of advancing this energy carrier.[17] However, the strategy does not provide specific figures regarding the extent of cost reductions. The scope of this chapter is limited to the hydrogen transport only, with the focus on the pipeline transportation. This is due to the fact that the strategy stresses the importance of efficient transport of hydrogen for the 'harmonious development of an economy based on hydrogen'.[18] Furthermore, the document points out that as customer demand for hydrogen increases, existing gas infrastructure or dedicated hydrogen pipelines will be used for transportation.[19] Accordingly, this chapter will be focused on the repurposing of existing gas infrastructure for hydrogen transportation and the construction of dedicated hydrogen pipelines.

1.2 Development of Dedicated Hydrogen Pipelines and Repurposing Natural Gas Pipelines

Despite substantial differences between natural gas and hydrogen, research has shown that existing natural gas pipelines can be adapted for transporting hydrogen.[20] A study by the Agency for the Cooperation of Energy Regulators (ACER) notes that the energy density of gaseous hydrogen is only slightly lower than that of natural gas.[21] ACER identifies two primary alternatives for transporting hydrogen: *developing new hydrogen pipelines*, or *repurposing existing natural gas pipelines*.[22] While there are technical challenges with repurposing gas infrastructure for hydrogen, the legal challenges are also substantial.[23] This chapter will address the permitting processes for both the construction of new hydrogen pipelines and the repurposing of existing natural gas pipelines.

[14] ibid 4.
[15] ibid 3.
[16] ibid 21.
[17] ibid.
[18] ibid.
[19] ibid 21.
[20] Liv Malin Andreasson, Kars de Graaf and Martha Roggenkamp, *Regulatory Framework: Legal Challenges and Incentives for the Development of Hydrogen Infrastructure in Port Areas* (New Energy Coalition, 31 December 2020) 32 https://www.newenergycoalition.org/custom/uploads/2021/04/Havenschets-Report-Final-Regulatory-Framework-Liv-Malin-Andreasson-1.pdf accessed 1 September 2024.
[21] European Union Agency for the Cooperation of Energy Regulators, *Transporting Pure Hydrogen by Repurposing Existing Gas Infrastructure: Overview of Existing Studies and Reflections on the Conditions for Repurposing* (ACER 2021) 6 https://www.scribd.com/document/697691738/Transporting-Pure-Hydrogen-by-Repurposing-Existing-Gas-Infrastructure-Overview-of-studies accessed 1 September 2024.
[22] ibid 3.
[23] Evans-Pritchard Jayanti (n 1) 815.

As it stands, the Polish regulatory framework for hydrogen transport is fragmented, relying on various pieces of legislation. The Polish Energy Act, as noted in the Hydrogen Strategy, lacks a precise definition of hydrogen.[24] However, the Amendment addresses this by incorporating hydrogen within the provision that covers gaseous fuels.[25] This approach is based on the understanding that hydrogen is considered to be a gaseous fuel under the current Energy Act, which includes 'other types of combustible gas, supplied via the gas network, … regardless of their intended use'.[26] Since hydrogen is a highly flammable gas and can technically be transported through the gas network, it falls under this category.[27] Furthermore, the Amendment includes definitions of three types of hydrogen in the Energy Act—low-emission hydrogen, renewable hydrogen and renewable hydrogen of non-biological origin.[28]

A noteworthy technical specification of hydrogen pipelines is that they typically operate at pressures between 500 psi and 1200 psi (approximately 3.44–8.27 MPa), similar to natural gas transmission pipelines, which operate at 200–1500 psi (about 1.38–10.34 MPa).[29] In Poland, natural gas networks which operate at pressures between 0.5 and 1.6 megapascals (MPa) are classified as elevated pressure pipelines (*gazociąg podwyższonego ciśnienia*) and those exceeding 1.6 MPa are classified as high pressure pipelines (*gazociąg wysokiego ciśnienia*).[30] Until the Amendment is enacted, hydrogen transport is regulated by the provisions applicable to gaseous fuels, with a focus on the permits required for high-pressure natural gas pipelines.

Since the Amendment has not yet entered into force, the Strategic Investments Act currently serves as the primary legal framework for the permitting regime for dedicated hydrogen pipelines. This act governs transmission networks under the Energy Act, defining them as 'high and medium pressure gas networks functionally connected with each other, excluding mining and direct gas pipelines'.[31] The Strategic Investments Act further defines a strategic investment within the scope of the transmission network as an investment task, including the necessary construction works under the Construction Act.[32] This classification of a hydrogen pipeline as a strategic investment

[24] Polish Hydrogen Strategy (n 5) 26.

[25] Amendment art (1)(1)(b).

[26] Act of 10 April 1997—Energy Act (Consolidated Version Journal of Laws 2024 item 266 with amendments) [*Ustawa z dnia 10 kwietnia 1997 roku—Prawo Energetyczne (tj Dz U 2024 poz 266 ze zm)*] (Energy Act) art 3(3a).

[27] Gawlik and Mokrzycki (n 9) 2.

[28] Amendment art 1(1)(c).

[29] Michael Penev, Jarett Zuboy, and Chad Hunter, 'Economic Analysis of a High-Pressure Urban Pipeline Concept (HyLine) for Delivering Hydrogen to Retail Fuelling Stations' (2019) 77 Transportation Research Part D 92, 93; Pipeline Safety Trust, 'Pipeline Basics & Specifics About Natural Gas Pipelines' (2024) 2 Pipeline Briefing Paper 1, 1.

[30] Regulation of the Minister of Economy of 26 April 2013 on the Technical Requirements to Be Met by Gas Networks and Their Location (Journal of Laws 2013 item 640) [*Rozporządzenie Ministra Gospodarki z dnia 26 kwietnia 2013 r. w sprawie warunków technicznych, jakim powinny odpowiadać sieci gazowe i ich usytuowanie (Dz U 2013 poz 640)*] art 6(1)(c) and (d).

[31] Energy Act art 3(11a).

[32] Act of 24 July 2015 on the Preparation and Implementation of Strategic Investments in Transmission Networks (Consolidated Version Journal of Laws 2024 item 1199 with amendments) [*Ustawa z dnia 24 lipca 2015 r. o przygotowaniu i realizacji strategicznych inwestycji w zakresie sieci przesyłowych (tj Dz U 2024 poz 1199 ze zm)*] (Strategic Investments Act) art 1(2)(4).

is crucial for the discussion of the first relevant permit in section 3. The chapter will be structured alongside three major permits that are required for the repurposing and/or building of new hydrogen pipelines in Poland—in section 3.

The first relevant permit to be discussed is the decision on the location of a public purpose investment, which is the starting point for the construction of dedicated hydrogen pipelines. The Strategic Investments Act recognizes a strategic investment as a public purpose investment, and the 'decision on the location of a strategic investment' is synonymous with the 'decision on the location of a public purpose'.[33] For clarity, this chapter will use the term 'decision on the location of public purpose' (decision on the location), as it is commonly referenced in other Polish legal acts. This section will also address the local spatial development plan (local plan), closely interrelated with the first permit. The second permit examined is the decision on the environmental conditions, and the third and final permit is the construction permit, which is interrelated with the first two. The construction permit application must include the decision on the location (if issued), and the decision on environmental conditions for projects requiring an Environmental Impact Assessment (EIA).[34] Finally, the chapter will offer recommendations to enhance the efficiency of the processes associated with the construction of both dedicated hydrogen pipelines and repurposing of existing natural gas pipelines.

The three permits discussed in this chapter were selected due to their potential to cause challenges to entities involved in hydrogen transportation networks. The complexity lies in determining when these permits are applicable for planned projects. It is important to acknowledge that while further additional permits may be necessary for constructing dedicated hydrogen pipelines or repurposing natural gas pipelines, this chapter focuses on the three named. This is due to their crucial relevance for the procedure and the fact that they will be required for almost all hydrogen-related pipeline projects in Poland and therefore form the backbone of the permitting regime.

Prior to examining these three permits and the underlying legislation that makes them necessary in detail, an overview of the relevant administrative bodies will be provided, explaining key terms essential for initiating hydrogen transport pipeline projects in Poland.

Each section of this chapter will be subdivided into four subsections—the procedural and substantive legal aspects, dedicated hydrogen pipeline development, and the repurposing of existing natural gas infrastructure. This structure aims to clarify the different legal dimensions and permitting regimes involved.

[33] Strategic Investments Act arts 3 and 24.

[34] Act of 3 October 2008 on Providing Information on the Environment and its Protection, Public Participation in Environmental Protection and Environmental Impact Assessment (Consolidated version Journal of Laws 2024 No 1112 with amendments) [*Ustawa z dnia 3 października 2008 r. o udostępnianiu informacji o środowisku i jego ochronie, udziale społeczeństwa w ochronie środowiska oraz o ocenach oddziaływania na środowisko (tj Dz U 2024 poz 1112 ze zm)*] (EIA Act) art 3(1)(8).

2. Brief Overview of the Polish Administrative Landscape

To understand the administrative arrangements in Poland, it is important to understand Poland's territorial division. The country has three main administrative layers, with the basic units being communes, poviats, and voivodeships—communes constituting the smallest units and voivodeships the largest.[35]

The relevant administrative bodies discussed in this chapter are commune head (*wójt*, executive body in a commune),[36] mayor (*burmistrz*, executive body in a commune where the administrative seat is a city within its territory),[37] a starost (*starosta*, administrative authority in a poviat),[38] city president (*prezydent miasta*, executive body in cities with over 100,000 inhabitants),[39] and voivode (*wojewoda*, decision-making body in voivodeship).[40] Furthermore, the permit-specific bodies discussed in this chapter are the Regional Director for Environmental Protection (at the voivodeship level), as well as central bodies, namely the General Director for Environmental Protection and Chief Inspector of Construction Supervision, both of whom act at the national level.

The permits discussed in this chapter must be obtained separately, and their interrelation stems from the fact that the requirement for one permit depends on obtaining another. The first permit required is the decision on the location, accompanied by the decision on the environmental conditions, unless for dedicated hydrogen pipelines. For repurposing natural gas pipelines, the decision on environmental conditions may be necessary, depending on the administrative body's determination of whether an EIA is required. Finally, a construction permit application must include the decision on the location if issued, and the decision on environmental conditions for projects requiring an EIA.

3. Local Spatial Development Plan (Local Plan)/Decision on Location of a Public Purpose Investment (Decision on the Location)

The first potentially relevant permit is the local plan together with a decision on the location, as outlined in the Spatial Planning Act. It is an act 'specifying the principles

[35] Act of 24 July 1998 on the Introduction of a Basic Three-Stage Territorial Division of the State (Consolidated Version Journal of Laws 1998 No 96 item 603 with amendments) [*Ustawa z dnia 24 lipca 1998 r. o wprowadzeniu zasadniczego trójstopniowego podziału terytorialnego państwa (tj Dz U 1998 nr 96 poz 603 ze zm)*] art 1(1) and (2).

[36] Act of 8 March 1990 on Local Self-Government (Consolidated Version Journal of Laws 2024 item 609 with amendments) [*Ustawa z dnia 8 marca 1990 r. o samorządzie gminnym (tj Dz U 2024 poz 609 ze zm)*] (Local Self-Government Act) art 26(1).

[37] ibid art 26(3).

[38] Act of 5 June 1998 on Poviat Self-Government (Consolidated Version Journal of Laws 2024 item 107 with amendments) [*Ustawa z dnia 5 czerwca 1998 r. o samorządzie powiatowym (tj Dz U 2024 poz 107 ze zm)*] (Poviat Self-Government Act) art 34(1).

[39] Local Self-Government Act art 26(4).

[40] Act of 23 January 2009 on the Voivode and Governmental Administration in the Voivodship (Consolidated Version Journal of Laws 2023 item 190 with amendments) [*Ustawa z dnia 23 stycznia 2009 r. o wojewodzie i administracji rządowej w województwie (tj Dz U 2023 poz 190 ze zm)*] art 2(1).

of shaping spatial policy by local government units and government administration bodies, and the scope and principles of procedure in cases covered by areas specified in the framework of establishing the principles of their use and development'.[41] It is noteworthy that this permitting step varies between the construction of new dedicated hydrogen pipelines and for the repurposing of natural gas pipelines.

3.1 Substantive Law

The local plan plays a crucial role in facilitating investments as it designates specific areas where projects can be planned and located.[42] Its primary function is to define land use, including the location of public purpose investments, and to establish conditions and methods for land development.[43] Consequently, the local plan has binding authority, serving as the foundation for decisions pertaining to real estate in the respective area.[44]

The creation of a local plan is not obligatory and lies at the discretion of the commune council, unless stipulated otherwise by law.[45] Furthermore, local plans are not typically prepared for so-called closed areas—areas restricted due to the defence and security of the state.[46] As a result, a significant part of Poland's territory is not governed by local plans.[47]

Compliance with the local plan (if one exists in the relevant area) is a prerequisite for obtaining a construction permit.[48] As will be explained further in this chapter, a construction permit is required for the construction of dedicated hydrogen pipelines. Therefore, aligning the planned investment with the provisions of the local plan forms an essential part of the permitting process.

3.2 Procedural Law

The distinguishing feature of local acts is their issuance by local authorities, which limits their applicability to the specific jurisdiction of the authority.[49] In absence of

[41] Act of 27 March 2003 on Spatial Planning and Development (Consolidated Version Journal of Laws 2024 item 1130 with amendments) [*Ustawa z dnia 27 marca 2003 r. o planowaniu i zagospodarowaniu przestrzennym (tj Dz U 2024 poz 1130 ze zm)*] (Spatial Planning Act) art 1.

[42] Karolina Muzyczka, 'Pozwolenie na Budowę a Miejscowy Plan Zagospodarowania Przestrzennego' (2017) 17 Zeszyty Naukowe Gdańskiej Szkoły Wyższej 279, 281.

[43] Spatial Planning Act art 4(1).

[44] Aleksander Lipiński, 'Miejscowy Plan Zagospodarowania Przestrzennego jako Źródło Prawa' (2017) 1 Prawne Problemy Górnictwa i Ochrony *Środowiska* 33, 34.

[45] ibid 35.

[46] Spatial Planning Act art 4(3); Act of 17 May 1989 on Geodetic and Cartographic Law (Consolidated Version Journal of Laws 2024 item 1151 with amendments) [*Ustawa z dnia 17 maja 1989 r.—Prawo geodezyjne i kartograficzne (tj Dz U 2024 poz 1151 ze zm)*] art 2(9).

[47] Lipiński (n 44) 36.

[48] Act of 7 July 1994—Construction Act (Consolidated Version Journal of Laws 2024 item 725 with amendments) [*Ustawa z dnia 7 lipca 1994 r.—Prawo budowlane (tj Dz U 2024 poz 725 ze zm)*] (Construction Act) art 35(1)(1)(a).

[49] Lipiński (n 44) 34.

local plans, land development methods and conditions would be determined by a separate administrative decision: either (i) a decision on the location of a public purpose investment or (ii) a decision on development conditions (for other planned projects).[50] The decision on the location specifies, *inter alia*, the type of investment and the conditions for land development based on the separate provisions.[51] The following focuses specifically on that decision on the location, which is required in a situation when no local plan is in place.

The locally competent voivode is then responsible for issuing the decision on the location.[52] If the public purpose investment spans two or more voivodeships, the decision is issued by the voivode in whose jurisdiction the longest section of the transmission network is located.[53] The relevant administrative authority has a month from receiving an application to issue a decision.[54]

A notable recent positive development in Polish legislation is the Strategic Investments Act, which regulates the preparation and implementation of strategic investments in transmission networks.[55] This act was introduced to facilitate and expedite the permitting process for projects that pass through multiple communes, each of which would otherwise need to comply with different local plans.[56] Consequently, projects classified as strategic investments are exempt from local plans and instead must obtain a decision on the location.[57]

3.3 Dedicated Hydrogen Pipelines

The hydrogen transportation pipeline infrastructure can be classified as a strategic investment, encompassing the construction of a transmission network within the meaning of the Energy Act.[58] Once classified as a strategic investment, the provisions of the Spatial Planning Act are no longer binding on the project.[59] Consequently, adhering to the local plans is not required, which can expedite the decision-making process, by eliminating the need to amend these plans. The relevant administrative body issuing the decision on the location is the locally competent voivode.[60]

[50] Spatial Planning Act art 4(2).
[51] ibid art 54.
[52] Strategic Investments Act art 5(1).
[53] ibid art 5(3).
[54] ibid art 6(1).
[55] ibid art 1(1).
[56] Jacek Łubecki, 'Realizacja Strategicznych Inwestycji w Zakresie Sieci Przesyłowych—Czyli Co i Komu Da Specustawa Przesyłowa?' (2015) 5–6 Nowa Energia 8, 9.
[57] Strategic Investments Act art 11(1).
[58] Strategic Investments Act art 1(2)(3) and art 1(2)(4); Energy Act art 3(11a).
[59] Strategic Investments Act art 11(1).
[60] ibid art 5(1).

3.4 Repurposed Natural Gas Pipelines

Regarding the repurposing of natural gas pipelines for hydrogen, the legislator does not explicitly require a new decision on the location. The Spatial Planning Act necessitates a decision on location for projects requiring a construction permit.[61] The repurposing of natural gas pipelines does not require a construction permit, meaning there is no need for a new decision on the location. However, it is possible that the original natural gas pipeline required a construction permit; for example, if its technical specifications classified it as a project requiring an EIA before construction. Repurposing of natural gas pipelines can sometimes necessitate an EIA, depending on technical thresholds or location. If a decision on the location was initially issued by one administrative body, it must be amended by the same administrative body, namely the voivode.[62]

The same process applies to pipelines constructed under the Strategic Investments Act. In such a scenario, the original decision on the location might need to be amended by the same body which issued it initially—again, the voivode.[63]

However, if the natural gas network was constructed according to a local plan, and not under the Strategic Investments Act, the repurposing rules differ.[64] For pipelines located in the areas with a local plan, the plan needs to be amended. The amendment process follows the same procedure as the original adoption of the plan, where the application needs to be filed at the commune responsible for the plan.[65] Notably, regulations do not provide for any procedures or deadlines for processing applications to amend local plans.[66]

Finally, since most of Poland is not covered by local plans, natural gas networks in these areas would have been built based on the decision on the location.[67] Accordingly, a new decision on location will be required, similar to the process for constructing dedicated hydrogen pipelines.

4. Decision on the Environmental Conditions

Since most hydrogen pipeline projects require a decision on the location, which in turn necessitates an EIA, it is crucial to determine the specific circumstances under which this assessment is required. This section focuses on the environmental aspects of the

[61] Spatial Planning Act art 50(2)(2).

[62] ibid art 27; Act of 14 June 1960 Code of Administrative Procedure (Consolidated Version Journal of Laws 2023 item 775 with amendments) [*Ustawa z dnia 14 czerwca 1960 r.—Kodeks postępowania administracyjnego (tj Dz U 2023 poz 775 ze zm)*] art 155; Construction Act art 82(3)(5a).

[63] ibid.

[64] Refers to natural gas network which did not necessitate EIA and decision on environmental conditions before its construction.

[65] Spatial Planning Act art 27.

[66] 'Miejscowy Plan Zagospodarowania Przestrzennego' (biznes.gov.pl, 29 September 2024) https://www.biznes.gov.pl/pl/portal/ou357 accessed 6 October 2024.

[67] The natural gas pipelines operating at pressures greater than 0.5 MPa are classified as public purpose investments.

permitting regime for the construction of dedicated hydrogen pipelines as well as the repurposing of existing natural gas for hydrogen transport. This regime ensures that environmental impacts are assessed and addressed throughout the pipeline development process.

4.1 Substantive Law

In Poland, the key legal act regulating environmental decisions is the EIA Act.[68] The decision on environmental conditions defines the environmental conditions for the implementation of the project and is required for the two types of projects: planned projects that may always have a significant impact on the environment or projects that may potentially have a significant impact on the environment.[69] The distinction between the two is that an EIA is mandatory for the first category of projects, while for the second category, the requirement for an EIA is determined by the administrative body.

An EIA is a comprehensive investigation aimed at predicting the environmental effects of a planned impact of an activity or a project.[70] The EIA Act defines the EIA procedure as including (i) verification of the environmental impact report, (ii) obtaining the necessary opinions and approvals, and (iii) ensuring public participation in the process.[71] An EIA is conducted as a part of proceedings to issue a decision on environmental conditions.[72]

Pipelines which fall under the scope of those always having a significant impact on the environment are pipelines with external diameter of 800 mm or more and length of 40 km or more, or these passing through Natura 2000 areas.[73] Therefore, these installations always necessitate an EIA and the decision on the environmental conditions.[74]

Gas transmission installations with outer diameter of less than 800 mm length of less than 40 km or less, as well as those operating at pressures exceeding 0.5 MPa are projects that may potentially have a significant impact on the environment.[75]

4.2 Procedural Law

Since hydrogen pipelines operate at pressures above the 0.5 MPa threshold, the decision on whether an EIA is required rests with the relevant administrative body, unless

[68] EIA Act.
[69] ibid art 71.
[70] Judith Rosales, *Environmental Impact Assessment* (Delve Publishing 2021) 2.
[71] EIA Act art 3(1)(8).
[72] ibid art 61(1)(1).
[73] Regulation of the Council of Ministers of 10 September 2019 on Projects That May Have a Significant Impact on the Environment (Journal of Laws 2019 item 1839) [*Rozporządzenie Rady Ministrów z dnia 10 września 2019 r. w sprawie przedsięwzięć mogących znacząco oddziaływać na środowisko (Dz U 2019 poz 1839)*] (EIA Regulation) art 2(1)(20)(c); EIA Act art 59(2).
[74] ibid.
[75] EIA Act art 3(1)(31).

the pipeline infrastructure is to pass through Natura 2000 areas or for which the outer diameter is 800 mm or more and length of 40 km and more, in which cases an EIA is mandatory anyway.[76] The location of the pipeline, thus, plays a significant role in deciding whether an EIA is required, or if the necessity of conducting an EIA depends on the body issuing the decision.[77] The relevant authority in both cases are the commune head, mayor or the city president; the decision on environmental conditions must be issued within thirty days following the submission of the application.[78] The Amendment points to the Regional Director for Environmental Protection as the decision-making authority for hydrogen transport projects classified as having a significant environmental impact.[79]

When a dedicated hydrogen pipeline crosses more than one voivodeship, the Regional Director for Environmental Protection overseeing the majority of the project area will issue the decision on environmental conditions.[80] This decision is made after consulting the Regional Directors responsible for the remaining area(s).[81]

4.3 Dedicated Hydrogen Pipelines

The construction of hydrogen pipelines does not necessitate the obtaining of a decision on the environmental conditions.[82] Instead, entities seeking to begin construction work on dedicated hydrogen pipelines must submit a request to the General Director for Environmental Protection to determine the scope of the environmental assessment.[83] The General Director has fourteen days to issue a decision on the conditions for the realization of strategic investment.[84]

4.4 Repurposed Natural Gas Pipelines

The repurposing of natural gas pipelines into hydrogen pipelines also requires compliance with the EIA regulations. Construction of pipelines that meet the technical thresholds of projects requiring an EIA after repurposing necessitates a decision on the

[76] Penev, Zuboy, and Hunter (n 29) 93; EIA Regulation art 2(1)(21); EIA Act art 59(2).
[77] EIA Act art 63(1).
[78] ibid art 65(1).
[79] Amendment art 6(1). The Amendment adds a hydrogen transport installation to the fourth point in art 75(1)(1)(a) of the EIA Act. A Regional Director for Environmental Protection is the competent body for issuing a decision on the environmental conditions in cases of projects that may always have a significant impact on the environment.
[80] EIA Act art 75(5).
[81] ibid.
[82] EIA Act art 103b; The chapter VA of the EIA Act aims at streamlining the permitting process for the construction of strategic investments. Accordingly, chapters III and V are not applicable to the projects which qualify as strategic investments, and fulfil conditions listed in art 103a of the EIA Act.
[83] ibid art 103c(1).
[84] ibid art 103c(7).

environmental conditions from the Regional Director of Environmental Protection.[85] The pipelines which do not meet the technical thresholds of pipelines requiring an EIA before and after repurposing are projects which may potentially have an impact on the environment.[86] An EIA may then be necessary, depending on the competent body issuing the decision, which in this scenario is the commune head, mayor or the city president.[87]

5. Construction Permit

Having established which projects require an EIA, it becomes easier to understand the conditions for obtaining the third and final permit that is discussed in this chapter: the construction permit.

5.1 Substantive Law

The Construction Act necessitates a construction permit before construction work can commence.[88] This permit enables an entity to commence construction of a building or carry out construction works on structures other than buildings.[89] The construction permit is understood as 'an unilateral administrative decision authorizing the commencement and execution or the performance of construction works other than the construction of a building structure', under the Construction Act.[90] Commencing construction without a construction permit is classified as an unauthorized construction within the meaning of the Construction Act and such construction might be demolished.[91] Importantly, the construction permit is always required for projects which necessitate a decision on environmental conditions.[92]

Under the Construction Act, 'a linear structure is a structure which characteristic parameter is length, in particular ... a pipeline'.[93] The Construction Act defines a construction (*budowla*) as any building object (which is not a building (*budynek*)) or a small architecture object, such as a linear structure.[94] Furthermore, a building object (*obiekt budowlany*) is defined as a building, construction (*budowla*) or a small architectural object.[95] Accordingly, the pipeline transporting hydrogen would fall under the

85 EIA Act art 75(1)(1)(a) and EIA Regulation art 2(2)(1); EIA is required for natural gas installations which reach the thresholds of 800 mm outer diameter and more and length of 40 km.
86 EIA Regulation art 3(2)(1).
87 EIA Act art 63(1) and art 75(1)(4).
88 Construction Act art 28(1).
89 ibid art 3(12).
90 ibid.
91 ibid art 48(1) and art 49(e).
92 ibid art 28(3a).
93 ibid art 3(3a).
94 ibid art 3(3).
95 ibid art 3(1).

scope of linear objects and, therefore, also under the scope of building objects (*obiekt budowlany*).

5.2 Procedural Law

The Construction Act designates the architectural and construction administration authority as the relevant administrative body, which consists of three entities: the starost, the voivode, and the Chief Inspector of Construction Supervision.[96] For strategic investments, such as hydrogen pipelines, the authority responsible for issuing the construction permit is the voivode with territorial jurisdiction.[97] Additionally, a construction permit may only be granted to an entity that has received a decision of the President of the Energy Regulatory Office, officially designating them as the operator of the gas transmission system.[98]

The decision concerning the construction permit must be issued within sixty-five days from the date the permit application is submitted, otherwise a fine is imposed on the issuing authority.[99] However, the Construction Act clarifies that this deadline does not apply to projects requiring an EIA.[100] Notably, the act does not provide any alternative deadlines for projects necessitating an EIA.

5.3 Dedicated Hydrogen Pipelines

A construction permit is always required for the construction of dedicated hydrogen pipelines. The Strategic Investments Act specifies that the construction permit for a strategic investment is equivalent to the construction permit regulated by the Construction Act.[101] Therefore, the standard procedures for obtaining a construction permit apply.

First, a construction permit is required for gas transmission pipelines that necessitate an EIA.[102] Second, even if a pipeline does not meet the technical thresholds to automatically require an EIA, the Construction Act mandates a construction permit for gas transmission pipelines operating at pressures exceeding 0.5 MPa.[103] For strategic investments, the application for the construction permit must be submitted to the locally competent voivode.[104]

[96] ibid arts 80(1), 82(2), 82(3), and 88(1).
[97] Strategic Investments Act art 13(1).
[98] Construction Act art 32(4)(3).
[99] ibid art 35(6)(1).
[100] Construction Act art 35(6a); projects requiring EIA include pipelines with an outer diameter of not less than 800 mm and length of not less than 40 km, unless passing through a Natura 2000 area.
[101] Strategic Investments Act art 3b(3).
[102] Construction Act art 29(6); pipelines which fall under the scope of projects that may always have a significant impact on the environment, thus with an outer diameter of 800 mm or more and a length of 42 km or more.
[103] ibid art 29(1)(2)(e); As explained in the introduction, hydrogen which is transported via pipelines is transported under a pressure over 0.5 MPa which means that the construction permit for hydrogen pipelines is required.
[104] Strategic Investments Act art 13(1).

It is noteworthy that the Amendment also established the requirement to obtain a construction permit before constructing hydrogen pipelines operating at pressures higher than 0.5 MPa.[105]

5.4 Repurposed Natural Gas Pipelines

The repurposing of natural gas pipelines for hydrogen transportation is governed by a different set of regulations than those applicable to the construction of dedicated hydrogen infrastructure. The Construction Act distinguishes between the terms 'change of use' (*zmiana sposobu użytkowania*) and 'reconstruction' (*przebudowa*).[106] A 'change of use' of a building or its part refers to altering the way a building or its part is used, particularly when the activities involved may have a significant environmental impact.[107] Such repurposing requires a decision on environmental conditions.[108] A construction permit is not required in these circumstances but the administrative body must be notified.[109] For natural gas pipelines that are classified as strategic investments, the relevant authority is the voivode, whereas for other pipelines, it is the starost.[110] The notification must specify the pipeline's current (transport of natural gas) and intended use (hydrogen transport).[111]

Additionally, the Construction Act defines 'reconstruction' as construction works that result in changes to the functional or technical parameters of an existing building object.[112] The building object includes 'installations ensuring the possibility of using the object in accordance with its purpose'.[113] As such, components of the natural gas infrastructure should be identified as 'installations' falling under this definition, as they are essential for the functioning of the pipeline infrastructure 'in accordance with their purpose', which is to transport natural gas. Accordingly, modifying these 'installations' would be essential for the new pipeline to function 'in accordance with its purpose', which in this case is to transport hydrogen. Therefore, the replacement of parts which would make the pipeline suitable for hydrogen transport would be classified as 'reconstruction' under the Construction Act. This classification arises from the fact that the functional parameters of the pipeline would change, as it will no longer transport natural gas but hydrogen. There is ambiguity regarding the extent of changes allowed under the definition of 'reconstruction'. Specifically, it is unclear where the boundary lies between reconstruction and initiation of a new project, which would necessitate a

[105] Amendment art 1(1)(a); The Amendment includes point f) after point e) in Construction Act art 3 pointing out the necessity of construction permit for hydrogen pipelines operating under pressure over 0.5 MPa.

[106] Construction Act art 71(1)(2) and art 3(7a).

[107] ibid art 71(1)(2); See EIA section on projects which might have significant impact on the environment.

[108] EIA Act art 72(1a).

[109] Construction Act art 71(2).

[110] ibid art 80(1); Strategic Investments Act art 5(1).

[111] Construction Law Act art 71(2).

[112] ibid art 3(7a).

[113] ibid art 3(1).

construction permit.[114] This uncertainty arises because the law is not clear and specific at this point.

As it stands, the interpretation of the term 'repurposing' in the context of hydrogen transportation pipelines remains unclear. It is uncertain whether repurposing under the Construction Act means 'change of use' or 'reconstruction'. It seems logical to assume that repurposing would encompass both definitions, as the pipelines are transitioning from transporting natural gas to hydrogen, while also undergoing modifications to support hydrogen transport, thus requiring reconstruction.

6. Recommendations

Following discussion on the three key permits that are required for the construction of dedicated hydrogen pipelines, as well as the repurposing of natural gas pipelines, recommendations on how to improve the process will now be provided. These recommendations are structured alongside the four key elements of this chapter: substantive law, procedural law, the construction of dedicated hydrogen infrastructure, and, finally, the repurposing of natural gas pipelines for hydrogen transport.

6.1 Substantive Law

The primary issue with Polish legislation governing the three permits is the ambiguity of terms and definitions, particularly within the Construction Act. This problem can be addressed by clarifying the definitions within the Construction Act in order to improve legal certainty.

The Polish Construction Act currently lacks a clear definition of 'repurposing' in the context of adapting natural gas pipelines for hydrogen transport. It does not specify whether such repurposing should be classified as a 'change of use', 'reconstruction', or something in between. While it is clear that administrative authorities need to be notified in either case, the repurposing of natural gas pipelines for hydrogen transport would require a decision on environmental conditions.[115]

Moreover, it remains unclear whether or not the repurposing of a natural gas pipeline for hydrogen transport would qualify as a new construction project under the Construction Act. Given that the lack of legal certainty could deter efforts to repurpose natural gas pipelines for hydrogen transport, this issue highlights the pressing need for further legislative clarification. Notably, the Amendment does not address this issue, potentially leading to complications in the future. Accordingly, this should immediately be changed in the current legislative process.

[114] The Construction Act art 3(6) defines a construction as 'construction of a building in a specific place, as well as reconstruction, expansion, superstructure of a building'.

[115] Hydrogen transport exceeds 0.5 MPa thus it necessitates EIA.

Therefore, including a clear definition of 'repurposing' within the context of adapting natural gas pipelines for hydrogen transport would provide much-needed legal clarity, ensuring a more robust and effective legal framework.

6.2 Procedural Law

A key recommendation for procedural law is streamlining the permitting process for the construction of dedicated hydrogen pipelines and repurposing of natural gas pipelines. This requires a regulatory framework that provides clear guidance on the procedural steps and the necessary authorizations, consolidating the relevant information.

It is important to note that certain permits may be contingent upon the fulfilment of other permitting requirements, with numerous provisions cross-referencing others within the same act or different statutes. This complexity causes navigating the regulatory landscape to be difficult. A potential solution to this issue could be the development of a digital platform for the entities involved or interested in hydrogen transport. Such a system could provide a clear overview of procedures, timelines, and required permits, simplifying the permitting process.

Furthermore, the permitting process could be significantly more efficient if the coordination between various administrative bodies involved was improved. For instance, in the case of dedicated hydrogen pipelines, the voivode's decision on the location is binding on the local authorities, effectively elevating the decision-making process to the regional level. Such coordination could be improved by establishing a single point of contact or a coordinating body that oversees all administrative actions related to hydrogen transportation pipelines.

6.3 Dedicated Hydrogen Pipelines

The regulatory framework governing dedicated hydrogen pipelines offers the most clarity of the ones that have been researched. The existing Strategic Investments Act provides clear procedures for obtaining a decision on the location, a requirement for an EIA, and a decision on the environmental conditions, as well as construction permits.

A potential recommendation for dedicated hydrogen pipelines would be the introduction of a fast-track or an integrated permit system specifically designed for this type of infrastructure. The Strategic Investments Act is a clear example of how the approval process for transmission networks can be effectively accelerated. Therefore, the next logical step would be to create a unified permitting system where a single application is submitted to the voivode (or another single point authority), to further speed up and streamline the entire permitting process.

6.4 Repurposed Natural Gas Pipelines

Repurposing natural gas pipelines has proven to be a rather complex operation under the current permitting regime. As demonstrated by the first discussed permit, many factors influence the process, including the pipeline's location, technical thresholds, and its classification as a public purpose project or not. The procedures and the responsible administrative bodies vary depending on whether the original pipeline was built in compliance with a local plan, or whether it was developed under the Strategic Investments Act.

This area of the permitting process requires significant legislative refinement and further research. Streamlining the natural gas pipeline repurposing process would substantially improve the efficiency of the permitting system. Establishing clear procedures that outline when new decisions are required or when existing permits need to be amended would contribute to a more transparent and effective process.

Finally, the permitting process for the repurposing natural gas pipelines for hydrogen transport involves decision-making at various levels and requires input from administrative authorities at both local and regional levels. Establishing a single authority responsible for the entire process would provide further clarity. If designating one authority is not possible, then at the very least, establishing a clear decision-making hierarchy would provide much needed transparency and consistency in the permitting process.

7. Conclusion

The legal framework governing hydrogen transportation pipelines in Poland remains complex and requires specialized expertise. Navigating the numerous laws and regulations can be challenging for those without professional legal knowledge. A positive development is the forthcoming Amendment, which provides some clarity on hydrogen regulation, addressing the current absence of a clear definition of hydrogen in the Energy Act.

By 2030, Poland intends to reach 2 GW of installed capacity from low-emission sources and processes, allowing for the production of 193,634.06 tonnes of hydrogen per year.[116] Achieving that goal and developing a hydrogen economy in Poland necessitates legislative reforms. Although EU law has an influence on the Polish legislation, the question whether or not EU law acts as a driver or an obstacle to legislative and procedural change for hydrogen transport in Poland lies beyond the scope of this chapter. It can be noted, however, that the EU is working intensively on the so-called EU Hydrogen Backbone initiative. Poland's participation in this initiative is likely to increase the pressure to align its legislative structure with that of the Hydrogen

[116] Polish Hydrogen Strategy 20.

Backbone.[117] Finally, while the new Polish government faces various challenges, prioritizing hydrogen economy, and at the same time hydrogen transportation infrastructure, is essential for the country's future, and should be given even greater priority than it has to this date.

Further Reading

Polish Acts

Act of 8 March 1990 on Local Self-Government (Consolidated Version Journal of Laws 2024 item 609 with amendments) [*Ustawa z dnia 8 marca 1990 r. o samorządzie gminnym (tj Dz U 2024 poz 609 ze zm)*].

Act of 7 July 1994—Construction Act (Consolidated Version Journal of Laws 2024 item 725 with amendments) [*Ustawa z dnia 7 lipca 1994 r.—Prawo budowlane (tj Dz U 2024 poz 725 ze zm)*].

Act of 10 April 1997—Energy Act (Consolidated Version Journal of Laws 2024 item 266 with amendments) [*Ustawa z dnia 10 kwietnia 1997 roku—Prawo Energetyczne (tj Dz U 2024 poz 266 ze zm)*].

Act of 3 October 2008 on Providing Information on the Environment and its Protection, Public Participation in Environmental Protection and Environmental Impact Assessment (Consolidated version Journal of Laws 2024 No 1112 with amendments) [*Ustawa z dnia 3 października 2008 r. o udostępnianiu informacji o środowisku i jego ochronie, udziale społeczeństwa w ochronie środowiska oraz o ocenach oddziaływania na środowisko (tj Dz U 2024 poz 1112 ze zm)*].

Act of 24 July 2015 on the Preparation and Implementation of Strategic Investments in Transmission Networks (Consolidated Version Journal of Laws 2024 item 1199 with amendments) [*Ustawa z dnia 24 lipca 2015 r. o przygotowaniu i realizacji strategicznych inwestycji w zakresie sieci przesyłowych (tj Dz U 2024 poz 1199 ze zm)*].

Regulation of the Council of Ministers of 10 September 2019 on Projects That May Have a Significant Impact on the Environment (Journal of Laws 2019, item 1839) [*Rozporządzenie Rady Ministrów z dnia 10 września 2019 r. w sprawie przedsięwzięć mogących znacząco oddziaływać na środowisko (Dz U 2019 poz 1839)*].

Resolution No 149 of the Council of Ministers of 2 November 2021 on the Adoption of the 'Polish Hydrogen Strategy until 2030 with an Outlook until 2040' (Polish Monitor—Official Journal of the Republic of Poland, Warsaw 7 December 2021, item 1138) [*Uchwała nr 149 Rady Ministrów z dnia 2 listopada 2021 r. w sprawie przyjęcia 'Polskiej strategii wodorowej do roku 2030 z perspektywą do 2040 roku' (Monitor Polski—Dziennik Urzędowy Rzeczypospolitej Polskiej, Warszawa dnia 7 grudnia 2021 r., poz 1138)*].

Books

Judith Rosales, *Environmental Impact Assessment* (Delve Publishing 2021).

Journal articles

Jayanti S Evans-Pritchard, 'Repurposing Pipelines for Hydrogen: Legal and Policy Considerations' (2022) 8 Energy Reports 815.

L Gawlik and E Mokrzycki, 'Analysis of the Polish Hydrogen Strategy in the Context of the EU's Strategic Documents on Hydrogen' (2021) 14(6382) Energies 1.

A Lipiński, 'Miejscowy plan zagospodarowania przestrzennego jako źródło prawa' (2017) 1 Prawne Problemy Górnictwa i Ochrony Środowiska 33.

F Moreno-Brieva, J Guimón, and J C Salazar-Elena, 'From Grey to Green and from West to East: The Geography and Innovation Trajectories of Hydrogen Fuel Technologies' (2023) 101 Energy Research & Social Science 1.

K Muzyczka, 'Pozwolenie na budowę a miejscowy plan zagospodarowania przestrzennego' (2017) 17 Zeszyty Naukowe Gdańskiej Szkoły Wyższej 279.

[117] ibid 22.

M Penev, J Zuboy, and C Hunter, 'Economic Analysis of a High-Pressure Urban Pipeline Concept (HyLine) for Delivering Hydrogen to Retail Fuelling Stations' (2019) 77 Transportation Research Part D 92.

Online journals

E Kochanek, 'Evaluation of Energy Transition Scenarios in Poland' (2021) 14(6058) Energies 1, 1.

A Kovač, M Paranos, and D Marciuš, 'Hydrogen in Energy Transition: A Review' (2021) 46(16) International Journal of Hydrogen Energy 10016, 10021.

J Łubecki, 'Realizacja strategicznych inwestycji w zakresie sieci przesyłowych—czyli co i komu da specustawa przesyłowa?' (2015) 5–6 Nowa Energia 8, 9.

Pipeline Safety Trust, 'Pipeline Basics & Specifics About Natural Gas Pipelines' (2024) 2 Pipeline Briefing Paper 1, 1.

Websites

'Miejscowy plan zagospodarowania przestrzennego' (biznes.gov.pl, 29 September 2024) https://www.biznes.gov.pl/pl/portal/ou357 accessed 6 October 2024.

LM Andreasson, K de Graaf, and M Roggenkamp, 'Regulatory Framework: Legal Challenges and Incentives for the Development of Hydrogen Infrastructure in Port Areas' (New Energy Coalition 31 December 2020) https://www.newenergycoalition.org/custom/uploads/2021/04/Havenschets-Report-Final-Regulatory-Framework-Liv-Malin-Andreasson-1.pdf accessed 1 September 2024.

European Union Agency for the Cooperation of Energy Regulators, 'Transporting Pure Hydrogen by Repurposing Existing Gas Infrastructure: Overview of Existing Studies and Reflections on the Conditions for Repurposing' (ACER 2021) https://www.scribd.com/document/697691738/Transporting-Pure-Hydrogen-by-Repurposing-Existing-Gas-Infrastructure-Overview-of-studies accessed 1 September 2024.

International Energy Agency, 'Poland 2022 Energy Policy Review' (International Energy Agency 2022) https://iea.blob.core.windows.net/assets/b9ea5a7d-3e41-4318-a69e-f7d456ebb118/Poland2022.pdf accessed 19 August 2024.

XII
Legal Barriers in the Dutch Permitting Regime for the Rollout of Hydrogen for Industrial High-Temperature Heating Processes

Jeanette Maria Jansen

1. Introduction

As the global shift towards clean energy accelerates, hydrogen is gaining recognition as a crucial piece of the puzzle for decarbonizing hard-to-abate sectors.[1] This chapter explores a key example to highlight the legal challenges associated with its use. The focus is on industries in the Netherlands that rely on high-temperature heating processes such as steel, cement, glass, and ceramics, which require heating at temperatures above 400°C. For these sectors, electricity-based solutions may not be viable, requiring hydrogen as one key alternative to fossil fuels. As such, it may be argued that hydrogen application should be prioritized for these sectors.[2] Although over 60 million tonnes of hydrogen are produced globally each year for use as chemical feedstock, its direct application in high-temperature heating remains at the early stages of development.[3]

[1] International Energy Agency, *Global Hydrogen Review 2023* (2023) 18.

[2] European Environmental Bureau, *Policy Brief: A Sustainable Hydrogen Strategy for the EU* (2023) 8.

[3] Gregory P Thiel and Addison K Stark, 'To Decarbonize Industry, We Must Decarbonize Heat' (2021) 5 Joule 531; Max Wei, Colin A McMillan, and Stephane de la Rue du Can, 'Electrification of Industry: Potential,

This will change in the coming years. The EU's REPowerEU plan aims for domestic renewable hydrogen production of 10 million tonnes by 2030, and for import of another 10 million tonnes.[4] The purpose is to decarbonize existing hydrogen production (eg industry feedstocks), but also 'facilitating take up of hydrogen consumption in *new end-use applications* such as *other industrial processes*'.[5] Electrolysis is considered to be a key technology with high potential for decarbonization towards building a carbon-neutral society if applied on a large scale.[6]

In the Netherlands, hydrogen is an integral part of the national strategy to achieve net-zero emissions, as stipulated in the Dutch Climate Act of 2019 and the Climate Agreement.[7] The Climate Act establishes emission-reduction targets for 2030 and 2050, while the Climate Agreement outlines measures to achieve these goals. In 2023, the national ambitions were raised due to more ambitious EU targets. The new aim is to cut greenhouse gas (GHG) emissions by 55% by 2030 (compared to 1990 levels) and achieve climate neutrality by 2050. Hydrogen deployment is considered crucial to meeting these objectives, with a specific goal of deploying 3–4 GW of electrolyser capacity by 2030.[8]

The Climate Agreement thus sets the groundwork for the future role of hydrogen in the Netherlands, which is further developed in the country's National Hydrogen Programme.[9] The programme shows that the Dutch hydrogen decarbonization strategy targets various applications. This also includes high-temperature industrial processes (eg furnaces, ovens, and kilns), which are recognized to be particularly challenging to decarbonize.[10]

Challenges and Outlook' (2019) 6 Springer 140, 141; Ankica Kovač, Matej Paranos, and Doria Marciuš, 'Hydrogen in Energy Transition: A Review' (2021) 46 International Journal of Hydrogen Energy 10015; Steve Griffith and others, 'Industrial Decarbonization via Hydrogen: A Critical and Systematic Review of Developments, Socio-technical Systems and Policy Options' (2021) 80 Energy Research & Social Science 1, 2.

[4] European Commission, *Hydrogen* (2022) https://energy.ec.europa.eu/topics/energy-systems-integration/hydrogen_en#:~:text=The%20REPowerEU%20Strategy%20of%202022,processes%20and%20the%20transport%20sector accessed 24 May 2025.

[5] European Commission, *Communication from the Commission to the European Parliament, the Council, the European Economic and Social Committee and the Committee of the Regions: A Hydrogen Strategy for a Climate-Neutral Europe* COM (2020) 301 final; European Commission, *Communication from the Commission to the European Parliament, the European Council, the Council, the European Economic and Social Committee, and the Committee of the Regions: REPowerEU Plan* COM (2022) 230 final.

[6] ibid.

[7] Rijksoverheid, *Klimaatakkoord* (2019) https://open.overheid.nl/documenten/ronl-7f383713-bf88-451d-a652-fbd0b1254c06/pdf accessed 24 May 2025; Wet van 2 juli 2019, houdende een kader voor het ontwikkelen van beleid gericht op onomkeerbaar en stapsgewijs terugdringen van de Nederlandse emissies van broeikasgassen teneinde wereldwijde opwarming van de aarde en de verandering van het klimaat te beperken (Klimaatwet), Staatsblad 2019, 253; Tweede Kamer, *Wijziging van de Klimaatwet afgerond* (2023) https://www.tweedekamer.nl/kamerstukken/plenaire_verslagen/kamer_in_het_kort/wijziging-van-de-klimaatwet-afgerond-1 accessed 24 May 2025. See also OECD, 'Hydrogen Governance in the Netherlands' *Risk-based Regulatory Design for the Safe Use of Hydrogen* (OECD Publishing 2023) 85.

[8] Rijksoverheid, *Waterstof* (n.d.) https://www.rijksoverheid.nl/onderwerpen/duurzame-energie/waterstof accessed 24 May 2025.

[9] Nationaal Programma Waterstof, *Routekaart Waterstof* (2022) https://nationaalwaterstofprogramma.nl/documenten/handlerdownloadfiles.ashx?idnv=2339011 accessed 24 May 2025.

[10] Cross-sectorale werkgroep waterstof, *Werkplan Nationaal Waterstof Programma 2022-2025* (2021) https://open.overheid.nl/documenten/ronl-47be8733-0b7f-4d80-a293-79031070271c/pdf accessed 24 May 2025, annex D.

While the Dutch government's National Hydrogen Programme and the broader EU plans outline ambitious aims for scaling up hydrogen production and usage across industrial sectors, '[t]here is a disconnect between the large hydrogen pledges ... and the relatively limited progress in its deployment in practice'.[11] Indeed, in the Netherlands, the use of hydrogen as a fuel in high-temperature heating processes is currently at a pilot stage, and there is relatively little experience with permitting for this type of activity.[12] This could imply that hydrogen is subject to more constraining legislation than its 'hydrocarbon competitors'—because of the lack of a targeted legal framework it could end up being regulated as more high-risk activity than oil and gas, with stricter provisions.[13]

Facilitating a seamless transition to hydrogen use in high-temperature heating processes will require a robust legal and regulatory framework.[14] Therefore, the anticipated expansion of hydrogen applications requires an understanding of potential legal barriers in the existing governance structure. In this light, it is interesting to assess an important prerequisite for the application of hydrogen in practice: the permitting procedures.

Hydrogen use in high-temperature applications requires two steps: (i) the *production* of hydrogen itself—which is discussed in the first part of this book in more depth and will only be briefly discussed in this chapter where relevant, and (ii) the *end use* of hydrogen in high-temperature processes. The latter will be the focal point of this chapter, identifying legal barriers in the Dutch permitting regime.

The chapter proceeds as follows: section 2 provides a broad overview of the context, explaining relevant characteristics of hydrogen and industrial processes. Section 3 delves into the Dutch permitting regime for industrial consumers seeking to integrate hydrogen into high-temperature heating processes. It begins with procedural issues before addressing substantive issues related to using hydrogen as a fuel in high-temperature heating processes. The focus is on two key aspects in the permitting regime: environmental and safety considerations for industrial hydrogen consumers. By examining these aspects, this section highlights that hydrogen may still face unnecessarily stringent regulations, particularly for small-scale experimental projects. These projects are crucial for industrial consumers, supporting a learning phase in which they navigate the complexities of fuel-sensitive operations and products. Section 4 offers three key recommendations to address the issues identified in Section 3 regarding the Dutch permitting regime. Section 5 concludes the chapter.

[11] OECD, 'Hydrogen in Context' in OECD (n 7) 59.

[12] Nationaal Programma Waterstof (n 9) 66.

[13] OECD, 'Hydrogen Applications in Practice' in OECD (n 7) 100.

[14] OECD, 'Regulatory Governance and Delivery in the Energy Transition' in ibid 65, 70; International Energy Agency, *Energy Technology Perspectives* (2023) 24–25 https://www.iea.org/reports/energy-technology-perspectives-2023 accessed 24 May 2025.

2. Scope and Characteristics

This chapter focuses on the permitting considerations surrounding hydrogen integration into high-temperature industrial processes, assuming hydrogen is produced through electrolysis at the industrial site where it is stored (temporarily) and used. This simplifies the analysis by excluding spatial planning and infrastructure-related legal challenges, such as permits for pipelines or transportation. Instead, the goal is to understand the general permitting rules and requirements for hydrogen usage to decarbonize industrial processes. The analysis remains eclectic regarding the 'colour' of hydrogen, as any type capable of decarbonizing high-temperature processes could be relevant.[15]

2.1 Hydrogen Characteristics

The characteristics of hydrogen, along with the technologies used in its deployment, distinguish it from conventional fuels.[16] Hydrogen is a gas that is colourless, odourless, tasteless, non-toxic, and environmentally benign, possessing distinctive physical and chemical properties that are key to its production, storage, and utilization.[17] While hydrogen has a high energy content per kilogram, its low density results in a relatively low energy content per cubic meter.[18]

Hydrogen's broad flammability limits compared to natural gas (methane) mean it can ignite or explode over a wider range of concentrations in air. These properties may lead to a perception of being more hazardous than methane, which could result in stricter permitting requirements.[19] This perception, and its impact on permitting procedures, is discussed in section 3.

2.2 On-site Storage

When electrolysers are placed at industrial sites, temporary hydrogen storage is often necessary. This enables a stable and reliable hydrogen supply to accommodate varying industrial demands throughout the day or operational cycles. It also offers operational flexibility, allowing continuous hydrogen production even during periods of low demand. Furthermore, hydrogen produced during periods of excess electricity (eg from renewable sources) can be stored for use when electricity is scarce or more expensive.[20]

[15] There are various methods for producing hydrogen, which determines its colour, see eg Ruven Fleming, 'Clear or Renewable—Hydrogen and Power-to-Gas in EU Energy Law' (2021) 39 Journal of Energy and Natural Resources Law 43, 44.
[16] OECD (n 11) 59.
[17] Griffiths and others (n 3) 3.
[18] OECD (n 11) 59.
[19] Griffiths and others (n 3) 3.
[20] ibid.

Given hydrogen's low density, efficient storage typically requires compression or liquefaction. For the purposes of this chapter, storage involves a compression and storage unit.[21] Noise emissions from compression units may have permitting implications (as discussed in the first part of this book), while environmental and safety considerations are also crucial when storing hydrogen under pressure.[22] This analysis assumes above-ground storage as underground storage is regulated by a different set of rules that lie beyond the chapter's scope.

2.3 Hydrogen Usage in High-Temperature Industrial Processes

In contrast to some industries where hydrogen has been widely used as a feedstock, there is limited experience with hydrogen as a fuel in the industry. It should be noted that the fuel switch required is complex, as industries using gases in high-temperature heating processes are marked by a high degree of diversity.[23] For example, some processes and products may be more sensitive than others, and some steps may depend on each other, needing to be timed exactly right and executed in precision.[24] The glass industry falls under the category of sensitive users, and considering the distinct characteristics of hydrogen in comparison to natural gas, it is considered imperative to discern the effects on material quality before large-scale implementation of hydrogen.[25]

For this reason, while large quantities of hydrogen are still unavailable due to the lack of a developed market, industries may choose to start with small-scale experimentation projects to gain insights. These projects could involve blending varying amounts of hydrogen into their processes. In the Netherlands, some companies are already conducting on-site, smaller-scale experiments with hydrogen admixtures to understand hydrogen's impact on their operations, products, and emissions.[26]

In principle, a mixture of hydrogen and natural gas can be used if the burners are compatible.[27] This can be done at low percentages without needing modifications to

[21] OECD (n 11) 59.
[22] Griffiths and others (n 3) 21.
[23] Jörg Leicher and others, 'Hydrogen in Natural Gas: How Does It Impact Industrial End Users?' (World Gas Conference 2018) 1–3 https://www.researchgate.net/publication/326199589_Hydrogen_in_natural_gas_how_does_it_affect_industrial_end_users accessed 20 September 2024.
[24] ibid.
[25] ibid 16.
[26] An example in the Netherlands is Getec Emmen, which operates on an industrial park where it places a small-scale electrolyser to produce hydrogen which is to be blended with natural gas on site. The aim is to learn what hydrogen does to the relevant process, installations, and products. Getec adapted its industrial burners in order to process hydrogen and blends of hydrogen with natural gas. The intention is to introduce hydrogen in the high-temperature heating process in phases, eventually operating on 100% hydrogen. See eg Platform Verduurzaming Industrie, *Getec Park Emmen stapt gefaseerd over naar waterstof* (2023) https://verduurzamingindustrie.nl/inspiratie/2460924.aspx accessed 5 November 2024; see also Ministerie van Economische Zaken en Klimaat, *Cluster 6 Connect Samen naar een Groene en Schone Regionale Industrie* (2023) https://www.ibknl.com/media/kbnfneq3/verslag-cluster6connect-002.pdf accessed 5 November 2024.
[27] ibid 4.

the installations. However, when hydrogen concentrations are higher, adjustments to the installations (such as industrial burners) become essential to prevent operational issues.[28] In addition, blending hydrogen with natural gas reduces the calorific value of the mixture, which can affect the furnace's gas flow and, if unadjusted, lower temperatures, risking issues with material quality.[29] Furthermore, higher hydrogen concentrations may increase nitrogen oxide (NOx) emissions, complicating environmental compliance and permitting procedures.[30] As a result, experimentation with hydrogen admixtures is crucial to understanding its effects before large-scale adoption can take place.

Though this chapter does not address the legal aspects of adapting installations for varying hydrogen qualities in detail, it stresses the need for small-scale experimentation to support the integration of hydrogen into industrial settings, a key consideration for permitting.

2.4 Analysed Permits

Three permits were analysed for this chapter: two for the placement and operation of an electrolyser unit.[31] Only one permit was found that considers the use of hydrogen in a high-temperature industrial heating process, albeit being a temporary permit for an experimental project.[32] Table XII.1 below provides an overview. It should be noted that these permits were issued before 2024, while on 1 January 2024 a new law came into place that significantly changed the permitting regime, the *Omgevingswet* (Environmental and Planning Act, hereafter Ow). Despite this, the permits remain relevant because many of the underlying rules persist, offering insights into the approaches of permitting authorities.

[28] Nationaal Programma Waterstof (n 9) 66.

[29] Leicher and others (n 23) 16.

[30] ibid 16; Nationaal Programma Waterstof (n 9) 66.

[31] Provincie Friesland, *Besluit Omgevingsvergunning* (Z2021–002320, 8 September 2021) https://www.planviewer.nl/imro/files/NL.IMRO.9921.EcomunityWaterstof-VA01/d_NL.IMRO.9921.EcomunityWaterstof-VA01.pdf accessed 24 May 2025 (hereafter Permit Friesland);

Omgevingsdienst Groningen, *Besluit Omgevingsvergunning* (Z2022–001022, 4 October 2023) https://bestanden.provinciegroningen.nl/bestanden-openbaar/publicatievoorstel/KIWI_PublicatieVoorstel_IPPC_000000210003/D2023-104321%20GEANONIMISEERD%20-%20DEFINITIEF%20-%20Besluit%20%20Kloosterlaan%2012%20te%20Farmsum.pdf accessed 24 May 2025 (hereafter Permit Groningen).

[32] Ministerie van Economische Zaken en Klimaat, *Ontwerpbesluit test geschiktheid waterstof als energiedrager inrichting WHC 1/2 Veendam* (7578719, 8 November 2023) https://mijnbouwvergunningen.nl/attachment/entity/44878037-4b9c-40f7-9815-a6f6e0ac2165 accessed 24 May 2025 (hereafter Permit Industry).

See also Ministerie van Economische Zaken en Klimaat, *Verzoek om aanvullingen vergunning waterstof* (April 2023) https://mijnbouwvergunningen.nl/attachment/entity/3a718b8e-778d-43b5-b761-588ea245e818 accessed 24 May 2025 (hereafter Supplement Permit Industry).

Note that in this particular case, it concerned a mining company for which a different permitting authority was responsible (Ministry of Economic Affairs and Climate Policy). This is a unique situation, because more generally the Province is the competent authority, which in turn delegates the permitting authority to Omgevingsdiensten. See eg Instituut Fysieke Veiligheid, *Kennisbundel waterstof in de gebouwde omgeving* (2021) https://nipv.nl/wp-content/uploads/2022/03/20210324-IFV-Kennisbundel-waterstof-in-de-gebouwde-omgeving.pdf accessed 4 November 2024, 11.

Table XII.1 List of approved permits for hydrogen production or usage analysed in this chapter

Location	Approval Date	Type of project
Oosterwolde, Friesland	8 September 2021	Electrolyser producing a maximum of 1.3 MW with storage and disposal facilities (tube trailers).
Delfzijl, Groningen	4 October 2023	The electrolyser has an electrical capacity of 20 MW. The setup consists of modular electrolysis units housed in containers. Each container has an electrical capacity of 2–2.5 MW.
Veendam, Groningen	8 November 2023	This permit involves an experiment using hydrogen as a fuel for a currently natural gas-fired heating installation (ie a high-temperature heating process). The natural gas burner is to be replaced by a dual burner suitable for natural gas, hydrogen gas, and mixtures thereof. The hydrogen gas is to be supplied in tube trailers. The total expected hydrogen gas consumption during the experimental period is estimated at 4,000 kilograms (10 tube trailers).

3. 'The' Dutch Permitting Regime for Hydrogen Use in High-Temperature Heating Processes

For simplicity, this chapter refers to the permitting regime in the Netherlands. However, there is currently no comprehensive framework specifically tailored to hydrogen applications in high-temperature heating processes. Section 3 is structured as follows: first, it outlines general procedural considerations; next, it examines substantive issues related to hydrogen end-use in high-temperature heating, with a focus on environmental and safety considerations. Both play a central role in the permitting regime and are essential for obtaining approval.

As mentioned in subsection 2.4, the permitting regime underwent significant changes on 1 January 2024, with the introduction of the Ow. References to the pre-2024 permitting regime are included where relevant to provide context and clarify the current state of play.

3.1 Procedural Aspects

Pre-2024, Dutch environmental regulations used to apply when there was an 'establishment', for example local production of hydrogen at a specific location is an establishment. The manufacturing and storing of the gases necessitated an environmental permit.[33]

[33] Besluit van 25 maart 2010, houdende regels ter uitvoering van de Wet algemene bepalingen omgevingsrecht (Besluit omgevingsrecht) Staatsblad 2010, 143 (repealed on 1 January 2024) (hereafter Bor) Annex I, Categories 1.1a and 2.1a.

Dutch legislation generally provides for two procedures to obtain an environmental permit. The *reguliere* ('simplified') procedure is short, as a decision is taken within eight weeks (unless more information is required, allowing for an extension of six weeks).[34] The *uitgebreide* ('extended') procedure is twenty-six weeks (with the potential of a six-week extension) and involves additional steps, such as environmental impact assessments (EIA) or public consultations. The exact timeline depends on the complexity of the project, the need for expert assessments, and the duration of public participation processes.[35]

Before 2024, one environmental permit was required for one establishment. A new combustion oven added to a steel factory would become part of the same establishment. This would 'only' require an adaptation of the existing environmental permit.[36] The duration of the procedure would depend on whether there was an 'environmentally neutral' modification of an existing environmental permit.[37] If a modification did not result in different or greater adverse effects on the environment than already allowed by an existing environmental permit, a permit could be granted through the simplified procedure. This was not allowed if an EIA had to be conducted, for which the rules are considered more extensively in subsection 3.2.[38]

Under the new regime of the Ow, the criteria for 'environmental neutrality' have not been taken over, and the term establishment has been repealed.[39] The current regime refers to '*milieubelastende activiteiten*' (Environmentally Harmful Activities, hereafter MBA).[40]

Similar to the pre-2024 regime, amendments to an existing permit generally follow the simplified procedure if there are 'no significant adverse effects on human health or the environment'.[41] This can be determined through an 'EIA screening', further discussed in subsection 3.2. However, if a *full* EIA is required, the extended procedure must still be followed.

The analysis of permits for this chapter reveals that, at least before 2024, the extended procedure was applied in cases that might have qualified for the simplified process. The authority had discretion in determining the procedure to be followed. For instance, in one permit reviewed, while the applicant asked for a simplified procedure

[34] *Algemene wet bestuursrecht* (2021) Staatsblad 2021, 135; see s 4.1 for the simplified procedure, and s 3.4 for the extended procedure.

[35] Kenniscentrum InfoMil, *Procedure Omgevingsvergunning* (n.d.) https://www.infomil.nl/onderwerpen/ruimte/ruimtelijke/wet-algemene/procedure/ accessed 4 December 2024.

[36] *Wet algemene bepalingen omgevingsrecht* (2010) Staatsblad 2010, 231 (repealed 1 January 2024) (hereafter Wabo) art 2.1(1)(e); see also BG.Legal, 'Uitspraak van de week; begrip 'één inrichting' in milieurecht' (2015) https://bg.legal/uitspraak-van-de-week-begrip-een-inrichting-in-milieurecht/ accessed 10 September 2024.

[37] Kenniscentrum InfoMil, *Wanneer wordt het milieugedeelte van een omgevingsvergunning gewijzigd met de reguliere procedure?* (n.d.) https://www.infomil.nl/onderwerpen/integrale/wet-algemene/vragen-antwoorden/wettelijk-kader/voorbereidingsproc/wanneer/ accessed 10 September 2024.

[38] Art 3.10(3) Wabo.

[39] Valérie van 't Lam and Jan R van Angeren, 'Milieubelastende activiteiten in de Omgevingswet: Gevolgen van de overstap van het begrip inrichting naar milieubelastende activiteiten voor de praktijk en de verhouding met het omgevingsplan. Een eerste verkenning op basis van de consultatieversies van de vier amvb's' (2016) 132 Tijdschrift voor Bouwrecht 840, 841–44.

[40] *Wet van 23 maart 2016, houdende regels over het beschermen en benutten van de fysieke leefomgeving* (2016) Staatsblad 2016, 156 (entered into force 1 January 2024) ('Omgevingswet'; hereafter Ow) annex 1.1 Ow.

[41] Translated from Dutch, see art 4.22(2)(d) Ow.

to be followed,[42] the authority justified using the extended procedure on the grounds that the proposed activity constituted 'an entirely new activity' (eg using a different fuel or fuel mixtures).[43] Notably, this procedure took even longer than the typical extended timeline of twenty-six weeks, despite the small scale of the project. This suggests that permitting authorities may perceive the novelty and associated risks of using hydrogen as a combustion fuel as warranting a more cautious (and lengthy) permitting process. This may be partly due to hydrogen's lack of explicit recognition as a fuel within the legislative framework, as discussed in the following section.

Finally, a relevant procedural aspect to note is that under Article 5.7 of the Ow, a single permit application can cover multiple activities, such as the installation of an electrolyser on an industrial site and the subsequent use of hydrogen. In principle, this provision could streamline the permitting process by consolidating related activities into one application and aligning them under a single decision-making period. However, the need for additional steps, such as environmental impact assessments, may still cause delays.

3.2 Substantive Aspects

3.2.1 Hydrogen fuel end-use

A key issue in the current legislative framework is that hydrogen is not explicitly recognized as a 'standard fuel'.[44] The *Besluit activiteiten leefomgeving* (Environmental Activities Decree; hereafter Bal) lists standard fuels such as natural gas, for which specific, relatively lenient rules apply.[45] A new permit is generally not required for using or altering a standard fuel in an industrial heating process; a simple notification to the competent authority may suffice.[46] However, hydrogen does not feature on this list. Hence, the Bal mentions 'non-standard fuels' (eg hydrogen), for which an environmental permit is required by definition—along with inspection/maintenance rules and specific emission limits for different types of industrial installations (Articles 4.1346 to 4.1350). Non-standard fuels, including hydrogen, require an extended permitting procedure by default.

There are exemptions to these rules. For example, Article 4.1343 of the Bal allows for exemptions to the emission limits and inspection/maintenance rules for heating installations if the installation operates for no more than 500 hours per year. However, this

[42] See Permit Industry (n 32) 3 and Supplement Permit Industry (n 32).
[43] Permit Industry (n 32) 2.
[44] See eg ibid. This is also recognized in other contexts—ie for the development of infrastructure, the *Gaswet* (hereafter Gas Act) is relevant. However, hydrogen gas is not considered a fuel in this law. In this context, this has temporarily been resolved with additional guidance documents. However, the Minister of Climate Policy recognizes that at some point, the explicit consideration of hydrogen as fuel in law is required. See *Wet van 22 juni 2000, houdende regels omtrent het transport en de levering van gas* (*Gaswet*) Staatsblad 2000, 305; Tijdo van der Zee, 'Rijk wil regie op waterstof' (2022) https://www.installatie.nl/nieuws/rijk-wil-regie-op-waterstof/ accessed 24 May 2025.
[45] *Besluit van 3 juli 2018, houdende regels over activiteiten in de fysieke leefomgeving* (*Besluit activiteiten leefomgeving*) (2018) Staatsblad 2018, 293 (entered into force 1 January 2024) (hereafter Bal).
[46] ibid s 4.1.6.

is not always applied in practice, highlighting the permitting authority's discretion in determining the procedure to be followed. One of the permits analysed in this chapter illustrates this point. Although the 500-hour exemption could have applied—given that the requested activity for hydrogen use as a fuel would only last eighty hours—the permitting authority opted for a more stringent approach. It required the application of the extended procedure, including additional information on emissions, and did not apply the 500-hour exemption. Instead, the authority imposed provisions to ensure the modified heating installation would still undergo inspections.[47] This approach was taken 'considering the nature of the experiment, the risks associated with hydrogen, and the modified burner'.[48] It underscores the perception of hydrogen as a potentially high-risk fuel, necessitating stricter regulations and increased monitoring. Thus, even when companies opt for relatively small-scale experimental projects, permitting authorities may adopt a cautious stance, requiring an extended procedure of up to twenty-six weeks (with possible extensions) due to the novelty of hydrogen use.

This situation highlights a potential disconnect between the Dutch government's ambitious goals for expanding hydrogen use in novel applications like high-temperature heating and the practical realities of the permitting regime. The lack of specific references to hydrogen in the legislation creates potential ambiguity about applicable standards,[49] while absence of clear recognition of hydrogen as a standard fuel could lead to unnecessary delays and complexities in the permitting process. These obstacles could hinder both industrial companies and permitting authorities, slowing the transition to hydrogen-based decarbonization solutions.

In addition to the uncertainties surrounding hydrogen's status as a fuel, there are key environmental considerations that must be taken into account when navigating the Dutch permitting process.

3.2.2 Environmental considerations

Until the revision of the Industrial Emissions Directive (IED) in 2024, even small-scale hydrogen projects were subject to its stringent environmental regime due to the absence of threshold values for inclusion. As a result, any hydrogen production project was considered to be 'at an industrial scale'.[50] However, the revised IED introduced threshold values that could simplify permitting.[51] Annex I on 'Categories of activities

[47] Permit Industry (n 32) 7. Note that even though the permit was issued under the pre-2024 regime, the 500-hour exemption already existed. Therefore, the old regime provides some insight into the interpretation of the Ow rules.

[48] Translated from Dutch, Permit Industry (n 32) 7.

[49] For additional context, it should be noted that there are some rules on hydrogen combustion and the registration of emissions, eg see Regulation (EC) No 166/2006 of the European Parliament and of the Council of 18 January 2006 concerning the establishment of a European Pollutant Release and Transfer Register and amending Council Directives 91/689/EEC and 96/61/EC, OJ L 33/1 (2006) (hereafter E-PRTR Regulation) annex I, point 4—where emission limits are mentioned, which if exceeded, must be reported.

[50] Category 4.2a of Annex I, Directive 2010/75/EU of the European Parliament and of the Council of 24 November 2010 on industrial emissions (integrated pollution prevention and control) (Recast), OJ L 334/159 (2010) (hereafter IED 2010).

[51] Directive (EU) 2024/1785 of the European Parliament and of the Council of 24 April 2024 amending Directive 2010/75/EU of the European Parliament and of the Council on industrial emissions (integrated

referred to in Article 10' now includes 'Electrolysis of water for production of hydrogen *where the production capacity exceeds 50 tonnes per day*'.[52] This marks a key change, as electrolysers producing less than 50 tonnes per day will no longer require an IED permit once this EU Directive is transposed into Dutch law. In practical terms, this threshold corresponds to an electrolyser capacity of approximately 90 MW, meaning that most existing electrolysers will no longer require an emissions permit.

However, Article 23.11 of the Ow states that the 2010 version of the IED continues to apply, meaning a stricter regime will remain in place, until the new legislation is transposed. The Dutch government must adopt these changes by 1 July 2026, so until then, small-scale projects may still face a strict permitting process.

Another potential factor leading to a more extensive permitting process is the EIA. The EIA Directive mandates that certain projects, which may have significant environmental effects due to their nature, size, or location, must undergo an environmental impact assessment before approval.[53] Activities listed in Annex I of the EIA Directive automatically trigger a full assessment, requiring the permit-requesting party to draft an environmental impact report.[54] For example, combustion installations with a heat output of 300 MW or more fall under this category.[55]

Hydrogen production and storage, however, are included in Annex II, for which Member States can determine whether a full EIA is needed, based on case-by-case evaluations or threshold values.[56] In the Netherlands, the EIA requirements are transposed into the Ow and further specified *Omgevingsbesluit* (Environment and Planning Decree, hereafter Ob).[57] The latter explains when a full environmental impact report is required, how it should be conducted, and when an informal, simplified EIA screening suffices.[58] A full EIA is required when certain activities exceed a specified threshold, and below that threshold, the competent authority must determine whether the potential environmental impacts are significant enough to warrant a full EIA (and consequently, an extended permitting procedure). If the impacts are not deemed significant, a screening is sufficient, allowing for a simplified permitting procedure.[59]

The relevant provisions of the Ob are outlined in the F and I lists, which specify the hydrogen-related activities subject to EIA requirements (Table XII.2). These include hydrogen production, processing, and storage. Notably, hydrogen combustion is not explicitly mentioned in this legislation. However, examining the hydrogen-related

pollution prevention and control) and Council Directive 1999/31/EC on the landfill of waste, OJ L 234 (2024) (hereafter IED 2024).

[52] Annex I IED (2024) under 6.6.

[53] Directive 2014/52/EU of the European Parliament and of the Council of 16 April 2014 amending Directive 2011/92/EU on the assessment of the effects of certain public and private projects on the environment, OJ L 124/1 (2014) (hereafter EIA Directive), see art 1(g)(iii) and annex III for the considerations to determine potential significant environmental consequences.

[54] Art 4 EIA Directive; art 16.39 Ow; art 16.74 Ow; art 16.43 Ow.

[55] EIA Directive, Annex I under 2a.

[56] EIA Directive Annex II, under 6a and 6c.

[57] Omgevingsbesluit (2018) Staatsblad 2018, 290 (entered into force on 1 January 2024) (hereafter Ob) s 11.1.

[58] ibid.

[59] Art 16.43(1)(b) Ow.

Table XII.2 Relevant parts of the *Omgevingsbesluit*

Activities	Text	Threshold
F 3	'The establishment of an integrated chemical installation, i.e., an installation for the industrial-scale production of substances through chemical conversion, where several units coexist and are functionally interconnected, intended for the production of: ... b. inorganic basic chemicals'.	This provision requires a complete EIA when a new installation is erected. A screening suffices only when an existing permit for that installation is adapted.
F 5	'Processing of intermediate products and manufacturing of chemicals'.	A full EIA is not required, only an EIA screening when permitting the creation or adaptation of an MBA.
I 3	'Installation intended for the storage of petroleum, petrochemical, or chemical products'.	This provision requires a full EIA in cases where the activity relates to a production capacity of 200,000 tonnes per year or more. Below, an EIA screening should be conducted.

Omgevingsbesluit as translated from Dutch. Annex V Categories F 3, F 5 and I 3 Ob.

activities subject to EIA obligations offers insight into how hydrogen is treated within this framework. Additionally, since this chapter assumes hydrogen production and subsequent use on an industrial site, which would follow the same permitting procedure under Article 5.7 Ow, this broader context should be considered.

It appears that a hydrogen production plant is treated as a conventional chemical production plant, as defined in category F 3 of Annex 5 of the *Omgevingsbesluit*, irrespective of the method of hydrogen production (eg protein exchange membrane (PEM) or alkaline), and irrespective of the type of hydrogen produced (eg grey or green). One report argues that '[t]his places a disproportionate burden on environmentally friendly production methods, as it subjects them to the same requirements as industrial, emission-emitting processes. There is no specific legislation for hydrogen production and it is considered as any other inorganic gas production facility'.[60]

An electrolyser can also fall into the scope of Category F 5. A full EIA used to be required pre-2024 if a production capacity threshold of 100,000 tonnes per year was met. This threshold has been repealed with the introduction of the Ow, and now only an EIA screening is required.[61]

Lastly, the storage of hydrogen, especially temporary above-ground storage at industrial sites (as discussed in subsection 2.2), also requires attention. A threshold of 200,000 tonnes is provided in Category I 3 of the *Omgevingsbesluit*. It is assumed that

[60] Jan Piet van der Meer, Remco Perotti, and Françoise de Jong, 'HyLaw, National Policy Paper—Netherlands' (2020) https://www.hylaw.eu/files/2019-03/HyLAW_National%20Policy%20Paper_Netherlands.pdf accessed 24 May 2025, 4.

[61] *Besluit milieueffectrapportage* (2020) Staatsblad 2020, 528 (repealed 1 January 2024) annex D, category D 34.4; annex V, category F 5 Ob.

at a lower production capacity no significant adverse environmental effects occur, allowing for a lighter, informal EIA screening. Interestingly, this threshold has been increased, as pre-2024, it was 100,000 tonnes. Still, even with that old threshold, one may question whether hydrogen production would even meet 100,000 tonnes a year. The plans of Shell to build a 200 MW electrolyser would produce around 50–60 tonnes of hydrogen per day, and with that, only 18.250–21.900 tonnes per year when producing continuously.[62]

Based on this analysis, it appears that the installation of an electrolyser would typically only require an EIA screening. Consistent with this, none of the permits reviewed in this chapter required more than an EIA screening. It is also noteworthy that only one of the permits involved the actual use of hydrogen in high-temperature processes. While an EIA was not necessary, the process still required an extended procedure, including additional monitoring and inspections, due to the novelty of using hydrogen as a fuel. If an application is submitted comprising both hydrogen production and its use as a fuel on an industrial site under Article 5.7 of the Ow, any complications related to the latter could extend the entire permitting process, as only one decision-making period applies. In this context, the simplified EIA screening process may not significantly expedite the overall procedure.

In fact, some authors contend that this system is not necessarily 'lighter', as the innovative nature of hydrogen in industrial heating applications prompts authorities still to thoroughly evaluate environmental impacts.[63] In this light, one may argue that it appears that 'the development of small production units is as complicated as large units. This severely limits the potential for development of localised production units….'[64]

The following subsection examines safety considerations, where similar issues can be observed.

3.3.3 Safety considerations

Safety considerations are paramount, especially in industrial settings. As explained in subsection 2.2, hydrogen poses specific safety risks due to its inherent properties, such as high flammability.[65] Like all flammable gases and vapours, the consequences associated with hydrogen releases depend on the specific situation and the presence of ignition sources. In outdoor environments, due to its low density, hydrogen typically rises and disperses. Conversely, indoors, hydrogen releases tend to accumulate near the ceiling, where ignition sources are less likely.[66] The implementation of robust

[62] Jan C van Oosten, Peter van Lingen, and Neeltje Walgemoed, 'Omgevingsrechtelijke besluitvorming voor de groene waterstofinfrastructuur. Nu en onder de Omgevingswet' (2022) 102 Tijdschrift voor Bouwrecht 683, 686–87; Shell, 'Kickstarting the Hydrogen Economy of the Netherlands' (2023) https://www.shell.nl/about-us/what-we-do/waterstof/_jcr_content/root/main/section_2001009258/call_to_action/links/item0.stream/1700559096526/0a5bcc38e8969b5b30bc923805b910b1722d63fc/shell-hydrogen1-mcw-v3.pdf accessed 24 May 2025.

[63] Van Oosten, van Lingen, and Walgemoed (n 62) 687.

[64] Translated from Dutch, Van der Meer, Perotti, and de Jong (n 60) 5.

[65] Griffiths and others (n 3) 3.

[66] ibid.

safety measures can significantly mitigate these risks.[67] Ongoing research augmented the understanding and introduced a range of technical solutions to address the more hazardous aspects of hydrogen.[68]

The permitting procedure will hinge, among other factors, on the implementation of appropriate safety measures. It is therefore important for industrial companies seeking to incorporate hydrogen into their operations to engage with permitting authorities at an early stage.[69] A lack of technical expertise among public servants may hinder the permitting process, particularly when dealing with relatively new end-use applications such as high-temperature heating. Authorities may act cautiously and request unnecessary studies or simulations, particularly when making decisions in the absence of a clear legal framework.[70] This challenge is important to consider when determining potential solutions in section 4.

A noteworthy observation is coming from one of the permits reviewed for this chapter. The permit states: '[r]egarding electrolysis installations and the resulting gases hydrogen and oxygen, there are currently no direct rules and regulations in the Netherlands for the protection of human health and the environment. This is because these developments are of recent origin'.[71] This highlights the emerging nature of hydrogen applications and the absence of clear regulatory guidance. However, for the handling and storage of hazardous substances, guidelines have been established in documents called *Publicatiereeks Gevaarlijke Stoffen* (Dangerous Substances Publication Series; hereafter PGS), which ensure an acceptable level of protection for human health and the environment.[72] As discussed in the first part of this book, PGS 35 (Hydrogen installations: delivery and use) provides good starting points for the safe and environmentally responsible use of electrolysers and the storage of hydrogen.[73] PGS 15 (storage of hazardous substances in packaging) is also applicable in the context of this chapter. Requirements established in these documents can be explicitly included in an environmental permit to ensure that the standards to be complied with are

[67] OECD (n 11) 59; interestingly, Permit Friesland (n 31) refers to the usage of a circulating potassium hydroxide solution for cooling and the supply of (fresh) water in electrolysis. The permit states that '[t]his technique is proven, robust, and has no particular risks other than the occasional release of hydrogen gas, oxygen, or potassium hydroxide solution. By applying techniques such as soil protection, strict separation of gases, and ventilation, the risks can be minimized and, therefore, negligible' (under 4.15.5, translated from Dutch). This illustrates how a permitting authority may take into account the minimization of risks through the application of proven techniques.

[68] OECD (n 11) 59.

[69] ibid.

[70] European Clean Hydrogen Alliance Permitting WG Report, 'Paving the Way for Permitting of Hydrogen Projects in the European Union: Barriers and Recommendations' (2023) 1, 9 https://ec.europa.eu/docsroom/documents/50514 accessed 24 May 2025.

[71] Translated from Dutch. Permit Friesland (n 31) under 4.15.6.

[72] The series of publications provide a guide for companies involved in the production, transportation, storage, or use of hazardous substances, as well as for authorities responsible for overseeing and granting permits to these companies. *Publicatiereeks Gevaarlijke Stoffen* https://publicatiereeksgevaarlijkestoffen.nl/ accessed 3 December 2024.

[73] 'Waterstofinstallaties voor het afleveren van waterstof aan voertuigen en werktuigen' (2021) https://publicatiereeksgevaarlijkestoffen.nl/publicaties/pgs35/ accessed 24 May 2025 (hereafter PGS 35).

clear.[74] Additional safety rules and regulations have been discussed in the first part of this book. However, in the context of this chapter it is important to note that there is no guidance thus far on the actual use of hydrogen as combustion fuel.

National policies recognize that there is a lack of targeted rules for hydrogen, and it has nonetheless been stressed that the absence of clear legal guidelines should not obstruct its deployment.[75] To address this, the *Rijksdienst voor Ondernemend Nederland* (Netherlands Enterprise Agency; hereafter RvO) has been tasked with creating an interim solution—a guidance document to assist permitting authorities, particularly concerning the safety aspects of hydrogen, until legislation has been updated.[76]

Although not a binding document, the guideline can offer valuable guidance for permitting authorities. Their purpose is to support the energy transition by promoting a 'responsible approach to managing risks and uncertainties surrounding hydrogen in pilot projects'.[77] There is a general guidance document, and one specifically focused on hydrogen use in buildings. More specific guidelines for other hydrogen applications are under development, but for now, the generic document is applied to non-building-related hydrogen uses.[78] The anticipated future guidelines will cover hydrogen pilot projects in sectors like mobility, production, transport and handling, storage, electricity supply, and applications in aviation and shipping.[79] Currently, there is no indication that specific guidance will be issued for hydrogen use in high-temperature heating, though the general document may still offer useful support for permitting authorities.

The generic guideline clarifies that existing safety standards for maximum allowable risks apply to hydrogen; however, where no specific standard exists, hydrogen technologies must at least meet the safety benchmarks of their fossil fuel counterparts. In cases where no direct comparison is possible—such as with new technologies and applications in industrial settings—an adequate level of risk control can be demonstrated by outlining the risk-reducing measures that will be implemented.[80]

The guideline stresses several times that the idea behind it is to facilitate pilot projects involving hydrogen. The guideline states that where relevant, insights gained from pilot projects on hydrogen safety risks and potential mitigation measures should be shared as widely as possible. This highlights the intent to reduce barriers to pioneering initiatives. It also acknowledges that current laws and regulations, which may not yet account for new hydrogen applications, could create unforeseen challenges. While

[74] *Publicatiereeks Gevaarlijke Stoffen* 15, 'Opslag van verpakte gevaarlijke stoffen' (2023) https://publicatiereeksgevaarlijkestoffen.nl/publicaties/pgs15/ accessed 24 May 2025 (hereafter PGS 15); see eg under 3.1, 3.2.1–3.2.3, 3.4, 3,6, 3.7, 3.11, 3.12, 3.12.2, 3.14.1, 3.14.2, 3.15, 3.15, 3.16, and 3.18. They contain detailed explanations of the safe handling and storage of hazardous substances. Permit Friesland (n 31) 10 and Permit Groningen (n 31) 28 explicitly reference specific PGS provisions, stating that the project must comply with them.

[75] Cross-sectorale werkgroep waterstof (n 10) Table 1, 8.

[76] Rijksdienst voor Ondernemend Nederland (RvO), 'Generiek richtsnoer waterstofveiligheid, eerste versie' (2022) https://www.rvo.nl/sites/default/files/2022-10/Generiek%20richtsnoer%20Waterstofveiligheid%20%28eerste%20vastgestelde%20versie%2C%205%20oktober%202022%29.pdf accessed 24 May 2025 (hereafter RvO Guidance Document).

[77] Translated from Dutch. RvO Guidance Document (n 76) 2, 3, 5.

[78] ibid.

[79] ibid 12.

[80] ibid 3 under 2.

these issues cannot always be resolved through guidance alone, the national government aims to explore all avenues to remove such barriers where possible.[81] The following recommendations discuss potential approaches.

4. Recommendations: Overcoming Legal Barriers in the Dutch Permitting Regime

We have seen that an important policy goal in the Netherlands is to prevent undue delays in the energy transition where specific legislation is still lacking.[82] For decarbonizing hard-to-abate industrial high-temperature heating processes, this goal is especially pertinent. Resulting from the analysis, three key recommendations can be made to improve the system.

4.1 Recommendation 1: Include Hydrogen Explicitly in Relevant Legal and Regulatory Frameworks

For hydrogen to realize its potential, it is essential to establish, customize, and regularly review regulations, standards, and oversight mechanisms to facilitate its implementation.[83] For industrial high-temperature heating processes, these frameworks must evolve to accommodate the unique characteristics of hydrogen as a combustion fuel.

Evidently, ensuring a sound consideration of environmental aspects and safety throughout the hydrogen lifecycle is crucial for secure production, transportation, utilization, and for fostering public confidence.[84] Conversely, overly complex legal barriers, excessively cautious rules, procedures, and requirements may require adjustments to facilitate the smooth development of the hydrogen sector.

At present, Dutch regulations often apply generic frameworks to the hydrogen sector rather than developing specific regulations suited to its use as a combustion fuel. While these regulations may provide temporary support for environmental and risk management, they may not be the most efficient or effective way to enable the deployment of hydrogen in novel applications, such as high-temperature industrial heating processes in hard-to-abate sectors. In other words, a more targeted regulatory approach is required.

In the Netherlands it would be particularly helpful to revise the list of standard fuels and to consider the inclusion of hydrogen in that list. At the very least, creating specific guidance for its use in industrial high-temperature heating processes would be a sensible step. Such guidance should address both the environmental implications of hydrogen use in high-temperature applications and the relevant safety considerations.

[81] ibid 7–8.
[82] RvO Guidance Document (n 76) 2.
[83] OECD (n 11) 54.
[84] RvO Guidance Document (n 76).

A targeted PGS for use of hydrogen as combustion fuel in this particular industrial setting would be helpful—so that the right safety considerations are taken into account.

In line with this, it is recommended to consider the prioritization of innovative hydrogen projects in national policies, to steer permitting authorities towards facilitating experiments by way of shorter procedures. This may additionally require further refinement of thresholds. As indicated, even small-scale demonstration projects are still considered to be of an 'industrial scale' in the sense of the IED (2010). In this light, it is recommended that the Netherlands prioritizes the prompt transposition into national law of EU legislative developments.

In parallel to hydrogen experimentation projects, it would be sensible for permitting authorities or more central authorities to conduct research into the potential complexities and challenges within the permitting regime. This research should focus on identifying key regulatory hurdles, procedural inefficiencies, and safety concerns that might arise during the experimentation phase. A proactive approach of this kind would allow authorities to develop targeted solutions to address these issues, ultimately streamlining the permitting process for future hydrogen-based projects.

4.2 Recommendation 2: Streamline the Permitting Process

The diversity of industrial processes makes standardization in permitting challenging, yet this complexity underscores the need for clear, practical frameworks. Permitting authorities in the Netherlands are already overburdened, and vague or complex legislation without specific guidance for novel hydrogen use cases risks exacerbating delays.[85]

Reducing the administrative burden on these authorities is crucial to expediting project implementation. Targeted guidelines for specific hydrogen applications could play a key role in this by clarifying legal requirements. In fact, the Netherlands has something of this kind already—guidelines for hydrogen refuelling stations.[86]

A comparable, dedicated guidance manual tailored to high-temperature heating applications would be beneficial.[87] As a practical interim measure, such a manual could be introduced more swiftly than legal reforms, offering immediate support while broader regulatory updates are in progress. The manual should also offer clear criteria on how the permitting process accounts for project-specific factors, such as scale (eg capacity, bulk storage) and location (eg industrial sites, urban areas). Additionally, it should outline pathways to fast-track pioneering pilot projects where feasible. Granting flexibility to certain categories—such as smaller projects below a defined threshold or those in

[85] Anna Collignon and Jake Tingen, 'Zes ongewenste wijzigingen door de Omgevingswet. Een bespreking van relevante wijzigingen voor de bouwpraktijk en aanbevelingen voor de toekomst' (2023) 64 Bouwrecht 419.

[86] See eg Instituut Fysieke Veiligheid (n 32); Instituut Fysieke Veiligheid, 'Bestuurlijke handreiking vergunningverlening waterstoftankstations' (2019) https://nipv.nl/wp-content/uploads/2022/02/20190619-IFV-Bestuurlijke-handreiking-vergunningverlening-waterstoftankstations.pdf accessed 24 May 2025. This document aims to help competent authorities handle permit requests for hydrogen refuelling stations, with the additional objective to streamline the approach throughout the Netherlands.

[87] As suggested by the European Clean Hydrogen Alliance (n 70) 5–15.

industrial zones that do not require a full EIA—could further streamline permitting and accelerate knowledge development.[88]

Essentially, the permitting approach should fit the scale of the project at hand. However, relying solely on decentralized permitting authorities to determine this could lead to inconsistencies and added complexity. Clear guidance is essential to ensure flexibility is applied effectively. It is of particular importance to provide a manual with clear differentiation of the processes between applications and uses of hydrogen (eg storage, use as feedstock, or combustion fuel). It would be sensible to state explicitly the required documents to be provided to authorities, time limits, and who the relevant authorities are.[89] In this way, a manual laying down the permitting procedure could increase predictability and improve the efficiency of the overall process.

A next step could be to eventually enshrine rules in legislation, making them binding and therefore alleviating the disparities that may arise between regions in the Netherlands. This will require consistent collaboration and knowledge sharing between relevant actors, which leads to the third recommendation.

4.3 Recommendation 3: Collaborating and Knowledge Sharing

Developing hydrogen-specific legislation will take time, but collaboration and knowledge sharing can address immediate challenges, particularly for industrial high-temperature heating processes, where both regulatory and technical expertise are still maturing. While permitting authorities play a central role, collaboration should extend beyond regulators to include heavy industries, which can benefit from sharing technical insights and permitting experiences.

Permitting authorities across regions in the Netherlands may encounter varying levels of familiarity with hydrogen-based industrial heating projects. If one authority has successfully issued a permit for an experimental hydrogen project, sharing its approach by disseminating expertise and best practices for permitting hydrogen projects—including safety risk assessment strategies, safety mitigation measures, and emissions considerations—could provide a blueprint for others. By pooling best practices and lessons learned, authorities can standardize procedures and reduce complexities in the permitting process. This could be facilitated through an internal information exchange forum in the Netherlands, fostering knowledge sharing at a national level.

In addition to collaboration among regulators, heavy industries themselves have a critical role to play. High-temperature industrial heating processes vary significantly across sectors, with differences in feedstock, production methods, and combustion conditions. This diversity means that each sector may face unique technical challenges and regulatory hurdles when adopting hydrogen as a combustion fuel. By creating a platform for dialogue, industries can share technical innovations, operational insights,

[88] ibid.
[89] ibid 5–15.

and solutions to common permitting challenges. For example, companies could share their experiences in adapting burners for hydrogen use in high-temperature heating processes, offering valuable insights into controlling NOx emissions and navigating the associated permitting challenges.

Once a robust knowledge base is established, it could serve as the foundation for developing a targeted permitting manual and in the long-term, hydrogen-specific legislation tailored to industrial high-temperature heating processes. This iterative approach would ensure that regulations are informed by practical experience and are adaptable to the unique needs of heavy industries.[90]

5. Conclusion

As the world transitions to clean energy, hydrogen is becoming a key solution for decarbonizing hard-to-abate sectors, such as those relying on high-temperature industrial heating processes. The Dutch permitting regime is crucial in determining how quickly hydrogen can be integrated into these processes.

This chapter identified some key gaps in the current Dutch permitting landscape, particularly the absence of a targeted legal framework and guidance for hydrogen usage in industrial high-temperature processes. Despite ambitious hydrogen goals set by both the government and the EU, the lack of clear, specific regulations creates uncertainty, often resulting in hydrogen being treated more restrictively than fossil fuels.

Additional challenges include limited experience with hydrogen applications and a complex permitting process that causes delays, even for small-scale experimental projects. Although interim guidance documents offer some relief, they do not fully address the systemic issues at hand. Comprehensive regulatory and legal reforms are therefore necessary.

To overcome these challenges, the following is recommended: first, hydrogen as a fuel should be explicitly included in the legal and regulatory frameworks, providing clarity and consistency. Second, streamlining the permitting process by developing targeted manuals would reduce complexity and encourage innovation. Tailored thresholds and prioritizing pilot projects can accelerate hydrogen deployment. Finally, fostering collaboration and knowledge sharing between authorities and industries will help exchange technical insights and in turn, improve the regulatory environment.

For the Netherlands to achieve its climate neutrality goals by 2050, hydrogen is expected to play a central role in decarbonizing high-temperature industrial heating processes. This will require not only technological advancements, but also a permitting system that encourages innovation while upholding rigorous safety and environmental standards.

[90] ibid 5–15.

Acknowledgements

The author wishes to thank Ruven Fleming for his helpful comments, and her family and Quemi for their unwavering support.

Further Reading

Instituut Fysieke Veiligheid, 'Bestuurlijke handreiking vergunningverlening waterstoftankstations' (2019) https://nipv.nl/wp-content/uploads/2022/02/20190619-IFV-Bestuurlijke-handreiking-vergunningverlening-waterstoftankstations.pdf accessed 18 February 2025.

Steve Griffiths and others, 'Industrial Decarbonization Via Hydrogen: A Critical and Systematic Review of Developments, Socio-Technical Systems and Policy Options' (2021) 80 Energy Research & Social Science 1.

Ministerie van Economische Zaken en Klimaat, 'Cluster 6 Connect Samen naar een groene en schone regionale industrie' (2023) https://ibknl.com/verslag-cluster6connect-002.pdf accessed 18 February 2025.

MultHyFuel, 'Permitting requirements and risk assessment methodologies for HRS in the EU (First version)' (2021) https://multhyfuel.eu/images/event-documents/deliverables/MHYF_WP1_D12_Permitting_requirements_and_risk_assessment_methodologies_20210930_03.pdf accessed 18 February 2025.

Platform Verduurzaming Industrie, 'Getec Park Emmen stapt gefaseerd over naar waterstof' (2023) https://verduurzamingindustrie.nl/inspiratie/2460924.aspx accessed 18 February 2025.

Waterstof Veiligheid Innovatie Programma, 'Lokale productie van waterstof bij een waterstoftankstation' (2021) https://www.nen.nl/media/wysiwyg/WVIP_vergunningverlening_Lokaleproductie_waterstoftankstation_sept21-1.pdf accessed 18 February 2025.

XIII
Conclusion

Ruven Fleming

1. Introduction

Europe's phasing in of hydrogen requires a fundamental and rapid ramping up of production capacity as well as transport and end-use infrastructure. While national governments can set ambitious targets, the actual implementation depends heavily on local authorities. Permitting can become a key obstacle in establishing future hydrogen economies, not only for production but also, as shown in this volume, along the entire hydrogen value chain.

A crucial element in addressing this challenge is cooperation, not only between EU institutions and national governments but especially between national governments, local authorities, and regions. A common feature is that local authorities need both support and the ability to act quickly to secure the infrastructure needed for efficient permitting of hydrogen projects. This is not a minor technical detail but a key issue: local authorities—those who will carry out the work on the ground—are neither equipped to handle the huge numbers of permits that will need to be processed (neither in terms of personnel nor in terms of expertise) nor does their general structure and regulatory infrastructure in many Member States encourage cooperation and knowledge sharing.

Discussions with several local authorities in different Member States covered in this volume indicate a clear willingness to engage, however they foresee a significant issue in terms of workload and feasibility. Digitalization in some local and regional authorities remains underdeveloped. For example, project applications submitted via an electronic system (which is not yet available in all Member States) may have to be printed, signed in ink by an official, and scanned again because digital signatures are not accepted.

Another issue is space and location. The main areas for wind energy production, for example, are in the north, a region that is generally less populated, whereas solar energy is particularly abundant in southern Europe. Thus, much green hydrogen production could take place in rural areas. The same is not necessarily true for grey or blue hydrogen, which are often better produced near industrial centres where they are used. This means that the rural energy transition is key, particularly for green hydrogen production, and permitting processes in rural areas must be streamlined and better guided.

A common feature across Europe is the multitude of actors in the permitting regime, especially at the local level. Whereas national governments in many Member States have at least a relatively well-established system of interplay and shared responsibilities with regional governments, identifying the correct local authority can be a real headache—and a time-consuming exercise—for project developers. In hydrogen permitting, local entities such as municipalities, counties, district governments or directorates, autonomous communities, and regional councils may all be involved. These terms can be confusing, however, because they often refer to similar levels of administration in different jurisdictions. For example, Germany does not use a single term for its regional authorities: some *Länder* have *Bezirksregierungen* (district governments), while others have *Regierungspräsidien* (regional councils) or *Landesdirektionen* (state directorates). All of these terms denote the administrative layer between a *Landkreis* (county) and the *Land* (federal state) under national ministries. This terminological variation illustrates that the core issue is identifying the proper authorities to contact, not differences in functional structure.

In fact, the complexity has led the German Federal Ministry for Economic Affairs and Energy (among others) to fund a three-year study (2017–2020). One aim of the study was to advise electrolyser project developers on which authority to submit their permit application to—specifically the emissions permit. The result was a fifteen-page list of the responsible authorities in the sixteen German *Länder*—again only for the emissions permit.[1] This was intended to serve as much-needed guidance for navigating the German administrative system. However, the list became outdated quickly (due to the reshuffling of competences and personnel changes), so that three years later the Ministry commissioned a follow-up study to update it.[2]

2. Key Observations on Hydrogen Regulation in Europe

One might hope that the German example was isolated, but unfortunately similar issues are not uncommon in other Member States. On the contrary, very few contributors

[1] Portal Green, *Genehmigungsrechtlicher Leitfaden für Power-to-Gas-Anlagen* (pp 143–158) https://www.dvgw.de/medien/dvgw/forschung/berichte/g201735-portalgreen-finaler-genehmigungsleitfaden-bd1.pdf accessed 17 February 2025.

[2] DVGW, *Portal Green II Project* https://www.dvgw.de/themen/forschung-und-innovation/forschungsprojekte/dvgw-forschungsprojekt-portal-green-ii/portal-green-ii#c77242 accessed 17 February 2025.

to this volume appeared satisfied with the administrative setup of permitting regimes in their countries for hydrogen production and infrastructure. A key lesson is that implementing these ambitious hydrogen plans will face an uphill struggle when it comes to permitting actual projects. Bureaucracy may be too slow and cumbersome to keep pace with the dynamics of the hydrogen market.

2.1 Hydrogen Upstream: Permitting Regimes for Electrolysers

There are, however, some positive examples. Osipov-Gipsh and Jansen illustrate in their chapter on the Netherlands how revamping the legal framework and unifying most substantive requirements for electrolyser permitting into a single Environmental and Planning Act can be very beneficial. The Netherlands now faces an interesting balancing exercise: it must ensure that not all large-scale electrolysers are excluded from substantial parts of the permitting regime. Osipov-Gipsh and Jansen clearly suggest how to align the Dutch nationally determined threshold for exemptions with the EU's Industrial Emissions Directive (IED). An additional observation is that although the Netherlands has harmonized and unified its permitting procedure, there is no guidance document available for electrolyser developers. This is surprising given that a similar document exists for hydrogen refuelling stations, indicating a clear need for research and practical guidance.

This contrasts with the proactive approach to guidance in Denmark, as Elkjær discusses in her chapter. Danish authorities make significant efforts to assist developers during the permitting process on at least two levels. First, they provide a comprehensive and free guide on the permitting procedure for electrolysers. Second, support is provided by the Power-to-X taskforce, which coordinates the permitting process, fosters market collaboration to address issues, and even holds workshops for project developers. However, as Elkjær notes, this is not an 'all-in-one' permit: developers still must engage with multiple authorities and apply for various permits, with the Danish Energy Authority serving only as an overarching guide to the process. Elkjær also suggests an innovative approach to the surplus heat produced by all current electrolysers: since Denmark has a well-developed system of district heating networks, it could consider requiring developers to include a waste heat reuse plan as a condition for obtaining environmental permits.

Germany has a relatively comprehensive permitting framework. It does not have a single integrated environmental and planning code like the Netherlands; however, it does apply the so-called concentration effect, a procedural tool that yields a partial all-in-one permitting regime. Germany's Energy Industry Act covers both electricity and hydrogen, indicating that the country is moving towards legal integration in this field. This integrated approach extends to hydrogen governance: when planning hydrogen production facilities like electrolysers, the associated transmission and distribution infrastructure are also considered. This integrated thinking stands in sharp contrast to the procedural hurdles and the nearly impossible to navigate maze of authorities that project developers may encounter. In conclusion, Germany has a sound substantive legal framework but it needs much improvement in practical procedures and guidance.

Poland is a Member State that exemplifies the limitations of high-level targets that are not underpinned by concrete administrative actions. Owidzki notes that by 2025 most of Poland's hydrogen targets are likely to have been missed. He attributes this in part to the lack of firm deadlines in the Polish legal system for processing electrolyser permit applications. From a substantive perspective, Poland needs a dedicated legal act on hydrogen that reinforces the country's policy plans. Owidzki specifically advocates that electrolysers below 10 MW, which currently do not require a construction permit in Poland, should similarly be exempted from mandatory environmental impact assessments (EIAs). Finally, attributing overriding public interest to hydrogen projects so that these project decisions take precedence over other development plans would make it easier to allocate suitable locations to the projects. He concludes that the multi-tiered nature of the permitting process, from spatial planning to environmental impact assessments, requires careful navigation through various administrative levels and compliance with a multitude of regulations that may not fully reflect the low environmental impact of electrolysers in particular.

Environmental impacts—particularly those associated with electrolysers—also constitute a significant issue in Spain, where the relevant legal framework has already undergone reform. The Integrated Environmental Authorization (*Autorización Ambiental Integrada*, AAI) now offers a form of 'one-stop shop' for permits. However, as del Guayo and Bucher observe in their chapter, improved coordination between the AAI process and regional and urban planning remains essential, as municipal interventions may obstruct the coherent development of renewable hydrogen projects. They conclude that a central question for Spain, moving forward, is how to reconcile centralized energy policy objectives with the decentralized decision-making powers of its Autonomous Communities. Striking this balance will require innovative governance models that enable meaningful participation by local stakeholders while safeguarding overarching national objectives.

A general observation emerging from this volume is that southern European countries have been particularly active in reshaping their legal frameworks and tailoring them to the evolving needs of hydrogen deployment. Italy constitutes another example where the permitting process has undergone notable improvements, including the introduction of a services conference mechanism and expedited environmental impact assessment procedures for green, or renewable, hydrogen production. Volpi concludes that these reforms could serve as a reference model for other jurisdictions. The recent legislative changes in Italy also included the unification of procedures for the authorization of the construction and operation of electrolysers into a single legal text. Nevertheless, Volpi notes that there remains scope for improvement, particularly due to persisting uncertainties in the legal definitions surrounding electrolysers. While the recent Italian National Hydrogen Strategy identifies the simplification of the permitting process as a key priority, Volpi cautions that this goal will not be realized without the adoption of detailed guidelines and explanatory circulars to support both local authorities and project developers.

A third southern European country with considerable potential for hydrogen production is Greece. In principle, Greece is well-positioned to become a key player in the European hydrogen economy. Its strategic location in the Mediterranean and abundant renewable energy resources—particularly solar and wind—render it a promising hub for green hydrogen production.

However, at the time of writing, Greece still lacks a national hydrogen strategy, making it one of only a few European countries without such a framework. This omission poses a significant challenge to the strategic direction and coordination of hydrogen deployment. As Kounelis and Douka observe, a wide range of hydrogen applications are feasible across Greece's industrial, transport, and energy sectors, yet the success of these endeavours is contingent upon the effective streamlining of the country's fragmented permitting processes. Encouragingly, administrative requirements have been consolidated to some extent into four umbrella permits, which aim to streamline the process in particular respects. Nevertheless, according to Kounelis and Douka, numerous permits or supporting documents must still be submitted multiple times across different permitting stages. The existence of numerous ministerial decisions and fragmented legislative instruments renders the process complex and burdensome, requiring developers to expend significant effort in identifying and complying with applicable rules. In addition, the requirement to interact with various authorities throughout the permitting procedure complicates coordination and increases the risk of delays. To mitigate these issues, the authors recommend enhancing guidance and transparency through the publication of detailed, step-by-step instructions on official government websites to support developers in understanding and fulfilling legal requirements.

This stands in interesting contrast to the legal situation in the United Kingdom, which has departed from the European Union. In their chapter, Goldberg and Jarvis focus specifically on England and Wales in relation to hydrogen production regulation. They observe that many of the challenges identified in continental European jurisdictions are equally present in the UK context, albeit alongside slightly more developed approaches to investment incentives—such as those found in the *Clean Power 2030 Action Plan*. Through this policy framework, the UK government is pursuing an ambitious decarbonizing agenda in which hydrogen is expected to play a central role.

However, at present, there is no dedicated consenting regime for hydrogen projects in the United Kingdom. Instead, developers must navigate a fragmented array of existing regulations and consents, originally conceived for other sectors, including chemical manufacturing, natural gas, and power generation. The lack of clear and consistent planning policy support for hydrogen production facilities has led to a consenting landscape that lacks the clarity and certainty needed to reasonably guarantee planning permission in appropriate locations. Goldberg and Jarvis further argue that local planning authorities are generally not resourced to process hydrogen-related applications effectively. This is attributable not only to the novelty of the technology and the complexity of its impacts—both of which require regulatory confidence—but also to broader capacity constraints within local planning bodies. They conclude that the existing consenting and licensing regime in England and Wales presents significant barriers and uncertainties for developers of low-carbon hydrogen systems, thereby potentially undermining the realization of the UK government's ambitions under the *Clean Power 2030 Action Plan*.

2.2 Hydrogen Downstream: Key Regulatory Issues

While the chapters of the first part of the book focused on hydrogen upstream, key regulatory issues for the downstream use of hydrogen were discussed in the following chapters, ranging from offshore transport to onshore transport and examples of hydrogen end-use, such as industrial high-temperature processes.

The discussions in the chapter by Afentoulis, Nordtveit, and Herrera Anchustegui focus on offshore hydrogen in another non-EU jurisdiction, Norway, which is associated with EU legislation by agreement. The authors are positive about repurposing offshore petroleum infrastructure for hydrogen production and transportation, presenting a promising avenue for advancing Norway's energy transition.

However, their analysis reveals a surprising absence of proper procedures for a seafaring nation like Norway, illustrating several regulatory shortcomings that must be addressed to facilitate this offshore hydrogen transition effectively. Both hydrogen production and transport are omitted by the current Norwegian legal framework, meaning its application relies on legal analogy and expansive interpretation. This creates uncertainty for stakeholders and regulators alike and may hinder the development of offshore hydrogen projects. Like other chapter authors covering EU Member States, Afentoulis, Nordtveit, and Herrera Anchustegui call for further guidance from the Ministry of Petroleum and Energy to ensure that hydrogen production, transportation and associated pollution risks are appropriately regulated without imposing undue burdens on developers. Administrative practices concerning the current petroleum decommissioning framework ought to be reviewed to incentivize and require circular practices beyond recycling.

Reform of the legal framework to properly address hydrogen transportation is also a key issue in Poland, as Radomska observes. She notes a forthcoming amendment to Polish law that provides some clarity on hydrogen regulation and addresses the current absence of a clear definition of hydrogen in the Polish Energy Act. However, this can only be a first step towards improved regulation of hydrogen transportation, as she observes that the legal framework governing hydrogen transportation pipelines in Poland will remain complex, requiring specialized expertise. Poland's participation in the European Hydrogen Backbone initiative is likely to increase the pressure to align its legislative structure with that of the EU and to streamline it.

At a procedural level, Radomska notes that the permitting process for repurposing natural gas pipelines for hydrogen transport involves decision-making at various levels and requires input from administrative authorities at both local and regional levels. Establishing a single authority responsible for the entire process would provide further clarity. If a single authority cannot be designated then Radomska suggests creating a clear decision-making hierarchy for hydrogen pipeline permits in Poland, a step that would provide much-needed transparency and consistency in the permitting process.

Ultimately, the production and transport of hydrogen serve one goal: increased use of hydrogen. The EU and various national hydrogen strategies want to deploy hydrogen primarily in so-called hard-to-abate applications. Jansen investigates this question in a case study on industrial high-temperature processes in the Netherlands, such as steel, cement, glass, and ceramics, which require heating at temperatures above 400°C.

Overall, Jansen in particular criticizes the absence of a targeted legal framework and guidance for hydrogen use in high-temperature industrial processes. Despite ambitious hydrogen goals set by the Dutch government and the EU, the lack of clear, specific regulations creates uncertainty; according to Jansen, hydrogen is often treated more restrictively than fossil fuels. Other challenges include limited practical experience with hydrogen applications and a complex permitting process that causes delays, even for small-scale experimental projects. Jansen concludes that the current permitting procedure in the Netherlands should be improved both substantively and procedurally and she makes three concrete recommendations. These recommendations effectively summarize the essence of this volume's chapters, providing a succinct description of what needs to change. First, she calls for the explicit inclusion of hydrogen in the relevant Dutch legal and regulatory frameworks. Second, she identifies ways to streamline the permitting process. Third, she highlights the importance of collaboration and knowledge sharing.

3. Conclusion

Streamlining the permitting processes across the entire hydrogen value chain will become a make-or-break factor for Europe's success with hydrogen. In many countries, a lack of clear separation of responsibilities, limited knowledge or experience within public authorities regarding hydrogen, and a complicated legal framework can all become roadblocks to the rapid rollout of hydrogen in Europe.

The good news is that most national governments—and also many local authorities—appear to recognize the possibilities and opportunities of reshaping authorization processes for hydrogen. Such willingness is crucial given the urgency of the situation.

Given this recognition of hydrogen as a key enabler of the energy transition in many sectors, it is surprising that this volume is the first comprehensive Europe-wide publication addressing the actual legal implementation of the 2030 hydrogen targets—less than five years before they must be achieved. This highlights another key theme emerging from this volume: reform of the legal framework and streamlining of processes are not only desirable but necessary. Equally important for the success of the hydrogen transition in Europe is capacity and knowledge-building within permitting processes. Guidance documents for project developers—containing basic information about relevant contacts and procedures—are often either unavailable or outdated. Resources should be rapidly dedicated to creating such guidance documents and to the establishment of knowledge-sharing platforms where authorities can exchange best practices for hydrogen permitting. The next logical step, consistent with the integrated European energy market, is knowledge sharing across borders between EU Member States. The issues and challenges are strikingly similar across Member States, so enabling the sharing of solutions between local authorities across borders should be a key area of action for EU institutions.

Many solutions already exist and many more could be realized through a bottom-up approach. All of this, however, must be undertaken urgently. The fact that some Member States have already missed their 2025 hydrogen targets should serve as an alarm bell. European institutions have established the legal infrastructure for regulating the hydrogen market between December 2021 and the end of 2024 through the Hydrogen and Decarbonised Gas Markets Package. The catch is that no market yet exists. Creating that market depends fundamentally on permitting regimes for hydrogen production, transport, and end-use applications in Member States. This volume calls for all hands on deck to use this key effectively to open the necessary doors for the hydrogen future in Europe.

Index

For the benefit of digital users, indexed terms that span two pages (e.g., 52–53) may, on occasion, appear on only one of those pages.